THE FUTURE OF AGENCY

CURRENT PERSPECTIVES IN SOCIAL THEORY

Series Editor: Harry F. Dahms

Previous Volumes:

Volume 1:	1980, Edited by Scott G. McNall and Garry N. Howe
Volume 2:	1981, Edited by Scott G. McNall and Garry N. Howe
Volume 3:	1982, Edited by Scott G. McNall
Volume 4:	1983, Edited by Scott G. McNall
Volume 5:	1984, Edited by Scott G. McNall
Volume 6:	1985, Edited by Scott G. McNall
Volume 7:	1986, Edited by John Wilson
Volume 8:	1987, Edited by John Wilson
Volume 9:	1989, Edited by John Wilson
Volume 10:	1990, Edited by John Wilson
Volume 11:	1991, Edited by Ben Agger
Volume 12:	1992, Edited by Ben Agger
Volume 13:	1993, Edited by Ben Agger
Volume 14:	1994, Edited by Ben Agger Supplement 1: Recent Developments in the Theory of Social Structure, 1994, Edited by J. David Knottnerus and Christopher Prendergast
Volume 15:	1995, Edited by Ben Agger
Volume 16:	1996, Edited by Jennifer M. Lehmann
Volume 17:	1997, Edited by Jennifer M. Lehmann
Volume 18:	1998, Edited by Jennifer M. Lehmann
Volume 19:	1999, Edited by Jennifer M. Lehmann
Volume 20:	2000, Edited by Jennifer M. Lehmann
Volume 21:	Bringing Capitalism Back for Critique by Social Theory, 2001, Edited by Jennifer M. Lehmann
Volume 22:	Critical Theory: Diverse Objects, Diverse Subjects, 2003, Edited by Jennifer M. Lehmann
Volume 23:	Social Theory as Politics in Knowledge, 2005, Edited by Jennifer M. Lehmann
Volume 24:	Globalization Between the Cold War and Neo-Imperialism, 2006, Edited by Jennifer M. Lehmann and Harry F. Dahms

Volume 25:	No Social Science Without Critical Theory, 2008, Edited by Harry F. Dahms
Volume 26:	Nature, Knowledge and Negation, 2009, Edited by Harry F. Dahms
Volume 27:	Theorizing the Dynamics of Social Processes, 2010, Edited by Harry F. Dahms and Lawrence Hazelrigg
Volume 28:	The Vitality of Critical Theory, 2011, by Harry F. Dahms
Volume 29:	The Diversity of Social Theories, 2011, Edited by Harry F. Dahms
Volume 30:	Theorizing Modern Society as a Dynamic Process, 2012, Edited by Harry F. Dahms and Lawrence Hazelrigg
Volume 31:	Social Theories of History and Histories of Social Theory, 2013, Edited by Harry F. Dahms
Volume 32:	Mediations of Social Life in the 21st Century, 2014, Edited by Harry F. Dahms
Volume 33:	Globalization, Critique and Social Theory: Diagnoses and Challenges, 2015, Edited by Harry F. Dahms
Volume 34:	States and Citizens: Accommodation, Facilitation and Resistance to Globalization, 2015, Edited by Jon Shefner
Volume 35:	Reconstructing Social History, Theory, and Practice, 2016, Edited by Harry F. Dahms and Eric R. Lybeck
Volume 36:	The Challenge of Progress, 2019, Edited by Harry F. Dahms
Volume 37:	Society in Flux: Two Centuries of Social Theory, 2021, Edited by Harry F. Dahms
Volume 38:	Mad Hazard: A Life in Social Theory, 2022, Edited by Stephen Turner
Volume 39:	The Centrality of Sociality: Responses to Michael E. Brown's The Concept of the Social in Uniting the Social Sciences and the Humanities, 2022, Edited by Jeffrey A. Halley and Harry F. Dahms
Volume 40:	Planetary Sociology: Beyond the Entanglement of Identity and Social Structure, 2023, Edited by Harry F. Dahms

EDITORIAL ADVISORY BOARD

EDITOR

Harry F. Dahms
*University of Tennessee – Knoxville
(Sociology)*

ASSISTANT EDITOR

Anthony J. Knowles
*University of Tennessee – Knoxville
(Sociology)*

ASSOCIATE EDITORS

Robert J. Antonio
University of Kansas (Sociology)

Lawrence Hazelrigg
Florida State University (Sociology)

Timothy Luke
*Virginia Polytechnic Institute and
State University (Political Science)*

EDITORIAL BOARD

Amy Allen
*Pennsylvania State University
(Philosophy)*

Kevin B. Anderson
*University of California, Santa
Barbara (Sociology)*

Molefi Kete Asante
*Temple University (African-American
Studies)*

David Ashley
University of Wyoming (Sociology)

Robin Celikates
Free University Berlin (Philosophy)

Pradeep Chakkarath
Ruhr University Bochum (Social Psychology)

Steven P. Dandaneau
Colorado State University (Sociology)

Norman K. Denzin
University of Illinois at Urbana – Champaign (Sociology)

Tina Deshotels
Jacksonville State University (Sociology)

Arnold Farr
University of Kentucky (Philosophy)

Nancy Fraser
New School for Social Research (Political Science)

Martha Gimenez
University of Colorado – Boulder (Sociology)

Robert Goldman
Lewis and Clark College (Sociology and Anthropology)

Elizabeth Goodstein
Emory University (English and Comparative Literature)

Mark Gottdiener
State University of New York at Buffalo (Sociology)

Jeffrey Halley
University of Texas – San Antonio (Sociology)

Reha Kadakal
California State University – Channel Islands (Sociology)

Douglas Kellner
University of California – Los Angeles (Philosophy)

Daniel Krier
Iowa State University (Sociology)

Lauren Langman
Loyola University (Sociology)

Eric R. Lybeck
University of Manchester (Sociology)

Sarah Macmillen
Duquesne University (Sociology)

John Levi Martin
University of Chicago (Sociology)

Paul Paolucci
Eastern Kentucky University (Sociology)

Ilaria Riccioni
Free University of Bozen-Bolzano (Sociology)

Lawrence Scaff
Wayne State University (Political Science)

Steven Seidman
State University of New York at Albany (Sociology)

Jon Shefner
University of Tennessee – Knoxville (Sociology)

Helmut Staubmann
Leopold Franzens University, Innsbruck (Sociology)

Alexander Stoner
Northern Michigan University (Sociology)

Michael J. Thompson
William Paterson University of New Jersey (Political Science)

Stephen Turner
University of South Florida (Philosophy)

CURRENT PERSPECTIVES IN SOCIAL THEORY
VOLUME 41

THE FUTURE OF AGENCY: BETWEEN AUTONOMY AND HETERONOMY

EDITED BY

HARRY F. DAHMS

University of Tennessee – Knoxville, USA

United Kingdom – North America – Japan
India – Malaysia – China

Emerald Publishing Limited
Emerald Publishing, Floor 5, Northspring, 21-23 Wellington Street, Leeds LS1 4DL

First edition 2025

Editorial matter and selection © 2025 Harry F. Dahms.
Individual chapters © 2025 The authors.
Published under exclusive licence by Emerald Publishing Limited.

Reprints and permissions service
Contact: www.copyright.com

No part of this book may be reproduced, stored in a retrieval system, transmitted in any form or by any means electronic, mechanical, photocopying, recording or otherwise without either the prior written permission of the publisher or a licence permitting restricted copying issued in the UK by The Copyright Licensing Agency and in the USA by The Copyright Clearance Center. Any opinions expressed in the chapters are those of the authors. Whilst Emerald makes every effort to ensure the quality and accuracy of its content, Emerald makes no representation implied or otherwise, as to the chapters' suitability and application and disclaims any warranties, express or implied, to their use.

British Library Cataloguing in Publication Data
A catalogue record for this book is available from the British Library

ISBN: 978-1-83608-979-7 (Print)
ISBN: 978-1-83608-978-0 (Online)
ISBN: 978-1-83608-980-3 (Epub)

ISSN: 0278-1204 (Series)

INVESTOR IN PEOPLE

CONTENTS

About the Editor											xi

About the Contributors										xiii

INTRODUCTION

Surviving (in) a World of Contradictions: Conceptualizing Agency Between Autonomy and Heteronomy			3
Harry F. Dahms

PART I
THE PERSISTENT PROBLEM AND CHALLENGE OF AGENCY (SOCIOLOGICAL THEORY)

What Do We Need "Agency" for? A Critical Analysis of Reasons for the Use of "Agency" in Sociology			15
Axel van den Berg and Emre Amasyalı

What Do We Use "Agency" for? A Critical Empirical Examination of Its Uses in the Sociological Literature		43
Emre Amasyalı and Axel van den Berg

Curiously Footnoted Conceptualizations of Agency						77
Steven Hitlin

Agency Between Freedom/Action and Determinism/Structure: Comment on van den Berg and Amasyalı			91
John Levi Martin

The Great Agency Muddle										103
Stephen Turner

Why Do We Need to Discuss Agency?								117
Axel van den Berg and Emre Amasyalı

PART II
THE PROBLEM AND CHALLENGE OF AUTONOMY (CLASSICAL AND CONTEMPORARY THEORY)

Erik Olin Wright's Selective Interpretation of Weber and Exploitation: A Discussion and Evaluation *129*
Sandro Segre

A Lost Horizon: Revisiting "the Societal Rationalization of the Economy" (Translator's Introduction) *147*
Anthony J. Knowles

The Societal Rationalization of the Economy: Guaranteed Minimum Income as a Constitutional Right *153*
Harry F. Dahms

PART III
THE PROBLEM AND CHALLENGE OF HETERONOMY (APPLIED CRITICAL THEORY)

Authoritarianism From Below: Why and How Donald Trump Follows His Followers *189*
David Norman Smith and Eric Allen Hanley

Project 2025 Environmental Policy: Postfactual Ecocatastrophe *237*
Robert J. Antonio

Filmmaking as Pedagogy and Praxis: An Interview With Garry Potter *257*
Daniel M. Harrison

Index *265*

ABOUT THE EDITOR

Harry F. Dahms (New School for Social Research, 1993) is a Professor of Sociology, a Codirector of the Center for the Study of Social Justice, and a Cochair of the Committee on Social Theory at the University of Tennessee in Knoxville. He also has taught at Florida State University, University of Göttingen (Germany), and University of Innsbruck (Austria) and is the editor of *Current Perspectives in Social Theory*, the director of the International Social Theory Consortium, and a task force member of the AI TENNessee Initiative. In 2021, he received the Senior-Level Excellence in Teaching Award (UTK College of Arts & Sciences). A collection of essays, *The Vitality of Critical Theory*, appeared in 2011. Dahms also edited and coedited numerous volumes and special issues of journals. Among his current book projects are *Modern Society as Artifice: Critical Theory and the Logic of Capital* (Routledge) and a monograph on Adorno, *Beyond Regression: Adorno's Sociology of Late Capitalism*.

ABOUT THE CONTRIBUTORS

Emre Amasyalı is a postdoctoral research fellow at the Institut Barcelona d'Estudis Internacionals (IBEI) in Barcelona. His research examines topics in political sociology, comparative historical sociology, and history and is substantively concerned with nationalism and processes of nation-building over long periods. He has published in *Social Science History*, the *International Journal of Comparative Sociology*, and the *European Journal of Sociology*. At IBEI, he is involved in Ethnicgoods, a 5-year research project funded by the European Research Council (ERC) Consolidator Grant.

Robert J. Antonio (PhD Notre Dame) is a Professor of Sociology at the University of Kansas and specializes in social theory, globalization, macroscopic sociology, economy and society, and climate change. His writings have focused on Marx, the Frankfurt School, Weber, Dewey, Habermas, and others in the classical and continental tradition. In recent years, he has focused on the global neoliberal regime and inequality, financial instability, and ecological degradation. Among his many publications are *Marx & Modernity* (2002), "When History Fails Us: Immanent Critique of Capitalism to the New Right and Beyond" (2021), "Social Theory in the Anthropocene: Ecological Crisis and Renewal" (2020; with Brett Clark), and "The Climate Change Divide in Social Theory" (2015; with Brett Clark).

Eric Allen Hanley (PhD UCLA) is an Associate Professor in Sociology at the University of Kansas and specializes in economic, environmental, and political sociology. His recent research focuses on political behavior in the United States, specifically the rise of white nationalism. Other projects also include analyses of the anti-mining movement in Peru and the political and economic processes contributing to land degradation in western China. Recent publications include "State Corporatism and Environmental Harm: Tax Farming and Desertification in Northwestern China" (with KuoRay Mao, *Journal of Agrarian* Change, 2018) and "The Anger Games: Who Voted for Donald Trump in the 2016 Election, and Why?" (with David Smith, *Critical Sociology*, 2018).

Daniel M. Harrison is a Professor of Sociology at Lander University in Greenwood, SC. His BA degree is from New College of the University of South Florida, and his MS and PhD degrees are from Florida State University. He is the author of *Making Sense of Marshall Ledbetter: The Dark Side of Political Protest* (University Press of Florida, 2014) and *Live at Jackson Station: Music, Community, and Tragedy in a Southern Blues Bar* (University of South Carolina Press, 2021). His essay "Sociology at the End of History: Profession, Vocation, and Critical

Practice" was published in *Current Perspectives in Social Theory, Vol. 36: The Challenge of Progress* (2019, pp. 133–155).

Steven Hitlin is a sociological social psychologist whose work spans morality, self and identity, the life course, and social theory. Before his faculty position at Iowa, he was a postdoctoral fellow at the University of North Carolina at Chapel Hill and received his PhD from the University of Wisconsin-Madison. He is an author or coauthor for several books and academic articles including *The Science of Dignity* (Oxford), *Unequal Foundations: Inequality, Morality and Emotions across Cultures* (Oxford), and *Moral Selves, Evil Selves: The Social Psychology of Conscience* (Palgrave Macmillan).

Anthony J. Knowles is a lecturer in sociology and a postdoctoral researcher at the Center for Transportation Research at the University of Tennessee – Knoxville. He was also a guest researcher at the University of Bielefeld for his dissertation research, which involved a comparative historical and theoretical analysis of automation and technological displacement in the United States and Germany. His research interests include automation and transformations of labor, critical theory, basic income, queer theory, and political theory and democracy. His work has appeared in *Current Perspectives in Social Theory* and *Social Justice*, and he is preparing a book manuscript based on his dissertation research for publication by Brill, within their series, *New Scholarship in Political Economy*.

John Levi Martin teaches Sociology at the University of Chicago. His most recent book is *The True, the Good, and the Beautiful: On the Rise and Fall and Rise of an Architectonic for Action*, in press with Columbia University Press. He is also the author of *The Explanation of Social Action*, as well as other books and articles on sociological theory.

Garry Potter is a social theorist and a filmmaker at Wilfrid Laurier University in Waterloo, ON. He is the author of *Dystopia: What is to be Done?* (New Revolution Press, 2010); *The Philosophy of Social Science: New Perspectives* (Routledge, 2017), and *The Bet: Truth in Science, Literature, and Everyday Knowledges* (Routledge, 2020). He is also the writer, producer, and director of more than 20 films, including: *Luxury Eco-Communism* (2020); *Sociology at the End of the World* (2018); *Contract Faculty: Injustice in the University* (2016); *Ideology: Marx, Althusser, Gramsci* (2015); *Marx's Theory of Alienation and Species Being* (2013); and *Whispers of Revolution* (2012).

Sandro Segre (born in 1945) was a Professor of Sociology and Sociological Theory at the University of Genoa (Italy) before his retirement in 2017. He received a PhD in Sociology in 1978 and a Master of Arts in Sociology in 1972 (both from New York University, Dept. of Sociology). In 1970, he received a "Laurea in Economia e Commercio" from the Università Bocconi of Milan. His recent publications (2008–2023) include several books, articles, and contributions, such as *Bauman, Elias and Latour on Modernity and Other Options* (London: Anthem Press, 2020); *Business Groups and Financial Markets: A*

Weberian Analysis (London: Routledge, 2018); *Contemporary Sociological Thinkers and Theories* (Aldershot: Ashgate, 2014) – Italian edition: *Le teorie sociologiche contemporanee* (Carocci, 2020); *Introduction to Habermas* (Lanham, MD: University Press of America, 2012); *Talcott Parsons: An Introduction* (Lanham, MD: University Press of America, 2012); *A Weberian Analysis of Business Groups and Financial Markets: Trade Relations in Taiwan and Korea and Some Major Stock Exchanges* (London: Ashgate, 2008).

David Norman Smith is a Professor of Sociology at the University of Kansas. He publishes widely under two broad theoretical rubrics, the critique of political economy, on the one hand, and the critique of political psychology, on the other hand. Work on the former topic revolves around the concepts of commodity, money, and capital fetishism. Work on the latter topic, the subject of "Authoritarianism from Below" in this volume, encompasses inquiry into charismatic authority, authoritarianism, antisemitism, ethnocentrism, genocide, and the Rwandan genocide. With Eric Hanley and Robert McWilliams, Smith successfully proposed the inclusion of Right-Wing Authoritarianism (RWA) and Social Dominance Orientation (SDO) items in the 2012–13 American National Election Study (ANES) and, with Hanley, the inclusion of RWA items in the 2016 ANES survey. With Kevin Anderson, he successfully submitted a proposal to the National Endowment for the Humanities (NEH) which enabled the transcription of hitherto unpublished late texts by Karl Marx on patriarchy and ethnology that appeared, in 2024, in digitized online form, in Vol. 4/27 of the *Marx-Engels Gesamtausgabe* (MEGA).

Stephen Turner (1951) is a Distinguished University Professor at the Department of Philosophy, University of South Florida, where he is also a director of the Center for Social and Political Thought. His degrees, in Philosophy and Sociology, are from the University of Missouri. He was an Honorary Simon Visiting Professor at the University of Manchester, and he has held fellowships from the US National Endowment for the Humanities and the Swedish Collegium for Advanced Studies. He has written on action explanation for many decades. His more writings in this area include essays collected in *Brains/Practices/Relativism: Social Theory after Cognitive Science* (2002) and *Understanding the Tacit* (2014). He more recently published *Cognitive Science and the Social: A Primer* (2018), *Teoria social e Cienças Cognitivistas* (2021). A memoir, *Mad Hazard: A Life in Social Theory* (2022), and a festschrift edited by Christopher Adair-Toteff, *Stephen Turner and the Philosophy of the Social* (2021), also discuss action explanation.

Axel van den Berg is a Professor of Sociology at McGill University where he has taught since 1984. His research interests include social and labor market policy, sociological theory and the relation between sociology and economics. He has participated in several multi-nationally funded research networks conducting cross-national comparative research on current transformations of the welfare state. His most recent book, coauthored with several graduate students, is *Combating Poverty: Quebec's Pursuit of a Distinctive Welfare State*, published in 2017 by the University of Toronto Press. His work on sociological theory has dealt with, and criticized, various aspects of Marxist theory, critical theory, grand theory, public sociology, and rational choice theory. He is currently working on a systematic examination of whether and how widely held "post-positivist" tenets in sociological theory are integrated into or accommodated by actual sociological research practice. The first paper from this project, entitled "Cutting Off the Branch on Which We Are Sitting? On Postpositivism, Value Neutrality, and the 'Bias Paradox'," written with Tay Jeong, was published in December 2022 in *Society*. It examines how authors manage the tension between epistemological relativism and rejection of "value free" social science on the one hand, and their own validity claims on the other.

INTRODUCTION

SURVIVING (IN) A WORLD OF CONTRADICTIONS: CONCEPTUALIZING AGENCY BETWEEN AUTONOMY AND HETERONOMY

Harry F. Dahms

University of Tennessee – Knoxville, USA

> Whatever experience the reader may register has to be thought out on the basis of the reader's own experience. Understanding has to find a foothold in the gap between experience and concept. Where concepts become an autonomous apparatus ... they need to be brought back into the intellectual experience that motivates them and be made vital, as they would like to be but are compulsively incapable of being.
>
> – Theodor W. Adorno (1963/1993, p. 166)

ABSTRACT

Agency is a concept whose status as a social-theoretical tool in and for the 21st century is a challenging question. Sociological *theorists endeavor to identify agency's analytical and systematic usefulness for social research.* Social *theorists and critical theorists are less concerned with agency as concept and tool but may be more dedicated to assessing and tracking the fate and future of agency as a historically and socially variable phenomenon. While social theorists recognize the importance of socio-historical variations, critical theorists also are concerned with how modern societies are inherently contradictory and problematic, especially when accounts try to balance a society's "official" validity claims with the realities they obscure. Many sociologists study the societal conditions that have a bearing on whether, how, and to what extent individuals are able to engage in self-determined actions and practices. Correlating a person's location in the social structure with the status of agency in human and social life, within the matrix of race, class, gender, sexual orientation, geographic location, education, and similar indicators, is essential to delineating individuals' ability to pursue opportunities for success and to take advantage of life chances. In societies that are reproducing, fraught with, and burdened by myriad contradictions and proliferating corollary dangers and threats, individuals' locations within the social structure effect their chances for and modes of survival. In the end, agency as a function of socio-historical specificity visualizes how individuals are making decisions and choices (agency ~ autonomy) within contexts that are beyond their control or understanding (determinism ~ heteronomy).*

Keywords: Theoretical sociology; social theory; sociological theory; critical theory; classical theory; politics

AGENCY AS A CONCEPT

"Agency," like many other social-theoretical and sociological concepts, is a notoriously amorphous and contested word that refers to an equally ambiguous and disputed phenomenon or genus of phenomena. Generally, agency is of interest to social scientists as it is located at the intersection of voluntary action and determinism: to what extent and how are individuals capable of determining their own conditions and fate, as opposed to "society" determining their choices and lives? Theoretically oriented social scientists often use and treat *agency* as a *word*, whereas recognizing its importance and potential value as a *concept*, along with its history and implications as a theoretical tool, is much more appropriate and productive. On the one hand, conceptual clarity and focus are preconditions for careful and pertinent research and analysis. Yet, on the other hand and by their very nature, socially and sociologically important phenomena appear in many different forms and variations, which often overwhelms even narrowly focused efforts to capture reality. Moreover, most languages and terminologies are too limited and limiting to facilitate capturing social phenomena in accurate and satisfactory fashion. There are many reasons for corollary difficulties. For instance, absent rigorous related training, the problem of interpretation is a major hurdle to recognizing the gravity of context, both as far as social situations are concerned, and the need to appreciate a social theorist's works and overall objective. Furthermore, the size of the human population today is larger than ever, which has been producing a relatively new type of contradictory effect, among many others. The more persons there are, the greater the opportunity for conflicting and countervailing patterns to take hold and persist. On the one hand, many pervasive patterns pertain to and reflect differences, divergences, disagreements, conflicts, incongruities, misunderstandings, and misinterpretations. On the other hand, the greater the variety and opportunities for differentiation, the stronger the impulse among many persons to insist on their distinctiveness and "singularity" while also seeking a semblance of security in conformity with and to others who appear to be similar to oneself. In the early 21st century, little remains that has not been contested, controversial, or offensive in one form or another, to members of certain segments of a population, and in many different forms.

In any case, all social and sociological phenomena of any import are far too multifarious for a concept, however refined, to be able to capture their nature or to do them justice. As the classics of social theory pointed out in different ways, as far back as Hegel, Marx, Durkheim, and Weber, the notion that modern societies can be in tune with themselves, well ordered, stable, immune to crises, is inconsistent with their very nature *as* modern societies. Any working definition of modernity must include acknowledgement that this type of society has a proclivity toward disorganization, instability, crises, and so forth. Even if certain types of government or modes of governance are successful at integrating a specific society sufficiently to "maintain order" (or to create the impression, which largely is the same), they can do so only for a certain period of time. Yet, maintaining order in any society is neither straightforward, nor is it possible to grasp at an intuitive level how order is being maintained, appearances to the contrary notwithstanding.

As far as "agency" is concerned, both the concept and the phenomenon directly relate to issues and challenges theorists and social researchers have struggled to acknowledge, consider, confront, and address, in the course of efforts to grasp the human condition in modern society under changing societal circumstances. Who or what influences, shapes, or determines how we exist and live, individually or as members of the human species? What is the balance between individual freedom and autonomy, on the one hand, and heteronomous societal forces and patterns that individuals may or may not be aware of and contemplate but must contend with throughout their lives, on the other? The importance of revisiting, refocusing, or revising specific established or neglected concepts is an indispensable task in social theory, to keep track of social change and to enhance our understanding of social and societal conditions, or both, together or separately.

Yet, for the most part, and perhaps categorically, the social and societal phenomenon or challenge a concept such as *agency* denotes and makes accessible typically is extremely difficult to capture, identify, or delineate. This difficulty precisely is the main reason why concepts nevertheless are indispensable, as opposed to terms or words, not least because rigorously conceptual thinking is rare in the social sciences, albeit slightly less so in social theory. Most practicing social scientists and many social theorists view concern with concepts as part of the domain of philosophy, despite the undeniable prominence of such works as Max Weber's "Basic Concepts in Sociology" (1913/1962). The methodological purpose and potential productivity of Weber's concepts, when deployed for the purpose of focusing and enhancing empirical social research, appears to be lost on many sociologists today. Especially in the aftermath of Hegel's influence, the reluctance of social scientists to engage in careful conceptual reflection, analysis, and application appears to be made of the same cloth as the refusal to consider the power of dialectical thinking.

Part of the reason for the difficulty to capture a social and societal phenomenon with the help of a corresponding concept is that the social world in general, but especially under modern conditions, is not static but inherently dynamic. What appears to be stable in fact rests on an ongoing process (or set of processes) prone to being self-sustaining, but this stability does not adhere to, nor is it directly a function of, human standards or values. Nor is it a generic dynamic and without identifiable qualities but tied to specific ways of doing things, including "doing business" (see, e.g., Postone, 1993). Concordantly, virtually every aspect of our reality involves a historical (and historically specific) dimension, and increasingly so, including what we term "nature." Yet without a probing, focused, and powerful concept, addressing effectively a particular phenomenon or an issue it refers to, in the singular or in its diverse multiplicity, would be impossible, absent the persistent search for more powerful concepts. Thus, advocating the usefulness of an established or a newly introduced concept to denote, delineate, or circumscribe a phenomenon largely is suggestive. Whether a promising attempt or an experiment that is bound to be preliminary is successful also is impossible to determine "objectively" but depends to a large extent on its impact on other members of one's discipline, the productivity and relevance of new insights it has the potential of engendering, or the direction of historical change. A concept's continuing or newly discernible usefulness often has less to do with its inherent worth (however it may be determined, according to what kind of criteria?) than with whether fellow social theorists and social scientists find it useful, intriguing, legitimate, compelling, or disturbing, often in comparison or support of, or in competition with, their own work and efforts.

Typically, in social theory, and especially in sociological theory, the concept of "agency" is associated with particular types of "action": generally speaking, human action in society or social action, i.e., action that is socially consequential or relevant. More specifically, agency also may refer to types of action along a spectrum, e.g., from reproductive to productive, from regenerative to transformative, or from regressive to progressive. Types of action that affirm, support, revert to, or protect an existing social structure or order may fall into the category of "agency," as well as types that reject, try to subvert, to change, or to improve a social structure or order. Agency that belongs into the first category may fall under a continuum from "conservative" or "reactionary," while agency that belongs into the second category may range from "liberal" to "revolutionary." In both cases, however, it is important to retain a certain amount of skepticism about whether either type of agency truly amounts to genuinely "conservative," "liberal," "reactionary," or "revolutionary" forms of action, as actors often are prone to imagining (and projecting) that their or their opponents' and enemies' actions are consonant or consistent with such designations. Yet, are these distinctions relevant for the sociological study of agency?

Agency in the 21st Century

Since the beginning of the 21st century, as the totality of social and societal life has been going through major reorientations, upheavals, and convulsions at an accelerating pace, the future of agency in the broader sense has become increasingly unclear. One mode of approaching *agency* would be to conceive of it in proximity to autonomous action or self-possession: agency would apply to *actors who know what they do, why they do it, in what context, for what reasons, for which purpose, how, and with what kind of goal in mind.* Under currently emerging circumstances, agency in this sense of an individual's circumspection about their actions and activities would appear to be increasingly difficult to sustain, as even the vision of such a stance towards action would seem to be incongruous with the state of the human species, the proliferating challenges we are facing, and the future of humankind. On the other hand, does this larger context and its problematic condition even matter as far the place of agency in sociological theory is concerned? Should this larger context be part of the equation? Who today is truly "in control" – of themselves or their environment, not to mention anyone else? The very idea of any individual being in control does not seem to resonate with but may impede an adequate understanding of the character of social and societal life today.

The so-called "anxiety epidemic" draws attention to the fact that the 21st century has been a time when especially many younger persons are feeling less and less well-prepared or able to face the many uncertainties, threats, and dangers the future is holding. The intensity of experiences of cognitive dissonance appears to be reaching a breaking point for many, especially in the absence of schooling that should have prepared them to manage such experiences constructively and productively. At the same time, segments of the elites and political classes in many countries are adopting stances vis-à-vis many of their own societies' institutions and traditions which they used to endow with proto-religious qualities and which they were committed "to protect against all enemies foreign and domestic," until doing so became inconvenient or a hurdle to amassing power. Given that it is categorically impossible to keep at bay the future as a source of uncertainties in highly complex, integrated, and contradictory politico-economic societies, whether "people" or many individuals are determined to "prevent" uncertain futures is of little consequence. Making the future more predictable and reliable, e.g., by "turning back" the clock on progress, is bound to aggravate further the element of uncertainty, although in the short term, doing so may come with certain direct and indirect benefits for some, perhaps for many.

Unsurprisingly, the future of agency, too, is fraught with uncertainty and ambiguity, both the concept and the multiplicity of phenomena to which the concept refers. The projection of a better future has enabled modern societies to compel individuals to act in ways that appear to be consonant with the possibility of continuous progress, but what we are observing today is a process of inverted progress overtaking the potential for actual progress – the opposite of regression – that remains. The resulting field of intensifying tensions has a direct bearing on "agency" and its meanings, purposes, and forms in the 21st century. Agency refers to types of *action* whose specific manifestations and underlying intentions require careful analysis and examination. The meaning, role, nature, status, and legitimacy of human agency currently is undergoing major changes, along with and as part of the totality of modern social and societal life, even though at the level of surface appearances, everyday life may seem to be flowing along at it has for decades, if not longer.

AGENCY IN THEORETICAL SOCIOLOGY: SOCIOLOGICAL THEORY, SOCIAL THEORY, AND APPLIED CRITICAL THEORY[1]

As a concept that has been especially prominent in sociological theory, agency has been at the center of efforts to pin down its meaning for analytical and systematic purposes in social research. *Sociological* theorists especially have been concerned with agency as an abstract concept intended to illuminate aspects of modern societies that are located at the intersection of voluntarism and determinism and the question of whether, how, and to what extent individuals' actions are the result of free will or of structural and systematic features that prefigure human actions or inaction. By contrast, *social* theorists and *critical* theorists appear to be less prone to reference and address agency explicitly in their works and possibly more concerned with assessing and tracking the fate and future of human and/or social "agency" across time and space, in history and particular societies. By implication, social and critical theories treat agency and its variable uses as a tool intended to capture specific conditions and circumstances as they find expression in individuals' ability or inability to make choices on their own rather than on society's terms. Social and critical theorists often provide insights that rely on and pertain to empirical specificity in a manner that typically is not part of the purview and self-understanding of sociological theorists. To be sure, most "theorists of the social" in the broader sense do what they do without clearly and rigorously distinguishing between sociological, social, and critical theory: concern with the nature of the social is the driver, and the underlying motivation often remains just that, *underlying* and *implicit*. Although theoretical sociologists by definition study the modern condition, it is not uncommon to refrain from making related distinctions, instead purporting to study "society in general." Yet, the kind of society sociologists are interested in resulted from the parallel spread of capitalist market economies and the industrial revolution, and the entire apparatus of methods and tools sociologists developed to study this genus of society co-emerged with the spread of this type of society.

Many sociologists engaged in social research regard it as part of their charge as social scientists to delineate the societal conditions that have a bearing on whether, how, and to what extent individuals are able and have the opportunity to engage in agency. Correlating a person's location within the matrix of race, class, gender, sexual orientation, geographic location, education, and similar indicators, with the status of agency in human and social life is essential to delineating a person's ability to pursue opportunities for success and to take advantage of life chances.[2] Increasingly, in the context of social structures that are fraught with and burdened by myriad contradictions and proliferating corollary dangers and threats, individuals' locations within the matrix also impact their chances for and modes of *survival*. In every instance, concern with agency would need to consider historical and comparative specificity and how exactly, in what ways, and to what extent individuals, depending on their position within the social structure, are able to make independent decisions and choices. How autonomous are we, how much agency do we have, within contexts that are beyond our control or understanding, especially if we lack rigorous theoretical and social-scientific training? Do we shape the circumstances of our lives, or do those circumstances influence ("determine") both our lives and ability to grasp our circumstances, within contexts that are fraught with heteronomous forces and processes that shape humans, and which humans do not have the power to shape in turn? In highly complex, industrialized, bureaucratic societies that rely on corporate forms as well as ongoing permutations of the logic of capital, humans may be able to take advantage of emerging and transient opportunities, but humans cannot abolish organizational or economic forms and modes, at least not without risking our own existence, individually and collectively.

Social and critical theorists often provide insights that are not part of the purview and self-understanding of sociological theorists who focus on identifying and establishing tools for social research meant to apply across the range of socio-historical contexts. But the tools are intended to facilitate illumination of, not to reflect specific socio-historical contexts (even though, practically speaking, it is impossible to develop tools for sociologists in whose conception and construction specific socio-historical contexts are not present in some form or other). Social theory (as an ideal type) is concerned with socio-historical and comparative specificity – how exactly a particular society is constituted, with what kind of implications for individual and social life and existence within force fields that include economic, political, social, cultural, environmental, and psychological challenges and circumstances. By comparison, critical theory takes the further step to consider what bearing a society's constitution has on the work of social scientists and theorists of the social, how the society maintains stability and functions. Critical theory also is concerned with the specific ways in which a society is problematic and predictably requires systematic critique. How *exactly* does a particular society place all individuals in double-binds and impose forms of cognitive dissonance, contradictions, and violations of the principles according to which it is supposed to be organized, and how it purports to work and bestow success and failure in structurally unequal ways on members of different groups in society.

Sociological theorists tend not to be concerned primarily with the socio-historical embeddedness of their work. Most sociologists, however, regard identifying, delineating, and scrutinizing the concrete societal conditions that have a bearing on how humans live and coexist, as part of their charge as social scientists, and – in the present context – whether and how and to what extent individuals are able to engage in agency. Specifically, in different ways, most sociologists illuminate the place of agency within the matrix of race, class, gender, sexual orientation, geographic location, education, and similar indicators, to delineate individuals' ability to pursue personal and professional success, reconciliation between the norms and values that guide their lives and the larger material conditions in which they exist, and – if so – equal life chances. Such pursuits are key to *survival*, not only bare biological survival, but survival as human and social beings within contradictory social structures that provide opportunities and come with constant dangers and challenges to personal well-being and social membership.

Thus, in every instance of social research, concern with agency would need to consider historical and comparative specificity and how exactly individuals, depending on their position within the social structure, are or are not likely to be able to make independent decisions and choices within contexts that are far beyond their control or grasp. Part of the self-understanding and purpose of sociology as an emergent discipline in the late 19th and early 20th century was to establish knowledge about the forces that situate and shape individual's lives. In the works of such classics as Emile Durkheim, Max Weber, and Georg Simmel, this objective is tangible, as well as in the writings of precursors like Georg Wilhelm Friedrich Hegel and Karl Marx, and less well-known proponents of sociology like Lester F. Ward, the "father of American sociology." How are humans prone to misinterpret their life stories as mostly their own responsibility and doing, and to persistently endeavor to understand and "explain" society in human terms, as extensions and transpositions of human values, desires, modes of behavior and interaction? Individuals generally are inclined to view forms of social life as functions of human existence, rather than the unsettling and disturbing reverse: modes of human existence and life goals, and social coexistence, as functions of societal needs and requirements, well above the circumspection of what individuals possibly could conceive of. This tension between the need to organize and conduct our lives as if we were *autonomous* decision-makers capable of determining the conditions of our individual lives, and the fact that modern societies are far too complex and contradictory to allow for and tolerate such autonomy, is precisely what necessitated sociology as a social science. Persistent efforts to illuminate modern circumstances with regular innovations in our reliance on theoretical frames and tools to keep up with the accelerating pace of social change are required to stress how heteronomy is the unpleasant secret of our lives. One key illustration of the power of heteronomy may well be that even and especially individuals who think of themselves as immune to the workings of social, economic, and technological forces often are more likely to support and amplify the latter, further diminishing opportunities for human and social autonomy, frequently in the name of individual freedom and self-determination. Governments typically are the targets of such insistence on freedom, as if governments were "in control of society," a profound and momentous misunderstanding. Paradoxically, most governments are efforts to balance the normative desire for autonomy with an inescapably practical understanding that heteronomous forces do their own bidding, regardless of what this or that person, or the government, might think of them.

In turn, at the current historical juncture, an equally intricate (in its manifestations) and complex (in each instance) phenomenon such as agency may necessitate historically sensitive analyses within theoretical sociology as itself a field of tensions. Concordantly, assessments of early, either implicit or explicit, contributions to the study of agency, along with its status and condition in time and space (i.e., in specific societies or types of society), would belong to the domain of social theory. Scrutinizing how changing political trends and conditions have a bearing on the ability of individuals to engage in agency would belong to critical theory. The pursuit of conceptual clarity, and how it ought to translate into the study of agency in social research, would belong to sociological theory.

The main (first) part of this volume takes the form of "author-meets-critics" and is dedicated to examining the concept of agency within the context of *sociological* theory, centered on two chapters by Axel van den Berg and Emre Amasyalı on the need for and uses of *agency*. One chapter is focused on the need for this concept, the other on related uses. Both chapters ask whether the concept in fact does the work its proponents claim it does. In response, Steven Hitlin, John Levi Martin, and Stephen Turner provide assessments of how van den Berg and Amasyalı answer their own questions. In turn, van den Berg and Amasyalı reply to their "critics."

Parts Two and Three do not address the concept of agency explicitly, but they provide treatments of the phenomenon's importance and context. Part Two includes treatments at the intersection of classical and contemporary *social* theories. Sandro Segre provides an assessment of Erik Olin Wright's interpretation of Max Weber's work on class. To be sure, in the social-theoretical and sociological theory literature, "class" consistently has served as a frame for addressing the tension between autonomy and heteronomy, and between agency and determinism, but rarely in explicit terms. Typically, discussions of class have been at the center of questions pertaining to whether and under what conditions individuals may have the opportunity to escape their circumstances as defined and determined by social structures, and how class position corresponds with related difficulties. In more recent decades, particularly in relational approaches in social theory and sociology (which also play an important role as far as the study of agency is concerned), the view has taken hold that constellations of individual and class often are rather dialectical in nature. Class defines the opportunities individuals do or do not have available in pursuing life chances, but class structures persist because during their socialization and early education, individuals internalize their class position (as part of acquiring a self, an identity), thus potentially reinforcing the conditions that are limiting or enhancing their opportunities and access to acquiring abilities, skills, social knowledge, etc. Depending on one's particular position in the class structure, one is able to access the means for a relatively autonomous life, or deprived of the same. The second part of this volume also includes an introduction by Anthony J. Knowles to his translation of an article I published more than 30 years ago, in one of the leading German sociology journals edited at the time by social theorist Ulrich Beck. The article is an attempt to trace the idea of a guaranteed minimum income (or universal basic income) through relevant writings by Georg Wilhelm Friedrich Hegel, Eduard Heimann, Ralf Dahrendorf, Claus Offe, and Jürgen Habermas, focusing on this idea at the legal-constitutional level as a means to increase individual autonomy for all citizens, not least as a precondition for greater overall societal rationality.

Finally, Part Three includes two chapters that draw theoretical insights from the present political situation in the United States, and one chapter that is about communicating critical social knowledge to large audiences. All three chapters are instances of *applied critical theory*. The first chapter is by David Smith and Eric Allen Hanley and examines, in terms of the literature sparked by the famous study of the authoritarian personality in 1950, the symbiotic relationship between Donald Trump and his followers. Although not addressed explicitly, reactions to social and societal circumstances and developments visualize in dramatic fashion the potentially explosive tension between autonomy and heteronomy, and agency and determinism, as it practically is playing out in American society and arguably transforming its very fabric – politically, socially, and economically. In similar fashion and referring to precisely the same case, Robert Antonio provides a critical social analysis of "Project 2025" and its far-reaching potential implications for American society if pursued and implemented, with an emphasis on environmental policy. The third chapter is an interview by Daniel Harrison, with Canadian social theorist Garry Potter. The theme of the interview is Potter's production of documentaries as means to communicate important sociological and critical social-theoretical concepts, ideas, and tools to larger audiences than social theorists typically have access to.

NOTES

1. For present purposes, I am distinguishing between the three main types of theoretical sociology: social theory, sociological theory, and critical theory. Nicos Mouzelis (1995, pp. 3–8; see also Dahms, 2007, pp. 197–200) has suggested that we should differentiate these types as follows: *sociological theories* are analytical and heuristic devices ("tools") whose purpose it is to examine a phenomenon (or question); *social theories* are socio-historically descriptive representations of societies at certain stages of their development ("end-product"); and *critical theories* are identifying critical standards for determining which tools and representations are most adequate for understanding the significance of a phenomenon, action paradigm, or historical reference frame. Whereas critical theories are concerned with identifying, analyzing, and scrutinizing the gravity concrete socio-historical circumstances exert on the process of and agenda of social research, sociological theory typically has no related concerned, nor does social theory, in most instances (see Dahms, 2008).

2. I am using the concept as developed by Ralf Dahrendorf (1979).

REFERENCES

Adorno, T. W. (1963/1993). *Hegel: Three studies* (S. W. Nicholsen, Trans.). MIT Press.
Dahms, H. F. (2007, Fall/Winter). Confronting the contradictory nature of modern social life. *Soundings: An Interdisciplinary Journal*, 90(3/4), 191–205.
Dahms, H. F. (2008). How social science is impossible without critical theory: The immersion of mainstream approaches in time and space. In H. F. Dahms (Ed.), *No social science without critical theory. Current perspectives in social theory* (Vol. 25, pp. 3–61). Emerald Publishing Limited.
Dahrendorf, R. (1979). *Life chances: Approaches to social and political theory*. Weidenfeld & Nicolson.
Mouzelis, N. (1995). *Sociological theory: What went wrong?* Routledge.
Postone, M. (1993). *Time, labor, and social domination: A reinterpretation of Marx's critical theory*. Cambridge University Press.
Weber, M. (1913/1962). *Basic concepts in sociology* (H. P. Scherer, Trans.). Philosophical Library.

PART I

THE PERSISTENT PROBLEM AND CHALLENGE OF AGENCY (SOCIOLOGICAL THEORY)

WHAT DO WE NEED "AGENCY" FOR? A CRITICAL ANALYSIS OF REASONS FOR THE USE OF "AGENCY" IN SOCIOLOGY[1]

Axel van den Berg[a] and Emre Amasyalı[b]

[a]*McGill University, Canada*
[b]*IBEI — Barcelona, Spain*

> We have to believe in free will. We've got no choice.
>
> – Isaac Bashevis Singer

ABSTRACT

Since its introduction by Anthony Giddens in the early 1980s, the use of the concept of "agency" as a way to accommodate an irreducible element of voluntarism into sociological explanations has grown exponentially in the literature. In this chapter, we examine the most prominent theoretical justifications for adopting the notion of "agency" as an integral part of such explanations. We distinguish three broad sets of justifications: the meaningfulness/intentionality of social action, the need for "agency" to explain change in social structures, and the link between agency, social accountability, and human dignity. We find that none of these provides a convincing rationale for the analytical utility of agency. This raises the question of what work it actually does *perform in the sociological literature.*

Keywords: Agency; voluntarism; theoretical justifications; explanatory use; social accountability; human dignity

INTRODUCTION

Philosophers have struggled with the concept of Free Will for millennia and continue to do so (see, e.g., Kane, 2011; Swindal, 2012; see, e.g., the contributions in Watson, 2003). By contrast, among sociologists, the notion of "agency" appears to be as unproblematic as it is popular, as shown by the massive and growing wave of sociological publications treating it as a central explanatory concept. A simple search on the *Web of Science* database for "agency" as a topic in sociology publications produces 5,277 articles and papers published since 1985, the annual numbers swelling continuously from 3 publications in 1985 to 432 in 2020 (see Appendix 1).

To be sure, sociology, too, has wrestled with the philosophical paradox of voluntarism vs determinism. The tension within Marxism between the inexorable structural forces of advancing modes of production on the one hand and the proletariat's unwillingness to execute its historical mission, on the other, is well-known (Anderson, 1976, 1980; van den Berg, 2004; Gouldner, 1980; Parkin, 1979; Thompson, 1978). So is Talcott Parsons' notorious slide from his initial commitment to a "voluntaristic theory of social action" (Parsons, 1937) to a much-criticized relentless determinism (Garfinkel, 1967; Gouldner, 1970; Homans, 1964; Wrong, 1961; see also Barnes, 2000, pp. 21–24; Loyal & Barnes, 2001, pp. 508–512).

Parsons' critics were primarily concerned with what Garfinkel aptly called his "cultural dope" view of social actors (Garfinkel, 1967, pp. 66–75) or his "oversocialized conception of man" (Wrong, 1961), which takes "conformity to norms for granted" (Homans, 1964, p. 814) and assumes that "human conduct is *totally* shaped by common norms" (Wrong, 1961, p. 186, our emphasis). In other words, these critics objected specifically to Parsons's *cultural* determinism rather than to his determinism *as such*.

The principal exception among Parsons' critics is Herbert Blumer whose critique was explicitly based on his Meadian voluntarism. According to Blumer:

> …joint activity and individual conduct…are not mere expressions or products of what people bring to their interaction or of conditions that are antecedent to their interaction. The failure to accommodate to [sic] this vital point constitutes the *fundamental deficiency of schemes that seek to account for human society in terms of social organization or psychological factors, or of any combination of the two*. By virtue of symbolic interaction, human group life is necessarily a formative process and not a mere arena for the expression of pre-existing factors. (Blumer, 1969, p. 10, emphasis added)

In other words, unlike Parsons' other critics, Blumer insists on an irreducible element of voluntarism over and beyond the effects of "social organization or psychological factors, or of any combination of the two."[2]

But it was only in the 1980s, in the wake of Anthony Giddens' recasting of the issue as the agency vs structure *problématique*, that the wave of sociological writings referring to "agency" really took off. Giddens, too, takes Parsons' alleged slippage into determinism as his point of departure:

> The use of the term 'voluntarism' suggests that Parsons wished to try to build into his own approach a conception of the actor as a creative, innovative agent. For Parsons the very same values that compose the *consensus universal*, as "introjected" by actors, are the motivating elements of personality. If these are the "same" values, however, what leverage can there

possibly be for the creative character of human action as nominally presupposed by the term 'voluntarism'? Parsons interprets the latter concept as referring simply to 'elements of a normative character'; *the 'freedom of the acting subject' then becomes reduced – and very clearly so in Parsons' mature theory – to the need-dispositions of personality.* In the 'action frame of reference', 'action' itself enters the picture only within the context of an emphasis that sociological accounts of conduct need to be complemented with psychological accounts of 'the mechanisms of personality'. The system is a wholly deterministic one.[3] (Giddens, 1993, p. 103, emphasis in original)

Giddens' much-debated resolution of the apparent antinomy between agency and structure – positing a "duality" of structure and agency according to which agents and social structures *mutually* constitute each other – will not detain us here.[4] Nor will we consider the rather odd circumstance that the concept of "structure," for all its centrality in sociological thinking since at least Marx and Durkheim, has remained remarkably ill-defined in Giddens' and others' attempts to specify its relation to "agency" (see, e.g., Jenkins, 2010; Sewell, 1992). What concerns us here is the notion of agency itself and its supposed role in sociological explanations.

Although he treats it at some length (Giddens, 1993, pp. 78–82, 1984, pp. 3–16, 281–285), Giddens' concept of "agency" remains surprisingly nebulous. But its voluntaristic intent, explicitly adopted from symbolic interactionism and ethnomethodology (Giddens, 1984, pp. 2–3), is quite clear.[5] "Agency," he writes, "concerns events of which an individual is the perpetrator, in the sense that the individual could, at any phase in a given sequence of conduct, have acted differently" (Giddens, 1984, p. 9).

By contrast, instead of rejecting Parsons' theory, Jeffrey Alexander seeks to amend it by incorporating a suitably voluntaristic concept of agency. He conceives Parsons' three systems (the psychological, cultural and social) as "environments" of action which constrain and inspire but do not wholly determine it. These environments:

…do not exhaust the contents of a person's subjectivity. There remains the extremely significant dimension of agency. Philosophers may understand agency, or free will, as an existential category; for sociologists it can be conceived as process, one that involves invention, typification, and strategization. These processes give pragmatic shape to the exercise of free will. (Alexander, 1998, pp. 215–216)

In other words, and importantly for our purposes, action contains an element of voluntarism that is not in any way causally reducible to personality, culture or social relations, or any combination thereof (see also Alexander, 1988, Chap. 10, 1993, 1998, pp. 210–216).

By far the most elaborate attempt to nail down the notion of agency is a much-cited article by Emirbayer and Mische, appropriately titled "What Is Agency?" (Emirbayer & Mische, 1998). The article begins with the following observation:

The concept of agency has become a source of increasing strain and confusion in social thought. At the center of the debate, the term *agency* itself has maintained an elusive, albeit resonant, vagueness; it has all too seldom inspired systematic analysis, despite the long list of terms with which it has been associated: selfhood, motivation, will, purposiveness, intentionality, choice, initiative, freedom, and creativity. (1998, p. 962, emphasis in original)

In proposing to clear up the confusion, Emirbayer and Mische explicitly "build upon Alexander's highly useful categorization, which opens up theoretical space for analyzing the inventive and critical aspects of agency" (Emirbayer & Mische, 1998, p. 967). But they define agency in terms of the temporal orientation of actors:

> What, then, is human agency? We define it as the temporally constructed engagement by actors of different structural environments – the temporal-relational contexts of action – which, through the interplay of habit, imagination, and judgment, both reproduces and transforms those structures in interactive response to the problems posed by changing historical situations. (Emirbayer & Mische, 1998, p. 970, emphasis in original)[6]

This temporal view of agency encompasses three analytically distinct "constitutive elements," the "iterational" orientation toward the past, the "projective" one oriented toward the future, and the "practical-evaluative" element concerned with the present (Emirbayer & Mische, 1998, pp. 970–971). The remainder of their long article is primarily devoted to identifying different subprocesses for each of these three temporal dimensions and to showing how the sociological literature is replete with explanations of social action in terms of such temporal orientations of the actors.

At this point, we are not concerned with whether or to what extent Emirbayer and Mische's recasting of agency as a configuration of temporal orientations succeeds in clarifying the concept and establishing its explanatory import.[7] What matters to us here is that like all other theorists of agency, Emirbayer and Mische consistently emphasize its voluntaristic, creative, and reflexive character. Not even the iterational dimension, they insist, can be reduced to the notions of habit, routinization, and tradition emphasized by other theorists. For it, too, contains an important "agentic dimension" consisting of "how actors selectively recognize, locate, and implement such schemas [from their past] in their ongoing and situated transactions" (Emirbayer & Mische, 1998, p. 975). The same holds a fortiori for the obviously more "agentic" temporal orientations of projection and evaluation. As they put it in a programmatic statement at the beginning of their article, "[w]e claim that, in examining changes in agentic orientation, we can gain crucial analytical leverage for charting varying degrees of maneuverability, inventiveness, and reflective choice shown by social actors in relation to the constraining and enabling contexts of action" (Emirbayer & Mische, 1998, p. 964).

In short, like Blumer, Giddens, Alexander, and even the early Parsons before them, Emirbayer and Mische take the distinctive feature of agency to be that it points to the element of choice and creativity of actors facing the constraints and opportunities offered by the structural contexts of action, which include the actors' own sociopsychological predispositions. In one way or another, these authors all reject a model of causal explanation that takes action to be the fully determined joint product of actors' environments and their psychological predispositions. Beyond these, they insist on an element of choice, of free will. "All social action is a concrete synthesis," Emirbayer and Mische conclude, "shaped and conditioned, on the one hand, by the temporal-relational contexts of action and, on the other, by the dynamic element of agency itself. The latter guarantees that empirical social action will never be *completely* determined or structured" (Emirbayer & Mische, 1998, p. 1004).

This is the key point we wish to make in this introductory section. Sociological calls for "bringing agency back in" are not merely meant to point to the importance of social processes at the microlevel, nor are they intended to highlight the causal significance of the actions of specific individuals. Both of these could in principle be accommodated in an entirely deterministic causal explanatory model that takes action and its outcomes as the wholly determined effect of the confluence of "structural" conditions and the actors' psychological predispositions. By contrast, the authors cited here subscribe to what Pleasants has called the "categorical" libertarian view "that at least some of our actions are not causally determined by antecedent states and events" at all (Pleasants, 2019, p. 9), whether these be social-structural or psychological or a combination of the two. To them, the distinctive and appealing feature of the notion of agency is that it holds the promise of allowing us to incorporate an element of free will, creativity, unpredictability, choice, etc., into our explanatory models.[8]

WHY DO WE NEED "AGENCY"?

In the next three sections of this chapter, we systematically assess the principal theoretical arguments in the literature supporting these calls for bringing agency back in. We distinguish three broad sets of justifications for incorporating "agency" in sociological explanations: that social action is meaningful, intentional, and (to some degree) the result of deliberation; that some voluntaristic element like "agency" is required to be able to explain change in social structures; and the need for a concept like "agency" as part of the socially inescapable assignment of social responsibility. We find that none of these provide a satisfactory justification for incorporating such a voluntaristic notion of agency into sociological explanations. This raises the question of what role the notion of "agency" really *does* fulfill in the growing literature claiming to employ it.

Meaning, Intention, and Deliberation

Max Weber famously declared the object of sociology to be the explanation of social action by means of an interpretive understanding of the meanings actors attribute to their actions (Weber, 1978, p. 4ff) since "explanation requires a grasp of the complex of meaning in which an actual course of understandable action thus interpreted belongs" (Weber, 1978, p. 9). In contrast to the natural sciences which must treat their objects externally as the passive products of the push and pull of antecedent forces, sociology is able to access the meaning actors attach to their actions through empathic understanding or *verstehen* (Weber, 1978, p. 15). And since the meanings and purposes of the actions are in effect *chosen* by the actors, it would seem to follow that a *verstehende* sociology would have to take into account the fact that actors have agency, that is, that they make choices that are to some extent free.

According to some of his interpreters, this was precisely the voluntaristic position taken by Weber himself. Thus, Freund argues that Weber's *verstehende* sociology implies that social phenomena cannot "be accounted for satisfactorily by causal explanations, that is by other, antecedent phenomena...because, to account for them, it is also necessary to understand their motives; that is, the reasons which have led men to act and the goals which they are pursuing...This is because human action is based on *will*, on a capacity, therefore, for anticipation or resistance, which takes us beyond simple material conditions" (Freund, 1979, p. 168).

However debatable this interpretation of Weber's own views may be, the linkage made between meaning and agency is a central feature of the interpretative tradition to which Weber was responding.[9] Thus, in one *locus classicus* (Taylor, 1971), Charles Taylor argues that the fact that social action is inherently a matter of meaning as interpreted by the actors implies that the "human sciences" must be hermeneutical. In social science, explanation necessarily consists of interpretation with the aim of achieving an adequate understanding of the actors' motives, given *their* practices and institutions. This, in turn, rules out the kind of prediction based on causally deterministic models of explanation since "man is a self-defining animal. With changes in his self-definition go changes in what man is, such that he has to be understood in different terms" (Taylor, 1971, p. 49, see also 1985 Chap. 2). Similarly, Blumer argues that to take meaning seriously means that rather than treating human beings as the mere products of pre-existing forces, sociology must conceive "of the individuals themselves as existentially free agents who accept, reject, modify, or otherwise 'define' the community's norms, roles, beliefs, and so forth, according to their own personal interests and plans of the moment" (in Lewis & Smith, 1980, p. 24). And again, Emirbayer and Goodwin criticize network analysis which, they argue, "either neglects or inadequately conceptualizes the crucial dimension of subjective meaning and motivation...and thereby fails to show exactly how it is that intentional, creative human action serves in part to constitute those very social networks that so powerfully constrain actors in turn" (1994, p. 1413).

But, one might ask, why should we treat the meanings, motivations, and intentions of social actions as arising *ex nihilo*, as uncaused causes? Why does the mere fact that actors have intentions and attach meanings to their actions imply that these intentions and meanings are themselves impervious to causal explanation? No doubt the hermeneutic exercise of trying to understand the actors' motives within their own sociocultural context is an important part of the explanatory enterprise. But this in no way precludes the causal explanation of these motives as the result of a particular configuration of external circumstances and internal psychological dispositions, the kind of explanation which, as we saw in the introduction, advocates of agency find unsatisfactory.[10]

Some authors would concede in principle that the mere existence of beliefs and intentions need not be incompatible with such a causally deterministic approach (Greenwood, 1988, pp. 104–106; Sharrock, 1987, p. 148) but add the Wittgensteinian point that the rules, norms, and prescriptions actors seek to apply are never wholly determinate. In each concrete situation, the actor needs to *interpret* them as best she can, and this means there can be different interpretations even by seemingly very similar actors in very similar contexts.[11] This, in turn, means that choices must be made and, therefore, that at least some actions are self-determined by the actors rather than wholly "determined by internal or external stimulus conditions" (Greenwood, 1988, p. 110). Blumer, too, insists on the centrality of "the process of interpretation" which "...should not be regarded as a mere automatic application of established meanings but as a formative process in which meanings are used and revised as instruments for the guidance and formation of action" (Blumer, 1969, p. 5). Similarly, Charles Taylor asserts that "we have to think of man as a self-interpreting animal. He is necessarily so, for there is no such thing as the structure of meanings for him independently of his interpretation of them; for one is woven into the other" (Taylor, 1971, p. 16).[12]

The idea that interpretation of meaning is to some extent inherently voluntaristic is made explicit by several authors who link the notion of agency to (the degree of) deliberation involved in social action. Simply put, the argument is that humans have the ability to reflect upon and deliberate about alternative courses of action before deciding which course to follow and that, hence, until the moment of decision, courses of action *other than* the one eventually chosen *could have been* chosen instead. Therefore, so the argument goes, action based on reflection or deliberation necessarily contains an element of free will.[13]

Thus, Anthony Giddens and Margaret Archer, who otherwise disagree profoundly on how to conceive of the relation between agency and structure,[14] "both define agency in terms of an actor's reflexivity, because we are agents precisely at the point of consciously choosing a course of action in circumstances where we could have acted otherwise" (Burkitt, 2016, p. 323). Inspired by "the major contributions of interpretative sociologies," Giddens heavily emphasizes "the specifically reflexive form of knowledgeability of human agents" (Giddens, 1979, pp. 55–58, 1984, pp. 2–3, see also p. 30, 1993, p. 163), which implies, as we have seen already, "that the individual could, at any phase in a given sequence of conduct, have acted differently" (Giddens, 1984, p. 9). Similarly, for Margaret Archer, the key to human agency is the "'inner conversation' as the process which generates our concrete singularity" (2000, p. 10). Through this inner conversation, "human beings have the powers of critical reflection upon their social context and of creatively redesigning their social environment, its institutional or ideational configurations, or both...[enabling] human beings to become agentially effective in these ways" (Archer, 2000, p. 308, see also 2007, 2012). Emirbayer and Mische, too, "ground [the] capacity for human agency in the structures and processes of the human self, conceived of as an internal conversation possessing analytic autonomy vis-à-vis transpersonal interactions" (Emirbayer & Mische, 1998, p. 974). And, as we have seen already, a central theme in symbolic interactionism, from Blumer (see, e.g., Blumer, 1969, pp. 13–15) to Wiley (Wiley, 1994), is that the processes of interpretation and "self-interaction" are at the root of human freedom and creativity.

An interesting corollary of the association of agency with deliberation, one most explicitly pursued by Margaret Archer, is that "agenticness" is a matter of degree.[15] After all, the amount of reflection or deliberation that informs our actions is exceedingly variable, as is the inclination of different actors to engage in such reflection. According to Archer, the lifelong "inner conversation" produces a wide range of degrees of reflexivity and dispositions to consciously deliberate among different individuals and, consequently, widely differing degrees to which they can become "agentially effective" (Archer, 2000, p. 308, see also pp. 222–249). While some individuals eventually attain the status of fully fledged, autonomous, self-conscious, and effective "social actors," many remain stuck at the level of "primary agents," passively resigned in their given social location, "at the mercy of first-order pushes and pulls" (Archer, 2000, p. 246). In subsequent work, Archer has tried to document the existence of different levels of reflexivity through in-depth interviews with individuals from different social backgrounds, yielding a hierarchy of levels of agenticness (Archer, 2003, 2007, 2012). She distinguishes several types of lesser "reflexives" from the "meta-reflexives" located at the agential pinnacle. Only the latter are fully self-directed and capable of developing their own independent assessments and projects in accordance with the concerns and commitments they have developed through their lifelong inner conversations (Archer, 2007, Chap. 6, 2012, Chap. 6; see also Burkitt, 2016, pp. 327–330). Not entirely surprisingly, lesser reflexives tend to be more prevalent among the less educated and lower social strata, whereas "meta-reflexives" primarily hail from highly educated upper-middle class backgrounds (Archer, 2007, pp. 158, 192, 229, 2012, Chap. 6).

Now, what are we to make of this deliberation-entails-agency argument? Unquestionably, it corresponds to something quite familiar in everyday experience. Whenever we are consciously deliberating on what action to take – and not just when we face the moral dilemmas mentioned by Greenwood (1988, pp. 108–109) – it certainly feels as though we are weighing the alternatives and deciding more or less freely between them. And the more consciously we deliberate, the stronger is this sensation of momentary indeterminacy, an inescapable feeling that the outcome is, so to speak, still up in the air. In a sense, that feeling is what deliberation *is*. But that feeling in and of itself in no way proves that the deliberative process is self-directed and causeless in some sense or to some degree independent from the processes of interaction between psychological dispositions and social interactions that produce the final outcome. There is no obvious reason why this feeling on the part of the actor should preclude that those processes fully *caused* her to terminate her deliberations by favoring one option rather than another. There is no obvious reason why as observers, or, a fortiori, as social scientists, we should treat the process of deliberation as random, intrinsically indeterminate, or an uncaused cause.[16]

In fact, one should ask: what kind of *explanatory work* can the observation that the action in question was preceded by deliberation possibly do? What does the bare fact that this or that action was the result of (some) deliberation add to our explanation of it? Perhaps, as Margaret Archer suggests, deliberation produces different kinds of decisions. Or perhaps – although this, too, is by no means self-evident – deliberation produces a greater variety of action outcomes than, say, blind conformity to norms, impulse, or emotion. But in either case, this just begs the further question of what accounts for the options the deliberators end up choosing, as compared to nondeliberators or different deliberators. And so we naturally return to causal explanations involving, say, the different social backgrounds, cultural commitments, perceived interests, beliefs, etc., of the members of different social groups.[17]

It is worth noting that *every one* of the authors we have cited above considers the idea that deliberation implies some degree of voluntarism to be so self-evident as to require no further justification or explanation.[18] But surely one of sociology's principal aims is to explain what *makes* actors make the choices that they make. It would be a very odd sociology indeed that would rule out consideration of any anterior causal factors for the explanation of all actions that happen to be preceded by (some) deliberation. Seen from this perspective, it is not a little ironic that sociologists of all people should so unreflectively adopt the commonplace assumption that reflection entails free agency, while philosophers, neuroscientists, and behavioral psychologists have long found this "reflectivist" notion of agency exceedingly problematic (see, e.g., Doris, 2015, Chaps. 2 and 3; Watson, 2003; Wegner, 2002).

The same is true for the apparently equally self-evident claim that an actor "could have done otherwise." On closer inspection what exactly this could mean is far from obvious. There seem to be two possible ways of interpreting it. One is based on the empirical observation that different actors respond differently to similar situations. The fact that, under similar conditions, actor A did X while actor B did Y shows, according to this interpretation, that actor B *could have* done X and vice versa. Hence, so it is argued, these actors have agency.

But again, the fact that people respond differently to similar situations merely begs the eminently sociological question: what *causes* them to do so? Is there something in their social background that may account for the difference? Or perhaps, there are some hitherto unnoticed differences in the seemingly "similar" situation they faced which account for the different choices. In other words, differences in actors' responses call for an explanation and to chalk the difference up to something called "agency" and leave it at that does not do anything to advance such an explanation. In fact, it amounts to simply abandoning the effort to explain.

A second, philosophically more radical interpretation of the claim that actors "could have done otherwise" is to take it quite literally. On this interpretation, it means that what is sometimes called a duplicate actor, that is, an actor with exactly the same history, motives, inclinations, and so on, and faced with exactly the same situation, might have acted differently. But this amounts to declaring the action chosen to be fundamentally "random, capricious and irrational" (Pleasants, 2019, p. 8) and thus quite inexplicable. As Weber once remarked, this conception of agency renders it "the privilege–of the insane" (Weber, 1949, p. 124). Paradoxically, it turns agency into the very opposite of the rational, reflexive, self-conscious view of the actor that its sociological proponents seem to have in mind.[19]

Finally, what are we to make of the idea that there are different levels or degrees of "agenticness" by virtue of the different amounts or depths of deliberation and reflection that inform our various actions? There is something oddly elitist about assigning levels of "agenthood" on this basis. For many academics and intellectuals, the Socratic ideal of the well-examined life may be the only life worth living. But it is not clear what purpose is served by relegating to lower levels of human agency, or even lower orders of "humanity" (Archer, 2000), those of us who lack either the leisure or the inclination to regularly reflect deeply on their motives and motivations. In fact, it is hard to view such a claim as anything other than the expression of a rather awkwardly elitist value judgment and a rather shockingly unreflective one at that.[20]

To recapitulate this section, then, there is no obvious reason why sociologists, or psychologists for that matter, should take the seemingly natural intuition that our deliberations are *sui generis* at face value and allow it to short-circuit their attempts to explain what *causes* us to choose one intention or meaning over another, and what *causes* our deliberations to be resolved in one direction rather than another. Neither the meaningfulness of social action nor the occurrence of deliberation in human decision-making imply anything at all about "agency" in the voluntaristic sense in which its advocates intend the term.

Agency as the Capacity to Change "Structures"

The "legacy of theories of agency," according to Sztompka, is "that the ultimate motor of change is the agential power of human individuals and social collectivities" (Sztompka, 1993, p. 200). As already suggested above, the reassertion of the importance of agency in recent decades was, first and foremost, a rebellion against the seemingly implacable determinism of structural functionalism and other versions of social structuralism which appeared to be unable to account for social change (see, e.g., Sales, 2012, pp. 51–52; Sztompka, 1993, pp. 193–200, 1994, pp. 30–43). After all, if the value consensus underwriting the existing social structures is as solidly internalized by actors as Parsons claims, or if actors are nothing more than Althusserian "träger" (carriers) of those structures, then what could possibly motivate such actors to seek to change those structures? This was the gist of Giddens' criticism of Parsons quoted earlier (Giddens, 1993, p. 103). According to Emirbayer and Mische, only agents have the capacity to "exercise...imagination and judgment," allowing them to "gain reflective distance from received patterns" (Emirbayer & Mische, 1998, p. 973) and to envisage the possibility of transforming those patterns. And again, for Archer agency is what gives "human beings...the powers of critical reflection upon their social context and of creatively redesigning their social environment" (2000, p. 308).

While some authors recognize that the *maintenance* of existing structures requires actors to act as well (e.g., Mouzelis, 2008, p. 33), there is an unmistakable tendency to associate active agency with the *transformation* of those structures. Thus, throughout his work on agency and structure, Giddens systematically associates agency with the capacity of actors to *change* structures and relegates the "reproduction" of those structures to the relatively passive, unreflective, mechanical enactment of existing routines and practices, as do several other advocates of "agency" (for more examples see, e.g., Loyal & Barnes, 2001, pp. 513–515; King, 2010, pp. 161–164). And again, Emirbayer and Mische emphasize throughout how actors can "assume greater or lesser degrees of transformative leverage in relation to the structuring contexts of action" (Emirbayer & Mische, 1998, p. 973) depending on how successfully they manage to distance themselves "from the schemas, habits, and traditions that constrain social identities and institutions" (Emirbayer & Mische, 1998, p. 1004).[21]

But not all agents are equally capable of bringing about change in the structures they face. In an oft-quoted passage, Giddens slides from the idea that agents "could have done otherwise" to a quite different concept of agency:

> To be able to 'act otherwise' means being able to intervene in the world, or to refrain from such intervention, with the effect of influencing a specific process or state of affairs...Action depends upon the capability of the individual to 'make a difference' to a pre-existing state of affairs or course of events. An agent ceases to be such if he or she loses the capability to 'make a difference', that is, to exercise some sort of power. (Giddens, 1984, p. 14)

Clearly, not all actors dispose of the same amount of such power. Similarly, in his influential article on the nature of social structure, Sewell declares that "[t]o be an agent means to be capable of exerting some degree of control over the social relations in which one is enmeshed, which in turn implies the ability to transform those social relations to some degree" (Sewell, 1992, p. 20). Note Sewell's emphasis on the *degree* of control over social relations here. This would seem to imply that some people have more "agency" than others by virtue of the way they are "enmeshed" in their respective social relations. This is indeed the implication drawn by a number of authors.

Thus, Mouzelis argues that the extent to which actors are capable of affecting existing structures varies according to their location within social hierarchies. Different actors "possess different amounts of economic, political, social or cultural capital" as a result of which "[s]tructures whose main features are unchanging from the point of view of actors with small amounts of capital can be more manipulable from the point of view of more powerful actors involved in the same game" (Mouzelis, 2008, p. 227; see also Chaps. 12 and 14). As a concrete example, Mouzelis contrasts high-ranking administrators with mere professors and students at the London School of Economics (Mouzelis, 2008, pp. 121–127), where the former have the power to set the rules by which the latter must play.

As we have seen already, Archer assumes that those with the highest degree of "agenticness" are, *ipso facto*, the most capable of transforming social structures for the better. Moreover, the degree of agenticness does not only vary depending on where one is located in the social structure. It also varies over historical time. According to Archer, while the overwhelming majority of the population in premodern societies remained confined to mere "primary agency," the hallmark of modern society is the ever-increasing numbers of ordinary people who can, by forming or joining "corporate agents" representing their interests, "aspire to become active participants in society's decision-making" and thus become more truly agents than their premodern forebears (Archer, 2000, p. 269 see also pp. 269–282, see also 2007, Chap. 1, 2012).[22]

In an influential critique of feminist conceptions of agency, Chafetz defines agency "as *the extent to which* people enjoy a variety of opportunities/options for behavior, among which they can choose with minimal social penalty" (Chafetz, 1999, p. 147, italics in the original) and then continues to argue that:

> ...in some times and places people are highly constrained and enjoy relatively few (never no) degrees of agenic [sic] freedom, while in others they enjoy substantially more choices among alternative lines of action (e.g., compare citizens of Nazi Germany with those in contemporary Germany). More importantly for purposes of this paper, in most, if not all societies, some categories of people (e.g., gender, class, racial/ethnic) enjoy more agency than others. (Chafetz, 1999)

These quotes hint at an additional element. The appeal of "agency" was not only due to its promise as an antidote to the determinism of Parsonian structural functionalism but also to what was seen as its inherent conservatism (Gouldner, 1970). The "transformation" and "alternatives" that agency advocates envisage have unmistakably "progressive" overtones. Thus, for Archer, the most "agentic" actors that she encounters in her interviews are those who are suitably critical, in true Habermasian fashion, of *both* the state and markets (Archer, 2012, Chap. 6). This is entirely in line with the emancipatory intent of the Bhaskarian "critical realism," of which she is a major proponent (see, e.g., Bhaskar, 1989, p. 4), as it "directs the attention of people who want to make the world a better place to the task of transforming these structures" (Collier, 1994, p. 16).[23]

The theme of "agency" as the source of resistance to oppressive social structures is quite widespread, particularly, but by no means only in the feminist literature (Burke, 2012, pp. 123–126; McNay, 2000).[24] In much of that literature, "agency" is treated "as a synonym for resistance to relations of domination" (Mahmood, 2001, p. 203). And again, symbolic interactionists with a commitment to social justice also tend to equate "agency" with "progressive" social change, emphasizing the "subjective struggle" through which agents achieve the ability to overcome oppressive "structures of domination" (Musolf, 2017, pp. 11, 12). Agency is based on "epistemological emancipation" which "inspires actors to define selves as incompatible with ruling-class representations, and to envision a more socially just society" (Musolf, 2017, p. 13).

There are, then, three linked but somewhat distinct aspects to the arguments that associate "agency" with the capacity to bring about change in social "structures." First, there is the claim that agency is indispensable for the explanation of change in those structures. Second, agency consists of a socially and historically *variable* capacity to bring about structural change. And third, agency is associated with emancipatory change in bringing down structures of oppression. We will briefly address each of these.

Perhaps the oddest thing about the assertion that it would not be possible to explain change in social structures without the intervention of agency is that it unwittingly seems to accept the very same Durkheimian/Parsonian conception of social structures "as real material social facts that are external to and coercive over actors" (Ritzer, 2005, p. 764) that its proponents claim to criticize. They appear to have fallen victim to the "architectural analogy" (Jenkins, 2010, p. 137; see also Martin & Dennis, 2010, p. 6; Mouzelis, 2008, pp. 204–205) implying that social structures, like the structures of steel-and-concrete buildings, invariably support each other as well as the overall edifice of which they are thought to be a part (Kemp & Holmwood, 2012). But, *pace* Parsons, for *social* structures, such imagery is utterly misleading. Quite to the contrary, *social* structures – regular patterns of behavior and their concomitant beliefs – are subject to myriad tensions and conflicts between them as well as within them, and the social changes these bring about are the very bread and butter of everyday sociology. The idea that there is a need to invoke some extra-structural *deus ex machina* in order to account for such changes seems to rest on a very oddly reified, externalized notion of "structures" indeed.[25]

Far from being the external constraints suggested by the false analogy, social structures exist only in and through the actors' actions and beliefs. Just as it takes human actions for them to change, it takes human actions for them to exist and persist in the first place.[26] And dignifying either, or for that matter both types of action with the label "agency," gives us no additional analytical handle whatsoever on *why* some act to maintain while others act to change those "structures."[27] In short, the notion of agency is not needed to account for change in social structures nor does it help us in any way to do so.

But then, does not the obvious fact that actors have widely different capacities to affect "structures" point to varying degrees of "agency"?[28] The problem with this usage is that it is simply redundant. It effectively confuses or conflates "agency" with differences in structurally determined social power. No doubt *some* individuals' decisions have a greater impact on the lives of others than the decisions of other individuals do. But this is due to the differences in their positions within the structure of social relations. And these relations and the power they confer on some to take decisions that have a major impact on others are, of course, the nuts and bolts of all of sociology.

Consider Mouzelis' example above: a university president who may decide, say, to abolish formal exams versus a first-year undergraduate who decides not to show up for her final exam. Certainly, the former's decision has far greater ramifications for far more people than the latter's. But that doesn't make the president's choices any more "agentic" than the student's. Mouzelis describes these more and less powerful actors as "actors involved in the same game." But they simply are not. They may be members of the same organization or institution, but they are *definitely* playing quite *different* games within it. Within their own "games," the more socially powerful actor is in no sense "freer" to choose than the less powerful one – as any university administrator, high or low, will readily attest. In other words, this use of the notion of "agency" simply confuses its voluntaristic feature with the perfectly ordinary, socially determined notion of "power."

At the same time in ordinary parlance, we do tend to speak of actors with more social resources and hence often a wider range of palatable options as having greater "freedom of choice," as Chafetz points out. But the operative word here is "palatable." As Chafetz puts it, they have a greater "variety of opportunities/options for behavior, among which they can choose with minimal social penalty." Yet here again, the severity of the social penalties a given actor faces in response to the choices she makes is a function of that actor's social resources, that is, the actor's location in the social structure, not a feature of her choice-making per se. Take a trivial example of a rich person who has the choice of buying a Mercedes or a Rolls Royce and a poor person having to choose to travel by bus or by subway. The poor person would certainly face serious social penalties if she pretended that she could afford to buy a Rolls Royce. But this just tells us something about the less privileged social position she occupies. It does not in any sense render her less of a choice-maker. Barnes sums up the obvious category mistake here, which he calls the "naturalization" of status: "[t]hus it is that individuals with rights to choose are easily rendered as individuals natively imbued with powers of choice" (Barnes, 2000, p. 149).

In short, whether we are talking about actors whose decisions have more momentous ramifications for others, or actors who enjoy a larger range of agreeable options than others, we are talking about social structure, *not* "agency." The use of the term in this context, with all its voluntaristic connotations, does not add anything of analytic value to what is simply a matter of relative social power or privilege.[29]

At this point, it is worth briefly considering where this peculiar contrast between rock-solid structures and free agents wielding their agentic sledgehammers might have come from. As several authors have noted, it has a peculiarly Western modernist ring to it, pitting the heroic individual against the heavy weight of tradition and custom (e.g., Honneth, 2014; Meyer & Jepperson, 2000; see also Hitlin & Elder, 2007, p. 171).[30] And while tradition and custom may have receded as the principal oppressive "structures," they have been replaced by the faceless institutions of modern society: the state, the market, and large, impersonal organizations that today appear to confront and constrain us individually.

The widespread identification of agency with "progressive" change of social structures in the literature seems to rest on the tacit assumptions that, first, those "structures" are inherently oppressive and, second, that it takes actors with exceptional consciousness (an "epistemological emancipation," in fact) and willpower to successfully resist their relentless pressures to conform. From the vantage point of the early 21st century, there is something charmingly *soixante-huitard* about these assumptions. As Collins remarks wryly discussing Giddens' implicit assumption that all we need is awareness of the causes of inequality to be able to eliminate it, "[t]he lessons of sociology, since the days of Weber and Michels, have been rather bitter on this point" (Collins, 1992, p. 87).[31]

Be that as it may, the point here is that the advocates of progressive change appear to think they need the voluntaristic concept of agency either to explain or promote desirable social change. At first sight, it seems to make some sense to attribute a measure of "agency" to actors who appear to possess the requisite consciousness and courage to resist pressures for conformity to existing social structures. One might even grant, quite plausibly, that in many cases, it is "harder" to challenge a widely accepted pattern or rule than to comply with it at least in the sense that it may require more self-conscious and maybe agonizing deliberation than does conformity. But to credit the former with the moniker "agency" on such grounds merely takes us back to the nonsequitur that deliberation is necessarily more indeterminate/agentic than more or less routine following of the rules. On the other hand, crediting *both* resistors *and* conformists with "agency" as several authors do, albeit mostly *pro forma* (see, e.g., Alexander, 1998, p. 215; Giddens, 1993, p. 6), adds literally nothing to our ability to explain the difference between them.

To summarize, there is no need to resort to the extra-structural *deus ex machina* of "agency" in order to be able to explain change in social structures. Second, replacing the relatively well-understood concept of social power with the much more nebulous one of "agency" serves no analytical purpose whatsoever. Third, the association of "agents" with "progressive" change appears to be a normative evaluation rather than offering anything of analytical value. And in any case, it is not clear what the notion of "agency" could possibly contribute to the sociological task of explaining why and how some "structures" change and others do not.

Accountability, Dignity, and Agency

Now let us turn briefly to two justifications for the importance of "agency" that are less prominent in the sociological literature but are thought to be of great significance in everyday life as well as in philosophical discussions of voluntarism and determinism. The first line of defense of the notion of "agency" one encounters in everyday discourse is the idea that agency is an indispensable part of the "institution of responsibility" (see Barnes, 2000). Surely, so the argument goes, we can only hold our fellow actors to account to the extent that we can attribute some measure of free will to them. There is no point, after all, in blaming or praising a person for (in-)actions when she could not have done otherwise. This is, of course, the basic rationale for distinguishing voluntary actions from those involving diminished capacity in the courtroom. And it is perhaps not surprising that criminology happens to be the one sociological field in which this particular defense of the notion of agency does appear explicitly (see, e.g., Agnew, 2011, Chap. 3; Black, 2016; see also D'hondt, 2009).[32]

It would seem to make some intuitive sense that to hold someone responsible for her actions amounts to treating her as "an uncaused cause of whom it may be said: it was you, and you alone, who did it" (Barnes, 2000, p. 61). But does this necessarily commit us to the kind of partly causeless voluntarism advocated by the proponents of "agency"? Not really. For when we distinguish between actions for which a person can be held responsible from those which they cannot be held responsible for because they had "no choice," we are not comparing an uncaused cause with one impelled by some anterior force. We are comparing two different types of causal configurations. To deem a person not responsible for her actions is to attribute those actions to causes which we cannot readily influence by ordinary symbolically interactive means. By contrast, treating an actor as responsible for her actions amounts to saying that we are able to intervene in the forces that impelled her to act in the way she did by such ordinary means (which may well include disapproval, threats, fines, incarceration, and so on) so as to persuade her to act differently, that is, so as to *cause* her to act differently. Such actors are deemed to be susceptible to "reason." As Barnes puts it, in our everyday practice, to identify an action as freely chosen "implies that the action was performed by a normal, susceptible agent, and that it was accordingly an action possibly modifiable by symbolic intervention" (Barnes, 2000, p. 70), whereas "[c]ausation may be attributed to courses of action precisely to indicate the futility of any attempt at symbolic intervention" (Barnes, 2000; see also Loyal & Barnes, 2001, p. 521; Kusch, 2008, p. 139).[33]

At the same time, the routine employment of voluntaristic assumptions may well be an inescapable part of "the practical business of orienting ourselves to others and defining what we expect of them" (Barnes, 2000, p. 14), that is, of social life.[34] But the business of sociology is a different one. Sociology "should be concerned to understand actions in terms of their antecedents, and sequences of actions in terms which include the continuing pressures and influences bearing upon those who perform them" (Barnes, 2000, p. 61). By unreflectively importing from everyday discourse the notion of the individual actor as an uncaused cause sociology simply "cripples itself as far as the pursuit of its own proper and distinctive purposes are concerned" (Barnes, 2000, p. 61). It arbitrarily puts a causally inexplicable entity as an obstacle to sound causal explanation.

But then, there may be moral rather than analytical reasons for insisting on doing so. Authors in the hermeneutic and interpretivist traditions often express the view that treating humans as objects driven by causal forces just like any other natural phenomenon is morally repugnant, an affront to human dignity. For them, the whole point of hermeneutic approaches is to treat subjects as fellow humans whose motives and lifeworlds we should attempt to *understand and respect* rather than treating them as mere objects of causal forces (see, e.g., Bleicher, 1980, 1982). Thus, Sharrock notes, the "attempt to conceive of human relations in much the same way as physicists think of connections between physical objects seems repugnant to many and perhaps as contributing to an all too common tendency to 'dehumanize' human beings" (Sharrock, 1987, p. 128). We could easily multiply similar quotes (e.g., Layder, 1985, pp. 268–269; Tibbetts, 1982, p. 182), expressing an evidently deep "aversion to ordinary causal explanation in the human realm" (Barnes, 2000, p. xii; see also pp. x, 25–26, 77, 105). While such sentiments do resonate with broadly Kantian ethical injunctions about not treating others in a way that we would not have them treat ourselves, is that sufficient to persuade sociologists to abandon causal explanation, in part or in general?

We think not for at least two reasons, one philosophical and one methodological. The philosophical reason is that the argument is plainly arbitrary. It simply prohibits the pursuit of a certain kind of knowledge not because it is invalid but because it is morally repugnant. The insistence on elevating humans above the realm of "mere" natural necessity on moral grounds may stem from a certain Enlightenment anthropocentrism, but it certainly appears a little dated now, and it does not, at any rate, provide any good *sociological* grounds for treating humans as to some extent impervious to causation.

Methodologically, the problem is that there is no way of actually drawing the line between human behaviors that are caused as opposed to those that are not. "[T]here is no fact of the matter, no evidence, however tentative or questionable, that will serve adequately to identify actions as 'chosen' or 'determined' for the purposes of sociological theory" (Loyal & Barnes, 2001, p. 508). As we have already seen, the mere presence of meaning, reflection, or deliberation does not provide us with such evidence either.

Alternatively, one might argue that actions for which the actor can give reasons that appear plausible or sensible to us should be treated as the result of those reasons alone and that we should thus abstain from probing any further. This is, after all, how we often treat each other's actions, and the accounts given for them, in everyday life. Once a reasonable account has been provided, we would usually consider further probing about what causal factors *made* the actor adopt this particular rationale as fairly insulting. This is what Fuchs refers to as the "common sense" approach to "personhood" (Fuchs, 2001, p. 30 see also pp. 31–34).

But the fact that we feel uncomfortable questioning a seemingly reasonable actor in this way in everyday social interaction does not imply that *as sociologists*, we should be forbidden to do so. For one thing, what sounds like a reasonable justification of an action to one person sounds like something puzzling, to be explained by what *caused* the actor to adopt that account, to another, depending on one's cultural biases and assumptions. Disallowing any further causal probing of actions that make "sense" in terms of one set of cultural preconceptions rather than another would amount to an entirely arbitrary imposition of one group's cultural values over the other.[35] In fact, a good case can be made for the proposition that sociology's principal mission is precisely to overcome that kind of arbitrary cultural imposition.

In sum, the practice of treating actors' actions as their own for the purpose of holding them accountable makes perfect sense in everyday life. But it provides no reason for sociologists to treat such actions as having no anterior causes. Similarly, there may well be very good reasons in everyday life for us to demonstrate our respect for our fellow humans' justifications for their actions by refraining from probing further. But, again, to import this perfectly civil everyday attitude toward our fellow humans' actions into sociology simply amounts to imposing an arbitrary interdiction on their sociological explanation. On the other hand, the common association of the notion of agency with responsibility and human dignity does throw an interesting light on some of the uses of the term that we have considered in the previous sections. This association would go a long way toward explaining the strong appeal of the notion of "agency" among sociologists of hermeneutic and interpretivist approaches, the regular rebellions against "determinism" in the discipline, and the practice of reserving the label of "agency" for actors and actions that one approves of that we have encountered above.

CONCLUSION

Let us briefly recapitulate our argument. Theorists of "agency" insist that there is an irreducible element of voluntarism in (some) social action that must be accommodated in sociological explanations. We have examined the main theoretical justifications given in the literature for this claim and have found each seriously wanting. First, the fact that social action is defined by its meaning to the actor in no way implies that the choice of that meaning is in some sense beyond causation. The observation that such meanings cannot be mechanically derived from societal norms and values does not imply that they somehow emerge *ex nihilo* either. Second, while it is no doubt true that action that is preceded by some deliberation or reflection may not be predictable *to the actor herself* until she has concluded her deliberations, this does not imply in any way that the course of the deliberative process and its outcome are in some sense fundamentally unpredictable and impervious to causal explanation. Moreover, the claim that the actor "could have acted otherwise" turns out to be sociologically entirely incoherent. Third, the idea that agency is needed to explain change in "structures" appears to be based on an unacknowledged and quite mistaken reification of *social* "structures." The "progressive" variant of this idea, which equates "agency" with resistance to "oppressive" structures, boils down to a plainly normative stance without adding any analytical content. Fourth, the equation of agency with the social impact of a person's actions simply conflates it with social power and, again, adds nothing of analytical value to any conventional analysis of such power and its effects. Fifth, the notions of agency and free will may well constitute an integral part of the everyday social practice of holding one another accountable for our actions. But this in no way contradicts the simultaneous applicability of causal explanations, nor does it require the importation of such everyday notions into sociological explanations. Sixth, finally, in everyday life, we tend to take actors' good reasons for their actions as sufficient explanations, and it is considered rude to further question their origins. But such everyday *politesse* hardly precludes further causal probing by sociologists.

Finally, we need to address one major objection that might be raised against our entire argument. This is that our main point is entirely trivial. After all, it is practically true by definition that the invocation of free will does not and cannot contribute to *causal* explanation. In fact, as we have seen, the whole point of advocating the sociological recognition of "agency" is to insist that social action is to some extent *beyond* causal explanation. Indeed, the most thorough-going hermeneutic or interpretivist critics of conventional "positivism," who have partly inspired the arguments in favor of "agency" we criticized above, deny the appropriateness or at least the primacy of causal explanations altogether for the human sciences (e.g., Rabinow & Sullivan, 1979; Reed, 2011; Taylor, 1971, 1985; Winch, 1958).

The arguments for or against causal explanation as opposed to hermeneutic description and understanding in the human sciences are many and complex (Hall, 1999; Reed, 2011; Roth, 1987). Suffice it to say here that the sociological literature employing the notion of "agency" in the sense analyzed here does not reject causal explanations in the human sciences outright. Much to the contrary, "agency" is invariably introduced as a necessary component that *improves* upon what are otherwise causal explanatory exercises. Consequently, the question of what exactly the notion of "agency" contributes to the sociological enterprise remains entirely legitimate.

As a matter of fact, when advocates of "agency" actually *do* try to provide explanations for the actions of the agents they study, they invariably fall back on conventional causal, that is, broadly "structural" ones. This was notoriously the case for Talcott Parsons who abandoned his initial voluntarism for a rather robust cultural determinism when he was faced with the problem of explaining social order and regularity. But just like Parsons, Giddens turns from the ability "to do otherwise" of *his* agents to a pervasive psychological fixation with maintaining "ontological security" when he tries to explain the existence and relative predictability of social structures.[36] And again, when Emirbayer and Mische try to *explain* where the different "agentic orientations" they distinguish come from, they call for the identification of "which sorts of social-structural, cultural, and social-psychological contexts are more conducive to developing the different modalities of agency" (Emirbayer & Mische, 1998, p. 1005).[37] In short, agency simply does not seem to do any explanatory work, and when such work is called for, even the advocates of agency themselves are compelled to resort to factors that are, in a broad sense, "structural."[38] At this point, Barnes' conclusion seems to us to be inescapable:

> The only essential point here is that social theorists have no adequate technical rationale for their references to choice and agency, and no account of how to distinguish actions involving choice or agency from other actions or behaviours. All too often their theories are an eclectic concoction of causal and voluntaristic notions immiscible with each other, but mixed nonetheless, as it were, by shaking hard. And while the causal components of the resulting potion may have a useful role, it remains obscure what positive work the voluntaristic notions are supposed to do. (Barnes, 2000, p. 31)

Let us make one final philosophical point. We are in no way suggesting that there is no such thing as agency or free will. Nor are we willing to take any position whatsoever on any version of determinism, social, cultural, or otherwise.[39] Whether or not causal explanations will eventually necessarily encounter some inexplicable residual and whether or not such a residual can reasonably be ascribed to an uncaused "agency" is not a question that is of any practical or sociological significance at this time, if it ever will be.[40] And, as Barnes' quote notes, we do not even have any adequate way of recognizing when such a point of hard-core inexplicability will actually have been attained. But in any case, until we do encounter it, the question of whether the (social) world is fully causally determined or partly co-determined by an uncaused "agency" must remain of philosophical interest at best. Meanwhile, we sociologists are fated to try and use our causal explanatory tools as best we can to explain as much as we can.

NOTES

1. Earlier versions of this paper were presented at seminars at the Departments of Sociology of the University of Victoria, Western University, Universitat Autònoma de Barcelona, and the University of Stockholm, as well as at the 'Shoptalk' seminar at McGill University. We wish to thank the participants for their many helpful comments. We also thank Steven Davies, Maike Isaac, Chris Lorenz, Frédéric Mérand, Ignacio Nazif, Alain Noël, Charles Plante, Jeffrey Reitz, Eran Shor, Jane Stewart, Neil Stewart and Morton Weinfeld for their careful reading of earlier drafts and their many helpful comments and suggestions. The research for this paper was partly supported by a Social Sciences and Humanities Development Grant of McGill University.

2. Some social psychologists treat "agency" as a psychological trait equating it with an individual's sense of control, self-efficacy, and the like. While they may invoke the Meadian conception of the self as encompassing a spontaneous, innovative "I," there is no implication that such psychological traits are to some extent uncaused causes. Quite to the contrary, this literature seeks to explain what combinations of psychological predispositions and social locations produce more or less of a sense of self-efficacy. As Hitlin and Elder put it in an influential statement within this tradition, "Mead's 'I' is conceptualized as a fundamentally spontaneous aspect of the self. It is, however, far from random – idiosyncratic, possibly, but not unpredictable. If our responses were, in fact, completely random, much social science would be untenable" (2007, p. 178; see also Hitlin & Long, 2009).

3. The work from which we take this quote was first published in 1976. Our quotations are from the 2nd edition.

4. For some of the contributions to these debates, see, e.g., Archer (1982, 1995, Chap. 4, 2000), Bagguley (2003), Campbell (2009), Dépelteau (2008), Emirbayer and Mische (1998), Emirbayer and Goodwin (1994), Giddens (1979), Mouzelis (1989), Mouzelis (2008, Chap. 12), Newman (2018), Piiroinen (2014), Pleasants (2019), and Sewell (1992). The list is far from exhaustive.

5. As Barnes among others has noted (Barnes, 2000, pp. 21–31; Loyal & Barnes, 2001), much like Parsons, Giddens, too, effectively abandons this voluntarism in the end. We will return to this point below.

6. Henceforth, emphases in quotations shall be from the original unless stated otherwise.

7. From a Meadian social-psychological perspective, Hitlin and Elder similarly propose a threefold classification of types of agency based on different time horizons which are, in turn, they insist, anchored in a fourth type, the "existential capacity for exerting influence on our environments" (Steven Hitlin & Elder, 2007, p. 175). "This capacity for self-directed action," they write, "underlies all of the types of agency we discuss and refers to a fundamental level of human freedom, Giddens's (1984) notion that one might have acted otherwise. At this level, we are fully free within the constraints of physical reality" (Hitlin & Elder, 2007, p. 177).

8. As noted, there is a social-psychological approach that tends to equate "agency" with the individual's *sense* of it, that is, with some measure of self-efficacy, sense of control, and the like, as measured through psychological questionnaires. While authors in this tradition will routinely invoke Meadian and Giddensian claims implying some underlying free will (see footnote 7 above), the psychological states they measure are not obviously in any way uncaused causes. In fact, much of this literature deals with the social circumstances and life experiences that *lead* individuals to have a given sense of efficacy in, or control over, their environments. See, e.g., Black (2016), Clausen (1991), Eccles (2008), and Hitlin and Long (2009).

9. See, e.g., Beiser (2011, pp. 540–544).

10. This is also, it seems to us, the most plausible interpretation of what Weber meant when he declared sociology "a science concerning itself with the interpretive understanding of social action and thereby with a causal explanation of its course and consequences" (Weber, 1978, p. 4), thus seeking explanations that are both "subjectively" and "causally adequate" (Weber, 1978, pp. 11–12; see also Beiser, 2011, pp. 540–544).

11. Throughout this chapter, we use "she" and "her" as the generic gender-neutral pronoun.

12. For similar arguments from a wide range of different theoretical perspectives, see, e.g., Bleicher (1982, pp. 52, 105, 123), Layder (1985, pp. 266–270), and King (2006, p. 470).

13. For an influential philosophical argument along these lines, see Kane (1999).

14. See Archer's forceful critiques of the "central conflation" at the heart of Giddens' structuration theory (Archer, 2000, pp. 6–7, 1995, Chap. 4).

15. Mouzelis (2008, pp. 68, 232) attributes a similar "degrees-of-reflexivity" position to Alexander (Alexander, 1998, p. 218). But while we can see how Alexander's assertion that agency should be seen as a *dimension* of action could lead down this path, we see no evidence of this in the passage cited, and Alexander certainly has not taken the point as far as Archer has.

16. Some authors, particularly those inspired by symbolic interactionism, seem to take it for granted that such subjective experiences are sufficient to establish the existence of free will. Thus, for instance, Manis and Meltzer present the propositions that "1) human beings play an active role in shaping their own conduct; 2) human consciousness involves a creative interaction with oneself; and 3) human beings construct their behavior in the course of its execution" as "accepted truisms…which are testable chiefly through everyday experience" (Manis & Meltzer, 1994, p. 51).

17. The point is even more obvious in the case of "agency" attributed to animals by some authors on the grounds that their behavior is characterized by some "intentionality" (see, e.g., Carter & Charles, 2013; Pearson, 2013).

18. Archer, for instance, simply asserts, without bothering to justify, that the "inalienable powers of human reflexivity would generate variations in action responses even if it were possible to achieve conditions of laboratory closure" (Archer, 2007, p. 11).

19. A point made long ago by John Stuart Mill (1872, Chap. II; see also Copleston, 1985, Vols. VII, VIII and IX, Vol. VIII, pp. 44–49).

20. On this point, see also van den Berg (2003, p. 237).

21. Interestingly, a quite similar theoretical movement has occurred in the so-called "neoinstitutionalist" literature. Its heavy emphasis on institutional stability – itself a reaction against rational choice theory's focus on individual actors – led to growing unease about its seemingly static implications. To remedy this, a number of authors have come to invoke institutionally relatively autonomous "entrepreneurs" in an effort "to explain change endogenously" (Weik, 2011, p. 466; see also Beckert, 1999; Campbell, 2004; Clemens & Cook, 1999; Dimaggio, 1988; Djelic, 2010; van der Heijden & Kuhlmann, 2017; Madama, 2013). Likewise, the field of management and organization studies has recently become enamored with Giddens' structuration theory for its emphasis "on the transformative capacity of human agency that makes change possible" (den Hond et al., 2012, p. 239). This is not the place to criticize this theoretical move in detail. Suffice it to say that the notion of "entrepreneur" as a free-floating source of institutional "change" suffers from exactly the same weaknesses as the notion of the structure-changing "agent" we analyze here.

22. Habermas (1992) similarly assumes that modern humans possess greater agency and reflectiveness than their convention-bound ancestors in traditional societies. For a thorough critique of this remarkably unreflective assumption, see Barnes (2000, pp. 90–92). In a similar vein, Perry Anderson attempted to settle the Marxist dispute between E.P. Thompson's voluntarism and Althusser's structuralist determinism by suggesting that the degree of agency, that is, the ability of actors to intervene in and change "structures," is historically variable, rising to unprecedented levels in the past 150 years or so (Anderson, 1980, Chap. 2, but especially pp. 20–24).

23. Likewise, Dessler (1989, p. 473) argues that in the field of international relations, Bhaskar's "scientific realist" emphasis on agency "provides the conceptual basis…for situating possibilities of action that might lead to freedom from unwanted sources of structural determination."

24. Interestingly, here, too, the notion of "agency" was introduced to counter what was seen as the excessive determinism implied by "the rather one-sided language of patriarchal oppression that characterized first wave feminism" (McNay, 2003, p. 139).

25. For a good example of the philosophical knots such reification can get one into, see Glynos and Howarth (2008).

26. On this, see also Moore (2011).

27. As Barnes (2000, p. 139) notes, "If it is recognised that traditions exist and persist only through the continuing collective efforts of the social agents who inhabit them, then entirely routine activities within a tradition and non-routine encounters with those outside it stand revealed as having just the same form and demanding just the same skills, powers and susceptibilities" (for his examination of the strong temptation among sociologists to commit this kind of reification, see Barnes (2000, pp. 150–153).

28. Hitlin and Long consider "the extent that individuals *actually* have the situated capacity to exert influence" as one aspect of agency, the other being "their subjective belief about their personal capacity to exert influence" (2009, p. 139).

29. Cheong et al. (2017) provide a nice example. They attempt to quantify degrees of agency based on questions to married women about who takes certain household decisions and whether or not they require permission from a family member to go out. But what they are measuring, of course, is the amount of power, or lack thereof, these women have within their marital relationships.

30. There is some anthropological literature suggesting that notions of "agency" vary across cultures (Ahearn, 1999, 2001; Imberton, 2012; Markus & Kitayama, 2003).

31. The assumptions in question have a long Marxist pedigree. As Frank Parkin notes, the Marxist assumption "that the proletariat was endowed with massive usurpatory powers" created the puzzle of "why workers failed to actualize it for their own political ends. This paved the way for a succession of Marxist theorists, from Lukacs and Gramsci to the Althusserian and Frankfurt schools, offering a diagnosis implying in the most oblique and scholarly manner that the proletariat was suffering from a kind of collective brain damage" (Parkin, 1979, p. 81; see also, e.g., Anderson, 1976; Gouldner, 1980).

32. As well as in historiography, particularly where the culpability of actors is at stake. See, e.g., Pleasants (2017, 2019). For a recent example of the issue's continued salience in philosophy, see Sehon (2016).

33. This also explains the remarkably "easy-going compatibilism of most everyday discourse" (Barnes, 2000, p. 111) when it comes to reconciling "free will" with the causal nature of the world.

34. Smilansky's contributions to the philosophical debates about free will are remarkably close to Barnes,' although there is no evidence that either author was aware of the work of the other. Smilansky speaks of a "community of responsibility" (Smilansky, 2005, p. 252). He argues that in order to be able to treat each other with the respect due to fellow humans, we have no choice but to embrace the *illusion* of free will in the face of thorough determinism (see Smilansky, 2000, 2002). We thank Darren Abramson for drawing our attention to this. We should note though that while Smilansky appears to accept some version of "hard determinism," we see no reason to take any position about the ultimate validity of either voluntarism or determinism as we explain below.

35. The point is nicely illustrated within social science by the diametrically opposed qualities different perspectives associate with the notion of sensible agency. Contrast James Duesenberry's famous quip that "[e]conomics is all about how people make choices. Sociology is all about how they don't have any choices to make" (Duesenberry, 1960, p. 233) with one economic sociologist's ambition to "overturn erroneous understandings of individuals as robots who focus their attentions on making more money" (Wherry, 2012, p. 119). See also, e.g., Coleman (1990, p. 31) versus Sica (1992, pp. 253, 261) and Mouzelis (Mouzelis, 2008, p. 88) among many other possible examples. As Emirbayer and Mische rightly note, these fundamentally contradictory notions of "agency" reflect a tension that can be traced to at least "the Enlightenment debate over whether instrumental rationality or moral and norm-based action is the truest expression of human freedom" (Emirbayer & Mische, 1998, p. 964).

36. For a thorough analysis of this remarkably recurrent slippage from initial "voluntarism" to eventual determinism, see Barnes (2000, pp. 21–31) and Loyal and Barnes (2001, pp. 508–519).

37. As Weik (2011, pp. 474–475) notes, as soon as questions in the managerial literature are raised about the *conditions under which* "entrepreneurs" shake things up, explanations fall back on perfectly straightforward "structural" factors.
38. Among which we include actors' psychological predispositions.
39. Or on the question of the role of "chance" in social life and its explication. For an interested exchange on this issue, linking it in part to the concept of "agency," see Manis and Meltzer (1994), Meltzer and Manis (1995), and Martin (1995).
40. In this respect, we fully agree with Pleasants (2019) who argues that social scientists need not take any position on the metaphysics of free will versus determinism at all, although we come to the argument from a somewhat different angle.

REFERENCES

Agnew, R. (2011). *Toward a unified criminology: Integrating assumptions about crime, people and society*. NYU Press.
Ahearn, L. M. (1999). Agency. *Journal of Linguistic Anthropology*, 9(1/2), 12–15.
Ahearn, L. M. (2001). Language and agency. *Annual Review of Anthropology*, 30(1), 109–137.
Alexander, J. C. (1988). *Action and its environments: Toward a new synthesis*. Columbia University Press.
Alexander, J. C. (1993). More notes on the problem of agency: A reply. *Swiss Journal of Sociology*, 19, 501–506.
Alexander, J. C. (1998). *Neofunctionalism and after: Collected readings*. Wiley.
Anderson, P. (1976). *Considerations on Western Marxism* (Vol. 6). New Left Books.
Anderson, P. (1980). *Arguments within English Marxism*. Verso Books.
Archer, M. S. (1982). Morphogenesis versus structuration: On combining structure and action. *British Journal of Sociology*, 33(4), 455–483.
Archer, M. S. (1995). *Realist social theory: The morphogenetic approach*. Cambridge University Press.
Archer, M. S. (2000). *Being human: The problem of agency*. Cambridge University Press.
Archer, M. S. (2003). *Structure, agency, and the internal conversation*. Cambridge University Press.
Archer, M. S. (2007). *Making our way through the world: Human reflexivity and social mobility*. Cambridge University Press.
Archer, M. S. (2012). *The reflexive imperative in late modernity*. Cambridge University Press.
Bagguley, P. (2003). Reflexivity contra structuration. *Canadian Journal of Sociology [Cahiers Canadiens de Sociologie]*, 28(2), 133–152.
Barnes, B. (2000). *Understanding agency: Social theory and responsible action*. Sage.
Beckert, J. (1999). Agency, entrepreneurs, and institutional change. The role of strategic choice and institutionalized practices in organizations. *Organization Studies*, 20(5), 777–799.
Beiser, F. C. (2011). *The German historicist tradition*. Oxford University Press.
Bhaskar, R. (1989). *Reclaiming reality*. Verso.
Black, J. E. (2016). An introduction to the moral agency scale. *Social Psychology*, 47(6), 295–310.
Bleicher, J. (1980). *Contemporary hermeneutics: Hermeneutics as method, philosophy, and critique*. Routledge & Kegan Paul.
Bleicher, J. (1982). *The hermeneutic imagination: Outline of a positive critique of scientism and sociology*. Routledge.
Blumer, H. (1969). *Symbolic interactionism; perspective and method*. Prentice-Hall.
Burke, K. C. (2012). Women's agency in gender-traditional religions: A review of four approaches. *Sociology Compass*, 6(2), 122–133.
Burkitt, I. (2016). Relational agency: Relational sociology, agency and interaction. *European Journal of Social Theory*, 19(3), 322–339.
Campbell, J. L. (2004). *Institutional change and globalization*. Princeton University Press.
Campbell, C. (2009). Distinguishing the power of agency from agentic power: A note on Weber and the 'black box' of personal agency. *Sociological Theory*, 27(4), 407–418.
Carter, B., & Charles, N. (2013). Animals, agency and resistance. *Journal for the Theory of Social Behaviour*, 43(3), 322–340.

Chafetz, J. S. (1999). Structure, consciousness, agency and social change in feminist sociological theories: A conundrum. *Current Perspectives in Social Theory, 19*, 145–164.
Cheong, Y. F., Yount, K. M., & Crandall, A. A. (2017). Longitudinal measurement invariance of the women's agency scale. *Bulletin of Sociological Methodology [Bulletin de Méthodologie Sociologique], 134*(1), 24–36.
Clausen, J. S. (1991). Adolescent competence and the shaping of the life course. *American Journal of Sociology, 96*(4), 805–842.
Clemens, E. S., & Cook, J. M. (1999). Politics and institutionalism: Explaining durability and change. *Annual Review of Sociology, 25*(1), 441–466.
Coleman, J. (1990). *Foundations of social theory*. Harvard University Press.
Collier, A. (1994). *Critical realism: An introduction to the philosophy of Roy Bhaskar*. Verso.
Collins, R. (1992). The romanticism of agency/structure versus the analysis of micro/macro. *Current Sociology. La Sociologie Contemporaine, 40*(1), 77–97.
Copleston, F. C. (1985). *A history of philosophy (Vols. VII, VIII and IX)*. Doubleday.
Dépelteau, F. (2008). Relational thinking: A critique of co-deterministic theories of structure and agency. *Sociological Theory, 26*(1), 51–73.
Dessler, D. (1989). What's at stake in the agent-structure debate? *International Organization, 43*(3), 441–473.
den Hond, F., Boersma, F. K., Heres, L., Kroes, E. H. J., & van Oirschot, E. (2012). Giddens à La Carte? Appraising empirical applications of structuration theory in management and organization studies. *Journal of Political Power, 5*(2), 239–264.
D'hondt, S. (2009). Good cops, bad cops: Intertextuality, agency, and structure in criminal trial discourse. *Research on Language and Social Interaction, 42*(3), 249–275.
Dimaggio, P. (1988). Interest and agency in institutional theory. In L. Zucker (Ed.), *Institutional patterns and organizations* (pp. 3–21). Ballinger Publishing Company.
Djelic, M.-L. (2010). Institutional perspectives—Working towards coherence or irreconcilable diversity? In G. Morgan, J. L. Campbell, C. Crouch, O. Kaj Pedersen, & R. Whitley (Eds.), *The Oxford handbook of comparative institutional analysis* (pp. 15–40). Oxford University Press.
Doris, J. (2015). *Talking to our selves: Reflection, skepticism, and agency*. Oxford University Press.
Duesenberry, J. S. (1960). Comment on Gary S. Becker's 'An Economic Analysis of Fertility'. In NBER (Ed.), *Demographic and economic change in developed countries* (pp. 231–234). Princeton University Press.
Eccles, J. S. (2008). Agency and structure in human development. *Research in Human Development, 5*(4), 231–243.
Emirbayer, M., & Goodwin, J. (1994). Network anlaysis, culture and the problem of agency. *American Journal of Sociology, 99*(6), 1411–1454.
Emirbayer, M., & Mische, A. (1998). What is agency? *American Journal of Sociology, 103*(4), 962–1023.
Freund, J. (1979). German sociology in the time of Max Weber. In B. T. N. Robert (Ed.), *A history of sociological analysis* (pp. 149–186). Heinemann.
Fuchs, S. (2001). Beyond agency. *Sociological Theory, 19*(1), 24–40.
Garfinkel, H. (1967). *Studies in ethnomethodology*. Prentice-Hall.
Giddens, A. (1979). *Central problems in social theory: Action, structure, and contradiction in social analysis*. University of California Press.
Giddens, A. (1984). *The constitution of society: Outline of the theory of structuration*. University of California Press.
Giddens, A. (1993). *New rules for sociological method* (2nd ed.). Basic Books.
Glynos, J., & Howarth, D. (2008). Structure, agency and power in political analysis: Beyond contextualised self-interpretations. *Political Studies Review, 6*(2), 155–169.
Gouldner, A. W. (1970). *The coming crisis of western sociology*. Basic Books.
Gouldner, A. W. (1980). *The two Marxisms: Contradiction and anomalies in the development of theory*. Seabury Press.
Greenwood, J. D. (1988). Agency, causality, and meaning. *Journal for the Theory of Social Behaviour, 18*(1), 95–115.
Habermas, J. (1992). *Postmetaphysical thinking: Philosophical essays* (William Mark Hohengarten, Trans.). Cambridge University Press.
Hall, J. R. (1999). *Cultures of inquiry: From epistemology to discourse in sociohistorical research*. Cambridge University Press.

Hitlin, S., & Elder, G. H., Jr. (2007). Time, self, and the curiously abstract concept of agency. *Sociological Theory*, *25*(2), 170–191.
Hitlin, S., & Long, C. (2009). Agency as a sociological variable: A preliminary model of individuals, situations, and the life course. *Sociology Compass*. https://onlinelibrary.wiley.com/doi/abs/10.1111/j.1751-9020.2008.00189.x?casa_token=IYkXmJd-NsAAAAA:wayPOTpJUlJIyelv-GTSBVkp2zhY14IEJz8-M9horgrTgDIWllcciUL8tnBrfkDHE6MsDMo_uj4uno0
Homans, G. C. (1964). Bringing men back in. *American Sociological Review*, *29*(6), 809–818.
Honneth, A. (2014). *Freedom's right: The social foundations of democratic life*. Columbia University Press.
Imberton, G. (2012). Chol understandings of suicide and human agency. *Culture, Medicine and Psychiatry*, *36*(2), 245–263.
Jenkins, R. (2010). Beyond social structure. In P. J. Martin & A. Dennis (Eds.), *Human agents and social structures* (pp. 133–151). Manchester University Press.
Kane, R. (1999). Responsibility, luck, and chance: Reflections on free will and indeterminism. *The Journal of Philosophy*, *96*(5), 217–240.
Kane, R. (2011). *The Oxford handbook of free will*. Oxford handbooks. Oxford University Press.
Kemp, S., & Holmwood, J. (2012). Questioning contingency in social life: Roles, agreement and agency. *Journal for the Theory of Social Behaviour*, *42*(4), 403–424.
King, A. (2006). How not to structure a social theory: A reply to a critical response. *Philosophy of the Social Sciences*, *36*(4), 464–479.
King, A. (2010). Two kinds of social theory: The myth and reality of social existence. In P. J. Martin & A. Dennis (Eds.), *Human agents and social structures* (pp. 152–165). Manchester University Press.
Kusch, M. (2008). Barnes on the freedom of will. In Massimo Mazzotti (Ed.), *Knowledge as social order: Rethinking the sociology of Barry Barnes* (pp. 131–146). Ashgate.
Layder, D. (1985). Beyond empiricism? The promise of realism. *Philosophy of the Social Sciences*, *15*(3), 255–274.
Lewis, J. D., & Smith, R. L. (1980). *American sociology and pragmatism: Mead, Chicago sociology, and symbolic interaction*. University of Chicago Press.
Loyal, S., & Barnes, B. (2001). 'Agency' as a red herring in social theory. *Philosophy of the Social Sciences*, *31*(4), 507–524.
Madama, I. (2013). Beyond continuity? Italian social assistance policies between institutional opportunities and agency. *International Journal of Social Welfare*, *22*(1), 58–68.
Mahmood, S. (2001). Feminist theory, embodiment, and the docile agent: Some reflections on the Egyptian Islamic revival. *Cultural Anthropology: Journal of the Society for Cultural Anthropology*, *16*(2), 202–236.
Manis, J. G., & Meltzer, B. N. (1994). Chance in human affairs. *Sociological Theory*, *12*(1), 45–56.
Markus, H. R., & Kitayama, S. (2003). Models of agency: Sociocultural diversity in the construction of action. *Nebraska Symposium on Motivation*, *49*, 1–57.
Martin, J. L. (1995). Chance and causality: A comment on Manis and Meltzer. *Sociological Theory*, *13*(2), 197–202.
Martin, P. J., & Dennis, A. (2010). Introduction: The opposition of structure and agency. In P. J. Martin & A. Dennis (Eds.), *Human agents and social structures* (pp. 3–16). Manchester University Press.
McNay, L. (2000). *Gender and agency: Reconfiguring the subject in feminist and social theory*. Polity Press.
McNay, L. (2003). Agency, anticipation and indeterminacy in feminist theory. *Feminist Theory*, *4*(2), 139–148.
Meltzer, B. N., & Manis, J. G. (1995). Agency, chance, and causality: A rejoinder. *Sociological Theory*, *13*(2), 203–205.
Meyer, J. W., & Jepperson, R. L. (2000). The 'actors' of modern society: The cultural construction of social agency. *Sociological Theory*, *18*(1), 100–120.
Mill, J. S. (1872). *The logic of the moral sciences*. Open Court Publishing.
Moore, A. (2011). The eventfulness of social reproduction. *Sociological Theory*, *29*(4), 294–314.
Mouzelis, N. P. (1989). Restructuring structuration theory. *The Sociological Review*, *37*(4), 613–635.

Mouzelis, N. P. (2008). *Modern and postmodern social theorizing: Bridging the divide*. Cambridge University Press.
Musolf, G. R. (2017). Oppression and resistance: A structure-and-agency perspective. In G. R. Musolf (Ed.), *Oppression and resistance: Structure, agency, transformation, studies in symbolic interaction* (Vol. 48, pp. 1–18). Emerald Publishing Limited.
Newman, J. (2018). Morphogenetic theory and the constructivist institutionalist challenge. *Journal for the Theory of Social Behaviour*, *28*(December), 464.
Parkin, F. (1979). *Marxism and class theory: A bourgeois critique*. Columbia University Press.
Parsons, T. (1937). *The structure of social action: A study in social theory with special reference to a group of recent European writers*. Free Press.
Pearson, C. (2013). Dogs, history, and agency. *History and Theory*, *52*(4), 128–145.
Piiroinen, T. (2014). For 'central conflation': A critique of Archerian dualism. *Sociological Theory*, *32*(2), 79–99.
Pleasants, N. (2017). Ordinary men: Genocide, determinism, agency, and moral culpability. *Philosophy of the Social Sciences*, *48*(1), 3–32.
Pleasants, N. (2019). Free will, determinism and the 'problem' of structure and agency in the social sciences. *Philosophy of the Social Sciences*, *49*(1), 3–30.
Rabinow, P., & Sullivan, W. M. (1979). *Interpretive social science: A reader*. University of California Press.
Reed, I. (2011). *Interpretation and social knowledge: On the use of theory in the human sciences*. University of Chicago Press.
Ritzer, G. (2005). Social structure. In G. Ritzer (Ed.), *Encyclopedia of social theory*. SAGE.
Roth, P. A. (1987). *Meaning and method in the social sciences: A case for methodological pluralism*. Cornell University Press.
Sales, A. (2012). A reappraisal of agency – Structure theories to understand social change. In A. Sales (Ed.), *Sociology today: Social transformations in a globalizing world* (pp. 49–94). SAGE Publications Ltd.
Sehon, S. (2016). *Free will and action explanation: A non-causal, compatibilist account*. Oxford University Press.
Sewell, W. H., Jr. (1992). A theory of structure: Duality, agency, and transformation. *American Journal of Sociology*, *98*(1), 1–29.
Sharrock, W. W. (1987). Individual and society. In R. J. Anderson, J. A. Hughes, & W. W. Sharrock (Eds.), *Classic disputes in sociology* (pp. 126–156). Allen and Unwin London.
Sica, A. (1992). The social world as a countinghouse. *Theory and Society*, *21*(2), 243–262.
Smilansky, S. (2000). *Free will and illusion*. OUP.
Smilansky, S. (2002). Free will, fundamental dualism, and the centrality of illusion. In R. Kane (Ed.), *The Oxford handbook of free will* (pp. 489–505). Oxford University Press.
Smilansky, S. (2005). Free will and respect for persons. *Midwest Studies In Philosophy*, *29*(1), 248–261.
Swindal, J. (2012). *Action and existence: A case for agent causation*. Palgrave Macmillan UK.
Sztompka, P. (1993). *The sociology of social change*. Blackwell.
Sztompka, P. (1994). Evolving focus on human agency in contemporary social theory. In P. Sztompka (Ed.), *Agency and structure* (pp. 25–60). Gordon and Breach.
Taylor, C. (1971). Interpretation and the sciences of man. *The Review of Metaphysics*, *25*(1), 3–51.
Taylor, C. (1985). *Human agency and language*. Philosophical Papers. Cambridge [Cambridgeshire]. Cambridge University Press.
Thompson, E. P. (1978). *The poverty of theory and other essays*. Monthly Review Press.
Tibbetts, P. (1982). The positivism-humanism debate in sociology: A reconsideration. *Sociological Inquiry*, *52*(3), 184–199.
van den Berg, A. (2003). Review of *Being human, the problem of agency*. *Canadian Review of Sociology and Anthropology*, *40*(2), 233–238.
van den Berg, A. (2004). *The immanent Utopia: From Marxism on the state to the state of Marxism*. Transaction Publishers.
van der Heijden, J., & Kuhlmann, J. (2017). Studying incremental institutional change: A systematic and critical meta-review of the literature from 2005 to 2015. *Policy Studies Journal: The Journal of the Policy Studies Organization*, *45*(3), 535–554.

Watson, G. (Ed.). (2003). *Free will*. Oxford University Press.
Weber, M. (1949). In E. Shils & H. A. Finch (Eds.), *The methodology of the social sciences*. Free Press.
Weber, M. (1978). In G. Roth & C. Wittich (Eds.), *Economy and society*. University of California Press.
Wegner, D. M. (2002). *The illusion of conscious will*. MIT Press.
Weik, E. (2011). Institutional entrepreneurship and agency. *Journal for the Theory of Social Behaviour*, *41*(4), 466–481.
Wherry, F. F. (2012). *The culture of markets*. Polity Press.
Wiley, N. (1994). *The semiotic self*. University of Chicago Press.
Winch, P. (1958). *The idea of a social science and its relation to philosophy. Studies in philosophical psychology*. Routledge & Kegan Paul; Humanities Press.
Wrong, D. H. (1961). The oversocialized conception of man in modern sociology. *American Sociological Review*, *26*(2), 183–193.

APPENDIX 1: SOCIOLOGY PUBLICATIONS WITH "AGENCY" IN THE TITLE

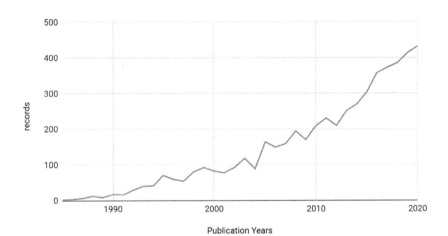

WHAT DO WE USE "AGENCY" FOR? A CRITICAL EMPIRICAL EXAMINATION OF ITS USES IN THE SOCIOLOGICAL LITERATURE[1]

Emre Amasyalı[a] and Axel van den Berg[b]

[a]*IBEI — Barcelona, Spain*
[b]*McGill University, Canada*

ABSTRACT

The use of the concept of "agency," in the sense of action that is to some extent free of "structural" constraints, has enjoyed enormous and growing popularity in the sociological literature over the past several decades. In a previous paper, we examined the range of theoretical rationales offered by sociologists for the inclusion of the notion of "agency" in sociological explanations. Having found these rationales seriously wanting, in this paper we attempt to determine empirically what role "agency" actually plays in the recent sociological literature. We examine a random sample of 147 articles in sociology journals that use the concept of "agency" with the aim of identifying the ways in which the term is used and what function the concept serves in the sociological explanations offered. We identify four principal (often overlapping) uses of "agency": (1) purely descriptive; (2) as a synonym for "power"; (3) as a way to identify resistance to "structural" pressures; and (4) as a way to describe intelligible human actions. We find that in none of these cases the notion of "agency" adds anything of analytical or explanatory value. These different uses have one thing in common, however: they all tend to use the term "agency" in a strongly normative sense to mark the actions the authors approve of. We conclude that "agency" seems to serve the purpose of registering the authors' moral or political preferences under the guise of a seemingly analytical concept.

Keywords: Agency; sociological literature; normative vs. explanatory uses; power; structure

INTRODUCTION

Ever since Anthony Giddens introduced the agency vs. structure *problématique* in the late 1970s, there has been a seemingly unstoppable rise in the frequency with which sociologists have adopted the notion of agency as a way to inject an element of voluntarism into their analyses. And, if anything, the trend appears to be accelerating, with every year seeing a larger number of sociological research articles prominently employing the concept than the preceding year.

It is worth noting that Giddens' initial formulation provoked a considerable amount of theoretical debate. The central issue in these debates has been, and continues to be, the exact manner in which we should understand the relationship *between* "agency" and "structure."[2] This is, of course, but a Giddensian reformulation of the ancient conundrum of voluntarism vs. determinism that has plagued philosophy since close to its inception. And the conundrum does not appear to have come closer to a resolution than it was when it was first raised.

But for all the lengthy contributions to these debates, the very concept of agency, and *a fortiori* its analytical purpose in sociological explanations, have remained fairly nebulous. At the same time, this unsettled state of theoretical affairs does not appear to have prevented empirical sociologists from adopting the notion of "agency" with growing abandon. To be sure, they invariably invoke a number of theorists to justify their use of the notion of agency in their work. But given the profound theoretical discord among those theorists this does not help much in clarifying the meaning or uses of the concept in practice. Nor have any of the participants in the theoretical debates bothered to examine how "agency" is *actually* used in the empirical sociological literature.

This somewhat curious disjunction between sociological theory and practice is all the more remarkable as the theoretical rationale for the inclusion of "agency" in sociological accounts is far from self-evident. In the previous chapter we have examined the principal theoretical arguments given for the analytical importance of "agency" in such accounts. There we show that none of them provides a convincing rationale for incorporating the notion of "agency" in sociological explanations, nor do they provide any satisfactory account of what analytical function "agency" can possibly fulfill in such explanations. But this only raises the question we address in this paper with greater urgency: if neither reasons for its employment nor the nature of its analytical purpose are at all clear, what *do* sociologists use "agency" for in their empirical work?

A few authors have questioned the explanatory utility of the notion of "agency" and have suggested that it serves some ulterior purpose in the literature instead. Some argue that the notion of "agency" is primarily used to celebrate heroic individual actors (Alexander, 1993) or to express the sensibilities of "60s anti-establishment romanticism" (Collins, 1992). Yet others treat the notion of "agency," for all its popularity in the social scientific literature, as something of a comforting illusion, an expression of the quintessentially Western modernist celebration of individual freedom and action (Barnes, 2000; Fuchs, 2001; Honneth, 2014; Loyal & Barnes, 2001; Meyer & Jepperson, 2000). But none of these commentators provides anything beyond anecdotal evidence to support these claims.

There is some literature that considers the empirical uses of "agency" more systematically. The influential article by Emirbayer and Mische (1998), for instance, lists a vast number of sociological studies that, the authors claim, implicitly or explicitly employ their conceptualization of "agency." Some authors propose operational definitions of "agency" to be used in specific research fields such as social work (Parsell et al., 2017) or the sociology of the workplace (Goller & Harteis, 2017). Others offer prescriptions on how to solve the "agent-structure problem" (Dessler, 1989, p. 443) in specific issue domains such as foreign policy analysis (Carlsnaes, 1992) or the study of regime change (Mahoney & Snyder, 1999, p. 4). There is one study that we are aware of which does systematically examine the extent to which core concepts of Giddens' "structuration theory," rather than "agency" specifically, have been adopted in the management and organization studies literature (den Hond et al., 2012). But what all these studies share is an unquestioned assumption that incorporating "agency" is an important analytical step forward in increasing the explanatory power of empirical sociological research. By contrast, having questioned the very rationales for its explanatory use, in this paper we systematically address the question of whether and to what extent "agency" is *actually* used for explanatory purposes in the empirical research literature. We do this by examining a random sample of research articles in sociological journals in which the notion of "agency" figures prominently.

METHODS

The purpose of this study is to systematically assess how the recent and current literature uses the concept of agency in empirical social science research. Accordingly, we aimed to identify all empirical studies claiming to employ the notion of agency from the years 2000 to 2016. We chose the year 2000 as our starting point after a preliminary search showed that the number of articles employing agency grew exponentially from that time onward. We started collecting our data in May 2015 by searching in the Web of Science's Core Collection for literature that had the term "agency" in the title. Only English peer-reviewed articles with a subject area central to social science studies were included for the review.[3]

The literature search and sampling procedure consisted of two basic steps: generating a large pool of potentially relevant articles and then randomly selecting a smaller subset of articles deemed relevant based on our inclusion criteria.[4] To be included as relevant in our final review, a source must specifically use "agency" as it relates to the agency-structure debate in the social sciences, and must refer to empirical findings, that is, not be purely theoretical. Control over quality was achieved by limiting the search to peer-reviewed publications only.

Prefaces, editorial notes, book reviews, and interviews in addition to any articles from trade magazines or industry publications were excluded. If a sampled source did not meet these specifications the following article in the sampling pool was selected and a fixed, numeric interval was applied from there on. The search was completed on May 1st, 2018.

Sampling took place in three distinct phases. In the first phase, which started in May 2015, we sampled every 10th article that contained the key terms "agency" and "structure" in its title for the date range of 2000–2016. An initial keyword search for articles revealed that there were more than 470 articles present in the database. However, it soon became apparent that including both terms yielded a bias in the search results. Specifically, almost all of these articles dealt in one way or another with the *interaction* between structures and agency. To get a more comprehensive survey of the diversity of ways in which scholars use agency we decided to run a more unrestrained search. The second phase narrowed the focus on articles published between 2012 and 2016 and included articles that contained *only* the term "agency" in its title. This search produced a pool of 1,708 articles, from which we selected every 20th article. Finally, in order to cover the full period in the last phase we selected all articles published in 2000–2012 that included agency in their title. This search produced 2,600 articles of which we sampled every 100th article. The total sample produced this way contained 147 articles for our analysis.[5]

One possible objection to our sampling procedure might be that our selection criterion is biased because it focuses on the use of agency in the title, and thus leaves out some articles that do address agency but do not use the term in their title. However, we have no reason to believe that this could bias our sample of articles in any substantial way that is relevant to our concerns. In fact, our criterion is more likely to select articles that more self-consciously use agency than those that may only be using the notion of agency in an ad hoc, casual manner. Hence, we believe that our sample is most likely to contain the most reflective, theoretically self-conscious uses of agency.

In order to identify the diversity of ways in which the articles in our sample used the notion of agency, we undertook thematic content analysis with the aim of generating a simple classification of patterns within the data (Braun & Clarke, 2006). We each analyzed the content of the articles and how they defined agency. We initially approached this task with a list of seven types of agency use derived from our reading of the theoretical literature on agency: normative, descriptive, weak voluntarism, power, strong voluntarism, strong structures and reflexivity.[6] But after several rounds of coding and re-coding the material, which is usually involved in conducting this kind of classificatory analysis (see Braun & Clarke, 2006, p. 86), our thematic map was reduced to four broad categories of agency use. While we identify these four uses as clearly distinct from one another, we also found that a large number of articles employed two, three or even all four of them simultaneously.

ANALYSIS: FROM REDUNDANT DESCRIPTION TO NORMATIVE APPROVAL AND BACK AGAIN

The smallest of these four main groups of articles used "agency" simply as a synonym for "action" or "choice." In these articles, the plain fact that similar actors in similar environments do not all act the same way is taken to be proof of the existence of "agency." We called this use "purely descriptive." A second somewhat larger group of articles equates "agency" with the power to effect change in one's fate or one's environment. Interestingly, the power in question is either due to the actors' ability to mobilize social resources or it is attributed to the actors' *will*power. This latter use comes with clearly normative overtones. It also shades over into another rather larger group of articles in which "agency" is identified with the ability to resist or overcome particularly powerful obstacles or structures of oppression. Again, the normative dimension is particularly prominent here. Finally, within the literature extolling those capable of resisting oppressive structures an intriguing evolution has taken place in recent years with authors extending the label of "agent" to groups of actors less and less obviously engaged in heroic resistance to oppression. As a result, a fourth group of articles emerged from our analysis which in some interesting respects returns to the vernacular use of the notion of "agency."

Making Choices as Agency

There are several uses of the term "agency" in the literature that are entirely redundant in that they simply use the term as a new label for a phenomenon that already has a well-understood term to describe it. Such uses add nothing of analytic value and only insert terminology that suggests some kind of voluntarism where none is needed for analytical purposes.

The most straightforward example of this is the use of "agency" simply as a synonym for "action" or "choice." We found that a good third of our sample of articles (56) used "agency" in this way. In these articles the authors claim that the mere fact that different people respond differently to similar stimuli shows that they have "agency." Thus, for instance, different responses by workers to the introduction of new management practices in different pulp and paper plants is taken to be evidence of their "agency" (Vallas, 2006). Or the fact that consumers respond in a variety of ways to interactive media products is said to signal "agency" (Reinhard, 2011). Or "agency" is called for to explain how different actors' responses to crises produce different outcomes in terms of regional economic resilience (Bristow & Healy, 2014). Or "agency" is seen to be manifested by male and female health care workers responding differently to work pressures (Husso & Hirvonen, 2012), by young scientists adopting different career strategies (Lam & de Campos, 2015), by adolescents responding in different ways to stressors in different countries (Seiffge-Krenke et al., 2012), by pregnant women following different health trends (Burton-Jeangros, 2011), by the different "modes of agency" social workers employ in crisis interventions (Smith, 2014, p. 408), by the fact that social policy beneficiaries respond in varying and complex ways to incentives (Wright, 2012), or, finally, the different strategies followed by parties of the radical populist right (Zaslove, 2012).[7]

We could continue to multiply examples. Our point here is that in all these cases "agency" simply stands for "action" without in any way implying that the actors' actions were in some sense the product of an uncaused free will.[8] To the contrary, whenever the authors do try to explain why different actors acted in different ways they invariably attempt to do so by reference to differences in context or circumstances which *made* the actors act differently. Thus, for instance, Husso and Hirvonen (2012) explain gendered "agency" by reference to the different emotional habitus – a notoriously deterministic and "structural" notion – that male and female care workers bring to the job. Similarly, Seiffge-Krenke et al. (2012) explain cross-national differences in how adolescents respond to stressful situations as the result of different national contexts. In other words, in all these cases, the invocation of "agency" does not contribute to a sociological explanation. Instead, it *calls* for such an explanation in perfectly conventional sociological, that is, "structural" terms. Since "agency" here simply is a substitute for "action" without adding any meaning, it is entirely redundant and, given its voluntaristic associations, only confusing.

But this does raise the question: what *do* these authors use the term "agency" for? As it turns out, the overwhelming majority, 47 out of the 56 articles we coded as "purely descriptive," actually turned out not to be *purely* descriptive in their use of the notion of "agency" at all. In these articles the term "agency" takes on a clearly normative hue as well. The "agency" in question is almost always exercised in opposition to evidently malign "structural" pressures. Thus, true agency is manifested in the different forms of "resistance" during the Greek austerity crisis (Chalari, 2013), in newsroom editors who defy the rules and norms prescribed by their news organization (van Rooyen, 2013), in "good" teachers who reflect, innovate and engage in ways that sometimes go "against the grain" (Leibowitz et al., 2012, p. 362), in some heavy cannabis users managing to quit (Liebregts et al., 2015), or in children who are supportive of their battered mothers (Katz, 2015).

In fact, there is a whole subcategory of articles that, while seemingly equating "agency" simply with different choices made by different people, actually focuses entirely on behavior that is seen by the authors as commendable, wise or appropriate. These include articles on "agents" making wise life or career choices (Hitlin & Johnson, 2015; Lam & de Campos, 2015; Lehmann, 2005), people engaging in healthy or appropriate sexual practices (Christianson, 2015; Dodsworth, 2014; Hammers, 2009; Levin et al., 2012) including resisting "heteronormative discourses" (Burkett & Hamilton, 2012), people managing to quit smoking marijuana (Liebregts et al., 2015) or tobacco (McCullough & Anderson, 2013), individuals deciding to go to college (Smyth & Banks, 2012), citizens resisting ethnic strife (Mac Ginty, 2014), and former delinquents desisting from delinquency (Lloyd & Serin, 2012; Zdun, 2012).

In a large proportion of these articles the commendable behavior turns out to be so because it conforms to the authors' *political* preferences. In them the "agents" are the actors who "resist" various malign "structural" pressures and are implicitly or explicitly contrasted with those who acquiesce, with the resisters clearly enjoying the authors' approval.[9] A number of these articles highlight different responses to authority, repression, austerity, and so on, and/or seek to identify specifically *political* "agency." Thus, Akram (2014) sees preconscious political "agency" in the actions of rioters in the United Kingdom in 2011, Ranganathan (2014) discovers political "agency" among the Indian peripheral urban middle class in response to state demands for payment for a new water provision system, and Paret and Gleeson (2016) uncover the "agency" in the actions of migrants aiming for "progressive" change. It is clear in all these examples that the authors strongly approve of the political agency in question, particularly the "progressive" kind.

Again, we could go on. But the point here is that while using the term "agency" adds nothing of analytical value in these articles, it does frequently seem to serve a normative purpose, namely, to register the authors' approval of the actions of *some* of the actors. We will have to return to this point below.

"Making a Difference"

Another essentially redundant use of the term "agency" consists of its conflation with (social) power. As we have shown in our companion paper, this usage looms rather large in the theoretical debates about the meaning of "agency." We found it to be present in a sizeable minority of articles in our sample, 64 in total.[10]

The equation of social power with "agency" goes back to Giddens' widely cited definition of agency as "the capability to 'make a difference', that is, to exercise some sort of power" (Giddens, 1984, p. 14). Several articles in our sample point to situations in which the characteristics of individual decision makers had important social ramifications and consider this evidence for the importance of "agency." To give some examples, Rodriguez (2009) documents how the characteristics of individual Commissioners mattered in the formulation of the United States Sentencing Commission's sentencing guidelines in the early 1990s; Madama (2013) interprets the pivotal role of the Italian minister of Social Solidarity in pushing through a major reform of the Italian social assistance regime in 2000 as proof of the importance of "agency"; Darlington (2012) argues that strike activity depends on the leadership characteristics of union activists as much as on objective structural conditions; Mukhtarov et al. (2013) see the role of individual and collective "policy entrepreneurs" in promoting two "global conservation narratives" in Vietnam as a manifestation of "agency"; Deegan-Krause and Enyedi (2010) show how political elites are able to shape the structure of political party competition; Edwards and Brehm (2015) examine the ability of civil society organizations to influence educational governance structures in Cambodia; Kirton (2006) detects "agency" in the clever ways in which political leaders design their international agreements at G8 summits to maximize subsequent compliance; and Brummer purports to "bring agency back" in the foreign policy literature by highlighting "the influence of personalities and idiosyncrasies of individual decision-makers" in Germany's decision to join NATO's air campaign against Yugoslavia (2012, p. 274).

No doubt, in each of these cases, the actions of the actors had a considerable impact on the world. Their actions certainly "made a difference" for a lot of people. And, no question, the personal characteristics of these actors on which the authors focus – the Commissioners' styles and ideologies; the German decision-makers reasoning style; the union leaders' left-wing militantism – affected the decisions they took. But the social impact of those decisions is entirely due to the places they happen to occupy in the social structure of which they are a part. Thus, as the authors of the article on Vietnamese "policy entrepreneurs" put it quite explicitly and correctly, in all these instances "[a]gency is the ability to exercise authority and influence policy change" (Mukhtarov et al., 2013, p. 115). But that ability is entirely the product of the social positions of power that these actors occupy and has nothing to do with their being especially more "agentic" than anyone else. After all, when these same actors have to decide, say, how much to tip a waiter in a restaurant, or what groceries to buy for tonight's dinner, they bring the exact same idiosyncrasies and "agentic" qualities to the event, yet their social impact is likely to be rather more modest than when they were deciding on joining a NATO bombing campaign or on revisions of US sentencing guidelines.

In short, this particular use of the term "agency" simply refers to the social impact that certain actors' actions have *by virtue of their location in the social structure*. Again, the use of the term adds nothing of analytic value to the argument, only some confusion due to its voluntaristic connotations. This may be obvious in the case of actors who clearly occupy positions of structural power or authority such as the examples discussed above, but it is equally true of many examples of humbler individuals who are credited with "agency" because their actions "made a difference." And, in fact, the larger number of articles conflating "agency" with social power in this way deals with ordinary actors succeeding in some way in achieving some desired goal.

Examples include young Swedes who are able to write letters to object to decisions by the authorities (Nordlander et al., 2015), dual earner couples who more or less effectively prepare themselves for possible job loss (Sweet & Moen, 2012), migrant children from Eastern Europe managing to access social services (Sime & Fox, 2015), successful English language learners in an urban high school (Wassell et al., 2010), resilient students from economically underprivileged backgrounds (Clegg, 2011), indigenous women coping with the effects of armed conflict in Columbia (Tovar-Restrepo & Irazábal, 2014), working parents in different European countries availing themselves of the benefits of work–life balance policies (Hobson, 2011), and the ability of workers in a Nike factory in Pakistan to act "collectively through trade unions with the aim of defending their rights and improving their conditions of work" (Lund-Thomsen & Coe, 2013, p. 276). The fairly extensive literature in the sociology of health equating "agency" with people's ability to exercise different options and gain control over their health (see, e.g., Shipman Gunson, 2010; Rütten & Gelius, 2011; Veenstra & Burnett, 2014; Williams, 2003) also belongs in this category.

In all these examples, the actors succeed in obtaining some desired goal, at least to some limited extent. But the reason why they succeed is, invariably, because they happen to have access to the socially structured resources and opportunities that enable them to do so. The Swedish youth most able to write letters protesting decisions by authorities, the dual earner couples best prepared for the possibility of job loss, the East European children most successful in accessing social services, the most proficient English learners, and the resilient lower class students, they all came, it turns out, from relatively higher income families, with higher levels of education and similarly advantaged social networks. The degree of "agency" the Columbian indigenous women and the working parents in the different European countries were able to exercise was the result of patriarchal structures being disrupted by military conflict for the former and differences in the institutional, societal, and individual resources available to the latter. In other words, in each of these cases the degree to which the actors were able to achieve what they were aiming for, that is, their "agency," wholly depended on the societally determined resources they happened to command. In this sense, their ability "to make a difference" was just as much a consequence of their location within the social structure as was that of the influential policy makers discussed earlier.

The same can be said of the considerable number of articles that treat "agency" as the absence of certain socially determined obstacles or constraints to the actors' ability to accomplish what they desire, or the reverse, the presence of such obstacles as a *lack* of "agency." Thus, Hezbollah's "agency" is secured through its deft navigation of its relations with its powerful sponsors, Iran and Syria (Knio, 2013); the Russian regime-friendly Nashi youth movement is more independent from the Kremlin, and has thus more "agency," than is widely assumed (Atwal, 2009); while seemingly a dependent periphery to Malta's core, Gozo islanders show their agency by cleverly exploiting their natural resources and political clout to protect their tourism industry against Maltese exploitation (Chaperon & Bramwell, 2013). Or, in reverse, President Obama was prevented from exercising "African agency" by the constraints imposed by "dominant institutions" (Howard, 2010, p. 380); labor organizers' "agency" was undercut by a variety of social factors in Long Beach, CA (Hytrek & Hernández Márquez, 2013); and the "agency" of Indian women trying to adequately feed their young children is limited by their poverty and gender inequality (Sridhar, 2008).

As Choby and Clark state quite explicitly, what all these examples have in common is that they "define agency as an individual's positioning within a network of power relations, which defines a set of limits and freedoms shaping action" (Choby & Clark, 2014, p. 90).[11] In short, actors manage to get (some of) what they want, or fail to do so, by virtue of the economic, political and social resources they command, that is, *because of their location in the relevant social structure.*

But this in effect amounts to little more than traditional, run-of-the-mill "structural" sociology. And it just raises the question again: what *do* these authors think they need the notion of "agency" for? The fact that only four of the 64 articles using "agency" as a stand-in term for effective social power or resources were *not* also coded as "normative" suggests the same answer we have already encountered above.

Once again, in most of these articles the reference to "agency" is not neutral but heavily normative as well. "Agents" here are actors who engage in obviously commendable or admirable actions. Examples include the leadership qualities of successful environmental and sustainability activists (Wolfgramm et al., 2015); creative, inspirational teachers who step outside the standard curriculum (Leibowitz et al., 2012; Schweisfurth, 2006); actively engaged citizens (Bifulco, 2013); homeless people finding homes (Parsell et al., 2014); women who have suffered domestic violence "'transcending' certain patterns of dependency" (Samelius et al., 2014, p. 270); resilient Bangladeshi childless women facing stigmatization (Nahar & van der Geest, 2014); resourceful itinerant street vendors evading local authority repression (Steel, 2012).

Among these there is a sizeable sub-genre of authors who, following such theorists as Archer (2000, 2003) and Emirbayer and Mische (1998), identify "agents" as actors who are seen to be particularly reflective and thoughtful. In each case the authors clearly view this as a praiseworthy attribute. Thus, the formerly homeless mentioned above are praised for "the role that [they] play in reflecting on and explaining their pasts, and determining and shaping the conditions of their future outcomes" (Parsell et al., 2014, p. 300). It is through their capacity to plan and project that dual earners preparing for possible job loss show their "agency" (Sweet & Moen, 2012). Lam and de Campos celebrate the "intention and forethought" in the "agency" of young scientists who successfully negotiate their collaborations with senior colleagues (Lam & de Campos, 2015, p. 816). Similarly, Scambler (2013) extols the virtues of Archerian "dedicated meta-reflexives" who can be mobilized to resist the injustices of health inequalities in a neoliberal age.

This latter example points to a second sub-genre which we have already encountered as well. Quite often the authors equate "agency" with actions that are *politically* desirable or admirable, particularly from a "progressive" point of view. Many authors, following writers like Archer and Emirbayer and Mische to some extent, equate "agency" with the ability to bring about "real," "fundamental" change. Thus, the "African agency" that President Obama failed to pursue is defined as "implementing policy that effectively redresses racial inequity" (Howard, 2010, p. 386). In a study of different career strategies of female and minority lawyers Tomlinson et al. treat "reforming the system" as the most "agentic" strategy since it is "the only strategy that directly challenges structural inequalities and provides potential for change" (2012, p. 247). Jabri (2014, p. 372; see also Hamati-Ataya, 2012) celebrates "the transformative potential of post-colonial agency" in the "ideational construction of the international" (Hamati-Ataya, 2012, p. 373). Björkdahl and Selimovic (2015, p. 166) "point out instances of transformative, critical, and creative agency performed by women that challenge or negotiate patterns of gendered relations of domination" in the aftermath of the conflict in Bosnia-Herzegovina. These are but a few of the examples we could give from the sub-sample we coded as equating "agency" with social power.

But let us reiterate our main finding here. Once again, we find that while the term "agency" in this subsample does no identifiable analytical work – serving merely as a synonym for wholly "structurally" determined social power or "capability" – it seems to have a pervasive *normative* purpose: to allow the authors to impart their stamp of approval to certain actors or actions.

Choice Within Structural Limits

We ended up classifying a very large proportion of our sample, some 119 out of the 147, as "weak voluntarism" because they offered something along the lines of Marx's famous dictum that "[m]en make their own history, but they do not make it just as they please" (Marx [1852] 1963, p. 15). A typical statement of this sort is: "[h]owever, decisions on a future course of action are not made in a political, economic or social vacuum, instead decisions are made in the context of a particular structural environment, which restricts the options available for actors" (Ploberger, 2013, p. 1028, emphasis deleted). In effect these articles, too, belong in the descriptive category in that they take evidence that people make choices as obvious proof that those choices are in some sense, or to some extent, "free."[12] But they share some interesting additional features that are worth pointing out here. They all claim to address the relationship *between* "agency" and the "structure" that limits actors' choices.[13] More interestingly, what most of the articles in this category single out as "agency" is action that in some way *defies* "structural" pressures. They point to actors who manage to resist, circumnavigate, negotiate, manipulate, or ingeniously cope with the "structural" conditions in which they find themselves in ways one would *prima facie* not expect from the apparent "structural" pressures they face. In other words, they point to actors who turn out to have more options for action than the initial "structural" account would lead one to expect.[14]

Instances of this way of using "agency" include a remarkable range of (types of) actors and social situations. Thus, to give just a few examples, we are told about African nuns resisting standard planning and auditing practices (Scherz, 2013); newsroom editors flaunting the regulations of their news organizations (van Rooyen, 2013); Chinese villagers circumnavigating government policies (Chen, 2016); Indian citizens asserting a surprising degree of freedom of action in the tightly monitored Indian borderlands with Bangladesh and China (Banerjee & Chen, 2013); Filipina entertainers resisting control by their traffickers in Korean gijich'on clubs and bars (Yea, 2016); human resource managers acting humanely despite strong pressures not to (Wilcox, 2012); Ontario school teachers finding ways to prioritize "global citizenship issues in their teaching" despite restrictive curricula (Schweisfurth, 2006, p. 41); low-income rural Texans responding creatively to "structural" pressures on their food buying practices (Dean et al., 2016); and elderly Germans who respond far less passively to the anti-aging movement than "Foucauldian gerontology" would have us believe (Schweda & Pfaller, 2014; see also Flaherty, 2013).

The apparent underlying reasoning is particularly clearly in evidence in articles pointing to *political* actors who, in one way or another, manage to evade or break through what would initially appear to be tight political constraints. Thus, as noted, Brummer (2012) claims to "bring agency back in" to counter the "structural approaches" that dominate the foreign policy literature. Chaperon and Bramwell show how, *contrary to the deterministic assumptions of dependency theory*, Gozo islanders manifest their "agency" against dominance by the Maltese core (Chaperon & Bramwell, 2013). And again, according to Harriss (2009) different developmental trajectories in the era of globalization show that there is more "space for political agency" than predicted by dependency theory. Jabri, finally, extolls the unacknowledged "potentiality of postcolonial agency" (2014, p. 387) in shaping the norms of "the international."

As we already mentioned in our critique of theoretical rationales for the analytical deployment of "agency" ("What Do We Need Agency For?" fn. 15) an interesting parallel can be found in the "neoinstitutionalist" literature. Starting from the theory-driven expectation of institutional stability and "path dependency," authors in this tradition have tended to attribute unanticipated change to "policy entrepreneurs." Madama (2013) provides a good example of this when she notes that a "path-shifting" departure in Italy's social assistance legislation cannot easily be explained by neoinstitutionalist theory and must *hence* be attributed instead to the "agency" of a particularly energetic minister of social solidarity playing "the role of policy entrepreneur" (Madama, 2013, p. 66). Or again, Wilmsmeier and Monios (2016) argue that where "institutional structure" and "path dependency" fail to explain differences in port development policies in Latin America this *must* be due to the presence of "agency."[15] In a similar vein, Jacobides and Winter (2012) effectively *define* "agency" as the ability of some economic actors to reshape the institutional "transactional environments" in which they operate.

But by far the largest subgroup of articles we initially coded as manifesting "weak voluntarism" focuses on actors who at first sight *appear to be* particularly powerless and/or marginalized. In these cases, the authors describe how the actors manage to exercise a surprising amount of latitude in the face of apparently daunting "structural" odds. They are part of what we might refer to as the "they are not really passive victims" literature, a vast body of work covering virtually every imaginable underprivileged social group.

Children are one such less-powerless-than-you-might-think group that was prominent in our sample. In most cases these were children from particularly disadvantaged social origins. Examples include the "agency" available to migrant Sudanese and Kenyan children in a Swedish cultural orientation program (Muftee, 2015); migrant children in Britain resourcefully employing social capital to obtain services (Sime & Fox, 2015); Palestinian children using religion to resist "Western perceptions and Israeli oppression" (Habashi, 2013, p. 155); everyday coping in Zambian child-headed households (Payne, 2012); the surprisingly "transformative practices" of children of inter-ethnic marriages among the Wampar of Papua New Guinea (Schwörer, 2012, p. 333); preschool children in Kyrgyzstan exhibiting self-assertion and even opposition in defiance of tightly hierarchical social structures (Bühler-Niederberger & Schwittek, 2013); and "marginalized youth" clinging to hope "in the face of massive uncertainty" (Bryant & Ellard, 2015, p. 486).[16]

Another category of actors much in evidence in the literature pointing to unexpected signs of "agency" are migrants and refugees. In spite of their often precarious situation, migrants exercise their "agency" through a variety of choices and actions (Paret & Gleeson, 2016). Allegedly powerless Romanian

Roma migrating to Western Europe turn out to be able "to mobilize resources to make a difference" (Vlase & Voicu, 2014, p. 2419). Contrary to "the powerful paradigm of migrants' victimisation, marginalisation, and exclusion," Chinese and Bangladeshi migrants in fact play an important role in the shaping of the urban spaces in the cities they migrate to (Bork-Hüffer et al., 2016). Nearly captive Filipina marriage migrants in South Korea manage nevertheless to give their difficult experiences meaning (Kim, 2013). Refugees in Kenya and Malaysia exhibit varying degrees of resilience when offered antiretroviral therapy (Mendelsohn et al., 2014). And refugees of the Bengal diaspora manifest their "agency" in the various ways they are able to deploy their "mobility capital" (Chatterji, 2013).

There were several other marginalized or underprivileged groups whose surprising resilience, resourcefulness or assertiveness are presented as evidence of their "agency." These included the homeless (Parsell et al., 2014; Watson, 2012), low-income families (Dean et al., 2016), and Indigenous peoples (Eickelkamp, 2011; Tovar-Restrepo & Irazábal, 2014; Walker, 2012). But by far the largest group of articles pointing to the unexpected "agency" of disadvantaged actors deals with women, particularly women in highly constrained social settings. The "agency" of Nordic suffragettes was required during the late 19th century to challenge "the gendered meaning of political citizenship as well as core elements in the understandings of masculinity and femininity" (Blom, 2012, p. 600). Contrary to the "victim or survivor" narrative, women who have experienced violence exhibit "agency in the sense of 'transcending' certain patterns of dependency, violence and harmful vulnerability" (Samelius et al., 2014, p. 270). Ukrainian women migrants in Naples manifest their "agency" through "various stages of resistance, action, reception and adaptation" (Näre, 2014, p. 223) to their difficult circumstances. Adult and even underage sex workers turn out to have considerably more "agency" than they are generally given credit for (Bungay et al., 2011; Dodsworth, 2014). Contrary to the "Eurocentric logic" that treats them as passive receptors of family planning campaigns, poor Third World women exercise a significant amount of "agency" in their fertility decisions (Basnyat & Dutta, 2012, p. 274; Beutelspacher et al., 2003). Nepalese widowed household heads and Bangladeshi childless women resist stigmatization and exclusion (Nahar & van der Geest, 2014; Ramnarain, 2016) and Indian surrogate and adoptive mothers challenge the prevailing "bio-centric paradigm of mother-making" (Nandy, 2015, p. 129), in defiance of seemingly stifling social norms and practices. Despite the multiple levels of oppression they face, educated Palestinian women manage to exploit cultural resources from both sides to challenge both Palestinian patriarchy and Israeli oppression (Abu-Rabia-Queder & Weiner-Levy, 2013). Contrary to the conventional view of them as "passive victims in need of protection" women in postconflict Bosnia-Herzegovina contributed actively and importantly to peace-building and transitional justice processes (Björkdahl & Selimovic, 2015). And Indian women's "indigenous feminisms," which have been "invisibilized" by the "dominant and explicit feminisms of the West," are revealed in how "everyday practices become the locus of both resistance and agency in subverting patriarchy and/or the State" (Datta, 2016, pp. 770, 769).[17]

The latter type of argument is particularly prominent in the now quite large literature identifying unanticipated forms of "agency" among women in Muslim-majority countries and cultures. In one way or another all these articles claim to reveal the many subtle ways in which women in those societies manifest their "agency" by challenging, resisting, subverting and renegotiating the "dominant tenets of patriarchy" that they are subjected to (Schütte, 2014, p. 1187), contrary to the Western liberal (and feminist) view of them "as silent, passive and oppressed subjects" (Schütte, 2014, p. 1176; see also Shively, 2014, pp. 463–464). Thus, Muslim women subtly mobilize seemingly orthodox piety as a way to claim greater Islamic authority for themselves (LeBlanc, 2014) and to legitimize their critical egalitarian claims (Rinaldo, 2014). That is, what may appear to the Western eye as submission to "structural" pressures are actually subtle forms of "agency" resisting those pressures (see also Ahmed, 2014; Chapman, 2016; Menin, 2015; Nahar & van der Geest, 2014; Nisa, 2012; Shively, 2014).

At first sight it seems to make some sense to point to these cases as instances of a surprising degree of "agency" on the part of the actors in question. But it is not at all clear what *explanatory* purpose is served by attaching that label to their actions. To the contrary, "agency" appears to be a kind of *deus ex machina* that provides a name for the initially unexpected outcome without providing any explanation for it. Even if it would make sense at all to claim that the actors acting in ways the observers initially did not expect exhibited a greater degree of "free will" than the actors that did act in accordance with those initial expectations – something which is by no means self-evident – this would still merely beg the question of what *caused* or *permitted* the noncompliant actors to act in that way.[18]

In fact, the attribution of "agency" to actors acting in ways that surprise the observer does not give us any new information about those actors at all. Instead, it tells us something about the observers, or, rather, about the observers' initial conception of the "structural" pressures the actors face. It just tells us that that initial conception was wrong, or too simple, or misguided. Whether one's starting point is dependency theory, the assumption that children are passive recipients of adults' perspectives, or the Western liberal feminist view that relatively compliant women in Muslim-majority societies must do so as a matter of passive submission to dominant values, these stories of unexpected "agency" tell us that those starting points were mistaken, pure and simple. The only thing these accounts show is that the *initial* conception of the "structures" and the limitations they impose on the actors was plainly too narrow or simplistic.

In other words, for all the talk about "agency," the story here is entirely and exclusively "structural." What all these examples show is that the *structure* of pressures and opportunities the actors face turned out to be more complex than was assumed by the simpler structural models criticized by the authors. To attribute some greater degree of willfulness to the actors who did *not* conform to the predictions of those simpler models than to those that did does not advance our sociological understanding of the situation by one iota. It merely returns us to the problem we noted with respect to the uses of "agency" that we coded as "purely descriptive": it just begs the question of what ("structural"?) factors caused the two groups of actors to behave in different ways.[19] But this once again raises our recurring question: if "agency" does not serve any explanatory or analytical purpose in these articles, what purpose, if any, *does* it serve?

By now, our answer is probably fairly obvious. In virtually *all* the examples we have given the actors' resistance, subversion, or circumnavigation of the seemingly overwhelmingly constraining "structures" is clearly *a good thing* in the authors' eyes. This is most obviously the case for actors who are thought to resist, circumnavigate, etc., what the authors consider to be oppressive "structures," particularly those of patriarchal societies. Thus, Blom's (2012) Nordic suffragettes, South-Asian women fighting stigmatization (Nahar & van der Geest, 2014; Nandy, 2015; Ramnarain, 2016), Palestinian women challenging patriarchy as well as Israeli oppression (Abu-Rabia-Queder & Weiner-Levy, 2013), peace-building women in Bosnia-Herzegovina (Björkdahl & Selimovic, 2015), young women resisting the "terms of sexuality set by heteronormative discourses" (Burkett & Hamilton, 2012, p. 817), and the "indigenous feminism" of Indian women (Datta, 2016), all represent political or moral "agency" that the authors clearly strongly approve of. The same is obviously the case for the whole range of articles on women in Muslim-majority societies, however openly or subtly they are said to challenge the "dominant tenets of patriarchy" (Schütte, 2014, p. 1187; see also Ahmed, 2014; Chapman, 2016; Menin, 2015; Nisa, 2012; Rinaldo, 2014; Shively, 2014; Nahar & van der Geest, 2014; LeBlanc, 2014).[20]

One interesting variant of the identification of "agency" with politically congenial action takes its inspiration from Archer's emphasis on reflexivity (2000, 2003) to argue that true "agency" requires the kind of "meta-reflexivity" that predisposes people to combat inequality and injustice (Scambler, 2013). Similarly, while not directly derived from Archer's work, for Ghorashi and Ponzoni "agency means emancipation from one's discursive position by focusing on previously unreflected relations" so that one may challenge those relations (Ghorashi & Ponzoni, 2014, p. 164). In these cases, it is in fact the politically "progressive" views of the actors that earns them the distinction of having "agency."

But even where the actions in question are not so evidently political or moral in nature, the authors' admiration for those they credit with "agency" is quite clear and often quite explicit. Our sample of articles is replete with references to the admirable character traits of the actors engaged in "agency," their resourcefulness, ingenuity, initiative, perseverance, resilience, foresight, and so on. The "agency" of working class kids choosing to learn a manual trade is manifested in the "ingenuity and resourcefulness" of the justifications they provide for their choices (Lehmann, 2005, p. 345). Children of migrants and Zambian children heading households are praised for the resourcefulness with which they mobilize their and their families' meagre resources (Muftee, 2015; Payne, 2012; Sime & Fox, 2015), as are the surprisingly "transformative practices" of inter-ethnic children in Papua New Guinea, Kyrgyzstani preschoolers challenging traditional hierarchies (Bühler-Niederberger & Schwittek, 2013; Schwörer, 2012), and Aboriginal children at play in Central Australia (Eickelkamp, 2011). Migrants and refugees exhibit their "agency" in the resilience, resourcefulness and ingenuity with which they confront their difficult situation (Chatterji, 2013; Gomberg-Muñoz, 2010; Kim, 2013; Mendelsohn et al., 2014; Paret & Gleeson, 2016; Vlase & Voicu, 2014). The same is true for resourceful homeless people (Parsell et al., 2014; Watson, 2012), members of low-income families (Dean et al., 2016) and Indigenous peoples (Tovar-Restrepo & Irazábal, 2014; Walker, 2012). Again, we could go on.[21]

In many cases it appears to be the actors' *will*power that the authors equate with "agency." This is particularly apparent in the literature on subjects desisting from (a life of) crime (Healy, 2013; Lloyd & Serin, 2012), battling various addictions (Liebregts et al., 2015; McCullough & Anderson, 2013), and engaging in what the authors view as "healthy" sexual activity (Burkett & Hamilton, 2012; Hammers, 2009; Levin et al., 2012).[22] In fact, the considerable literature on "sexual agency" quite nicely illustrates our main point here. The types of behavior that are identified as "agency" in that literature vary all the way from assertiveness and willingness to take risks to restraint and abstinence, from resisting patriarchal heteronormativity to hypersexuality, depending on which type of behavior the authors in question approve of (see, e.g., Allen et al., 2008; Binswanger & Davis, 2012; Froyum, 2010; Jackson & Cram, 2003; Lehr, 2008).

It is certainly reasonable to talk about the *will*power of these actors as they exhibited admirable fortitude against difficult odds. But this is not the same thing as attributing some kind of *free* will to them, as opposed to the actors that did *not* act in the same way. In fact, the term willpower is one of admiration, not explanation. It does not provide us with any new information that would help us explain why the actors in question did have this willpower while others do not. Moreover, as we shall see in the next section, the implicit complementary assumption that those actors who comply with the assumed "structural" pressures do so automatically and mindlessly is itself far from self-evident.

In short, rather than adding something of analytical value to their accounts of the actions and actors they study, in these articles that we coded as "weak voluntarism" the term "agency" is, again, overwhelmingly used for normative purposes, to allow the authors to put their stamp of approval upon the actions they favor. In fact, we felt we needed to code no fewer than 104 of the 119 "weak voluntarism" articles as being "normative" in their use of "agency." So, like the authors who appeared to use "agency" simply as a synonym for action or choice and those who equate "agency" with social power, these articles claiming to address the interplay between "agency" and "structure" actually merely end up using "agency" as a term of approval, an expression of the authors' own preferences or values.

Agency for All?

As we saw in the previous section, there is a large feminist literature that employs the term "agency" specifically to denote actors and actions that resist, subvert or at the very least circumnavigate a variety of oppressive patriarchal social structures. But at the same time, there is a growing literature as well that documents the actions of women in highly constrained patriarchal settings, particularly Muslim-majority countries, in which the opportunities for circumnavigation and subversion, let alone active resistance, would seem to be very limited indeed. As we have seen, in such cases it is often still possible to celebrate the actions of the women being studied as "agency" as a way to mark the resilience, resourcefulness and cleverness with which they manage to cope with the difficult conditions they face (see also Mahmood, 2012, pp. 5–8). But what about women who actively support the very patriarchal structures which, at least from a Western, liberal-progressive feminist perspective, oppress them and apparently do so willingly?

The paradox appears to be particularly glaring in the case of women who join various fundamentalist movements, most of which are profoundly patriarchal in their tenets and practices, and, at least from the liberal-progressive point of view, often shockingly retrograde. A number of ethnographic studies have attempted to dispel this apparent paradox by delving into what motivates such women as a way of salvaging their "agency." Thus, Bauer summarizes and concludes one influential collection of studies of this type by pointing to the trade-offs such women face (Bauer, 1997, p. 226). When one looks closely enough, she argues, one finds that women joining seemingly arch-patriarchal fundamentalist movements can derive a wide range of benefits from them, including "increased social status, even improved standards of living, and an oppositional position vis a vis the dominant majority" and much more (Bauer, 1997, p. 233 and pp. 226–232). So there is no reason to attribute "false consciousness" to such women, nor is there any "paradox" to be explained (Bauer, 1997, p. 225).[23]

But note that Bauer's description of fundamentalist women's "agency" still appears to imply a link with some form of resistance to, or at least effective coping with, seemingly profoundly oppressive "structures" of the type we analyzed in the previous section. The motivations she attributes to those women still imply that they are making the best of a very difficult situation, this being especially so "for those without family, for the working class or migrants without status or economic security, for unmarried or infertile women, for those desiring to make their lives more meaningful or in search of some measure of control over their lives they have not found through life outside" (Bauer, 1997, p. 233).

Not surprisingly, such re-evaluations of the "agency" of women who at least seemingly comply with, rather than resist, their own subordination has triggered considerable debate among feminist scholars about where exactly to draw the line between "agency" and its opposite (Bracke, 2003, 2008; McNay, 2000; Rinaldo, 2014). One particularly influential intervention in these debates is the work of Saba Mahmood based on an ethnographic study of women who have joined the Islamic revivalist mosque movement in Cairo, Egypt (Mahmood, 2012).

If we are to really understand what motivates women who join such movements, Mahmood argues, we must "detach the notion of agency from the goals of progressive politics" (Mahmood, 2012, p. 14). Even the most perceptive students of gender in the Middle East such as Lila Abu-Lughod (Abu-Lughod, 1990), who have rightly criticized the imposition of naïve, liberal-progressive feminist assumptions that are entirely alien to such settings, have not managed to fully free themselves from those assumptions, according to Mahmood: what they "fail to problematize is the universality of the desire – central for liberal and progressive thought, and presupposed by the concept of resistance it authorizes – to be free from relations of subordination and, for women, from structures of male domination" (Mahmood, 2012, p. 10).

If we are to understand "other modalities of agency whose meaning and effect are not captured within the logic of subversion and resignification of hegemonic terms of discourse" (Mahmood, 2012, p. 153), Mahmood argues, we need to conceive of "agency" not as individual, western-style autonomy but, following poststructuralism, as a matter of "subjectivation" as understood by Foucault. According to Foucault, the "subject," a.k.a. the "agent," far from being a force *sui generis*, is a *product* of the discursive structures within which she is embedded. Thus,

> The kind of agency I am exploring here does not belong to the women themselves, but is a product of the historically contingent discursive traditions in which they are located. The women are summoned to recognize themselves in terms of the virtues and codes of these traditions, and they come to measure themselves against the ideals furbished by these traditions; in this important sense, the individual is contingently made possible by the discursive logic of the ethical traditions she enacts. (Mahmood, 2012, p. 32)

Contrary to the "agonistic and dualistic framework" employed even by poststructuralists like Judith Butler, Mahmood argues that we should recognize "agency" in "the variety of ways in which norms are lived and inhabited, aspired to, reached for, and consummated" (Mahmood, 2012, p. 23). "In this sense, agentival capacity is entailed not only in those acts that resist norms but also in the multiple ways in which one *inhabits* norms" (Mahmood, 2012, p. 15, emph. in original).

Mahmood insists "that the meaning of agency must be explored within the grammar of concepts within which it resides" (Mahmood, 2012, p. 34). She wishes to understand her subjects in their own terms, to give them the respect that is due them, rather than impose alien western liberal-progressive feminist norms and judgments on them. She rejects such arbitrary Eurocentric impositions as a patronizing, authoritarian, and potentially violent form of "colonial feminism" (Mahmood, 2012, p. 36), and as entirely "unhelpful in the task of understanding what makes these [pious] practices powerful and meaningful to the people who practice them" (Mahmood, 2012, p. 37), a view shared by Mahmood's many admirers (see, e.g., Bracke, 2003, 2008; Kim, 2013; Menin, 2015; Rinaldo, 2014).[24]

Referring to other social contexts, a number of authors in our sample of articles expressed similar reservations about the dangers of equating "agency" with heroic resistance to oppressive "structures." And here, too, the principal objection is that such notions of "agency" are either simply irrelevant to some social settings or they fail to recognize the difficult constraints the actors in question face. Thus, Payne (2012), for example, points to the "everyday agency" that those looking for signs of "resistance" miss in the actions of children heading households in Zambia. Marston and McDonald (2012) criticize the exaggerated "heroic agency" attributed to social workers. Walker (2012) points to the inappropriateness of applying such a concept of agency to Amazonian Urarina. The tendency to attribute greater transformative power to actors than they really have, particularly in settings where trying to exercise such power would expose those actors to grave risks, is criticized by several authors as a deeply irresponsible imposition of Western, or even "neoliberal," notions of "agency" on vulnerable populations (Deomampo, 2013; Madhok & Rai, 2012; Näre, 2014; Scherz, 2013). Interestingly, by contrast, Parsell and Clarke (2019, p. 356) scold fellow sociologists for arbitrarily dismissing homeless people who endorse notions of autonomy and responsibility as "cultural dopes who have internalized neoliberal discourse." Somewhat relatedly, finally, in a study of women of different classes coping with infertility problems, Bell and Hetterly (2014) expose the blatant middle class bias of equating "agency" with assertiveness and treating the fatalism supposedly typical of the lower classes as the absence of "agency."[25]

These are certainly noble sentiments, at least for those of us who wish first of all to understand our subjects and their actions on their own terms rather than to judge them by our value commitments. But the resulting expansion of the scope of the concept of "agency" does raise some serious questions as to its precise boundaries. If, as Mahmood and her followers insist, "agency" is a "modality of action" that can range from "direct resistance against oppressive power" all the way to "consent…or even extreme deference to oppressive power" (Kim, 2013, p. 11), then what kind of behavior does *not* fit into this "modality" would seem to be a legitimate question to ask.

The point has not been lost on some commentators. Counting even compliance with patriarchal norms as "agency," Burke notes, risks turning the concept into "an all-encompassing term that offers little for productive research" (2012, p. 130). Others worry that Mahmood's inclusion of virtually *all* actions under the umbrella of "agency" risks losing sight of the "productive tension" between "agency" and "structure" so central to the field of "women's studies" (Bracke, 2003, p. 343; see also Rinaldo, 2014, p. 828).

To be sure, Mahmood herself occasionally hints at the kinds of behavior that she would *not* consider to be "agentival." She repeatedly states that one of her principal aims is to show that, contrary to widely held assumptions, her pietist subjects are *not* "unreflexively conformist and self-abnegating…passive, obsequious, and uncritical" (Mahmood, 2012, p. xii). She wants to show that "what may appear to be a case of deplorable passivity and docility from a progressivist point of view, may actually be a form of agency" (Mahmood, 2012, p. 15). In other words, and not unlike many of the other authors we have reviewed, for Mahmood it is the fact that her pietist subjects are reflective and conscious about what they are doing and active in the pursuit of their piety that marks them as "agents."[26]

But this just begs the question of what exactly the alternative, "non-agentive," docile, passive, etc. type of action would look like empirically. In the passages quoted above, Mahmood talks about how her subjects are "summoned" by the "historically contingent discursive traditions in which they are located" and how, consequently, their kind of agency "does not belong to the women themselves," and she repeatedly claims to want to explore "the variety of ways in which norms are lived and inhabited." But where exactly would one draw the line between the true "agents" who "inhabit their norms" actively and reflexively and those who do so "passively, obsequiously and uncritically"? Surely most people, no matter how arch-traditional their "discursive traditions" and no matter how dogmatically they "inhabit" them, would, if questioned, be able to come up with some reasoned account to justify those traditions and their adherence to them. How, then, would we distinguish their "docile" submission to their traditions from the "reflexive" one practiced by Mahmood's pietist women?

In other words, we seem to have arrived at a conception of "agency" that is effectively coterminous with action *as such*, or at least all actions for which the actors can produce intelligible motivations when questioned. This is remarkably similar to the way "agency" is used in everyday discourse. In our companion paper we present Barry Barnes' analysis arguing that in ordinary, everyday social interaction the attribution of "agency" serves the purpose of according our interlocutors the dignity of being a fellow human being who can explain, and therefore be held accountable for, her actions. This is precisely what Mahmood and her followers do by expanding the concept of agency from one designating morally or politically approved action to one referring to any action for which the actors can provide a reasoned, plausible account. It is hard to see what actions could be sensibly excluded from this conception of agency – after all, even purely impulsive or habitual actions can be plausibly accounted for in some way.

This result is perhaps not all that surprising as Mahmood et al. quite deliberately set out to try to understand their subjects in the latter's own terms. The implicit respect for one's interlocutors, and thereby the Barnesian everyday-like use of the notion of "agency," was, in a sense, already built into their efforts to understand what motivates the women they study. In this connection it is worth noting the important role played by ethnographic and life-history methodologies in this agency-expanding literature (see, e.g., Bauer, 1997, pp. 223, 234, 245–246; Bracke, 2008, p. 61). This makes perfect sense as these are the methodologies of choice for anyone interested in trying to understand how actors' actions are meaningful in their own terms rather than in passing moral or political judgments on those actions.

What we have here, then, is a nonjudgmental approach to explicating the beliefs and actions of people inhabiting particular social structures and "discursive traditions" in terms that respect the points of view of those people while being intelligible to an audience that inhabits different social structures and discursive traditions. That is, this is basically standard qualitative sociology or anthropology. But note that the use of "agency" here as a synonym for (intelligible) action has none of the voluntaristic connotations or implications given to the term by the theorists advocating its use. Quite to the contrary, there is more than a whiff of cultural ("discursive") determinism in Mahmood's adoption of Foucault's idea of "subjectivation" according to which the "agent" is really a creature of the "discursive" structures she inhabits. And second, what this approach shows, often quite convincingly, is that people who do not think and act exactly the same way we do are not necessarily mindless and thoughtless cogs in their own social-structural wheels but subscribe to plausible beliefs and act sensibly in circumstances and cultural traditions that are different from the ones we face. This is all to the good, though perhaps not the revolutionary discovery some seem to think it is.

All this, then, raises a final, and by now somewhat subversive question, one raised some time ago by Talal Asad (1996; see Bracke, 2008, p. 62): why is it so important to insist that fundamentalist believers are *also* "agents"? Could the very notion of "agency," too, be an alien, Western imposition onto non-Western social settings and discursive traditions where it has no proper place or meaning? Barnes suggests that *some* notion like "agency" may well be a cultural universal since it is an intrinsic part of human sociability, although the familiar individualistic conception of agency called "moral responsibility" may be especially characteristic of "our particular culture" (Barnes, 2000, p. 8). We are not in a position to address this claim here, but we can at least suggest the possibility that there is a distinctive Western liberal notion of "agency" which may not translate well into many non-Western settings *while at the same time* all "discursive traditions" have *some* notion of "agency" as a way to hold one another accountable for our actions.[27]

CONCLUSION: WHY AGENCY?

Let us briefly recapitulate. In this paper we try to address a question raised by our companion paper on the leading theoretical arguments for incorporating the notion of "agency" in sociological or social scientific explanations. In that paper we found that none of those arguments provided a satisfactory justification for such a move. But if the notion of "agency" does not have a useful role to play in sociological explanations, what *do* sociologists and social scientists use the concept for?

In an attempt to answer that question, we have drawn a random sample of 147 articles from a wide range of peer-reviewed social science journals that use the concept of "agency" as part of their explanatory approach, covering the period from 2000 to 2016, a period in which the use of "agency" in the literature has grown exponentially. On the basis of our initial survey of the theoretical arguments advocating the explanatory use of "agency" we had imagined that we would find seven more or less distinctive uses of the concept in the literature. After further consideration, however, we realized that these could be reduced to four more or less distinct uses.

One group of articles we found used "agency" simply as a synonym for "action" or "choice." Since the term confusingly introduces voluntaristic connotations without adding anything of value to the latter terms, this way of using it is entirely redundant. The same can be said of the second type, the conflation of "agency" with socially determined power. It introduces vaguely voluntaristic language while actually referring to entirely "structurally" determined outcomes. The third and largest category of articles using "agency" refers to situations in which actors act in ways that seem surprising in view of the structural pressures they are thought to be under. Again, the term "agency" does not add anything of explanatory value here as it simply signals the fact that the initial assumptions about the structural pressures the actors faced were mistaken. Finally, and somewhat in opposition to the third use of "agency," there is a growing literature of mainly feminist authors who wish to extend the designation of "agency" even to actors who quite clearly and fully comply with the pressures of the "structures" in which they are located. But this considerable expansion of the applicability of the concept of "agency" renders the concept practically compatible with any action whatsoever, thus in a sense returning to the redundancy of the first type of use which we had called "purely descriptive." We seem to have come full circle here, from initially equating "agency" to action *tout court*, to reserving it only for special actors who are doing the right thing in the authors' eyes, to discarding this authorial conceit in favor of a notion of "agency" which equates it to, well, action *tout court*.

But there does seem to be an underlying theme that runs through virtually all the uses of "agency" that we have examined: the use of "agency" as a way to mark actions and actors that the authors approve of. This is even the case for the fourth type of use of "agency" as it seeks to effectively restore a measure of dignity to actors whose actions might at first sight look like deplorable submission to "structural" pressures.

This raises a final question, however. What accounts for the immense popularity of this notion of "agency" when it is so utterly useless for all analytical intents and purposes? Our analyses throughout this paper suggest one obvious answer. To apply the concept of "agency" selectively to those actors and actions one approves of is one way of sneaking one's value judgments into the analysis under the guise of the application of a purely analytical concept. This would hardly be the first instance in which the ability to do so is a temptation too hard to resist for many social scientists.

But this apparent "agency" worship surely has deeper cultural roots as well. As noted, Barnes claims that *something like* "agency" may well be a cultural universal since it is so closely bound up with the institutions of mutual accountability that are at the core of all human social life. The argument sounds at least prima facie plausible to us. But Saba Mahmood and others are surely right that the *kind* of social structure-defying "agency" that is celebrated in the overwhelming majority of the articles that we have sampled does have a peculiarly Western, individualist and "autonomist" ring to it.[28]

As we mentioned in passing in our Introduction, this point has been made by several observers as well. Thus, Jeffrey Alexander has criticized the typically Western celebration of the heroic individual that characterizes much of the literature (Alexander, 1993, 1998, pp. 217–218). According to Randall Collins "this longing for agency is part of the romanticism of left intellectuals at the end of the 20th century, at a time when they are notably lacking in any effective power in the world" (Collins, 1992, p. 77). Meyer and Jepperson (2000, p. 100) trace the modern view of actors as "autochthonous and natural entities, no longer embedded in culture" to the secular rationalization of Western Christendom. Honneth (2014) has recently argued at length that the ideal of self-determination is the core value of Western modernity. And Emirbayer and Mische (1998), in their authoritative manifesto for "agency," trace the modern concept to the Enlightenment as it was intricately bound up with the idea of human reason as the antithesis of, and the antidote to, mindless tradition, custom, hierarchy, superstition, faith, and so on.

In other words, the norm-defying, tradition-challenging, hierarchy-resisting "agent" that is so prominently present in the current social-scientific literature looks an awful lot like the "Rational Man" of the European Enlightenment. Sabah Mahmood and others are surely right to point out that that particular conception of "agency" is a product of a particular time and place that may simply not (fully) apply to other times and places. And we may well agree with their insistence that other "modes of action," by people who do not necessarily share (all of) this Western, liberal, individualist outlook, deserve the same respect as do those engaging in actions that more obviously reflect that outlook. Yet even *that* sentiment may well be part of a culturally specific (Western? humanist?) outlook not necessarily shared by those to whom we would extend such respect.

But we are straying towards the domain of moral judgment in which we do not claim to have any special expertise. As sociologists our argument has to be that our primary responsibility is to try to *explain* the actions of different (kinds of) people and that the uses of "agency" we have documented here do not contribute towards furthering that task. What they do is to sneak in the authors' value judgments under the guise of what *appears* to be a purely analytical concept. Such a practice does not only fail to contribute anything of explanatory value but effectively serves to *de*value the explanations offered.

NOTES

1. An earlier version of this paper was presented at the 11th Annual Conference of the International Network of Analytical Sociology (INAS) at Stanford University. We wish to thank the participants, but especially Thomas Heinze, for their very helpful comments. The research for this paper was partly supported by a Social Sciences and Humanities Development Grant of McGill University.

2. For some of the contributions to these debates see, e.g., Archer (2000), Bagguley (2003), Campbell (2009), Emirbayer and Mische (1998), Emirbayer and Goodwin (1994), Giddens (1984), Mouzelis (1989), Mouzelis (2008, Chap. 12), Newman (2018), and Sewell (1992). The list is far from exhaustive.

3. These included Geography, Developmental Psychology, Urban Studies, Political Science, Social Issues, Criminology Penology, Philosophy, Sociology, Social Psychology, Social Work, Substance Abuse, Health Policy Services, Social Sciences Biomedical, Social Sciences Interdisciplinary, Anthropology, International Relations, Cultural Studies, Family Studies, Social Science Mathematical, Women's Studies.

4. Random selection was achieved by selecting every n-th article in our pool, where the number n was equal to the number of articles in the overall pool divided by the number of articles we wished to obtain as our final sample.

5. The final breakdown was 39 articles with both agency and structure in their titles published from 2000 to 2016, 26 articles with only agency in their titles published between 2000 and 2012 and 82 with only agency in the title from 2012 to 2016. While this means that we have slightly oversampled articles with both agency and structure and articles with only agency published in the more recent 2012–2016 period, we have no reason to believe this introduced any bias relevant to our main concerns here.

6. See Table A1 in the Appendix for a detailed distribution of categories contained in our sample.

7. Several authors treat the term "agency" as equivalent to "mode of action" or of taking decisions. See, e.g., Larson et al. (2016), Sun (2014), and Walklate and Mythen (2010).

8. In fact, Rütten and Gelius (2011, p. 954) do so explicitly, declaring that any (health promotion) action contains "agency" "by definition."

9. For some recent examples see, e.g., Bungay et al. (2011), Burkett and Hamilton (2012), Chalari (2013), Dodsworth (2014), Katz (2015), Nahar and van der Geest (2014), Samelius et al. (2014), Schütte (2014), and Vlase and Voicu (2014).

10. There is considerable overlap between this category and the others, with only 8 out of the 64 *not* also coded as either "descriptive" or "weak voluntarism" or both.

11. In a similar vein, some others equate "agency" with Amartya Sen's notion of "capabilities" (Bifulco, 2013; Hobson, 2011; Näre, 2014; Nordlander et al., 2015).

12. There is considerable overlap between the two groups of codings with about half of the articles coded as "descriptive" also coded as "weak voluntarism." In fact, only about 10 articles of the total sample of 147 were *not* coded as either one or the other, showing how pervasive and seemingly self-evident the assumption is that if some people act in one way and others in another then there must be some "free choice."

13. There may be a slight bias here due to the sequence in which we sampled our articles. As we noted, for the first 39 articles we sampled we used "agency" *and* "structure" as our key words. This may have led to a slight overrepresentation of articles in the overall sample of 147 articles contrasting the freedom of choice of the "agents" with the constraints imposed by the "structures" they find themselves in.

14. We thank Thomas Heinze for having drawn our attention to this important variant of "agency" attribution.

15. For an extensive treatment of the problem of explaining unanticipated change in the neoinstitutionalist tradition see Campbell (2004).

16. For additional examples that turned up in our sample see Dedding et al. (2015), Mascolo (2014), and Smith and Woodiwiss (2016).

17. But even animals, it turns out, can be said to have "agency" by virtue of the fact that they often "resist conditions which they do not like" (Carter & Charles, 2013, p. 322).

18. McLean presents an interesting ambiguous case. He first seems to take the fact that different favor seekers in Renaissance Florence manipulated available cultural frames to their best advantage in a variety of ways as evidence of "agency," but then emphasizes "the innovative gestural, written, or conversational agency of these actors" in doing so (McLean, 1998, p. 85).

19. The same can be said about the aforementioned neoinstitutionalists invoking "policy entrepreneurs" to account for unexpected deviations from the "path dependence" predicted by the initial theory. The point here is, again, that the observer-theorist deals with an event which her a priori theories would not have predicted by positing an *ex machina* "agency" to account for it. Mahoney has an instructive section on this in his article on path dependency where he argues that theories of path dependency tend to start with a "contingent" event, that is, an event that falls outside the domain of interest of existing theory and/or could not have been predicted by it (Mahoney, 2000, p. 514). But this in no way implies that such a "contingent" event was or needs to be an act of will *ex nihilo*, of course. In fact, he explicitly notes that the event might have been predictable by some *other* theory.

20. Renegar and Sowards (2009, p. 1), following Emirbayer and Mische (1998), equate agency with third-wave feminism employing contradictions to achieve "self-determination and identity...and counter-imaginations of a better future."

21. It is worth noting in passing here that we encountered a surprisingly large number of articles in our sample that equate "agency" with certain – always desirable and/or admirable – personality types that enhance people's (sense of) control of their lives. These were virtually all written from a social-psychological perspective in which the concept and measurement of "self-efficacy" tended to be treated as equivalent to "agency." Needless to say, there is no suggestion whatsoever in this particular strand of the "agency"-using literature pointing to anything like "free will" or actors making choices *ex nihilo* (see Black, 2016; Clausen, 1991; Eccles, 2008; Frye, 2012; see e.g., Healy, 2013; Hitlin & Johnson, 2015; Lam & de Campos, 2015; Lieblich et al., 2008; Liebregts et al., 2015; Lloyd & Serin, 2012; Poteat et al., 2016; Vlase & Sieber, 2016; Watson, 2012; Zdun, 2012). The same can be said for the related equation by social network theorists of individual character attributes with "agency" (see, e.g., Burt, 2012).

22. Interestingly, Rosenkrantz Lindegaard and Jacques (2014) argue, contrary to virtually all other criminologists using "agency," that crime can be the result of a conscious choice and thus "agency." But this effectively turns "agency" into a simple synonym for "choice" or "action" as such, like the articles mentioned in the first analytical section above.
23. For similar treatments of women and religious fundamentalism see also Franks (2001) and Griffith (1997).
24. For a particularly thoughtful intervention in the fraught feminist debates about the question of how to evaluate actions that seemingly perpetuate oppression without resorting to an objectionable paternalism see Khader (2012).
25. See also Stephens et al. (2011) who claim to show that the association of free choice with "agency" is part of the middle class but not the working class "model of agency."
26. Yet many of Mahmood's followers find it hard to resist the temptation of nevertheless discovering all kinds of subtle "resistance" even in the most seemingly submissive actions (see, e.g., LeBlanc, 2014; Rinaldo, 2014; Shively, 2014).
27. On this, see also, e.g., Imberton (2012).
28. See also Harmon (2014). Worse, according to Go it is "the analytic version of imperial imposition" of a "metrocentric" concept unto "the peripheral world" (2017, p. 142).
29. Includes articles both on social work and health care.

REFERENCES

Abu-Lughod, L. (1990). The romance of resistance: Tracing transformations of power through Bedouin women. *American Ethnologist*, *17*(1), 41–55.
Abu-Rabia-Queder, S., & Weiner-Levy, N. (2013). Between local and foreign structures: Exploring the agency of Palestinian women in Israel. *Social Politics*, *20*(1), 88–108.
Ahmed, F. E. (2014). Peace in the household: Gender, agency, and villagers' measures of marital quality in Bangladesh. *Feminist Economics*, *20*(4), 187–211.
Akram, S. (2014). Recognizing the 2011 United Kingdom riots as political protest: A theoretical framework based on agency, habitus and the preconscious. *British Journal of Criminology*, *54*(3), 375–392.
Alexander, J. C. (1993). More notes on the problem of agency: A reply. *Swiss Journal of Sociology*, *19*, 501–506.
Alexander, J. C. (1998). *Neofunctionalism and after: Collected readings*. Wiley.
Allen, K. R., Husser, E. K., Stone, D. J., & Jordal, C. E. (2008). Agency and error in young adults' stories of sexual decision making. *Family Relations*, *57*(4), 517–529.
Archer, M. S. (2000). *Being human: The problem of agency*. Cambridge University Press.
Archer, M. S. (2003). *Structure, agency, and the internal conversation*. Cambridge University Press.
Asad, T. (1996). Comments on conversion. *Conversion to Modernities* 26373. https://books.google.com/books?hl=en&lr=&id=s4GpAgAAQBAJ&oi=fnd&pgPA263&dq=Asad++Comments+on+Conversion&ots=UrUfM_nk_q&sig=LQlitesZPa7mv0fWiyWksVWiuiU
Atwal, M. (2009). Evaluating Nashi's sustainability: Autonomy, agency and activism. *Europe-Asia Studies*, *61*(5), 743–758.
Bagguley, P. (2003). Reflexivity contra structuration. *Canadian Journal of Sociology [Cahiers Canadiens de Sociologie]*, *28*(2), 133–152.
Banerjee, P., & Chen, X. (2013). Living in in-between spaces: A structure-agency analysis of the India–China and India–Bangladesh borderlands. *Cities*, *34*(October), 18–29.
Barnes, B. (2000). *Understanding agency: Social theory and responsible action*. Sage.
Basnyat, I., & Dutta, M. J. (2012). Reframing motherhood through the culture-centered approach: Articulations of agency among young Nepalese women. *Health Communication*, *27*(3), 273–283.
Bauer, J. (1997). Conclusion: The mixed blessings of women's fundamentalism: Democratic impulses in a patriarchal world. In J. Brink & J. Mencher (Eds.), *Mixed blessings: Gender and religious fundamentalism cross culturally* (pp. 221–246). Routledge.

Bell, A. V., & Hetterly, E. (2014). 'There's a higher power, but he gave us a free will': Socioeconomic status and the intersection of agency and fatalism in infertility. *Social Science & Medicine*, *114*(August), 66–72.
Beutelspacher, A. N., Zapata Martelo, E., & García, V. V. (2003). Does contraception benefit women? Structure, agency, and well-being in rural Mexico. *Feminist Economics*, *9*(2–3), 213–238.
Bifulco, L. (2013). Citizen participation, agency and voice. *European Journal of Social Theory*, *16*(2), 174–187.
Binswanger, C., & Davis, K. (2012). Sexy stories and postfeminist empowerment: From Häutungen to Wetlands. *Feminist Theory*, *13*(3), 245–263.
Björkdahl, A., & Selimovic, J. M. (2015). Gendering agency in transitional justice. *Security Dialogue*, *46*(2), 165–182.
Black, J. E. (2016). An introduction to the moral agency scale. *Social Psychology*, *47*(6), 295–310.
Blom, I. (2012). Structures and agency: A transnational comparison of the struggle for women's suffrage in the Nordic countries during the long 19th century. *Scandinavian Journal of History*, *37*(5), 600–620.
Bork-Hüffer, T., Etzold, B., Gransow, B., Tomba, L., Sterly, H., Suda, K., Kraas, F., & Flock, R. (2016). Agency and the making of transient urban spaces: Examples of migrants in the city in the Pearl River Delta, China, and Dhaka, Bangladesh. *Population, Space and Place*, *22*(2), 128–145.
Bracke, S. (2003). Author(iz)ing agency: Feminist scholars making sense of women's involvement in religious 'fundamentalist' movements. *European Journal of Women's Studies*, *10*(3), 335–346.
Bracke, S. (2008). Conjugating the modern/Religious, conceptualizing female religious agency. *Theory, Culture & Society*. https://doi.org/10.1177/0263276408095544
Braun, V., & Clarke, V. (2006). Using thematic analysis in psychology. *Qualitative Research in Psychology*, *3*(2), 77–101.
Bristow, G., & Healy, A. (2014). Regional resilience: An agency perspective. *Regional Studies*, *48*(5), 923–935.
Brummer, K. (2012). Germany's participation in the Kosovo war: Bringing agency back in. *Acta Politica*, *47*(3), 272–291.
Bryant, J., & Ellard, J. (2015). Hope as a form of agency in the future thinking of disenfranchised young people. *Journal of Youth Studies*, *18*(4), 485–499.
Bühler-Niederberger, D., & Schwittek, J. (2013). Young children in Kyrgyzstan: Agency in tight hierarchical structures. *Childhood*, *21*(4), 502–516.
Bungay, V., Halpin, M., Atchison, C., & Johnston, C. (2011). Structure and agency: Reflections from an exploratory study of Vancouver indoor sex workers. *Culture, Health and Sexuality*, *13*(1), 15–29.
Burke, K. C. (2012). Women's agency in gender-traditional religions: A review of four approaches. *Sociology Compass*, *6*(2), 122–133.
Burkett, M., & Hamilton, K. (2012). Postfeminist sexual agency: Young women's negotiations of sexual consent. *Sexualities*, *15*(7), 815–833.
Burt, R. S. (2012). Network-related personality and the agency question: Multirole evidence from a virtual world. *American Journal of Sociology*, *118*(3), 543–591.
Burton-Jeangros, C. (2011). Surveillance of risks in everyday life: The agency of pregnant women and its limitations. *Social Theory & Health*, *9*(4), 419–436.
Campbell, J. L. (2004). *Institutional change and globalization*. Princeton University Press.
Campbell, C. (2009). Distinguishing the power of agency from agentic power: A note on Weber and the 'black box' of personal agency. *Sociological Theory*, *27*(4), 407–418.
Carlsnaes, W. (1992). The agency-structure problem in foreign policy analysis. *International Studies Quarterly: A Publication of the International Studies Association*, *36*(3), 245–270.
Carter, B., & Charles, N. (2013). Animals, agency and resistance. *Journal for the Theory of Social Behaviour*, *43*(3), 322–340.
Chalari, A. (2013). The causal impact of resistance: Mediating between resistance and internal conversation about resistance. *Journal for the Theory of Social Behaviour*, *43*(1), 66–86.
Chaperon, S., & Bramwell, B. (2013). Dependency and agency in peripheral tourism development. *Annals of Tourism Research*, *40*(January), 132–154.

Chapman, M. (2016). Feminist dilemmas and the agency of veiled Muslim women: Analysing identities and social representations. *European Journal of Women's Studies, 23*(3), 237–250.
Chatterji, J. (2013). Dispositions and destinations: Refugee agency and 'mobility capital' in the Bengal diaspora, 1947–2007. *Comparative Studies in Society and History, 55*(2), 273–304.
Chen, N. (2016). Governing rural culture: Agency, space and the re-production of ancestral temples in contemporary China. *Journal of Rural Studies, 47*(October), 141–152.
Choby, A. A., & Clark, A. M. (2014). Improving health: Structure and agency in health interventions. *Nursing Philosophy: An International Journal for Healthcare Professionals, 15*(2), 89–101.
Christianson, M. (2015). 'Not used but almost...'—A gender and agency analysis of the grey zone between consensual and nonconsensual sexual intercourse. *Health Care for Women International, 36*(7), 768–783.
Clausen, J. S. (1991). Adolescent competence and the shaping of the life course. *American Journal of Sociology, 96*(4), 805–842.
Clegg, S. (2011). Cultural capital and agency: Connecting critique and curriculum in higher education. *British Journal of Sociology of Education, 32*(1), 93–108.
Collins, R. (1992). The romanticism of agency/structure versus the analysis of micro/macro. *Current Sociology [La Sociologie Contemporaine], 40*(1), 77–97.
Darlington, R. (2012). The interplay of structure and agency dynamics in strike activity. *Employee Relations Law Journal, 34*(5), 518–533.
Datta, A. (2016). Yeh Bhoogol Shastra Nahi Hai: On (in)visibilizing gendered geographies of resistance and agency in India. *Social & Cultural Geography, 17*(6), 768–772.
Dean, W. R., Sharkey, J. R., & Johnson, C. M. (2016). The possibilities and limits of personal agency: The Walmart that got away and other narratives of food acquisition in rural texas. *Food, Culture and Society, 19*(1), 129–149.
Dedding, C., Reis, R., Wolf, B., & Hardon, A. (2015). Revealing the hidden agency of children in a clinical setting. *Health Expectations: An International Journal of Public Participation in Health Care and Health Policy, 18*(6), 2121–2128.
Deegan-Krause, K., & Enyedi, Z. (2010). Agency and the structure of party competition: Alignment, stability and the role of political elites. *West European Politics, 33*(3), 686–710.
Deomampo, D. (2013). Transnational surrogacy in India: Interrogating power and women's agency. *Frontiers: A Journal of Women Studies, 34*(3), 167–188.
Dessler, D. (1989). What's at stake in the agent-structure debate? *International Organization, 43*(3), 441–473.
Dodsworth, J. (2014). Sexual exploitation, selling and swapping sex: Victimhood and agency. *Child Abuse Review, 23*(3), 185–199.
Eccles, J. S. (2008). Agency and structure in human development. *Research in Human Development, 5*(4), 231–243.
Edwards, D. B., & Brehm, W. C. (2015). The emergence of Cambodian civil society within global educational governance: A morphogenetic approach to agency and structure. *Journal of Education Policy, 30*(2), 275–293.
Eickelkamp, U. (2011). Agency and structure in the life-world of aboriginal children in Central Australia. *Children and Youth Services Review, 33*(4), 502–508.
Emirbayer, M., & Goodwin, J. (1994). Network analysis, culture and the problem of agency. *American Journal of Sociology, 99*(6), 1411–1454.
Emirbayer, M., & Mische, A. (1998). What is agency? *American Journal of Sociology, 103*(4), 962–1023.
Flaherty, M. G. (2013). Age and agency: Time work across the life course. *Time & Society, 22*(2), 237–253.
Franks, M. (2001). *Women and revivalism in the west: Choosing "fundamentalism" in a liberal democracy*. Springer.
Froyum, C. M. (2010). Making 'good girls': Sexual agency in the sexuality education of low-income black girls. *Culture, Health and Sexuality, 12*(1), 59–72.
Frye, M. (2012). Bright futures in Malawi's new dawn: Educational aspirations as assertions of identity. *American Journal of Sociology, 117*(6), 1565–1624.
Fuchs, S. (2001). Beyond agency. *Sociological Theory, 19*(1), 24–40.

Ghorashi, H., & Ponzoni, E. (2014). Reviving agency: Taking time and making space for rethinking diversity and inclusion. *European Journal of Social Work, 17*(2), 161–174.

Giddens, A. (1984). *The constitution of society: Outline of the theory of structuration.* University of California Press.

Go, J. (2017). Postcolonial thought as social theory. In C. E. Benzecry, M. Krause, & I. Ariail Reed (Eds.), *Social theory now* (pp. 130–161). University of Chicago Press.

Goller, M., & Harteis, C. (2017). Human agency at work: Towards a clarification and operationalisation of the concept. In M. Goller & S. Paloniemi (Eds.), *Agency at work: An agentic perspective on professional learning and development* (pp. 85–103). Springer International Publishing.

Gomberg-Muñoz, R. (2010). Willing to work: Agency and vulnerability in an undocumented immigrant network. *American Anthropologist, 112*(2), 295–307.

Griffith, R. M. (1997). *God's daughters: Evangelical women and the power of submission.* University of California Press.

Habashi, J. (2013). Children's religious agency: Conceptualising Islamic idioms of resistance. *Area, 45*(2), 155–161.

Hamati-Ataya, I. (2012). IR theory as international practice/agency: A clinical-cynical Bourdieusian perspective. *Millennium, 40*(3), 625–646.

Hammers, C. (2009). Space, agency, and the transfiguring of lesbian/queer desire. *Journal of Homosexuality, 56*(6), 757–785.

Harmon, B. (2014). The crisscrossed agency of a toast: Personhood, individuation and de-individuation in Luzhou, China. *The Australian Journal of Anthropology, 25*(3), 357–372.

Harriss, J. (2009). How much space is there for political agency in dependent economies? Reflections on papers on contemporary development inspired by Cardoso and Faletto's Dependencia Y Desarrollo En America Latina. *Studies in Comparative International Development, 44*(4), 435–440.

Healy, D. (2013). Changing fate? Agency and the desistance process. *Theoretical Criminology, 17*(4), 557–574.

Hitlin, S., & Johnson, M. K. (2015). Reconceptualizing agency within the life course: The power of looking ahead. *American Journal of Sociology, 120*(5), 1429–1472.

Hobson, B. (2011). The agency gap in work–life balance: Applying Sen's capabilities framework within European contexts. *Social Politics, 18*(2), 147–167.

den Hond, F., Kees Boersma, F., Heres, L., Kroes, E. H. J., & van Oirschot, E. (2012). Giddens à La Carte? Appraising empirical applications of structuration theory in management and organization studies. *Journal of Political Power, 5*(2), 239–264.

Honneth, A. (2014). *Freedom's right: The social foundations of democratic life.* Columbia University Press.

Howard, P. S. S. (2010). Turning out the center: Racial politics and African agency in the Obama era. *Journal of Black Studies, 40*(3), 380–394.

Husso, M., & Hirvonen, H. (2012). Gendered agency and emotions in the field of care work. *Gender, Work and Organization, 19*(1), 29–51.

Hytrek, G., & Hernández Márquez, A. (2013). Path dependency and patterns of collective action: Space, place, and agency in long beach, California, 1900–1960. *Urban Geography.* https://doi.org/10.1080/02723638.2013.790712

Imberton, G. (2012). Chol understandings of suicide and human agency. *Culture, Medicine and Psychiatry, 36*(2), 245–263.

Jabri, V. (2014). Disarming norms: Postcolonial agency and the constitution of the international. *International Theory, 6*(2), 372–390.

Jackson, S. M., & Cram, F. (2003). Disrupting the sexual double standard: Young women's talk about heterosexuality. *British Journal of Social Psychology/The British Psychological Society, 42*(Pt 1), 113–127.

Jacobides, M. G., & Winter, S. G. (2012). Capabilities: Structure, agency, and evolution. *Organization Science, 23*(5), 1365–1381.

Katz, E. (2015). Domestic violence, children's agency and mother–child relationships: Towards a more advanced model. *Children & Society, 29*(1), 69–79.

Khader, S. J. (2012). Must theorising about adaptive preferences deny women's agency? *Journal of Applied Philosophy, 29*(4), 302–317.
Kim, M. (2013). Weaving women's agency into representations of marriage migrants: Narrative strategies with reflective practice. *Asian Journal of Women's Studies, 19*(3), 7–41.
Kirton, J. (2006). Explaining compliance with G8 finance commitments: Agency, institutionalization and structure. *Open Economies Review, 17*(4), 459–475.
Knio, K. (2013). Structure, agency and Hezbollah: A morphogenetic view. *Third World Quarterly, 34*(5), 856–872.
Lam, A., & de Campos, A. (2015). 'Content to be sad' or 'runaway apprentice'? The psychological contract and career agency of young scientists in the entrepreneurial university. *Human Relations; Studies towards the Integration of the Social Sciences, 68*(5), 811–841.
Larson, R. W., Izenstark, D., Gabriel, R., & Cole Perry, S. (2016). The art of restraint: How experienced program leaders use their authority to support youth agency. *Journal of Research on Adolescence: The Official Journal of the Society for Research on Adolescence, 26*(4), 845–863.
LeBlanc, M. N. (2014). Piety, moral agency, and leadership: Dynamics around the feminization of Islamic authority in Côte d'Ivoire. *Islamic Africa, 5*(2), 167–198.
Lehmann, W. (2005). Choosing to labour: Structure and agency in school-work transitions. *Canadian Journal of Sociology [Cahiers Canadiens de Sociologie], 30*(3), 325.
Lehr, V. D. (2008). Developing sexual agency: Rethinking late nineteenth and early twentieth century theories for the twenty-first century. *Sexuality & Culture, 12*(4), 204–220.
Leibowitz, B., van Schalkwyk, S., Ruiters, J., Farmer, J., & Adendorff, H. (2012). 'It's been a wonderful life': Accounts of the interplay between structure and agency by 'good' university teachers. *Higher Education, 63*(3), 353–365.
Levin, D. S., Monique Ward, L., & Neilson, E. C. (2012). Formative sexual communications, sexual agency and coercion, and youth sexual health. *Social Service Review, 86*(3), 487–516.
Lieblich, A., Zilber, T. B., & Tuval-Mashiach, R. (2008). Narrating human actions: The subjective experience of agency, structure, communion, and serendipity. *Qualitative Inquiry, 14*(4), 613–631.
Liebregts, N., van der Pol, P., de Graaf, R., van Laar, M., van den Brink, W., & Korf, D. J. (2015). Persistence and desistance in heavy cannabis use: The role of identity, agency, and life events. *Journal of Youth Studies, 18*(5), 617–633.
Lloyd, C. D., & Serin, R. C. (2012). Agency and outcome expectancies for crime desistance: Measuring offenders' personal beliefs about change†. *Psychology, Crime and Law: PC & L, 18*(6), 543–565.
Loyal, S., & Barnes, B. (2001). 'Agency' as a red herring in social theory. *Philosophy of the Social Sciences, 31*(4), 507–524.
Lund-Thomsen, P., & Coe, N. M. (2013). Corporate social responsibility and labour agency: The case of Nike in Pakistan. *Journal of Economic Geography, 15*(2), 275–296.
Mac Ginty, R. (2014). Everyday peace: Bottom-up and local agency in conflict-affected societies. *Security Dialogue, 45*(6), 548–564.
Madama, I. (2013). Beyond continuity? Italian social assistance policies between institutional opportunities and agency. *International Journal of Social Welfare, 22*(1), 58–68.
Madhok, S., & Rai, S. M. (2012). Agency, injury, and transgressive politics in neoliberal times. *Signs, 37*(3), 645–669.
Mahmood, S. (2012). *Politics of piety: The Islamic revival and the feminist subject*. Princeton University Press.
Mahoney, J. (2000). Path dependence in historical sociology. *Theory and Society, 29*(4), 507–548.
Mahoney, J., & Snyder, R. (1999). Rethinking agency and structure in the study of regime change. *Studies in Comparative International Development, 34*(2), 3.
Marston, G., & McDonald, C. (2012). Getting beyond 'heroic agency' in conceptualising social workers as policy actors in the twenty-first century. *British Journal of Social Work, 42*(6), 1022–1038.
Marx, K. ([1852] 1963). *The 18th Brumaire of Louis Bonaparte*. International Publishers.
Mascolo, M. F. (2014). Politicizing childhood: A sociology of children's agency. *Publications, 35*(2), 118.

McCullough, L., & Anderson, M. (2013). Agency lost and recovered: A social constructionist approach to smoking addiction and recovery. *Addiction Research and Theory, 21*(3), 247–257.

McLean, P. D. (1998). A frame analysis of favor seeking in the renaissance: Agency, networks, and political culture. *American Journal of Sociology, 104*(1), 51–91.

McNay, L. (2000). *Gender and agency: Reconfiguring the subject in feminist and social theory*. Polity Press.

Mendelsohn, J. B., Rhodes, T., Spiegel, P., Schilperoord, M., Burton, J. W., Balasundaram, S., Wong, C., & Ross, D. A. (2014). Bounded agency in humanitarian settings: A qualitative study of adherence to antiretroviral therapy among refugees situated in Kenya and Malaysia. *Social Science & Medicine, 120*(November), 387–395.

Menin, L. (2015). The impasse of modernity: Personal agency, divine destiny, and the unpredictability of intimate relationships in Morocco. *The Journal of the Royal Anthropological Institute, 21*(4), 892–910.

Meyer, J. W., & Jepperson, R. L. (2000). The 'actors' of modern society: The cultural construction of social agency. *Sociological Theory, 18*(1), 100–120.

Mouzelis, N. P. (1989). Restructuring structuration theory. *The Sociological Review, 37*(4), 613–635.

Mouzelis, N. P. (2008). *Modern and postmodern social theorizing: Bridging the divide*. Cambridge University Press.

Muftee, M. (2015). Children's agency in resettlement: A study of Swedish cultural orientation programs in Kenya and Sudan. *Children's Geographies, 13*(2), 131–148.

Mukhtarov, F., Brock, A., Janssen, S., & Guignier, A. (2013). Actors and strategies in translating global conservation narratives to Vietnam: An agency perspective. *Policy and Society, 32*(2), 113–124.

Nahar, P., & van der Geest, S. (2014). How women in Bangladesh confront the stigma of childlessness: Agency, resilience, and resistance. *Medical Anthropology Quarterly, 28*(3), 381–398.

Nandy, A. (2015). Natural mother = Real mother? Choice and agency among un/natural 'mothers' in India. *Women's Studies International Forum, 53*, 129–138.

Näre, L. (2014). Agency as capabilities: Ukrainian women's narratives of social change and mobility. *Women's Studies International Forum, 47*(November), 223–231.

Newman, J. (2018). Morphogenetic theory and the constructivist institutionalist challenge. *Journal for the Theory of Social Behaviour, 28*(December), 464.

Nisa, E. F. (2012). Embodied faith: Agency and obedience among face-veiled university students in Indonesia. *The Asia Pacific Journal of Anthropology, 13*(4), 366–381.

Nordlander, E., Strandh, M., & Brännlund, A. (2015). What does class origin and education mean for the capabilities of agency and voice? *British Journal of Sociology of Education, 36*(2), 291–312.

Paret, M., & Gleeson, S. (2016). Precarity and agency through a migration lens. *Citizenship Studies, 20*(3–4), 277–294.

Parsell, C., & Clarke, A. (2019). Agency in advanced liberal services: Grounding sociological knowledge in homeless people's accounts. *British Journal of Sociology, 70*(1), 356–376.

Parsell, C., Eggins, E., & Marston, G. (2017). Human agency and social work research: A systematic search and synthesis of social work literature. *British Journal of Social Work, 47*(1), 238–255.

Parsell, C., Tomaszewski, W., & Phillips, R. (2014). Exiting unsheltered homelessness and sustaining housing: A human agency perspective. *Social Service Review, 88*(2), 295–321.

Payne, R. (2012). Extraordinary survivors' or 'ordinary lives'? Embracing 'everyday agency' in social interventions with child-headed households in Zambia. *Children's Geographies, 10*(4), 399–411.

Ploberger, C. (2013). China's adaptation challenges—A critical assessment of China's ability to facilitate a strategic shift towards a low-carbon economy by applying the structure–agency framework. *Journal of Contemporary China, 22*(84), 1028–1047.

Poteat, V. P., Calzo, J. P., & Yoshikawa, H. (2016). Promoting youth agency through dimensions of gay-straight alliance involvement and conditions that maximize associations. *Journal of Youth and Adolescence, 45*(7), 1438–1451.

Ramnarain, S. (2016). Unpacking widow headship and agency in post-conflict Nepal. *Feminist Economics, 22*(1), 80–105.

Ranganathan, M. (2014). Paying for pipes, claiming citizenship: Political agency and water reforms at the urban periphery. *International Journal of Urban and Regional Research, 38*(2), 590–608.

Reinhard, C. D. (2011). Studying the interpretive and physical aspects of interactivity: Revisiting interactivity as a situated interplay of structure and agencies. *Communications*, *36*(3), 110.
Renegar, V. R., & Sowards, S. K. (2009). Contradiction as agency: Self-determination, transcendence, and counter-imagination in third wave feminism. *Hypatia*, *24*(2), 1–20.
Rinaldo, R. (2014). Pious and critical: Muslim women activists and the question of agency. *Gender & Society: Official Publication of Sociologists for Women in Society*, *28*(6), 824–846.
Rodriguez, L. J. (2009). Regulatory decision making: Structure and agency in the development of the organizational sentencing guidelines. *Crime, Law and Social Change*, *51*(1), 109–125.
van Rooyen, M. (2013). Structure and agency in news translation: An application of Anthony Giddens' structuration theory. *Southern African Linguistics and Applied Language Studies*, *31*(4), 495–506.
Rosenkrantz Lindegaard, M., & Jacques, S. (2014). Agency as a cause of crime. *Deviant Behavior*, *35*(2), 85–100.
Rütten, A., & Gelius, P. (2011). The interplay of structure and agency in health promotion: Integrating a concept of structural change and the policy dimension into a multi-level model and applying it to health promotion principles and practice. *Social Science & Medicine*, *73*(7), 953–959.
Samelius, L., Thapar-Björkert, S., & Binswanger, C. (2014). Turning points and the 'everyday': Exploring agency and violence in intimate relationships. *European Journal of Women's Studies*, *21*(3), 264–277.
Scambler, G. (2013). Resistance in unjust times: Archer, structured agency and the sociology of health inequalities. *Sociology*, *47*(1), 142–156.
Scherz, C. (2013). Let us make god our banker: Ethics, temporality, and agency in a Ugandan charity home. *American Ethnologist*, *40*(4), 624–636.
Schütte, S. (2014). Living with patriarchy and poverty: Women's agency and the spatialities of gender relations in Afghanistan. *Gender, Place & Culture: A Journal of Feminist Geography*, *21*(9), 1176–1192.
Schweda, M., & Pfaller, L. (2014). Colonization of later life? Laypersons' and users' agency regarding anti-aging medicine in Germany. *Social Science & Medicine*, *118*(October), 159–165.
Schweisfurth, M. (2006). Education for global citizenship: Teacher agency and curricular structure in Ontario schools. *Educational Review*, *58*(1), 41–50.
Schwörer, D. B. (2012). Transformations in kinship, land rights and social boundaries among the Wampar in Papua New Guinea and the generative agency of children of interethnic marriages. *Childhood*, *19*(3), 332–345.
Seiffge-Krenke, I., Persike, M., Chau, C., Hendry, L. B., Kloepp, M., Terzini-Hollar, M., Tam, V., Rodriguez Naranjo, C., Herrera, D., Menna, P., Rohail, I., Veisson, M., Hoareau, E., Luwe, M., Loncaric, D., Han, H., & Regusch, L. (2012). Differences in agency? How adolescents from 18 countries perceive and cope with their futures. *International Journal of Behavioral Development*, *36*(4), 258–270.
Sewell, W. H. (1992). A theory of structure: Duality, agency, and transformation. *American Journal of Sociology*, *98*(1), 1–29.
Shipman Gunson, J. (2010). "More natural but less normal": Reconsidering medicalisation and agency through women's accounts of menstrual suppression. *Social Science and Medicine*, *71*, 1324–1331.
Shively, K. (2014). Entangled ethics: Piety and agency in Turkey. *Anthropological Theory*, *14*(4), 462–480.
Sime, D., & Fox, R. (2015). Migrant children, social capital and access to services post-migration: Transitions, negotiations and complex agencies. *Children & Society*, *29*(6), 524–534.
Smith, Y. (2014). Rethinking decision making: An ethnographic study of worker agency in crisis intervention. *Social Service Review*, *88*(3), 407–442.
Smith, M., & Woodiwiss, J. (2016). Sexuality, innocence and agency in narratives of childhood sexual abuse: Implications for social work. *British Journal of Social Work*, *46*(8), 2173–2189.
Smyth, E., & Banks, J. (2012). 'There was never really any question of anything else': Young people's agency, institutional habitus and the transition to higher education. *British Journal of Sociology of Education*, *33*(2), 263–281.
Sridhar, D. (2008). The role of structure and agency in hunger reduction in India. *Indian Journal of Gender Studies*, *15*(1), 81–99.

Steel, G. (2012). Whose paradise? Itinerant street vendors' individual and collective practices of political agency in the tourist streets of Cusco, Peru. *International Journal of Urban and Regional Research*, *36*(5), 1007–1021.

Stephens, N. M., Fryberg, S. A., & Markus, H. R. (2011). When choice does not equal freedom: A sociocultural analysis of agency in working-class American contexts. *Social Psychological and Personality Science*, *2*(1), 33–41.

Sun, W. (2014). Northern girls': Cultural politics of agency and South China's migrant literature. *Asian Studies Review*. http://www.tandfonline.com/doi/abs/10.1080/10357823.2014.901297

Sweet, S., & Moen, P. (2012). Dual earners preparing for job loss: Agency, linked lives, and resilience. *Work and Occupations*, *39*(1), 35–70.

Tomlinson, J., Muzio, D., Sommerlad, H., Webley, L., & Duff, L. (2012). Structure, agency and career strategies of white women and black and minority ethnic individuals in the legal profession. *Human Relations; Studies towards the Integration of the Social Sciences*, *66*(2), 245–269.

Tovar-Restrepo, M., & Irazábal, C. (2014). Indigenous women and violence in Colombia: Agency, autonomy, and territoriality. *Latin American Perspectives*, *41*(1), 39–58.

Vallas, S. P. (2006). Empowerment redux: Structure, agency, and the remaking of managerial authority. *American Journal of Sociology*, *111*(6), 1677–1717.

Veenstra, G., & Burnett, P. J. (2014). A relational approach to health practices: towards transcending the agency-structure divide. *Sociology of Health and Illness*, *36*(2), 187–198.

Vlase, I., & Sieber, R. (2016). Narrating well-being in the context of precarious prosperity: An account of agency framed by culturally embedded happiness and gender beliefs. *European Journal of Women's Studies*, *23*(2), 185–199.

Vlase, I., & Voicu, M. (2014). Romanian Roma migration: The interplay between structures and agency. *Ethnic and Racial Studies*, *37*(13), 2418–2437.

Walker, H. (2012). Demonic trade: Debt, materiality, and agency in Amazonia. *The Journal of the Royal Anthropological Institute*, *18*(1), 140–159.

Walklate, S., & Mythen, G. (2010). Agency, reflexivity and risk: Cosmopolitan, neurotic or prudential citizen? *British Journal of Sociology*, *61*(1), 45–62.

Wassell, B. A., Hawrylak, M. F., & LaVan, S.-K. (2010). Examining the structures that impact English language learners' agency in urban high schools: Resources and roadblocks in the classroom. *Education and Urban Society*, *42*(5), 599–619.

Watson, D. P. (2012). From structural chaos to a model of consumer support: Understanding the roles of structure and agency in mental health recovery for the formerly homeless. *Journal of Forensic Psychology Practice*, *12*(4), 325–348.

Wilcox, T. (2012). Human resource management in a compartmentalized world: Whither moral agency? *Journal of Business Ethics: Journal of Biological Education*, *111*(1), 85–96.

Williams, G. H. (2003). The determinants of health: structure, context and agency. *Sociology of Health and Illness*, *25*(3), 131–154.

Wilmsmeier, G., & Monios, J. (2016). Institutional structure and agency in the governance of spatial diversification of port system evolution in Latin America. *Journal of Transport Geography*, *51*(February), 294–307.

Wolfgramm, R., Flynn-Coleman, S., & Conroy, D. (2015). Dynamic interactions of agency in leadership (DIAL): An integrative framework for analysing agency in sustainability leadership. *Journal of Business Ethics*, *126*(4), 649–662.

Wright, S. (2012). Welfare-to-work, agency and personal responsibility. *Journal of Social Policy*, *41*(2), 309–328.

Yea, S. (2016). Everyday spaces of human trafficking: (In)visibility and agency among trafficked women in U.S. military-oriented clubs in South Korea. *Annals of the Association of American Geographers*, *106*(4), 957–973.

Zaslove, A. (2012). The populist radical right in government: The structure and agency of success and failure. *Comparative European Politics*. https://doi.org/10.1057/cep.2011.19

Zdun, S. (2012). The meaning of agency in processes of desisting from delinquent behaviour in prison: An exploratory study among juvenile inmates in Germany. *Journal of Social Work Practice in the Addictions*, *26*(4), 459–472.

APPENDIX

DESCRIPTION OF SAMPLE

The sample contained a diversity of social science subdisciplines (for details see Fig. A1 below). Amongst the most prevalent subdisciplines were gender studies (25%), social science of health[29] (12%), political sociology (11%), youth studies (10%), migration studies (8%), criminology and deviance (8%), religious studies (6%).

Table A1. Categorization of the Sample According to Agency Type.

Agency Categories	Number of Articles	Percentage (%) of Total Sample[a]
Normative	128	87.07
Descriptive	56	38.10
Weak voluntarism	119	80.95
Power/changing structures	64	43.54
Strong voluntarism	4	2.72
Strong structures	7	4.76
Reflexivity	17	11.56

[a]Percentage values in the table have been rounded up.

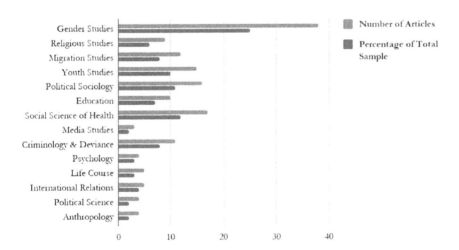

Fig. A1. Description of Sample According to Subdisciplines.

CURIOUSLY FOOTNOTED CONCEPTUALIZATIONS OF AGENCY

Steven Hitlin

University of Iowa, USA

ABSTRACT

Amasyali and van de Berg's discussions of Agency were edifying and scholarly, but curiously sideline some of the very pockets of sociology that might most fully address their concerns with this slippery concept. This response suggests some counterexamples to some of their strongest claims that deny the utility or the exploration of agency, ultimately suggesting that sociological social psychology, understood in its probabilistic format, helps address the lack of precision around this commonly employed concept.

Keywords: Agency; precision; probability; social psychology; Axel van den Berg; Emre Amasyali

Questioning the ultimate nature of human agency may be a peculiarly sociological preoccupation. A notoriously slippery term, agita about its reality is reemerging thanks to two forcefully argued papers by Amasyali and van den Berg (hereafter A&vdB). For brevity, I'll refer to this pair of papers as "need agency?" and "use agency?", though my pragmatist predilections suggest the distinction between needing and using is artificial.[1] We *use* the term "agency" to accomplish various situated tasks; by doing so, we demonstrate a potential *need*; it is up to the wider scholarly community to decide how effectively this was accomplished. There is a grain of truth to A&vdB's imputation of nefarious intent to authors who use the term to smuggle in notions of anti-structural heroism, but in a discipline focused on social forces, some sort of placeholder about individual social action has been needed and used since at least Weber's focus on types of social action. My concerns about these papers are twofold: (a) the footnoting of those of us who have, in fact, offered some precision as to what, when, and how "agency" (whatever it is) influences social life and (b) a vast underplaying of the notion of probability as key to their apparent goal of someday theorizing a fully determinative social universe. Ultimately, these authors impressively array how the term is inconsistently employed across the discipline, a contribution, but one that we – the footnoted – might consider a misdiagnosis of the nature of sociology, if not social action more broadly.

John Levi Martin, whose response to these articles I very much look forward to reading, stated one of his rules of sociology (Martin, 2015) as "some do, some don't," as strong a summary of how we approach our work as any longer treatise. Sociology, in the view I will be representing, is a probabilistic science, not a deterministic one. Insofar as that is true, the crucial aspects involve what and when and why and how people do things. Critiques of authors who use agency as dismissing the possibility that action is caused by external and internal regularities are...curious. Whether "agency" as a concept is "useful" or "needed" is determined by the success of various attempts to better explain the conditions of when things happen and when they don't than previous attempts, the process of cumulative science. Dismissing the possibility that some action is not directly caused by previous social forces does not mean advocating the sort of radical indeterminacy that these critics want to excise from sociology; it means that various forces probabilistically make other actions/responses/behaviors/reactions more or less likely. Agency may be a gloss in the more proximal factors that shift probabilities, but there is a reason the term has become more popular within a discipline so focused on extra-individual factors underlying human action. People do stuff, we want to know when and how and, in a particularly exciting paper, perhaps even why.

When asked to return to a topic I was more deeply engaged with a decade and a half ago by commenting on these two papers, I was intrigued to see what I could learn from this re-engagement. It is edifying to see some of that work referenced in these papers, but from my view, the solution to these "problems" is relegated to a pair of footnotes in "need agency?" and another in "use agency?" Entire disciplinary subfields concerned with probabilistic thinking about social action – social psychology, life course studies – are sidelined, precluding us from hearing what A&vdB believe about their capacity to address their concerns, which, following Loyal and Barnes (2001), see the term as a waste of time. In "need agency?" they claim agency is, for sociologists, "as unproblematic as it is popular," but I quibble with both aspects of this characterization; (a) it is, in fact, problematic for some of the scholars cited but not engaged with, here, or others who have previously dismissed the concept as superfluous, and (b) it may not be as popular in the last decade as it was in the three decades prior.

Greater precision in all things is a laudable goal, and perhaps the answer is to (a la Vaisey & Valentino, 2018) give up our disciplinary jargon and employ terms like other cognate fields (interests, preferences, constraints), to be better understood and more influential. For the time being, however, we still find the notion of agency that we once termed "curiously abstract" (Hitlin & Elder, 2007a, it's right there in the article title) and tried – perhaps unsuccessfully – to map out its different usages, not unlike "Use Agency?" but with less judgment about the intentions of the authors who draw upon this concept. The implicit assumption of our previous work, one that seems to bump up against A&vdB's treatises, is that social life is at some level indeterminate but not fully idiosyncratic or random. Finding patterns among the range of social forces that exist within and without people is a difficult, maybe hopelessly doomed, exercise, but it is the cursed realm of sociology. A&vdB criticize dozens of previous authors for "reject[ing] a model of causal explanation that takes action to be the fully determined joint product of actors' environments and their psychological predispositions." Guilty, I fear, in this construction. However, I work in a tradition (many of whom are cited here in our crowded footnote locations) that, far from rejecting it, focuses *entirely* on the probabilistic relationship of environmental and psychological predispositions. Perhaps there is room to find common ground.

PROBABILISTIC SCIENCE PROBABLY (!) NEEDS ELASTIC CONCEPTS

> In a pivotal moment of *The Pirates of the Caribbean*, the villain, upon seeing the heroes still alive despite his best attempts, shouts in a moment of pique "That's Impossible!" To which one of the heroes replies, "That's *Improbable*!"

Almost 40 years ago, fellow commenter Turner (1987) argued that sociological theories were destined to be "underdetermined," since any observable phenomenon has a myriad of potential theoretical explanations. In understanding social phenomena, we cannot "discard" less usable theories and concepts as they get replaced in the manner of the physical sciences; even old ideas might still be plausible in the face of new ones. This lack of agreed-upon standards for becoming a cumulative science is not a new problem (Freese, 1972), and I am not well positioned to weigh in on our potential to overcome this. An implication of A&vdB's work, however, seems to be that discussing and using "agency" is an obstacle toward a goal of finding a fully sociological understanding of human action, whatever that would mean in practice (Black, 2000).[2]

One of my mentors used to say that sociology was a probabilistic, not a deterministic, science. I found that incredibly helpful during my graduate training, and assumed it was more widely written about than seems to be the case. If we expect sociologists to develop a science that finds people's actions to "be fully determined" by anything, we are a long, long way from having that capacity. The physical science ideal of finding deterministic forces is not even successful in the physical sciences, as I understand it, where indeterminacy is built into a variety of models at different levels of physical reality. Do we think people, with our moods, changing incentives, subconscious beliefs, self-presentational concerns, lack of knowledge, and biased interpretive cognitive apparatuses, are somehow going to be MORE deterministically predictable than quarks, neutrons, lemurs, or beluga whales? A&vdB are convincing that "agency" is doing inconsistent work across treatments, but as a science, perhaps we "need" to "use" some placeholder for the (seemingly obvious to me) fact that similar people (based on whatever commonalities you like) do not always act similarly.

Again, I feel unqualified to enter too fully into this debate, though some (Glynn, 2010) suggest even deterministic worlds have inherent aspects of chance, and sociologists are less concerned with things like "luck" (Sauder, 2020) in our models than perhaps we should be. Recently, Strand and Lizardo (2021, 2022) have engaged issues of probability within the work of Bourdieu and Weber, showing how issues of chance and probability are inherent to these authors' understanding of reality. Details aside, Weber's and Bourdieu's works suggests probabilistic thinking as "a tool for sociological knowledge because such calculations can enable the restatement of sociological theories as 'probability statements' rather than the statement of laws" (Strand & Lizardo, 2021, p. 401). I do not read all agency-scholars as rejecting a model of causal action inasmuch as we are trying to refine such models with the understanding that even a fully specified model – never possible with human beings – needs to allow for some diversity in behavior, choice, understanding, capacity, and outcome. Probability statements, not causal ones. Some do, some don't.

A concern with probability is not a quantitative notion; all manner of sociological analysis can examine the personal, collective, interactional, and macro factors that make certain behaviors and outcomes more or less likely. What holds a disparate field together is what Martin (2001) considers the "sociological hunch," that somehow things "out there" get inside of people and influence their behavior, over and above rational choice or neurological or "cultural dope" sorts of models. Our best quantitative models rarely explain even a third of the variation in any outcome, and our best qualitative researchers are often discussing surprising or varied reactions to similar situations. Whether we call this variation "agency" is a legitimate question, but it necessitates being called something.

SOCIOLOGICAL SOCIAL PSYCHOLOGY: THE STUDY OF ENVIRONMENTS AND PSYCHOLOGICAL PREDISPOSITIONS

Fortunately, we have some theoretical and empirical tools to get purchase on this variation in probable influences and outcomes. I begin my undergraduate course and my contribution to our latest edition of our textbook, *Social Psychology 10th ed.* (DeLamater et al., 2024) drawing on Kurt Lewin's (1946) banal-yet-important observation that human behavior is a function of both the person and the environment. Literally, entire fields in sociology begin with the study of environmental and personal factors that influence social behavior; they simply assume probabilistic relationships, not deterministic ones. The "environment" for Lewin was proximal social space; for sociologists, it includes the cultural environment, historical era, structural resources, and so forth (McLeod & Lively, 2003). In both cases, these factors interact with personal characteristics and capabilities to probabilistically shape social behavior. Yet, as these authors dismiss the concept of agency (until they don't, confusingly), those of us trying to juggle external and personal forces in systematic ways get marginalized to these three footnotes.

It seems that A&vdB hold psychological processing as an uncaused cause, and/or as fully determinative of action. Philosophy majors for centuries have likely pondered if, when science gets advanced enough, we could know which particles bouncing off which objects would trigger which neurons to predict which actions and utterances would result. Even then, in a world of quantum physics, I'm skeptical such a model predicts everything. Short of that, however, the subfields that my fellow footnotes and I subscribe to try to specify what factors – external and psychological – interrelate and probabilistically influence various social outcomes and behavior. Most of us do not even use the term "agency," so maybe we have solved the problem?

Blumer, Giddens, Alexander, and the others that A&vdB suggest view agency as "choice" and "creativity" are the ones who (in these two papers) reject the possibility of causal explanation, viewed deterministically. Many trees have died (once upon a time, though journals still print on paper) in the service of finding sociologically sensitive patterns in the creation, reception, and implementation of these "uncaused causes." Beliefs and intentions, if they influence behavior, need not be "uncaused," especially within a probabilistic notion of the social universe. The notion that we are reflexively acting (a la Wittgenstein and Taylor, in A&vdB's telling a vague and overly conscious misconception) is not the only way to turn vague intentions into action; the entire point of Blumer, and others in that broad tradition, is that such actions emerge from the flow of interaction with others, a combination of locally produced social order (e.g., Garfinkel, 1967; see; Goffman, 1983; Rawls, 1987) and conscious and implicit reaction to the complicated alchemy of other actors, situational cues, and culture (whatever that is); to be a competent interactant is to properly demonstrate a moral commitment to emergent order regardless of the specifics (Rawls, 2010).

Apparently, I presciently published my responses to these two papers almost two decades ago (Hitlin & Elder, 2007a, 2007b; Hitlin & Long, 2009). Cited briefly here, our footnoted "tradition" elides the best potential routes for engagement. Agency, if I might speak for some social psychologists, is implied in the very notion of interaction.[3] Positing how much is "agentic" is a gloss on the observable facts that (a) people do things, (b) they often have reasons they believe for why they do things, (c) often these reasons appear unrelated to those things, even as people believe they are "causal," (d) some of these things can be measured – if inadequately, (e) those measures sometimes correlate with those behaviors, and (f) over time, we have an incomplete catalogue about how many phenomena (values, ideologies, status, identities, reciprocal obligations) systematically associate with those behaviors. Now, what these phenomena represent is an open and important question (see Martin & Lembo, 2020; Lizardo, 2017 for two notable engagements with this issue), but the work often operates without "agency" being invoked. Does that research pass muster? Is probabilistic work sans the term agency acceptable?

I take A&vdB's argument to be that agency is a useless gloss on top of all that work, but scholars who play closer to data have discussed this. It involves what Shanahan and Hood (1998) called "bounded agency," the very notion found in Marx and Mills and others that we make our history, but not under circumstances of our own choosing. An entire field of Life Course Studies (e.g., Elder, 1994) examines the how and when and where of these forces. We covered this (Hitlin & Elder, 2007a) in holding that sometimes, agency involves reproducing structures – which still involves creativity and sensitivity to interactants, norms, etc., what we called identity agency – and sometimes involves novel constructions of novelty (pragmatic agency) and sometimes involves, from a more macro perspective, important moments in a life that set future trajectories (life course agency). This all becomes antagonistic to causal models only if you view them in a prohibitively strict deterministic manner.

A THIRD PAPER MIGHT PROFITABLY ENGAGE WITH THE FOOTNOTES

A&vdB's papers interestingly map out different uses of agency, but the authors bail out before, in my view, engaging with the positive portion of their critique; what is the right way to talk about human action? Their mapping of the different treatments of this complicated term makes sense, but after this lengthy-but-convincing analysis, they state "we are not in a position to address this claim [of agency as a cultural construction]" (in Use Agency?) and "nor are we willing to take any position whatsoever on any version of determinism..." (in Need Agency?). But from the point of view of a veteran of the "agency" squabbles, these are precisely the issues left on the table; that agency is used differently (Emirbayer & Mische, 1998; Hitlin & Elder, 2007a), or potentially a useless concept (Alexander, 1992; Loyal & Barnes, 2001), is old news. We have categorizations of the usages of the term and other statements about its vacuity and ways of measuring its purported importance. Is the world deterministic in such a way as to preclude any of these forms of agency, as Loyal and Barnes and others maintain? Is it a Western gloss on action? These are more pressing, less engaged aspects of the term.

If I were reviewing these papers, I'd ask for the authors to apply their considerable insights on these questions, and perhaps shorten up the strangely critical review of the term across scholars who exhibit what they call "agency worship." They conclude by positing that agency sneaks in value judgments, which might be true, though I'd say some of those "values" are, in fact, disciplinary tenets that things outside people influence people, a larger problematic in sociology than for our economic and psychological neighbors. When studying the less powerful, these may constitute making some actions more "heroic" in the face of immense pressures, but criminologists, scholars of genocide, and others can also use the term to condemn the actions/choices of people, as well (e.g., Luft, 2023).

Put differently, some of these issues are a problem of a fit between theory and data and may be baked into the sociological enterprise (Turner, 1987). An inability to develop a single definition of agency that accurately captures the phenomenon of people doing stuff might be a flaw in the work of the scholars trying to fit theory to data, but it might also be a property of a difficult-to-study social world. If one's epistemology defends the proposition that all human action is deterministically caused, then certainly implications that people sometimes have "free will," or even that beliefs about one's free will, systematically influence a portion of their life course outcomes, then the dismissal of the term makes sense. But this is where data come in handy. I enjoy theoretical treatment as much as the next scholar, perhaps more given theory's relative declination in the field over the past 25 years, but as theorists tackle actual data, their definitions, measures, and outcomes are there for the rest of us to adjudicate. Whatever life-course scholars call "agency" (Hitlin & Elder, 2007b), and there are disagreements, those beliefs are correlated with various outcomes. Not in a strict causal sense, but people with more of these beliefs early in life have a greater probability of more "good" things (education, health) later in life. Did we discover "agency" just as physicists find new forms of matter? Maybe not, but we need to call it something. And in a field that has too much jargon, umbrella terms that signal relevance to other phenomena seem "useful," even "needed." Just be precise about how you meant the term to operate.

People lower on the SES ladder have fewer economic resources, and often score lower on psychological models of agency-like-beliefs than others (Mirowsky, 2013; Pearlin & Bierman, 2013), and those beliefs help predict longitudinal outcomes. Footnote 38 in "need agency?" says they consider psychological predispositions to be "structural," which perhaps concedes this point, but "structural" is attached to the phrase "does not seem to do any explanatory work," so I am not sure what the criteria are for agency, or "structural" psychological dispositions more generally, to be judged as effective. Removing these measures from statistical models worsens (some) models; people tell their life stories (McAdams, 2013) using related terms. How are we to know they do not do explanatory work if the evidence that they might is summarily dismissed?

In "agency for?", microsociology is once again relegated to a footnote (21 this time), with "social psychology" measuring some perception of one's agency, but A&vdB state "there is no suggestion whatsoever in this particular strand of the 'agency'-using literature pointing to anything like 'free will' or actors making choices *ex nihilo*..." I do not know exactly what that critique means, but it sounds damning. Except that, when I read (or write) articles cited here, I see work that theoretically posits what looks like "free will":

> The subjective aspect of agency, we argue, allows the development of a model of social actors that can reflectively influence their lives, rounding out influential theoretical models that minimize the place of conscious re-flection within understanding social action. (Hitlin & Kirkpatrick Johnson, 2015, p. 1434)

> But despite this awareness, they continue to strive for a college education because they associate unwavering ambition with a virtuous identity. (Frye, 2012, p. 1608)

> Those who were most mature and competent tended to assess the options available to them; they made more considered choices and they were better prepared to work through the problems of adaptation that marriage and careers require. (Clausen, 1991, p. 835)

Now, maybe these are choices made post nihilo, pre nihilo, ex nihilo, or nihilo but, in the framing of these authors, at least, choices are being made within some alchemy of available information coupled with unarticulated tacit beliefs within wider cultural edifices (Vaisey, 2009). Is this "agency"? I do not know, epistemologically, but the details and measurement and relationship to measurable outcomes are all offered in these sorts of projects, a move toward precision that I would like to know more about how they do or do not satisfy A&vdB.

AGENCY AND ITS DEBATES: PROBABILISTIC THINKING TONES DOWN EPISTEMOLOGICAL CERTAINTY

Three sets of explanations exist in "need agency?" to explain the use of the construct: (a) meaningfulness/intentionality of social action, (b) a need for "agency" to explain change in social structure, and (c) links between agency, accountability, and dignity. The authors argue none of these provides a convincing rationale for the analytical utility of agency. They seem not to like the voluntaristic notion of the concept and how it keeps room for unpredictable (my term) action. This carving of the problems with the overuse of the concept is interesting, and worthy of being out in the general literature, but then this paper skids into what to me seemed a strange (improbable?) ending; we don't know if/when we have solved this, so we are fated to use the tools as best we can.

But are we so fated? In "use agency?" we find a chart that convincingly shows the rise of the concept through 2015. However, these papers come out almost a decade later, and in some pockets, 8–10 years do not matter, but as someone whose work contributed to the upward trend of having "agency" in paper titles, my intuitive sense is that the concept – at least at this most metaphysical level – is getting sidelined. Giddens and Alexander are nowhere near as central as they were, anecdotally. I cannot in short order replicate A&vdB's more careful analysis, but two quick restrictions on a Web of Science search from 2021–2024 looking for "agency" in a title and "sociology" in the body of a paper gets 116 hits. Expanding that to "social" instead of "sociology" but limiting to social science publications (as defined by WoS) finds 71 articles. Dividing those numbers by three and a half years does not suggest that "agency" is still quite as strong a focus.[4] This does not mean it is a dead concept, but the spike in growth from their Figure represents a potential academic popularity wave that I was well in the midst of...and as I have shifted interests, perhaps I have also followed a wider trend. All of which is to say, one could look at this metadata and suggest the field is moving on from (or beyond) this debate. If we are to be a cumulative science – that is an entirely different can of worms – one might look at this as positive, even if we've cohered around three related forms of flawed explanation.

I write this comment not to necessarily defend specific instantiations of agency, and my own previously published defenses and critiques of the term may be outdated, misinformed, or useless. But the rhetorical approaches of these papers, which regularly refer to totalizing phrases like "none...provide," "some propose," "all these studies share an unquestioned assumption..." evidence a kind of omniscient summation of a literature that I read differently. After a decade of political appeals to "people are saying," a healthy skepticism is warranted about pretty much anything that gets grouped as "all scholars do (or do not do) X." One does not sell products by saying "this might be one of the best X's around, but might not," but in academia, the rhetorical view that "nobody" has this right, or "everybody" uses a term in a particular way, warrants skepticism. Some do, some don't. Giddens and Archer and Alexander apparently do.[5]

The notion of "agency" as heroism against malign structures echoes Alexander's (1992, 1993) notes three decades ago and certainly captures a general sociological slant toward the "heroic" battling of putatively dominant structures. This is, of course, a peculiarly sociological problem, the discipline most focused on these macro forces that shape individual action in some, often vaguely defined, way. So, blaming sociologists for focusing too much on the aspects of social action that often lay just outside of our purview is a choice, but is the alternative "pure" sociology? Loyal and Barnes and other scholars cited in these papers take versions of that position, but right when we get to the point for the affirmative position from A&vdB, they suggest at the conclusion of "need agency?" that maybe we are "fated to try and use our causal explanatory tools as best we can to explain as much as we can." For some, agency is that sort of multipurpose tool. I agree that, perhaps it is best not to look too closely, but does it substantively change the work to excise the term?

I have no quibble with the observation (not quite as new as suggested here) that many people use "agency" in ways that signal some diversion from a norm, or structures or other force that sociologists posit shapes action (Marshall, 2003, makes a similar point). The authors are correct to highlight that, some of the time, calling these "agency" does not add much explanation for the behavior. Perhaps using that term some of the time does tell us more about the author than the subject, to which my reaction is...ok? Disciplines have jargon, that jargon says something about the shared presuppositions of the author and readers in a particular field. There is a bias, as Alexander (1992) posited, toward agency's heroic instantiations and less so for the many terrible actions found in the world. That does say something about how the authors view power infused within institutions that marginalize some people who, in certain circumstances, do not mindlessly follow institutional or cultural dictates. But if that is an issue, the concern was present during the selection of study topic, not because of this overly abstract term.

CONCLUSION: DO WE NEED CRITIQUES ABOUT AGENCY? HOW DO WE USE THEM?

Years ago, we called this debate "curiously abstract" (Hitlin & Elder, 2007a), and I wish the intervening years had made things either less curious or less abstract. While this pair of papers walks the reader through a lot of this debate, I am not sure they have made things more concrete. So much of the work on this (Archer, 2000; Giddens, 1984) does stay at a curiously high level, and perhaps focuses too much in the abstract on deliberation, heroics, or unexplained behavior. But is "agency" the only problem in sociology? "Race," "Class," "Status," "Identity," etc., all these terms get used differentially for different projects, have some slippage across usages, and have the possibility of incorporating researcher biases toward individuals over structure into their analyses. We must label our phenomena somehow.

So let me conclude by (politely, I hope) turning the question around. What are the critiques of agency for? Why do we need them? If the issue is that sociology has a set of nebulous-but-important sounding terms, one might engage these terms (e.g., identity, values, morality, dignity, self) to push for more precision in their usage in specific studies.[6] This is not necessarily a sociological problem; the English Language offers "slippery" terms all over the place that are used as authors intend, sometimes in self-contradictory ways (e.g., Hitlin & Andersson, 2015). We are, as Collins (1994) holds it, a low-consensus field. If we are going to make the leap toward our own Nobel prize, or follow the dictates of the hard sciences, perhaps we should be making more explicit progress with our terms, or pruning them (e.g., Vaisey & Valentino, 2018) to line up with cognate fields.

But, short of that, scholars should be pressed to be precise about their use of a term within a specific project, but a discipline that studies "status," "legitimacy," "power," "identity," or "agency" will not immediately cohere on the precise, single definition of these terms to be applied in all cases. A&vdB themselves say, though these different "uses" of agency are conceptually distinct, they often overlap within the specific papers they surveyed. A term that does not have perfect clarity in definition thus demonstrates less clarity in usage but, for each of these studies, it is up to the scholarly reader to ascertain the paper's definition, treatment, and execution of the use of this (or any) concept. These two papers read as if the authors are discovering that this concept is a bit less powerful than its connotative meaning – calling something "agency" adds a legacy of heroism and powerful capacity to what otherwise might just be people "doing stuff" – but that is not fully a new critique, and where does gets us is not immediately evident.

To make this point, we have to go back to basic probabilistic logic; in a quantitative model, if a social scientist can explain 40% of the outcome in any meaningful variable (earnings, life span, voting behavior), we leap for joy and get published in elite journals. That leaves a lot of unexplained variance, and I suppose one way to read these critiques of agency is that the term gets us no closer to – and perhaps obscures – understanding those other factors. But the goal of science – short of a set of Issac Asimov novels – is not perfect prediction. Life is partially random, but probabilistically so, and people's intentions do not perfectly predict behavior (Ajzen, 1985). As a seminar classmate said years ago, if this were the case, the game of baseball would be useless, as pitchers have strong intentions of where the ball should go each and every pitch. The joy (for those who like the game) is in the imperfection of that thrown ball interacting with the simultaneous intention of a batter to redirect that ball. A fundamentally unknowable interaction, despite all the deterministic forces in play.

I may "intend" to overthrow a government, tell off my boss, or pick up someone at a bar; in an interactive context, those intentions and actions (agency?) intersect with others' intentions/actions, and that's the rub. Sociology at its best helps find a distribution of potentials along some dimensions that help us – admittedly imperfectly – get a bead on what is more or less likely to happen in these situations. Sometimes, referring to people's actions/beliefs/capacities as "agency" helps tell the story. In a probabilistic universe (or science), this helps organize a potentially infinite set of forces/pressures/neurons in play. So, dismissing these attempts but leaving the wreckage behind without an affirmative plan fails to leverage the powers of deduction demonstrated across these two papers. If we excised the term from the field today, what would change? Apparently, a nonsignificant number of academic article titles would have terminological gaps, but it isn't clear to me, after reading these two papers, what is at stake. Getting the entire field to agree on how to understand individual action is not impossible, improbable as it may be, but in a low-consensus field, that is a lofty goal, indeed.

NOTES

1. Pierce, largely hailed as pragmatisms' progenitor, did not like the direction taken by the more socially oriented scholars who also used his term. He redesigned his ideas around the notion of "pragmaticism," a term he suggested was too grotesque to be stolen.
2. I do not pretend to fully grasp Black's (2000) goal for a "pure" sociology, but perhaps A&vdB agree with this view.
3. Most of my microsociological friends, frankly, do not care about this argument at all; people do things for a variety of internal and external reasons, and the work involves studying and disentangling some subset of these reasons.
4. To be fair, changing the search to include all journals, this number is in the low 4 digits, suggesting 300 a year, but some of those articles are far afield of the kind of "agency" being analyzed, here.
5. Some of us, don't.
6. And I have.

REFERENCES

Ajzen, I. (1985). From intentions to action: A theory of planned behavior. In J. Hulh & J. Beckman (Eds.), *Action control: From cognition to behavior*. Springer.

Alexander, J. C. (1992). Some remarks on "agency" in recent sociological theory. *Perspectives, 15*(1), 1–4.

Alexander, J. C. (1993). More notes on the problem of agency: A reply. *Berliner Journal Fur Soziologie, 19*, 501–506.

Archer, M. S. (2000). *Being human: The problem of agency*. Cambridge University Press.

Black, D. (2000). Dreams of pure sociology. *Sociological Theory, 18*(3), 343–367.

Clausen, J. A. (1991). Adolescent competence and the shaping of the life course. *American Journal of Sociology, 96*, 805–842.
Collins, R. (1994). Why the social sciences won't become high-consensus, rapid-discovery science. In *Sociological forum* (pp. 155–177). Springer.
DeLamater, J., Collett, J., & Hitlin, S. (2024). *Social psychology* (10th ed.). Taylor & Francis.
Elder, G. H., Jr. (1994). Time, human agency, and social change: Perspectives on the life course. *Social Psychology Quarterly, 57*(1), 4–15.
Emirbayer, M., & Mische, A. (1998). What is agency? *American Journal of Sociology, 103*(4), 962–1023.
Freese, L. (1972). Cumulative sociological knowledge. *American Sociological Review, 37*(4), 472–482.
Frye, M. T. (2012). Bright futures in Malawi's new dawn: Educational aspirations as assertions of identity. *American Journal of Sociology, 117*(6), 1565–1624.
Garfinkel, H. (1967). *Studies in ethnomethodology*. Prentice Hall.
Giddens, A. (Ed.). (1984). *The constitution of society introduction of the theory of structuration*. University of California Press.
Glynn, L. (2010). Deterministic chance. *The British Journal for the Philosophy of Science, 61*(1), 51–80.
Goffman, E. (1983). The interaction order: American sociological association, 1982 presidential address. *American Sociological Review, 48*(1), 1–17.
Hitlin, S., & Andersson, M. A. (2015). Dignity as moral motivation: The problem of social order writ small. In E. J. Lawler, S. R. Thye, & J. Yoon (Eds.), *Order on the edge of chaos: Social psychology and the problem of social order* (pp. 268–285). Cambridge University Press.
Hitlin, S., & Elder, G. H., Jr. (2007a). Agency: An empirical model of an abstract concept. In R. Macmillan (Ed.), *Advances in life course research: Constructing adulthood: Agency and subjectivity in adolescence and adulthood* (pp. 33–67). Elsevier/JAI Press.
Hitlin, S., & Elder, G. H., Jr. (2007b). Understanding 'agency': Clarifying a curiously abstract concept. *Sociological Theory, 25*(2), 170–191.
Hitlin, S., & Kirkpatrick Johnson, M. (2015). Reconceptualizing agency within the life course: The power of looking ahead. *American Journal of Sociology, 120*(5), 1429–1472.
Hitlin, S., & Long, C. (2009). Agency as a sociological variable: A preliminary model of individuals, situations, and the life course. *Sociology Compass, 3*(1), 137–160.
Lewin, K. (1946). Behavior and development as a function of the total situation. In *Manual of child psychology* (pp. 791–844). John Wiley & Sons, Inc. https://psycnet.apa.org/doi/10.1037/10756-016
Lizardo, O. (2017). Improving cultural analysis: Considering personal culture in its declarative and nondeclarative modes. *American Sociological Review, 82*(1), 88–115.
Loyal, S., & Barnes, B. (2001). "Agency" as a red herring. *Philosophy of the Social Sciences, 31*(4), 507–524.
Luft, A. (2023). The moral career of the genocide perpetrator: Cognition, emotions, and dehumanization as a consequence, not a cause, of violence. *Sociological Theory, 41*(4), 324–351.
Marshall, V. W. (2003). Agency, events, and structure at the end of the life course. In *PaVie 2003 research colloquium, "Trajectories, stages, transitions and events of the life course: Towards an interdisciplinary perspective"*. https://www.academia.edu/5101391/Agency_Events_and_Structure_at_the_End_of_the_Life_Course
Martin, J. L. (2001). On the limits of sociological theory. *Philosophy of the Social Sciences, 31*, 187–223.
Martin, J. L. (2015). *Thinking through theory*. W. W. Norton.
Martin, J. L., & Lembo, A. (2020). On the other side of values. *American Journal of Sociology, 126*(1), 52–98.
McAdams, D. P. (2013). The psychological self as actor, agent, and author. *Perspectives on Psychological Science, 8*(3), 272–295.
McLeod, J. D., & Lively, K. J. (2003). Social structure and personality. In J. DeLamater (Ed.), *Handbook of social psychology* (pp. 77–102). Kluwer.
Mirowsky, J. (2013). Depression and the sense of control: Aging vectors, trajectories, and trends. *Journal of Health and Social Behavior, 54*(4), 407–425.

Pearlin, L. I., & Bierman, A. (2013). Current issues and future directions in research into the stress process. In *Handbooks of sociology and social research* (pp. 325–340). Springer.
Rawls, A. W. (1987). The interaction order sui generis: Goffman's contribution to social theory. *Sociological Theory*, *5*(2), 136–149.
Rawls, A. W. (2010). Social order as moral order. In S. Hitlin & S. Vaisey (Eds.), *Handbook of the sociology of morality* (pp. 95–122). Springer.
Sauder, M. (2020). A sociology of luck. *Sociological Theory*, *38*(3), 193–216.
Shanahan, M. J., & Hood, K. E. (1998). Adolescents in changing social structures: Bounded agency in life course perspective. In R. Silbereisen & E. Crockett (Eds.), *Negotiating adolescence in times of social change: Cross-national perspectives on developmental processes and social intervention* (pp. 123–134). Cambridge University Press.
Strand, M., & Lizardo, O. (2021). For a probabilistic sociology: A history of concept formation with Pierre Bourdieu. *Theory and Society*. https://doi.org/10.1007/s11186-021-09452-2
Strand, M., & Lizardo, O. (2022). Chance, orientation, and interpretation: Max Weber's neglected probabilism and the future of social theory. *Sociological Theory*, *40*(2), 124–150.
Turner, S. P. (1987). Underdetermination and the promise of statistical sociology. *Sociological Theory*, *5*(2), 172–184.
Vaisey, S. (2009). Motivation and justification: A dual-process model of culture in action. *American Journal of Sociology*, *114*(6), 1675–1715.
Vaisey, S., & Valentino, L. (2018). Culture and choice: Toward integrating cultural sociology with the judgment and decision-making sciences. *Poetics*, *68*, 131–143.

AGENCY BETWEEN FREEDOM/ ACTION AND DETERMINISM/ STRUCTURE: COMMENT ON VAN DEN BERG AND AMASYALI

John Levi Martin

University of Chicago, USA

ABSTRACT

Van den Berg and Amasyali make a persuasive (though not yet definitive) case that, in practice, appeals to ideas about agency do little to advance our sociological understanding. However, they seem to treat the antithesis of this (vague as it is) notion, explanatory determinism, as if it were stable. Not only are the two concepts equally paradoxical, but one calls out for the other, and we cannot criticize and dispense with one while retaining its twin.

Keywords: Agency; action theory; determinism; sociological theory; Simmel

As the notion of causality only arises on the ground of the observed regularity of appearances, so, too, its opposite, the idea of Freedom, stems from the ground of their observed irregularities. With both, we reach down below the appearances in order to explain their form through a transcendental potence; in both cases we really get no farther than to a condensation of the appearances, that, attaining a self-sufficient psychological life, appears as the primordial ground of the same, and so the problem is reproduced, disguised as its own solution.[1] – Simmel, Einleitung in die Moralwissenschaft, II, 227

INTRODUCTION

I admit to being somewhat puzzled, though also convinced, by this pair of pieces. It seems as though the authors have spent a great deal of time investigating a concept and its use that they were pretty sure, I think correctly, wasn't one that was likely to yield much fruit. One might ask, why bother? But I will argue that they actually may have helped push our thinking about the empirical study of agency forward, not killed it off. At the same time, however, I will argue that the concept of agency is part of a dyad, structure and agency, whose fundamental ontological incoherence has been well noted. Van den Berg and Amasyali highlight the problems only when attention is directed to agency, but not the reciprocal problems that arise when the other pole is taken seriously – which is just as improbable a venture. Finally, it is not clear to me that if there *were* any impressive uses of the concept of agency in empirical research, their procedures would have been likely to find it. Rather, it may be that by focusing on those who confound the empirical questions of relative agency with philosophical problems well-known to be intractable, they make it appear as though there is no room for the investigation of different types of action, a conclusion that I believe somewhat too dismal.

PARADOXES OF FREEDOM AND DETERMINISM
Ontological and Epistemological Solutions

One part of Van den Berg and Amasyali's argument is that sociologists using the idea of "agency" re-awaken classic paradoxes regarding freedom and determination that they are poorly equipped to handle. This seems to me a correct appraisal. Indeed, as far as I understand things, there are really only two types of resolutions to the problem of free will as it gets posed in western philosophy. On the one hand, there are the *ontological* resolutions, like that of Augustine. The fact that God knows what you will do does not, Augustine (*City of God* book V, ch 9; 1963: 183) argued, mean that your act is not fully voluntary. An act becomes voluntary not when you could have done otherwise, but when it is accompanied by the will. ("If we will, the will exists; if not, it does not.") When God foresees our action, He foresees not only our action but our *will* as well. We act with a will, even though there is no sense in which we have a "choice." This seems to me eminently sound, both on logical and on empirical grounds. The alternative idea, that the criterion by which we assess an act as *voluntary* must rest on our employment of an imagined counterfactual, and hence a criterion that makes references to worlds other than the one we are in, hardly seems a sound procedure.

On the other hand, there are *epistemic* solutions – those that have to do with a sophisticated critique of our own capacity for knowledge. The most important one of these is associated with Immanuel Kant (1996 [1787]). This argument, which I hold to be true, is that *cause* is, as far as we know, something that we as human beings develop in our engagement with the world, an engagement we undertake for practical purposes. As Nancy Cartwright (2004) has said, we are pretty sure that, in a world without humans, fire will burn: that's the sort of thing fire does. And we can imagine that rocks will tumble down hills when disturbed. But it is the human who comes up with a general idea about these, that fire *causes* burning, that gravity *causes* falling, and so on.

This second resolution is important as it accounts for the fact that there will be something inherently paradoxical in our attempt to work through our ideas about the universe consistently if we over-apply the concept of causality. As is so often the case, we confuse the *world* with our *statements about* the world. And it is certainly only humans – and perhaps in particular the rather hasty thinkers among them – who decide that from this, they are entitled to make an extrapolation that all changes in the universe come from a large or infinite set of such relations, whether or not they can ever be observed or demonstrated. This extremely unsound extrapolation then gives rise to puzzles that dissipate when one recognizes that *cause* and *determination* are anthropocentric concepts. Perhaps the whole world is determined, perhaps not, perhaps the very notion makes sense (I tend to doubt it), but what we certainly cannot do is declare that determinism is an axiom that we must treat as indubitable, and to which we must adjust all our other thoughts. And I am not sure that Amasyali and Van den Berg sufficiently appreciate this point – that the problem is not in the idea of agency alone, but also in the idea of determinism that, in the absence of an idea like agency, leads to paradox.

The Paradoxes of Determinism

First, a (true) corollary from Augustine's argument, but also derivable on other grounds, is that predictability does not imply determinism. If I say that I am going to go to the movies and then I do in fact go, there is very great predictive power from one datum to the other, but you would be mad to insist that this proves my determinism, and that I could only demonstrate that I was *not* determined and had free will if my statements about what I wanted to do had no relation to what I did later. Determination is an equivocal concept: if I am *determined*, it could be because I am determined by something outside me, or I may be determined to do exactly what, by gosh, I am going to do. More generally, in everyday terms, an act can be seen as highly determined and highly agentic. This is basically the view of Schopenhauer: our most willful acts are the ones that emerge from our character, and these are the ones that we are least able to imagine varying.

But it seems to me that Van den Berg and Amasyali accept the idea of a forced choice between willfulness and determinism – that is, they are still within the paradoxical dyad of freedom-determination. As Simmel says in the opening quotation, these are tightly bound as unsound ontologizations – Kant would call them amphibolies – of our thought. Indeed, the two are literal inverses. In his own attempt at developing a theory of agency, Michael Bell (2011) draws our attention to the fact that R^2 – the total amount of variance that can be attributed to supposedly exogenous predictors – was once called the "coefficient of determination," and $1 - R^2$ squared the "coefficient of alienation." These two are an exclusive and exhaustive partition of the covariance. So, too, bad ideas about determinism and causality necessarily generate equally bad ideas about agency, and vice versa.

Amasyali and Van den Berg are justly rather rough with those who misapply ideas of agency as irreducible freedom, but they pass over its sister concept, causation, in silence.[2] The notion of causation as generally used in sociology, that one's position in social structure – usually approximated by individual attributes – *causes* one to be or do this or that, makes no more sense than the idea that we are only free when we act randomly. If anyone can explain how these attributes have a causal effect on human action, I would be quite interested because I have not seen a coherent defense of this usage. Instead, Van den Berg and Amasyali seem to fall back on acknowledging that their use of causal language is, like that of the rest of social scientists, necessarily somewhat slipshod and impressionistic. At other times, however, they seem to me to be relying on a predetermined conclusion, that we basically live in a Laplacian world of total mechanical determination, which is perhaps the one thing that no contemporary scientists believe! But if there *is* determination, not as an epistemic matter (that is, determinism is a mental construct we extrapolate from successful patterns of cognitive intervention in our environments), but that it really is a part of the universe, including human action, then either there also is agency or we live in a very bizarre world indeed (or at least a Spinozan one).

Agency, in other words, is the dark matter of our anthropology: there's something a bit wrong with current theories of cosmology, so to make them balance out, we have to assume the existence of something that doesn't really make that much sense and can't be seen. So, too, we assume the causal determination of human actions, which is a bit screwy, and so we have to assume the occult quality of agency to make all things balance out. If this is a correct appraisal, perhaps what we want to do, along with analyzing what sociologists *do* with agency (as Amasyali and Van den Berg do), is to try to figure out how we can avoid relying on an explanatory our language that assumes a bizarre world that none of us would want to, or could, live in.

Simmel on the Empirical Turn

And perhaps we should follow Simmel, who proposed that, since the philosophical ideas of free will were themselves taken from the phenomenological experience of freedom, it is this variable experience that we should study. In this case, what might seem to be paradoxes in philosophical terms turn out to be nonparadoxical (Simmel, 1904 [1892–1893]: II, p. 237). If we focus on these states, we may avoid that need to partition our subjectivity into two ontologically antithetical portions, one agency, the other constraint. "The moral-scientific investigation of the problem of freedom will perhaps yield more fruit," Simmel wrote, "if it seeks to establish the role that the concept of freedom and its opposite play in the actual formation of psychic and ethical life than if it indulges in conceptual discussions whose elements ethics only drew from the empirical fact of mental life, and whose relative importance has been elevated into absolute principle; in that way it must, given that this elevation occurs on both sides, flow into deadly antitheses, the reconciliation of which now occupies all its efforts, even though it [ethics] itself probably created them in the first place" (II, p. 238).[3]

Similar elevation of concrete experience into abstract absolutes generates paradoxes for sociology as well. For one, in the social world, given that the materials of our action are other people, we must recognize that our freedom generally comes at the expense of someone else's *unfreedom* (Simmel, 1904 [1892–1893]: II, p. 233f). What from one side appears as constraint is, from the other side, freedom. This duality continues to be inherent in our thinking. The dominant understanding of causality in the social sciences today is one that is grounded in experimental treatments, which themselves are invalid if they are not the result of random assignments, meaning that in all but a very few cases, they rely on the deliberate (willful) assignment of cases to treatment and control groups. We can only prove the causal determination of action if we put some humans in settings in which *other* humans have free will (Martin, 2011). Simmel's proposal might let us carry out meaningful investigations without immediately grinding to a halt because of contradictions we have baked into our terms.

If we do decide to consider the phenomenological experience of free will, we might best understand it as pertaining to the degrees of *ownership* we feel regarding any act or event. And I want to note that this is basically how Aristotle thought about things. To him, the question of whether a person had exercised *forethought* and had made a *choice* (*Nic Eth*, 2011, 1135b1–1135b11) was different from the question of whether the act was *hekōn*, the word generally translated as "voluntary" – whether, say, the actor "knows both what he is doing and for the sake of what he does it" (*Nic Eth*, 2011, 1152a15). I think the best way to put it is that an action is *hekōn* to the extent that the actor would *happily own it* after the doing. A necessary response to an unhappy event (e.g., throwing cargo overboard in a storm) may be choiceworthy, but only partially voluntary, as much of the initiative here was external (since no one would wish for a storm).

If this reasoning is correct, then it might be that there is room for a fruitful exploration of empirical agency, one that does not get caught up in the paradoxes of determination. And, indeed, much of Amasyali and Van den Berg's work has to do with how sociologists fare when they attempt to do this. Their answer is, in short, not too well.

THE EMPIRICAL TURN

Attributions of Agency and People Like Us (PLUs)

Their overall argument is that *agency* seems to be used as a sort of blue ribbon that may be pinned to the actions of those whom the authors in question approve of, or want to dignify. This argument dovetails with an earlier work, based on a much smaller, and nonrepresentative, sample of sociologists, by Charles Kurzman (1991) who showed precisely this pattern in a wonderful ethnography of ethnographers.

And it gets worse – it isn't simply those we like, but PLUs, who disproportionately get that blue ribbon. Van den Berg and Amasyali are quite effective in skewering those thinkers for whom agency is basically a matter of "to what extent does this person see [actually, it would be more accurate to say *talk about* than *see*] the world the way I and my educated friends do?" Amasyali and Van den Berg highlight the illogical nature of the relationship between reflexivity and agency, one that assumes that humans' first impulse is an animalistic one, and only reflection leads to true self-consciousness: an idea which is familiar to us from Rousseau's anthropology, but, translated to social research, degenerates into mere class snobbery.

Their analysis is crushingly effective, and it should serve as a strong warning to us to always make sure that we understand the tendencies toward interpretive asymmetries that we sociologists bring to our studies, and to try to correct them. This is indeed a welcome contribution, but I think that there is a different sort of asymmetry in Amasyali and Van den Berg's analysis – a tendency to see the mote in the opponent's eye and miss the beam in our own.

First, they seem to assume that when authors are speaking of agency, they invariably mean it in philosophical terms of nondeterminism, and not, say, in Simmelian or Aristotelian terms – or, perhaps, in some cases, simply haven't yet quite thought it through, and so aren't really claiming all the philosophical arguments we might imagine they are. Amasyali and Van den Berg make the point that talking about the willpower of certain actors "is not the same thing as attributing some kind of free will to them." But are we sure that this identification is what the authors invariably intended? It isn't obvious to me that this is the case. Second, while Amasyali and Van den Berg pummel those who use the problematic concept of agency uncritically, they seem to pass over the problems in the other half of the dyad – structure, determinism, causality, call it what you will – in silence.

Structure Gets a Pass

Sometimes, this involves an empirical confidence that seems to me unwarranted. Somewhat like an overbold general unwilling to stop his army that has made a successful repulsion of an invader, Van den Berg and Amasyali chase the enemy back into his own stronghold, where they themselves become vulnerable. After reviewing some examples toured by others as proof positive of agency, Amasyali and Van den Berg claim that "the social impact of those decisions is entirely due to the places they happen to occupy in the social structure of which they are part." This seems to me remarkable: I am unaware of any social research that shows that any impact of any decisions is *entirely* due to anything! They seem to just be resting on their own assumptions and not reporting something all would conclude from an examination of the cases. One could of course try to take any case of a surprising success and make it appear as if it were fore-determined, but this seems no sounder than the practices they decry. One person might use the case of Greta Thunberg, a child on the autistic spectrum who became an international climate activist sensation, and argue that this illustrates exactly this sort of surprising "person from a most unlikely place making a difference" that establishes the significance of the concept of practical agency. And then, an anti-agentic theorist might emphasize the things that Thunberg had going for her – that she had parents who were already used to the limelight, that she convinced them to support her, that she was located in a country unusually receptive to such activism, and so on. It's a game in which each side declares the rules, and each side is convinced it wins. That can't be what we want.

But I think there are also real theoretical problems that Amasyali and Van den Berg run into and yet ignore. For example, Van den Berg and Amasyali say that even if we want to talk about practical agency, "this would still merely beg the question of what *caused* or *permitted* the non-compliant actors to act in that way." Let's let this sink in. Caused *or* permitted? Are these two things being equated? Perhaps – for many, causality is a statement about counterfactuals, and so anything that didn't stop someone from doing what they did is a valid cause. What permitted Greta Thunberg to become a climate activist? Well, the fact that her parents were eventually convinced to support her, the fact that the Swedish government didn't hire assassins to take her out, the fact that she was born, and so on and so forth. If Amasyali and Van den Berg are arguing that these are the sorts of things that social analysis *should* be focusing on, that is going to be an extremely hard sell. Again, considering another claimed case of agency, they say "this story here is entirely and exclusively 'structural'," but it seems that they just *call* whatever appears to them a legitimate explanatory factor *structural*, even if the factor is basically what *other* people are doing! It doesn't seem that promising to say that everyone's actions are caused, and no one has agency, but the causes of our actions are other people's actions. Yet that is usually the necessary result of employing ideas of causality in explanations of social action.

So the parts where Van den Berg and Amasyali make claims that in fact, contrary to what the authors say, this or that was wholly dependent on resources, and so on, seems no different from the absolutist language that they pitilessly (but perhaps appropriately) criticize in others. It is true their approach lacks the asymmetry of the others, who seem to only place the blue ribbon of *agency* on those they like, and this move toward symmetry is an important advance. Yet perhaps another critique they make, although (I believe) correct, might not be so damning as they think, namely that these theories really occupy an unstable halfway point on the way to universal agency.

A STUDY OF ACTION?

What Is Action, and How Do We Study It?

Van den Berg and Amasyali seem to assume that something is amiss if it turns out that by *agency*, social thinkers really turn out to mean *action*. It is not obvious to me that this is the case. After all, *action* and *agency* come from the same root! If by *action* we mean all forms of human behavior, then indeed, there might not be much in the concept, and if *agency* refers to the characteristics of such physical movement, it probably just means *activity* in the sense of self-directed motion. But there has been one theoretical tradition (including Weber, whom they cite) that begins by establishing a difference between certain forms of mere behavior done from habit, and those that we would grace with the name of action. And it is worth emphasizing that to Weber, this notion of action was not seen as incompatible with causality.[4] There are, of course, major differences between different thinkers who take the notion of action seriously, but I think it is worth considering Hannah Arendt's (1958, 1978) argument that what is fundamental about action is creating something new.

Van den Berg and Amasyali appear to me to try to deny that this is a possibility, and I find such arguments over-strong. If they are really claiming that Arendt is wrong, that *no one* ever does something new, that *everything* people do can be predicted from their location in social structure, I think they almost certainly exceed their evidentiary base.

If we do think that actions can be ordered or partially ordered by the degree to which they make something new appear, then, just as Simmel said, we could turn to the empirical issue of when and in what settings, and by whom, such novelty emerges. The piece by Emirbayer and Mische (1998) may be seen as such a Simmelian investigation – what are the modes in which we do new things?

Novelty seems one empirically varying aspect of actions; another is the extent to which we would "own" them (Aristotle's conception); a third, which, like Amasyali and Van den Berg, I am suspicious of, is the degree to which actors defend and justify their actions. (Empirical work in psychology [e.g., Wegner (2002); also Gazzaniga (1970)] demonstrates that people will give accounts for actions that they actually have *not* initiated, and there is nothing like a mildly antagonistic sociological interviewer to make even the best of us defensively justify things we actually regret having done.)

So if we are talking not about some ontological freedom, but some empirical issue of the degree to which some action should be seen as voluntary, then some of the work that Amasyali and Van den Berg criticize in their second paper may be more reasonable than it appears from their review. When women support patriarchal religious groups and no researcher talks to them, it might be believed that they don't really have much of a reflective subjectivity, or, I think more important, that they are doing what they're doing without "owning" it. That's the sort of dismissive snobbery that has substituted for analysis in the social sciences, and Van den Berg and Amasyali are justly opposed to allowing this back in. But when a researcher talks to the women and finds that they do reflect on it, and that, in many cases, they have, or at least can *appear* to have, very good reasons for doing what they are doing, then one is not wrong on empirical grounds to promote that action from nonagentic to agentic, just as a person who first appeared to be running blindly in a panic, and is then found to actually be to be running back and forth saving valuable heirlooms in a fire, would be promoted from nonagentic to agentic action. This could, then, be a step *away* from that sort of snobbery for which Amasyali and Van den Berg justly criticize many sociologists of agency. That is not to deny that there are still problems here, especially regarding separating defensive ownership after the fact from phenomenological experiences of will, of novelty, and so on. But this might better be seen as an incomplete step in the right direction, and not a leap in the wrong one.

And it may well be that the pieces in the sample that Amasyali and Van den Berg consider do not demonstrate much facility in pursuing these difficult questions. In some cases, Van den Berg and Amasyali show, authors work themselves into awkward *cul de sac*s, following paradoxical logic without being able to stop themselves. Submission becomes agentic, passivity becomes activity, defeat becomes victory, at least, when it is defended by a well-educated or sympathetic informant. Fortunately, the use of tautology to make a nonfinding seem impressive does not appear to characterize most of the stronger work on action in the social sciences, and it strikes me that when some of our colleagues do flail about, the polite option is to avert our eyes and give them plenty of space so that they do not hurt themselves or others.

We might even appreciate that the paradoxes that some of these authors talk about, if left in paradoxical form, may be related to deep insights that sociologists have long recognized. In his theory of autonomy, Durkheim (1961 [1902–1903]) argued that to be autonomous means to be autonomous within the laws of nature, laws that, to him, include sociological laws. This fundamental paradox – the one that gives rise to the dyad of structure and agency, a dyad that, as I have said, I do not think that Amasyali and Van den Berg have sufficiently criticized – then leads to the question of whether one can become autonomous by consciously, reflectively, voluntarily deciding to work within the laws of nature – to be, like Leibniz's rock, willfully falling according to the law of gravity.

Durkheim's answer was that yes, when we give the laws our enlightened allegiance, then, we are autonomous, but he argued that sometimes, we may accept that we *cannot* actually have an enlightened allegiance, for we cannot ourselves fathom these laws. But, added Durkheim, in such cases, we still can retain autonomy, but now through a sort of meta recognition – we understand why we cannot understand the reasons for our submission to laws. This might seem ridiculous, but many a soldier could explain that this is an empirically reasonable situation: one may understand why one cannot be trusted with the information as to why what one is being asked to do is rational, and yet one may, with full willfulness, pursue these actions, the reasons for which one does not know, without feeling that one is being irrational, because one understands the reasons why one does not understand the reasons. It is, as Simmel would emphasize, an empirical issue.

Open Possibilities for the Future?

Finally, Amasyali and Van den Berg may have been unduly negative about the potential of such studies to yield significant results. First, it might well be that a corpus of articles is not actually the best place to look for successful uses of the concept. If *agency* is a complex theoretical idea, then it might be the sort of thing better discussed in books, where one has the space (and the sort of reader) to allow one to unfurl a more complex theoretical structure. Second, searching for articles that use the word *agency* in their title also may not actually be the best place to get articles that use the term in a way that would meet Van den Berg and Amasyali's approval. If one has a study of some phenomenon that requires the *use* of the concept of agency, but successfully explains that phenomenon, one might choose a title about the explanatory factor. Without casting aspersions on the articles in their corpus, it might be that those that use the word *agency* are precisely those in which there is not much of a finding in traditional explanatory terms. It does appear that Amasyali and Van den Berg tended to draw from interdisciplinary journals more than ones where we might imagine that the authors would impress them with a sober and limited understanding of agency. Indeed, rather than examining many weak uses of agency, which is indeed proper for the question of what people in general *do* with the concept, it might make sense to focus on a single best example. I admit, however, that such an example of an empirical use is not actually coming to my mind. Yet I can think of many excellent empirical contributions that, from a resolutely sociological perspective, examine how something new came to be (a wonderful example is Reynold's [2022] analysis of the repurposing of Title IX).

And I also admit that the interesting empirical questions regarding agency – questions of, for example, when, against all apparent odds, someone does something new, someone initiates something, someone surprises others – may turn out not to be good sociological questions. Still, I don't think it will be possible to argue that they are inherently meaningless ones. If we stopped trying to *judge* people, to sort them into the great categories of PLU and non-PLU, we might find that there is something that empirical research could tell us about the structure, both inside and outside the person, of the experience of agency. Van den Berg and Amasyali's two-part analysis, intended to pound the last nail in the coffin of the use of agency, might actually have charted the way to free ourselves from old prejudices and rethink this question with greater rigor.

NOTES

1. "Wie die Vorstellung von Kausalität nur auf Grund der beobachteten Regelmässigkeit der Erscheinungen entsteht, so ihr Gegentheil, die Freiheitsidee, auf Grund der beobachteten Unregelmässigkeit derselben. Mit beiden greifen wir unter die Erscheinungen hinab, um ihre Form durch eine transszendentale Potenz zu erklären, in beiden Fällen kommen wir freilich auch nicht weiter als bis zu einer Verdichtung der Erscheinungen, die ein selbständiges psychologisches Leben gewinnend, als Urgrund derselben erscheint, und uns so das Problem als seine eigene Lösung verkleidet wiedergiebt."

2. I was delighted to see Van den Berg and Amasyali relying on the excellent work of Barry Barnes (2000), but they do not follow him far enough: it seems to me that taking Barnes seriously is incompatible with accepting the idea of agency versus structure-as-constraint. Barnes points out that very often social structure requires the utmost expenditure of agency. It is easy for a marching band to become disordered, hard for it to remain in lockstep and in time. I would also like to point to the structural similarity of Barnes's view of agency (we can attribute agency to an act when the actor could be persuaded to do otherwise) to Simmel's (we can attribute agency to an act when it makes sense to punish the actor for so doing).

3. "Die moralwissenschaftliche Ergründung des Freiheitsproblems wird vielleicht erfolgreicher werden, wenn sie sich an der Feststellung der Rolle versucht, die die Freiheitsvorstellung und ihr Gegentheil in der wirklichen Gestaltung des psychischen und sittlichen Lebens spielen – als wenn sie sich in begrifflichen Erörterungen ergeht, deren Elemente die Ethik doch nur aus der Thatsächlichkeit des Seelenlebens gezogen und deren relative Maasse sie zu absoluten Prinzipien gesteigert hat; auf diese Weise musste sie, indem die Steigerung nach beiden Seiten ging, an tötlichen Gegensätzen münden, auf deren Versöhnung nun ihr ganzes Bemühen geht, während sie selbst sie vielleicht erst geschaffen hat."

4. Amasyali and Van den Berg review without much discussion certain misinterpretations of Weber associated with the 1970's counter reading of Weber as touchy-feely, one that confused him with Dilthey. Although they seem to put some distance between these ideas and themselves, it is unclear whether they see these as incorrect or are endorsing them. Weber (1978) thought that sociology was most suited to doing a rational reconstruction of motives, and that that was indeed a form of understanding [*verstehen*] because it allowed the reproduction of the subjective components of an action orientation. Only when that failed was specifically empathic understanding to be brought into play. (The page they cite does not make the point they claim; they have inserted *empathic* here.) It is also strange to cite Weber as if he were a plausible aegis for the anti-causal movement, when he explicitly took a position that was compatible with (though it did not require) total causal determinism, and he did not think it was incompatible with action. Thus Weber: "Consider the categories of 'means' and 'ends,' without which teleological 'thought' would be impossible. Any scientific work undertaken with these categories rests upon discursive, nomological *knowledge*: which is to say, concepts and generalizations developed by employing the concept of *causality*" (Weber, 1975 [1903–1906], p. 144). A very useful examination of Weber's attempt to formulate a version of causality based on von Kries will be found in Heidelberger (2015).

REFERENCES

Arendt, H. (1958). *The human condition*. University of Chicago Press.
Arendt, H. (1978). *The life of the mind. Volume II: Willing*. Harcourt Brace Jovanovich.
Aristotle. (2011). *Nicomachean ethics* (R. C. Bartlett & S. D. Collins, Trans.). University of Chicago Press.
Barnes, B. (2000). *Understanding agency: Social theory and responsible action*. Sage Publications.
Bell, M. M. (2011). In A. Goetting (Ed.), *The strange music of social life: A dialogue on dialogic sociology*. Temple University Press.
Cartwright, N. (2004). Causation: One word, many things. *Philosophy of Science*, 71, 805–819.
Durkheim, E. (1961 [1902–1903]). *Moral education* (E. K. Wilson & H. Schnurer, Trans.). The Free Press.
Emirbayer, M., & Mische, A. (1998). What is agency? *American Journal of Sociology*, 103, 962–1023.
Gazzaniga, M. S. (1970). *The bisected brain*. Appleton-Century-Crofts.
Heidelberger, M. (2015). From Mill via von Kries to Max Weber: Causality, explanation and understanding. *Max Weber Studies*, 15, 13–45.
Kant, I. (1996 [1787]). *Critique of pure reason* (W. S. Pluhar, Trans.). Hackett Publishing Company.
Kurzman, C. (1991). Convincing sociologists: Values and interests in the sociology of knowledge. In M. Burawoy (Ed.), *Ethnography unbound: Power and resistance in the modern metropolis* (pp. 250–268). University of California Press.
Martin, J. L. (2011). *The explanation of social action*. Oxford.
Reynolds, C. (2022). Repurposing Title IX: How sexual harassment became sex discrimination in American higher education. *American Journal of Sociology*, 128, 462–514.
Simmel, G. (1904 [1892–1893]). *Einleitung in die Moralwissenschaft* (2 *Vols.*). J. G. Cotta'sche Buchhandlung.
Weber, M. (1975 [1903–1906]). *Roscher and Knies: The logical problems of historical economics* (Guy Oakes, Trans.). The Free Press.
Weber, M. (1978). In G. Roth & C. Wittich (Eds.), *Economy and society* (2 *Vols.*). The University of California Press.
Wegner, D. M. (2002). *The illusion of conscious will*. Bradford Books.

THE GREAT AGENCY MUDDLE

Stephen Turner

University of South Florida, USA

ABSTRACT

The concept of agency has a role in a variety of fields and theoretical traditions and has recently taken on the strange role that Emre Amasyali and Axel van den Berg discuss in their two papers, as a term of moral or political approbation and blame, in cases where people fail to act against a structure that is supposed to be blameworthy. But this role is confused. Structures are made up of agents. But the kind of intentionality that is being blamed is ascribed to the structure, as though it is the agent. But blaming, it turns out, is not closely connected to cause but rather to social conventions of justification. Action explanation itself is culturally relative and faces the problem that intentions are unknowable. Self-reports are based on a combination of public facts and inner feelings, which are private. But the reports follow cultural conventions, particularly of justification, which vary wildly. We can resolve the apparent muddle here and make reasons into causes by appealing to a cognitive science view of action as involving predictive processing: the potential justifications are part of the expectations that go into a causal account of action. But they do not determine actions, much less represent them.

Keywords: Action; agency; collective intention; will; justification; introspection; predictive processing

The concept of agency is a strange amalgam of culturally specific ways of talking about the causes of action and also about moral responsibility: blameworthiness or creditworthiness. The two are linked by the idea that blame or credit depends on the person causing something, even if the effect is internal to the person or is inaction. The issue of blame and credit requires a particular kind of causal theory: blame goes to the causer. But if blaming is linked to cause, it is to a special kind of cause. Though, as we will see, there is a lot of variation in which there is a blame or creditworthy moment, usually associated with the idea of free will. This seems like it should not belong in social science: there are no exceptions to the law of causality. But under the heading of agency, it is lodged there, notably in Giddens' use of the term in relation to structure (1984), but also in the empirical literature, which ascribes agency to particular kinds of actions and treats other kinds of action as not genuinely agential. In a sense, this relates to the ethical problem of agency, but in another it does not: acting according to the norms of the community, can be labelled as lacking agency. So it seems that these writers are not only making moral judgments in using the term agency, but asserting a higher level of evaluation than ordinary morality, and also higher level than the notions of action of ordinary people (in the West, at least), for whom intentional action and agency are the same thing.

The papers by Emre Amasyali and Axel van den Berg are an excellent overview of the post-Giddens uses of the concept in relation to structure and to the related writings of Margaret Archer and others (Archer, 1982, 1995, 2000, 2003; Emirbayer & Mische, 1998). In this comment, I do not propose to correct their effort in any way. The key question they pose, what exactly does the notion of agency add to explanation, is the right one. What they conclude is that it adds nothing explanatory but serves "to sneak in the authors' value judgments under the guise of what appears to be a purely analytical concept" (Amasyali & van den Berg, 2025, p. 64; van den Berg & Amasyali, 2025). The analytic concept is a second order one of a very special kind. It doesn't reject ordinary explanations of blameworthiness or creditworthiness in the name of causal determinism, which is certainly a possible social science stance. Instead, it builds on them, so that some kinds of intentional actions are agential and others are not. But there is a causal element to this second order sense of agency as well. People who are driven by the wrong causes – the structure – are not agents but a kind of self-willed moral prisoner of the system, neither free nor fully human.

BLAMING AND AGENCY

Although there are, as they show, different concepts of agency, this is the paradigmatic one. And it ends in a muddle, which I will try to explicate. The term self-willed is not theirs, but it is goes to the heart of the problem: to be an agent is to choose; but one can choose, in the prosaic sense, to be less than an agent. One can submit to the structure. And this choice is blameworthy. Why? Because the structure is itself blameworthy. The notion of structural racism captures this nicely: racism is blameworthy; individuals who conform to the structure, abide by the laws, and so forth are not blameworthy. The laws, the system, are the racist cause. It is only by defying or changing the system that one can be an anti-racist. And the structure is always bad. This makes the structure-agency relation into a moral drama: real agency is about changing, defying, or challenging the structure. Nonagency is mindlessly carrying out its demands or conforming to it: that is the self-willed choice to be less than an agent, in the second order sense.

My concern will be a little different: agency and its associated ideas, such as intention and free will, are both elusive and cognitively sticky. In semiotics, this is often called an empty signifier, which means that it signifies nothing precise, or nothing at all, and serves the speaker's purposes because it retains a discursive role: it appears to say something. There is a highly typical pattern of reasoning in social theory and indeed in social science that has the effect of producing these signifiers, and the idea of structure here is a good example. The pattern is this: one asserts a weak but plausible analogy, in this case between the institutions and practices of a society and a "structure"; one then ontologizes the analogical object, that is, asserts that it is real, that it has some sort of autonomous existence; one then asserts that it has actual causal powers rooted in its autonomous existence. Thus, we get structure. Then we can intentionalize structure, to attribute purposes to it that control its causal powers, so we can take an intentional concept, like racism, and attribute it to the analogical object.

This way of thinking has a use in a kind of ethics but a strange one. By granting structure a reality, an autonomous status, we get a new way of assigning blameworthiness and creditworthiness. The ordinary person whose willing behavior conforms to the structure lacks agency in the sense that it crucial to the paradigm case discussed above. But their willingness makes them responsible, and therefore blameworthy. Their conformity to the structure supports the structure – an odd notion to which I will return. But the reasoning also exempts the agential opponents of the structure from merely being willing conformists to their own structures – as a feminist agential resister might be to the structure of the women's movement. They retain agency and also moral credit as agents. Indeed, these movements, if they are of the right kind, become agency conferring movements, even if they are crowd-following. Moreover, the movements themselves become agential. All it takes is to be in conscious opposition to the larger structure.

WHAT IS A STRUCTURE?

Are structures also agents? This raises a key question. They are blameworthy, good or bad, and have consequences, so in that sense, they must be. They are analogous to agents in the sense that they have purposes, respond to changes in the environment by adapting to it and retaining their purposes. They are not merely fixed objects or environments. If they were, they could not be blameworthy. Nor would willing conformity to them have any moral significance. As Aristotle said, the rain falls on the just and the unjust alike: it has no moral significance and confers none. But the nature of this purposive, agential power is obscure. An oppressive structure is like an agent. But is it an agent?

One oddity of the intellectual landscape that van den Berg and Amasyali don't take up, reasonably enough, is that agency is being applied to all sorts of things that were never thought of as agents. Nor do they take up the anthropology of agents – the fact that in different cultures, there are different agents and the agency of individuals is divided up in different ways. These two extensions of the concept, and problem, of agency, raise a host of novel questions. The poster child for the extension of the concept is Bruno Latour, whose notion of "actants" subsumes the notion of structure itself: the world, for Latour, is composed of actants (1987), the physical world, animals, and objects, whose network relations mimic at least minimal human relations and have at least minimal "agency." This is the only "structure" needed.

Beyond this recherché example, there is the more familiar problem of collective agency. Do collectives have "agency," or is collective agency, such as speaking for a collectivity, merely a form of individual agents representing a supposed entity, such as the state, which is not itself an agent? Similarly, is an agent who is only an instrument of God an agent, and God the agent? Or is this a delusion about causality, and are similar claims when people speak on behalf of a "we" also delusions? Some philosophers of social ontology, for whom assigning moral responsibility to collectives is important, have gone on to argue that they too have agency, and therefore also free will, because "they" have the possibility of doing otherwise (List, 2023). This has long been standard in areas like business ethics, where it is claimed that the fact that businesses themselves can be said to learn through punishment shows that they are agents (French, 1995). But whether they do or not seems itself to be a causal question: when the Cardinals elect the Pope, do they have a choice, or is the "choice" merely the causal manifestation of the will of the Holy Spirit?

In what follows, I don't propose to solve the problems associated with these questions, but rather to show why they arise and some ways to think about them. In this way, I hope to explain to some extent the ubiquity of the problem van den Berg and Amasyali identify in sociology in relation to the problem of structure and agency. But I also want to clarify the problem itself.

THE INNER AGENT

It is hard to get rid of some version of originative control, implying ownership of one's actions. Autonomy, it seems, has to mean something like being an uncaused cause. But it is hard to figure out where it occurs, and how it works, if there even is such a thing. That is so to speak the "scientific" side of the problem: is there something casual left over from the ordinary course of causal processes, in this case neuroscientific ones? Is that something found someplace, in a homunculus, which directs "executive function"? This is part of the problem: in discussing the sources of action, we use the language of action itself. Attributing agency is attributing it to an inner agent.

The effect is to merely push the problem back to the supposed agentic functions of the parts of the brain, which only makes the mystery deeper: we more or less know what we think about agency and responsibility, for example, with paradigmatic human actions, where there is a context and a narrative structure that incorporates the context. For the executive function of the brain and the hypothetical homunculus sitting at the hypothetical executive desk in the brain barking orders, we have only inputs and outputs to go by. Worse, we know that we are strongly disposed to find agency where it does not exist. So we are chronically tempted to intentionalize what are merely complex caused outcomes. Ascribing an intention is a cognitive shortcut in the face of causal opacity or simply of random events.

One of the sources noted in the first of these two papers, Watson (2003), includes a famous article by Strawson ([1962] 2003) that radically separates the causal and the agential: responsibility, for him, is a term of conventional moral accounting relevant to social control, the justification for punishment, and so forth. "Cause" in the sense of a determinist account of human behavior is something else entirely. In another sense, the conventional or prephilosophical one which motivates the concept of agency combines the two: the agent causes their own behavior, and therefore is responsible for it. Agency and responsibility are inseparable and inseparable from cause. Yet another line of argument rejects the idea that reasons are causes and also denies that actions are in the appropriate category for causal explanation. This approach locates the "explanation" of action, as distinct from mere behavior, in the space of narrative or practical reason, and cause in a different space.

The motives for these arguments were various but deeply rooted in the intellectual history of the West. Theology poses famous puzzles: If God is omniscient, and it is blasphemous and perhaps incoherent to think of God as being less than omniscient, the future actions of people are known by God, and therefore determined. And for the people who believe in freedom of the will, there is the question of exactly where freedom enters into the process. Mill, for example, thought that actions were mostly determined by circumstance, character (which was his way of speaking about culture), and reason, determiners which left no room for freedom, but he did think that one could choose, to some extent, your character, which was thus the locus of freedom.

The sociological form of this problem discussed in these two papers is a subset of this larger problematic. As the papers make clear, the primary motivation for most of the writings appealing to agency is ideological or moral: to commend the actions that are the product of agency. They are at the same time attempts to identify the specific place in which freedom enters the normal stream of explanation, and in the papers they are concerned with, it is explanation which appeals to "structure." Structure is ill-defined, but in practice, it means little more than the ordinary course of events caused by the ordinary kinds of causes. And because the ordinary kinds of causes include the actions of other people – indeed aside from the scaffolding of the physical setting, which is itself partly made through the niche construction actions of other people, social structure consists of the actions of other people. Thus, if agency is the same as action, it is everywhere, and there is no contrast between agents and their environment. As Amasyali and van den Berg point out, to fail to act is also agency. But it follows that the actions of the people who act on behalf of the structure work in the same way: it is the mere possibility of their action that forms the constraint that makes up "structure."

RADICALLY EXPANDED AGENCY

But there is an even more complicated version of the problematic that goes to the heart of the question of what agency is. Most of the terms of the problematic are themselves culturally relative. One of the implications of the approaches of the past is that action, responsibility, and so forth are conceptually constituted by terms like reason, justification, and the whole range of related terms. And this is a problem for the sociologist: there is not going to be a nonrelative concept of action, and therefore agency, because the related terms that are used to define these things themselves vary. Some examples of this will be discussed below, but anyone who has read E. R. Dodds' *The Greeks and the Irrational* (1951), which discusses divine intervention in action that deprives the "agent" of control, knows this already. But the implications go far beyond the question of the peculiarities of Greek myth.

The Greeks were of course not alone in ascribing agency and agency interference to nonhuman and other forces. Animism is a continuing part of the world view of many people, as is the idea that ancestors are surrounding and watching and perhaps intervening in the world. If we follow W.I. Thomas in saying that if men define situations as real, they are real in their consequences (Thomas & Thomas, 1928, pp. 571–72); the social structure of such societies includes all of these beings, who "have agency." They are part of the structure, and agents, whether or not they exercise agency. Any thought that "structure" can be made objective and external to the agent is undermined by these ubiquitous facts. The elusiveness of agency thus implies the elusiveness of structure.

This is not the only problem for sociologists. Ascribing agency to demons may seem daft. But the effect of doing so is to displace responsibility. And this is a common trope. Some accounts in the sociological literature are intended to excuse behavior, especially criminal behavior, on the grounds that the social conditions of the agent had the effect of making them less than full agents and therefore not responsible in the way that full agents would be. The argument that racism causes specific mental problems leading to violence has a long history. It implies that the apparent agents are incapacitated in ways that make them less than fully responsible for their actions (Turner, 2020). But this line of argument can be extended to many other cases of societally generated incapacity. It is one straightforward implication of Frankfurt School psychoanalytic sociology, found, for example, in Erich Fromm's *Sane Society* (1955), that everyone in capitalist society is incapacitated in this way. And in a sense Freud goes further: that to a greater or lesser degree everyone is incapacitated by their subconscious drives to the point of not being full agents.

TURNING THE PROBLEM UPSIDE DOWN

These apparent oddities raise a question: why and how do we ascribe agency? This turns the question upside down – it does not assume that there is a correct view of agency but instead treats it as something we impose. The classic example of this comes from cognitive science, where random dots moving on a screen were characterized by their viewers as having purpose or direction. That the dead are acting in our lives, that objects have intentions, and so forth seem unsurprising given this. And that we can and are prone to the error of ascribing agency where there is none is also unsurprising. Daniel Dennett introduced the concept of "the intentional stance" as a way of talking about what we are doing when we think of people or other beings as thinking about something (Dennett, 1989), which is also a condition of acting intentionally toward something. This implies that intentional attributions are something we as observers impose on action, including our own actions, rather than its ultimate meaning as part of the causal world.

A radical approach to this problematic came from Rudiger Bittner, who made the obvious point that when we make claims about inaccessible mental processes as causes, we are doing no more than filling in the blank parts of a narrative that includes external and therefore accessible circumstances of action as well as external outcomes and related circumstances (Bittner, 2001; Turner, 2017). Our jobs as explainers and understanders can never go beyond constructing a narrative that includes it. But this and Dennett put the burden of ascribing agency back on us. And this puts the approaches to agency discussed in the two papers in a different light, in which it is not surprising that agency becomes moralized. We disdain certain actions as mindless. We regard as agential those that fit with our own sense of rightness.

As Archer's argument for deliberation as a criterion shows, there are preferred ways to be right. This is something that reappears in the larger literature on agency. Gary Becker, discussed by Foucault, regarded "any conduct which responds systematically to modifications in the variables of the environment" as rational agency (Foucault, [1979] 2008). The key word is systematic. There is a similar argument in Christine Korsgaard's ethics (2009) and in Alex Worsnip's book (2012) on structural rationality, which requires for full rationality a coherent structure of belief.

This is merely the more general form of the problem identified in the papers: it is "we" who are making these decisions about what is an agent and what actions are agential. Sociologists are caught in the dilemma produced by the conflict between the agent's point of view, or the cultural participants point of view, and the "scientific" point of view which suggests a different sense of agency. And this dilemma presents novel problems. Different cultures imagine the determiners of action in different ways: as a soul, as God's will, and so forth. But these concepts are themselves influencers of action. And this is one thing that makes them cognitively sticky.

Where is the correct or scientific view of agency in all this? It is not going to be found in an analysis of the explanations the individual gives of their conduct – with one caveat, to be discussed in the final section. The Western educated person does not refer to Voodoo or the promptings of dead ancestors to explain their conduct. The person for whom Voodoo is an intelligible narrative might. The Westerner might refer to their pangs of conscience, which derives from a different theological tradition. The Voodoo narrative may be intelligible to us or meaningless to us. But neither narrative is scientifically true. Both are subject to the limitation of the inaccessibility of the things being invoked – mental states, alien forces operating on the mind and so on.

If we as westerners do not invoke alien forces, what is our cultural model of the mind? Bittner argues that the west is dominated by the image of mind captured in the chariot metaphor by Plato. The individual is like a charioteer seeking to control the horses pulling the chariot but is being given impulses from both sides about what to do. Action is the result of the resolution of these conflicting inputs. But the horses themselves are the agents here: the charioteer has imperfect control over them, and they are in some sense independent, with minds of their own. So this is a principal–agent relation, with the charioteer as the principal, in relation to the horses, and the whisperers as principals in relation to them. Hume describes a similar imperfect relation when he says that reason is and should be slave to the passions. The "should be" is recognition of the fact that the passions have only imperfect control.

INVERTING REASONS AND CAUSES

Is there a way out of this muddle? The wrong way out is this: to think that we can analyze conduct back through a series of regresses to a homunculus who operates like our own conventional way of talking about action who actually has free will, sitting someplace in the brain. Whatever problems we have with agency just reappear with this mythical ultimate agent. The regress will simply reduplicate the problems we started out with: the means we have for making the agent intelligible are our only means for making the ultimate agent intelligible. This is why the long history of hidden motivations in the history of social science, notably in the examples of Freud and the various critiques of ideology deriving from Marx, ends by attributing unconscious motivations for the overt motivations professed by the agent.

A variant of this view however is more promising: there are philosophers who think that having a reason is a sufficient explanation for action that requires no antecedents. From a causal point of view, this amounts to saying that a reason has an autonomous act-producing causal power. In one sense, this is absurd: of course the reasons one has themselves come from someplace, like a culture. They are learned. And as Mercier and Sperber point out, "the implicit psychology – the presumption that people's beliefs and actions are motivated by reasons – is empirically wrong. Giving reasons to justify oneself and reacting to the reasons given by others are, first and foremost, a way to establish reputations and coordinate expectations" (Mercier & Sperber, 2017, p. 143). But if we dispense with the idea that these are causal explanations, and simply treat them as types, or narrative forms, we can think of our applying them to people not as explaining but as putting their behavior in a box or category that tells us what we need to know about what is going on in a given situation, including what its sequelae and circumstances were. In this sense, they are a sufficient explanation. A "reason" is not a mysterious causal force but a part of the narrative that links the conditions to the consequences. And most of the time when we are asking for a justification, we are asking what kind of act something was.

This severs the language of justification – reasons – from the actual causal processes that underlay action. But it does so in a problematic way: we are still faced with the fact that we experience such things as reflecting, choosing, making a decision, acting, accepting something as true, and so forth. These are the kinds of things that concern Margaret Archer. We experience, so to speak, our own agency. So we cannot simply discard it. And this leaves us with a trilemma. We need to reconcile three things: our inability to access our internal mental processes, except by applying conventions of mental talk that we know are placeholders for explanation rather than explanations, our phenomenological sense of our own agency, and the question of the causal status of our conventions of justification.

The core problem is our own sense of agency. It is perhaps useful to be reminded that this is subject to a large range of errors. The illusion of conscious will appears in a wide variety of situations, such as hypnosis, the one we will discuss shortly. So there is a fair question about the solidity of this sense. Nevertheless, there is a deeper problem here, which was discussed at length in the past. The problem went under the name of logical behaviorism, which held that descriptions of mental states are reducible to descriptions of behavioral states and implied that regardless of how we characterized action, it was not based on our knowledge of mental elements but was semantically reducible to external facts. The issue with this thesis was characterized by Wittgenstein's student Norman Malcolm in this way:

> The notion of verification does not apply to a wide range of first person psychological reports and utterances. Another way to put this point is to say that their reports and utterances *are not based on observations*. The error of introspectionism is to suppose they are based on observations of inner events. The error of behaviorism is to suppose that they are based on observations of outward events or of physical events inside the speaker's skin. These two philosophies of psychology share a false assumption, namely that a first person psychological statement is a report of something the speaker has, or thinks he has, observed. (Malcolm, 1964, p. 151; italics in original)

In short, when I report my intention to do something, I am neither observing my mental processes nor making an inference from my external behavior. We learn the use of psychological terms, such as pain, by observing others and the external manifestations of their pain. But then something new happens.

> The person who has satisfied our criteria of understanding [psychological] terms begins to use them in the absence of the former behavioral criteria. He says that he is *angry* at someone or *anxious* about something when we should not have supposed so from his demeanor. (Malcolm, 1964, p. 153; italics in original)

This is one source, perhaps *the* source, of our sense of the autonomy of the mental.

> This self-testimony has, one could say, an *autonomous* status. To a great extent we cannot check it against anything else, and yet to a great extent we credit it. I believe we have no reason to think it is even a theoretical possibility that this self-testimony can be supplanted by inferences from external and/or internal physical variables. (Malcolm, 1964, p. 153; italics in original)

Observation is an equivocal term here: we can't by definition observe our mental events because observe implies that others can also observe. "Inferences from internal physical variables" understood in the sense of measurements of such things as pulse rates are trickier. "Inferences" is also trickier. We can "observe" with special equipment lots of brain events and also bodily events. And thus, outsiders can perhaps infer such mental states as anger apart from demeanor. But to say we infer our own mental states from externals is a different matter.

Malcolm was concerned with inferences about mental states. If we treat these mental states terms as placeholders rather than terms that refer, we avoid this problem. The key to this way of thinking is to avoid treating inaccessible mental contents as explanations but to see intentional explanation as the application of a type concept. What the type recognizes is a pattern with typical antecedents and consequents, with enough elements to omit some of them but still regard it as an example of the pattern. The pattern is more or less a narrative. The explanation is narrative rather than nomic. If what has been said above is right, action attributions involving mental language is culturally variable, and action attributions involve patterns, with a loose kind of template. As we have discussed this kind of template or type explanation so far, it has been external – consistent with logical behaviorism and the idea that we attribute these types, adding in mental terms as culturally specific placeholders, to "explain" action. But the explanation is typification, or narrativizing, rather than a causal explanation involving these placeholder mental phenomena. But we don't derive our self-understanding entirely from externals. So where does it come from, and what is our inner knowledge of ourselves?

We can answer this using the model of pain. We know through our ability to sense our own bodily states – hunger, pain, and other subtle bodily correlates of a given type of action. We also know what we might say in response to a question or challenge – which is to say our beliefs. We can then project these beliefs on others in analogous situations and thus "understand" them. At no point do we access our beliefs or desires directly as objects of knowledge. Instead, they are ways of talking about types of action in which they serve as infillers to describe a mental content we don't have access to and which is described according to highly variable social conventions. We could just as well be describing the actions of inner demons as describing beliefs. But if these descriptions had the same kinds of internal bodily and external correlates as our descriptions of desires and reasons, they would also have the same phenomenological feel of being ours alone, of being private and also privately accessible. Indeed, part of the of the ensemble that makes up action, the feeling part, is in fact privately accessible only.

Attributing beliefs and desires seems more secure than this, especially if we can empathize, simulate, or introspect sympathetically. We know our own desires, in a special sense, and know what we might say if we were asked what we believe. This is a key distinction. There is something we own or have access to that others do not have direct access to. But what is the something? If we think it is the beliefs and desires themselves, we are faced with a myriad of problems. We would have to also concede that cultures with different mental entities also have access to different mental entities. But it is also the case that we do have something we have private access to: our bodily sensations and also feelings that might arise from cognitive inputs, surprise, bewilderment, anger, etc. These are accompaniments to, but for embodiment thinkers integral to, thinking itself. And when we recognize the pattern, we are also associating it with the action. This is consistent with "gut feeling" and much of the rest of the phenomenology of action.

A plausible account would be this. I can't feel your pain. But I can feel the analogous pain because I have internal bodily sensations. But the sensations are mine, based on my experiences, and limited by them. This kind of feeling is not "observation" in the sense of logical behaviorism, but it is nevertheless part of the experience we match up with others to attribute intentions and so forth to them. And it is closely related to our own sense of "agency" and therefore what we attribute to others. But it is asymmetric: on the one hand, we learn as toddlers to talk about these things (intention, pain, and so forth), simultaneously for ourselves and others, based on the external manifestations. But there is also a private part that is bound up with these manifestations. The common or public patterns are what make empathy, or simulation, or sympathetic introspection possible, but at the same time unreliable, because of this asymmetry, and because the private side of our associations with the language, which would be visible in brain activation networks, would not be a perfect match for others.

Where does this leave us with "agency"? What it does not require is the homunculus, the self-starting will, and so forth, that is implicit or explicit in the notion of agency. And this is not a loss. There is a considerable literature on the illusion of conscious will (Wegner, 2002). What this literature suggests is that there is a large gap between what we experience phenomenologically and the actual causal workings of action, including believing and cognizing. We have an occluded sense of ourselves in these domains. There is plenty of reason to believe that our conscious sense of making a decision or choosing to act comes at a late stage of a causal process that has determined the decision, and that our sense of ownership is a construction placed retrospectively on a process that is mostly unconscious (Beni, 2016; Metzinger, 2003; Turner, 2018, pp. 148–177). The feeling of agency, however vivid, is something we attribute to ourselves as "agency" based on our recognition that others behave like we do when we feel like agents. It is as much a filling-in as our attribution of mental steps to others. An undefinable and unidentifiable primary internal free agent solves an explanatory problem but nevertheless is just another fictional infilling construction. That it plays a normative role in customs of justification, punishment, and attributing guilt tells us more about social conventions than about the casual processes involved. But the conventions nevertheless depend on the fact that we have these feelings.

This points to another element in the trilemma. Conventions of justification are not just *ex post facto* additions to action. These social conventions do play a role in the causal explanation of action. But what is the role? The older view regarded the conventions as sources of reasons and the reasons as causes. Is there an alternative to this? One alternative comes from cognitive science, in the form of the idea that cognitive processes, including those which lead to action, are the result of the fact that our engagement with the world takes the form of predictive processing: as part of the process of engaging in the world, we anticipate multiple possible outcomes, and our behavior is guided by the confirmation of some of these predictions and the nonconfirmation of others (Clark, 2023). In short, we have a bag of hypotheses or expectations about the world that we revise continuously on the basis of their predictive failures and successes – all on the preconscious level.

This gives us an indirect way of making reasons into causes. When we see a stop sign and then stop, we have, among our predictive expectations, getting a traffic ticket or having a wreck. Predictive processing is a way of bringing these normative considerations, the basis of justification, into explanation. One expectation is the possible need to provide a justification. When we act, if the predictive processing thesis is correct, we anticipate multiple future possibilities, including a future in which we will be called upon to justify our action. That people do this is shown by a phenomenon of hypnosis, in which the subject is asked to explain an action of theirs that is the result of the hypnotist's suggestion. They are not flummoxed. They have many justifications at hand and trot them out on demand. They seem to construct these answers on the fly and can give contradictory ones. But these answers were also in the predictive processing toolkit: when they acted, they knew about these possibilities. When we answer the question "why did you stop at that stop sign?" and say "because it is the law," we are simply pulling this answer from the toolkit, even if our stopping at the sign is simply a matter of habit which we do not deliberate about or are even conscious of doing.

This gives us a plausible solution to the trilemma. The norms involved in justification play a role, typically an incidental one, in the predictive processing that governs our navigation of the world prior to action. Our sense of agency is partly private and unshared, partly shared through our common mental language that is the public part of action: the logical behaviorist part. Empathy is an unreliable guide to the unshared, private, part. And our sense of our own mental workings is equally unreliable, subject to the illusion of conscious will (Wegner, 2002). That the idea of agency as a sociological concept should collapse into a valuative preference for a particular kind of action should thus be no surprise. The private side is variable and connected to our personal experiences and dispositions.

The idea of agency, with its normative sense, is built upon the private side of the asymmetry between the public and personal parts of our sense of action, the side that involves the emotional and bodily connections between the action pattern as we experience it. Our feeling of agency is partly private: the connections based on our history of experiences and our bodily and mental make-up, which includes our expectations of a possible future need for justification, are ours. But they match up with a public pattern. The public pattern has no need for agency: making sense of action is a matter of narrative or typification based on externals. But a sense of the agency of others does appear when we analogize from our own experience, in an act of sympathetic introspection. But this commonplace mental activity, which we use to navigate the social world, is not a guide to causality. It is, instead, a projection based on our own occluded sense of our own mental and bodily processes, our culture, and the history that produced our personal sense of control over our actions. This does have implications for how we experience the world and others matters to how we understand them, experience them, and how we act as a result. But the phenomenology of action and its causes and effects is something that varies socially, is produced socially, and is changed and developed through learning, that is to say, with respect to human action, social learning. It thus needs itself to be explained in a way that includes its social aspects, rather than treated as an unmoved mover. Agency as a concept needs to be explained as well, with due respect to the radical variation in the way cultures treat action, rather than as a given.

REFERENCES

Amasyali, E., & van den Berg, A. (2025). What do we need 'agency' for? A critical analysis of reasons for the use of 'agency' in sociology. *Current Perspectives in Social Theory, 41*, 15–42.
Archer, M. S. (1982). Morphogenesis versus structuration: On combining structure and action. *British Journal of Sociology, 33*(4), 455–483.
Archer, M. S. (1995). *Realist social theory: The morphogenetic approach.* Cambridge University Press.
Archer, M. S. (2000). *Being human: The problem of agency.* Cambridge University Press.
Archer, M. S. (2003). *Structure, agency, and the internal conversation.* Cambridge University Press.
Beni, M. D. (2016). Structural realist account of the self. *Synthese, 193*, 3727–3740.
Bittner, R. (2001). *Doing things for reasons.* Oxford University Press.
Clark, A. (2023). *The experience machine: How our minds predict and shape reality.* Random House.
Dennett, D. (1989). *The intentional stance.* MIT Press.
Dodds, E. R. (1951). *The Greeks and the irrational.* University of California Press.
Emirbayer, M., & Mische, A. (1998). What is agency? *American Journal of Sociology, 103*(4), 962–1023.
Foucault, M. ([1979] 2008). "Neoliberalism redefined homo economicus," a lecture at the Collège de France, March 1979. In M. Senellart (Ed.), *The birth of biopolitics: Lectures at the Collège de France, 1978–1979* (Graham Burchell, Trans., pp. 267–290). Palgrave Macmillan. https://economicsociology.org/2020/11/18/foucault-neoliberalism-redefined-homo-economicus/#
French, P. (1995). *Corporate ethics.* Harcourt Brace College Publishers.
Fromm, E. (1955). *The sane society.* Rinehart.
Giddens, A. (1984). *The constitution of society: Outline of the theory of structuration.* University of California Press.
Korsgaard, C. M. (2009). *Self-constitution: Agency, identity, and intergrity.* Oxford University Press.
Latour, B. (1987). *Science in action.* Harvard University Press.
List, C. (2023, June). Do group agents have free will? *Inquiry.* https://doi.org/10.1080/0020174X.2023.2218721
Malcolm, N. (1964). Behaviorism as a philosophy of psychology. In T. W. Wann (Ed.), *Behaviorism and phenomenology* (pp. 141–162). University of Chicago Press.
Mercier, H., & Sperber, D. (2017). *The enigma of reason.* Harvard University Press.
Metzinger, T. (2003). *Being no one: The self-model theory of subjectivity.* MIT Press.
Strawson, P. ([1962] 2003). Freedom and resentment. In G. Watson (Ed.), *Free will* (pp. 72–93). Oxford University Press. https://people.brandeis.edu/~teuber/P._F._Strawson_Freedom_&_Resentment.pdf
Thomas, W. I., & Thomas, D. S. (1928). *The child in America: Behavior problems and programs.* Knopf.
Turner, S. (2017). The belief-desire model of action explanation reconsidered: Thoughts on Bittner. *Philosophy of the Social Sciences, 48*(3), 290–308. https://doi.org/10.1177/0048393117750076
Turner, S. (2018). *Cognitive science and the social: A primer.* Routledge.
Turner, S. (2020). Explaining away crime: The race narrative in American sociology and ethical theory. *European Journal of Social Theory, 24*(3), 356–373. https://doi.org/10.1177/1368431020982534
van den Berg, A., & Amasyali, E. (2025). What do we use 'agency' for? A critical empirical examination of its uses in the sociological literature. *Current Perspectives in Social Theory, 41*, 43–76.
Watson, G. (Ed.). (2003). *Free will.* Oxford University Press.
Wegner, D. (2002). *The illusion of conscious will.* The MIT Press.
Worsnip, A. (2012). *Fitting things together: Coherence and the requirements of structural rationality.* Oxford University Press.

WHY DO WE NEED TO DISCUSS AGENCY?

Axel van den Berg[a] and Emre Amasyalı[b]

[a]*McGill University, Canada*
[b]*IBEI — Barcelona, Spain*

ABSTRACT

Responding to Martin, Turner, and Hitlin, we clarify possible misunderstandings of our two papers on "agency." First, they do not presume or commit us to any form of universal determinism. We merely assume that the job of sociologists is to try and causally explain as much as we can of the variations in social life. Though our best efforts leave huge amounts of variance unexplained, there is no good reason for calling this unexplained variance "agency," and there are several good reasons for not doing so. Second, we acknowledge our use of "structure" is quite a loose one, simply referring to the combination of environmental and personal factors that can help us explain social phenomena. Our notion of "causation" is, admittedly, no less "slipshod" than that used by most social scientists. We are happy to leave questions as to the true nature of causation to the philosophers. Third, we do not see in what way using the notion of "agency" to describe, much less account for, novelty (Martin), or to help "organize" the potentially infinite number of forces in play (Hitlin), advances our understanding or explanatory power. The normative and voluntaristic connotations of the term only serve to muddy the explanatory waters. Fourth, this doesn't preclude empirically examining the sense of "agency" and its causes and consequences. Even if the current wave of enthusiasm for "agency" is waning, a thorough conversation remains worthwhile if only to help avoid the same confusions popping up again in the future.

Keywords: Causality; structure; sociology; human behavior; social action; sociological models

We wish to begin our reply by thanking Steven Hitlin, John Levi Martin, and Stephen Turner for their extremely thoughtful, as well as thought-provoking, comments. It is truly a pleasure and a privilege to have our work treated with such seriousness and genuine engagement. We hope that our reply will contribute to the continuing constructive discussion that Martin looks forward to at the end of his comment.

Let us start with what may be the most fundamental criticism of our work offered by Martin and Hitlin. They both attribute a kind of relentless determinism to us. Martin thinks our arguments rest on the assumption "that we basically live in a Laplacian world of total mechanical determination" (Martin, 2025, p. 94). Hitlin rejects our "apparent goal of someday theorizing a fully determinative social universe" (Hitlin, 2025, p. 78). But this is very far from the position we were actually trying to present. It was precisely this kind of criticism that we tried – obviously not clearly enough – to pre-empt in the final paragraph of "What Do We Need 'Agency' For?" (hereafter WDW*N*) where we try to distance ourselves from any firm position on the metaphysics of free will versus determinism. So let us try and clarify our view on the matter here.

We fully agree with Martin that adopting either side of those metaphysics inevitably leads to seemingly irresolvable paradoxes. In fact, we started an earlier version of WDW*N* with this epigraph quoting Stephen Pinker:

> Though space, time and causality (together with logic and substance) organise our world the paradoxes that infect these concepts – space and time being neither finite nor infinite, choices being neither caused nor uncaused – prove they are not part of the self-consistent world but part of our not-necessarily-consistent minds. (Pinker, 2007, p. 158)

This would also imply, it seems to us, that notions like cause and determination are anthropocentric concepts, as Martin argues. That is, we are quite prepared to accept that "*cause* is, as far as we know, something that we as human beings develop in our engagement with the world, an engagement we undertake for practical purposes" (Martin, 2025, p. 92). Consequently, we also have no problem acknowledging that our causal language is "like that of the rest of social scientists, necessarily somewhat slipshod and impressionistic," (Martin, 2025, p. 94) the true nature of causation being something better left to philosophers to debate.

The misunderstanding stems in part, it seems, from our perhaps imprudent references to specific explanatory attempts as "entirely and exclusively 'structural'" and to the rejection by the theorists we discuss in WDW*N* of "a model of causal explanation that takes action to be the fully determined joint product of actors' environments and their psychological predispositions," (WDW*N*, p. 18) which Martin and Hitlin cite as evidence of our apparent commitment to a thorough-going determinism.

Nothing is *entirely* explained or *fully* determined, we agree. And we agree with Hitlin that as sociologists, we are engaged in "the study of environmental and personal factors that influence social behavior" (Hitlin, 2025, p. 80). Does that mean we are committed to his probabilism? We suspect that the claim that the universe, or reality, are inherently "probabilistic" runs into the same kind of paradoxes or *petitio principii* as do hardcore voluntarism or determinism. As Hitlin points out, the amount of variance we are able explain in social phenomena remains pitifully low. But there is no way of knowing whether this is due to the existence of free will or to the intrinsically probabilistic nature of reality or to any other mysterious force, not now and probably not ever. Then again, it doesn't really matter. For now, as Hitlin rightly notes, "(f)inding patterns among the range of social forces that exist within and without people is a difficult, maybe hopelessly doomed exercise, but it is the cursed realm of sociology" (Hitlin, 2025, p. 79). Or, as we say in the final sentence of WDW*N*: "Meanwhile, we sociologists are fated to try and use our causal explanatory tools as best we can to explain as much as we can."

Nor do we ascribe anything like a commitment to a strong voluntarism or a rejection of causal models of action to any of the users of "agency" we analyze in "What Do We Use 'Agency' For?" (hereafter WDW*U*). Quite to the contrary, while the theorists we criticize in WDW*N* make strong and in our view unwarranted claims on behalf of voluntarism, the articles we analyze in WDW*U* actually practice the same kind of run-of-the-mill causalism as "the rest of social scientists," using "agency" not for explanatory purposes but as a kind of normative window dressing. And, as we try to argue in WDW*N*, it could hardly be otherwise because the voluntaristic concept of "agency" advocated by the theorists simply *cannot* add anything of explanatory value to the standard causal models.

This is nicely illustrated by the three examples Hitlin gives, somewhat self-contradictorily, of "work that theoretically posits what looks like 'free will.'" As we have argued at length in WDW*N*, that an action is based on conscious reflection, his first and third examples, does not at all preclude its causal explanation. Nor does the second example he gives, of actors' unwavering commitment to get a college education. And, as Hitlin himself goes on to point out, the authors in question do in fact exactly that: trying to come up with a causal explanation accounting for the choices made by the actors in question. We don't have the slightest objection to this. We just don't think inserting "agency" or any other reference to free will into these causal stories adds anything of explanatory value.

Related to the issues of determinism and causation, Martin takes us to task for giving "structure" a pass, that is, failing to address its conceptual problems. He makes three points here: first, in footnote 2, that maintaining social structure may well require a great deal of effort on the part of actors; second, that what we call "structure" really consists of other people's actions; and third, that we "just *call* whatever appears to [us] a legitimate explanatory factor *structural*, even if the factor is basically what *other* people are doing!" (Martin, 2025, p. 97).

Let us grant, first of all, that we use the term "structure" very loosely indeed, as the combination of environmental and personal factors that can help us explain social action, as Hitlin puts it. So, yes, that pretty much includes all legitimate explanatory factors. Moreover, we quite agree that *social* structure basically consists of (the expectation of) other people's behavior. We also agree that what is sometimes misleadingly called "reproducing" social structures may well require just as much effort and determination as does resisting them, a point we made ourselves in WDW*N* (p. 27). And, finally, we fully agree that viewing social structure as only a source of constraints is a mistake since what (we expect) other people do or do not do is a source of opportunities and choices as well, which is why we agree to participate in and uphold such structures to begin with. But we fail to see why the fact that the actors whose actions we try to explain are influenced by the actions of *other* actors implies that we have to attribute some kind of free will to either of them. We very much agree, in this connection, with Stephen Turner's remarks about structure being "ill-defined, but in practice it means little more than the ordinary course of events caused by the ordinary kinds of causes" mostly consisting of "the actions of other people" (Turner, 2025, p. 107).

As both Martin and Turner note, the moralization of the concept of "agency" is perhaps not that surprising given its close connection with notions of human dignity. We, laypersons and sociologists alike, naturally tend to accord that kind of dignity to actors and actions that make sense to *us*, the observers. So it isn't surprising that, as Martin puts it, agency tends to be used to reward a "blue ribbon" to people like us (Martin, 2025, p. 95) or that, in Turner's words, "[w]e regard as agential those that fit with *our own* sense of rightness," (Turner, 2025, p. 109, emphasis added) *not* the actors'. And since the observers in this case tend to be academics who, naturally, value reflection over mindless impulse or habit, such attribution of "agency" easily "degenerates into mere class snobbery" (Martin, 2025, p. 96). The tendency of identifying "agency" with "progressive" change that we mention in WDW*N* (p. 26) as well as the attribution of "false consciousness" to actors who fail to pursue such "progressive" change, which is its inverse, is but another form of the same kind of snobbery. The underlying assumption clearly is that if only the actors in question reflected deeply enough, they would surely come to the same conclusions that *we*, the academic observers, have come to. As Turner (2025, p. 110) notes, this is part of a "long history of hidden motivations in the history of social science." And we don't mind admitting that our work was partly motivated by our irritation with just this kind of class snobbery (see van den Berg, 2003; van den Berg & Jeong, 2022).

But for all his reservations about such snobbery, Martin still thinks that when actions appear to be based on conscious reflection and actors appear to have "very good reasons for doing what they are doing," it is "not wrong on empirical grounds to promote that action from non-agentic to agentic" (Martin, 2025, p. 98). In fact, following Durkheim, Martin insists that, even if we act for reasons we cannot know, we are "autonomous" to the extent that we do so "consciously, reflectively, [and] voluntarily" (Martin, 2025, p. 99). But we are afraid that this amounts to less of a "a step *away* from that sort of snobbery" (Martin, 2025, p. 98) than he thinks it is. For one thing, what are or are not "very good reasons" for doing something is still left to the observer to decide. But perhaps more importantly, human behavior no doubt ranges from unconscious reflexes to well-reflected action and many shades in between, and we may have good reasons for drawing useful distinctions along the continuum for various purposes. But we would hesitate to elevate the more reflected kind to some higher moral plane and to relegate more habitual forms of behavior to a lesser kind. In fact, in our view, one of our major tasks is precisely to try and uncover the "good reasons" underlying actions that to us appear initially to be of the latter type, as they may provide important clues to the possible causes of the behavior in question.

Another form of empirical agency Martin thinks worth exploring is the Aristotelian notion of an act being voluntary or *"hekōn* to the extent that the actor would *happily own it* after the doing" as opposed to merely responding to an unhappy event (Martin, 2025, p. 95). One problem with this is that, as Turner notes, "[t]here is plenty of reason to believe... that our sense of ownership is a construction placed retrospectively on a process that is mostly unconscious" (Turner, 2025, p. 113). But it is also not clear to us in what sense the happily owning of one's action is an attribute of the actor or the act rather than of the degree of (un)pleasantness of the options offered by the situation she finds herself in. We have tried to make this point in WDW*N* (p. 27) where we criticize Chafetz's notion of agency and freedom of choice as boiling down to whether or not the actor has the social resources ensuring a sufficiently wide range of palatable options to enable her to *happily* own her actions.

And what are we to make of "agency" as "action [that] is creating something new" (Martin, 2025, p. 98) as advocated by Hannah Arendt and emphasized by Emirbayer and Mische (1998)? We certainly do not deny the very possibility of novelty as Martin claims. In fact, in a trivial sense, every action is novel in *some respect*. But what we are presumably interested in studying are social actions, events, and phenomena that are, in some sense, *significantly* or *importantly* novel. And what we consider to be significant or important depends, of course, on what differences matter *to us*. Martin's example of Greta Thunberg's remarkable impact on the politics of climate change may help clarify the matter. From the standpoint of a hardline climate change denier, Thunberg's rise to prominence is nothing new: just another clever teenaged rabble-rouser having caught the attention of the liberal media. From the standpoint of someone interested in understanding the emergence of successful social movements, Thunberg's seemingly unlikely rise calls for a "turn to the empirical issue of when and in what settings, and by whom, such novelty emerges" (Martin, 2025, p. 98), that is, presumably by comparing it to other social movements. We see no problem in any of this.

Martin is surely right that the kind of counterfactualist free-for-all that he mocks in his discussion of the Thunberg case is pointless and, in fact, ridiculous. But at the same time, trying to explain some event or action involves an implicit or explicit comparison with *something*. The problem Martin points to is the use of *implausible* counterfactuals ("the fact that the Swedish government didn't hire assassins to take her out," Martin, 2025, p. 97). This is where comparisons with other, *actually existing*, cases of similar actors or conditions having produced different outcomes is crucial in helping us construct explanations that are worth our while. And the same can be said for distinguishing novelty from routine in social action: the routine from which the novelty is thought to deviate has to be a plausible one, preferably one that is well-documented.

As Hitlin, citing Martin, rightly notes the bread and butter of our craft consists of trying to figure out why "some do and some don't." Like many of the authors whose articles we analyze in the section of WDW*U* titled "Making Choices as Agency," Hitlin insists that we need "some placeholder for the (seemingly obvious to me) fact that similar people (based on whatever commonalities you like) do not always act similarly" (Hitlin, 2025, p. 80). We need some term to acknowledge the sheer variation in human behavior that precludes even the best of our explanatory models from explaining more than a fraction of the variation in outcomes. And, he adds, "[w]hether we call this variation 'agency' is a legitimate question, but it necessitates being called something" (Hitlin, 2025, p. 80). Perhaps. But what is wrong with just "diversity" or "variation"? Why insist on the philosophically loaded yet explanatorily entirely redundant "agency?"

After discussing the paradoxes of freedom and determinism, Martin proposes to treat "agency" as "the dark matter of our anthropology: there's something a bit wrong with current theories of cosmology, so to make them balance out, we have to assume the existence of something that doesn't really make that much sense and can't be seen" (Martin, 2025, p. 94). The analogy with astronomy is intriguing, but we are not wholly convinced. Astronomers know that they need to assume the existence of a mass of "dark matter" for their standard cosmological models to function and they even know precisely how much of it they need (26.8% according to Wikipedia!). Compared to this, invoking "agency" to account for the large amounts of unexplained variance in most of *our* explanations is like waving a magic wand. It amounts, as Turner puts it, to no more than a "cognitive short cut in the face of causal opacity" (Turner, 2025, p. 106) or "an empty signifier, which means that it signifies nothing precise, or nothing at all, and serves the speaker's purposes because it retains a discursive role: it appears to say something" (Turner, 2025, p. 105). We could just as well call it "X," or if that's too Musk-like, how about "unexplained variance?"

On the other hand, Turner's suggestion to treat actors' reasons for their actions not as uncaused causes but as a narrative form "that tells us what we need to know about what is going on in a given situation, including what its sequelae and circumstances were" (Turner, 2025, p. 110) points to something important, we think. He rightly points out that "most of the time when we are asking for a justification, we are asking what kind of act something was" (Turner, 2025, p. 110). And, as we briefly note in WDW*N* (p. 31), in ordinary interaction, if and when the reasons given strike us as reasonable, we tend not to ask any further questions. But as sociologists we cannot leave things there, not least because what is deemed to be "reasonable" is itself culturally highly variable, as Turner also notes (Turner, 2025, pp. 107–108). Instead, to sociologists knowing what kind of act something is constitutes the starting point as well as a crucial clue toward identifying its "typical antecedents and consequents" (Turner, 2025, p. 112), that is, toward explaining what its causes and consequences are.

This is also how we understand Weber's views of the relation between *verstehen* and causal explanation. *Zu verstehen* is to recognize what the action is about, to typify it. Explanation consists then of identifying the typical causes of that kind of action. In answer to Martin's question about our view (Martin, fn. 4), we definitely do *not* endorse the "touchy-feely" interpretation of Weber as an arch-voluntarist. To the contrary, while we are not exactly Weber scholars, Martin's rendition of Weber's views sounds entirely plausible to us. And, whether or not it is the correct interpretation of what Weber *really* meant, it sounds to us like the most sensible one for sociologists to adopt.

But while we do not think the notion of "agency" has a useful role to play in standard sociological explanations, that does not mean it cannot or should not be an appropriate topic of sociological analysis. All three of our commentators suggest varying aspects of the uses and experiences of "agency" that are well worth investigating sociologically. Martin and Turner both suggest we should be studying the variable "phenomenological experience of freedom" (Martin, 2025, p. 94), and Turner in particular emphasizes the "radical variation in the way cultures treat action" (Turner, 2025, p. 115) which deserves much closer sociological scrutiny. We wholeheartedly agree and note, at the end of WDW*U* (pp. 64–65), that the uses of "agency" in contemporary sociology have a peculiarly Western ring to them.[1] Barnes' (2000) argument that "agency," "freedom," and "choice" are notions that need to be understood within the framework of communicative interactions and social relations points in the same direction, it seems to us.

Hitlin in turn takes us to task for summarily dismissing the large social–psychological literature – of which he is one of the leading originators – that empirically studies the causes and consequences of "agency-like-beliefs" (Hitlin, 2025, p. 83). We definitely owe him an apology on this score. The "curious" footnotes in which we refer to his work and that of his fellow social psychologists were in no way intended to be dismissive of that particular tradition. Quite to the contrary, it has done an excellent job of uncovering and documenting both the causes and social consequences of varying degrees of a *sense* of "agency" – or "self-efficacy" as it is also widely called. Our point in those footnotes (with the exception of footnote 7 of WDW*N* where we do criticize Hitlin and Elder (2007) for invoking a Giddensian notion of free will) was simply that our criticisms of the concept and uses of "agency" in the sociological literature do *not* apply to this type of work. But we would add here that we think it would be much better to use terms like "sense of agency" or "self-efficacy" rather than "agency" *tout court* to avoid confusion as well as the occasional slippage into unnecessary talk about "free will."

As it happens, a number of articles using "agency" to mean the actors' subjective *sense* of being able to achieve some goal, that is, in essentially the way Hitlin et al. have treated it, turned up in our sample of articles with the term "agency" in their titles. We are not sure whether more might have turned up if we had chosen some other sampling criterion, as Martin suggests (Martin, 2025, p. 99). But our goal was to produce a random sample of articles whose authors are most likely to have some explicit rationale for using the term and we are not sure how else we would have been able to generate such a sample. Martin (Martin, 2025, p. 99) also wonders whether, given its theoretical complexity, books rather than articles might be the more likely places to find successful uses of the concept of "agency." It is certainly true that some of the book-length works (e.g., Alexander, 1988; Archer, 2000; Blumer, 1969; Giddens, 1984, 1993) and lengthier articles (esp. Emirbayer & Mische, 1998) offer more in-depth treatments but, as we try to show in WDW*N*, with the exception of Barnes (2000), they are not exactly "successful."

Finally, what is the point of all our critical work? According to Hitlin sociologists' enthusiasm for the notion of "agency" has already waned, so why continue to beat a dead horse? As he puts it, somewhat rhetorically, "[i]f we excised the term from the field today, what would change?" (Hitlin, 2025, p. 87). Besides, do we really expect to arrive at one, clear, and agreed-upon understanding of social action in a "low-consensus field" like sociology (Hitlin, 2025, p. 86), riddled as it is with contested concepts like "race," "class," "status," and "identity" (Hitlin, 2025, p. 86)?

It is certainly true that the meaning of many of the key terms in our discipline is ill-defined and more or less hotly contested. And quite often, the disagreements have a lot to do with underlying clashing political or ideological agendas. But that is hardly a reason to give up on the pursuit of greater clarity. Quite to the contrary, we would think.

But however nebulous the exact meaning of the term "agency," Hitlin still thinks that "[i]n a probabilistic universe (or science), [it] helps organize a potentially infinite set of forces/pressures/neurons in play" (Hitlin, 2025, p. 87). But as we have tried to show, in the literature that we have examined, it does not "organize" anything other than to display the authors' political/ideological colors. Then again, on the same page, after once more mentioning that most social science "leaves a lot of unexplained variance," he supposes that "one way to read these critiques of agency is that the term gets us no closer to – and perhaps obscures – understanding those other factors." That, as well as the annoying and in the long term quite damaging habit of so many sociologists to smuggle in their ideological commitments under the cover of seemingly neutral analytical terms, is exactly our concern!

Would it make any difference if we simply dispensed with the term "agency"? Hitlin may well be right that the enthusiasm for this particular term to express the voluntaristic urge may be past its prime.[2] But as we mention at the beginning of WDW*N*, this is just one of a repetitive series of such currents advocating some form of voluntarism. Without a serious and thorough consideration of what is and what is not at stake here, we can be quite sure that sooner or later, we will face another such wave of confusion driven by the half-conscious desire to exempt human action, or at least those human actions we approve of, from the indignity of causal explanation. Maybe this discussion triggered by our two papers is not a bad start. Again, we can only thank our commentators for their thoughtful and thought-provoking comments.

NOTES

1. Where we also cite Hitlin and Elder (2007) making a similar point.
2. A quick replication of our initial search for articles with "agency" in the title for the years after 2016 suggests that the number of such articles continued to rise through 2022, followed by a significant dip for 2023.

REFERENCES

Alexander, J. C. (1988). *Action and its environments: Toward a new synthesis*. Columbia University Press.
Archer, M. S. (2000). *Being human: The problem of agency*. Cambridge University Press.
Barnes, B. (2000). *Understanding agency: Social theory and responsible action*. Sage.
Blumer, H. (1969). *Symbolic interactionism: Perspective and method*. Prentice-Hall.

Emirbayer, M., & Mische, A. (1998). What is agency? *American Journal of Sociology*, *103*(4), 962–1023.
Giddens, A. (1984). *The constitution of society: Outline of the theory of structuration*. University of California Press.
Giddens, A. (1993). *New rules of sociological method* (2nd ed.). Basic Books.
Hitlin, S. (2025). Curiously footnoted conceptualizations of agency. In H. F. Dahms (Ed.), *The future of agency. Current perspectives in social theory* (Vol. 41, pp. 77–89). Emerald Publishing Limited.
Hitlin, S., & Elder, G. H., Jr. (2007). Time, self, and the curiously abstract concept of agency. *Sociological Theory*, *25*(2), 170–191.
Martin, J. L. (2025). Agency between freedom/action and determinism/structure: Comment on van den Berg and Amasyalı. In H. F. Dahms (Ed.), *The future of agency. Current perspectives in social theory* (Vol. 41, pp. 91–101). Emerald Publishing Limited.
Pinker, S. (2007). *The stuff of thought: Language as a window into human nature*. Viking Penguin.
Turner, S. (2025). The great agency muddle. In H. F. Dahms (Ed.), *The future of agency. Current perspectives in social theory* (Vol. 41, pp. 103–115). Emerald Publishing Limited.
Van den Berg, A. (2003, May). Review of Margaret S. Archer, being human: The problem of agency (Cambridge: Cambridge University Press, 2000). *Canadian Review of Sociology & Anthropology*, *40*(2), 233–236.
Van den Berg, A., & Jeong, T. (2022, December). Cutting off the branch on which we are sitting? On postpositivism, value neutrality, and the "bias paradox". *Society*, *59*(6), 631–647.

PART II

THE PROBLEM AND CHALLENGE OF AUTONOMY (CLASSICAL AND CONTEMPORARY THEORY)

ERIK OLIN WRIGHT'S SELECTIVE INTERPRETATION OF WEBER AND EXPLOITATION: A DISCUSSION AND EVALUATION

Sandro Segre

Università di Genova, Italy

ABSTRACT

This chapter discusses and evaluates Erik Olin Wright's reception of Max Weber. To this end, it presents Wright's and Weber's class theories and focuses on and counter poses their respective notions of emancipation, exploitation, inequality, and democracy. The article, furthermore, critically evaluates Wright's assessment of Weber by referring them to Weber's own texts and argues that Weber's notion of exploitation connotes the sphere of production, not that of exchange; that exploitation for Weber hinges on differences in life chances that cause obstacles in mobility between social classes; and that for Weber exploitation may be found in other modes of production in addition to capitalism. Finally, this chapter traces the differences in these authors' respective notions of exploitation to their different understanding of emancipation.

Keywords: Exploitation; capitalism; socialism; liberalism; emancipation

PREFATORY REMARKS

The late sociologist Erik Olin Wright (1947–2019) spent his scholarly life pursuing theory and research on two fundamental questions, namely, how to conceptualize social classes from a Marxist perspective, and what is the extent of, and what changes have occurred in, class-related inequality in the United States. In the last decades of his life, however, Wright also turned his attention to Weber's writings on classes, while remaining committed to a Marxist frame of reference. As Wright himself stated, he built his class theory on "the Marxist and Weberian traditions of class analysis" (Wright, 1997, p. xxviii). This chapter pursues the following aims: firstly, to outline Wright's stratification theory, which hinges on the related notions of exploitation and social class; second, to present his writings on Weber in the context of Wright's own class analysis; finally, to assess their consistency with Weber's writings on social stratification. The premise of this chapter is the conviction, which the present author shares with Wright and others, that "class is a pervasive social cause and thus it is worth exploring its ramifications for many social phenomena" (Wright, 1997, p. 1). Given the sociological significance of class analysis in the context of modern capitalism (cf. Giddens, 1971, p. xvi), assessing Wright's reception and interpretation of the Weberian writings on class may shed light on some central problems of social theory. A preliminary review of how the subject of exploitation has been discussed by some other contemporary prominent sociologists may serve as an introduction to Wright's analysis.

DIFFERENT CAUSES OF EXPLOITATION: ASYMMETRIC LIFE CHANCES, MONOPOLIZATION, AND EXCLUSION

Many contemporary sociologists have dwelt on this notion, each of them in his own way. Giddens has defined exploitation as "any socially conditioned of asymmetric life chances." Giddens thereby refers to the chances an individual has of sharing in "the socially created economic or cultural 'goods'" that "typically exist in any given society," but that are unevenly distributed (Giddens, 1973, pp. 130–131). Murphy views exploitation as the "more general phenomenon of monopolization and exclusion" rather than – more specifically – as the appropriation of labor in accordance with the Marxist conception of exploitation. He considers this view of exploitation, with its focus on social closure, closer to Weber than the one Marx-inspired, which lays emphasis upon the appropriation of labor and exclusion from productive labor (Murphy, 1988, p. 101). Parkin, while not rejecting out of hand the Marxist notion of exploitation, remarks that "all forms of exclusion are exploitative, by *whatever* criteria they are justified" (1979, p. 71; italics are in the original). Thus, these contemporary sociologists agree on viewing exploitation in the general terms of having exclusive access to social goods, broadly defined. Exploitation, in other words, presupposes for them the exclusion of some people or groups from having access to some goods to the advantage of others. As will be shown presently, both Weber and Wright concurred with this view of exploitation and agreed on considering it of crucial importance for the creation and upholding of the class structure. Their conceptions of exploitation differed otherwise, however.

WRIGHT'S CLASS THEORY

Building on earlier works by Ossowski (1963) and Poulantzas (1975), Wright proposed a revised model of Marxist class analysis. This model abides by Marx's fundamental notions of antagonistic relations of production and of exploitation as created and shaped in the market, for "markets are powerful engines for generating inequalities" even though "after-market income taxes can substantially redistribute income" (Wright, 2010, pp. 47, 263). Wright's model of class analysis, like the other authors that have been previously considered, lays emphasis upon asymmetric life chances but pursues two different ultimate aims. First, to emancipate society from capitalist exploitation, which is defined in Marxist terms as "the exclusion of direct producers from the means of production" (Wright, 2010, p. 150, note 84); and second, to further "the aspiration for an egalitarian and democratic future" (Wright, 1997, p. 519). As he wrote, "the struggle for human emancipation requires a struggle against capitalism" (Wright, 2010, p. 567). Emancipation, which was a key concept for Wright, was defined as a struggle for "the elimination of oppression and the creation of the conditions for human flourishing" (Wright, 2010, p. 10). A flourishing society is one in which "all people have unconditional access to the necessary means to ... the satisfaction of needs" (Wright, 2010, p. 13). Wright's "radical democratic egalitarianism" (Wright, 2010, p. 33) intended to challenge the conditions that promote unequal access to human flourishing.

Wright made two important distinctions in his notion of capitalism. One distinction is between relations of economic ownership and relations of production, which are in turn distinguished between the control of the means of production and the control of labor power. The second distinction is between different levels of control, from full control to partial, minimal, and no control at all. Wright first formulated this model in a seminal article he published with *The New Left Review* in 1976 (Wright, 1976). He did not depart from it subsequently but rather added further distinctions to his criteria of class location (cf. in particular Wright, 1980). With reference to this revised model, Wright proposed the notion of contradictory class location. Class location determines "the matrix of objective possibilities faced by individuals, the real alternatives people face to make decisions" (Wright, 1985, p. 144). Active choices of class, however, do not directly result from "the objective conditions of class location." They rather flow from the how the individual subjects mediate between these objective conditions and their own subjectivity (Wright, 1985, p. 145).

Active choices result, in other words, from the individuals' class consciousness, that is, from the realization by subordinate classes that the class structure – in the sense of "the interest-generating process linked to exploitation" (Wright, 1985, p. 186) – must be transformed in order to uphold their capacity to conduct class actions and the recognition on the part of the dominant classes that the existing class structure is necessary to preserve their power (Wright, 1985, p. 28). With the notion of contradictory class location, Wright referred to "positions which are torn between the basic contradictory class locations of capitalist society" (Wright, 1976, p. 26). Noncontradictory class locations in capitalist society are the bourgeoisie, the petty bourgeoisie, and the proletariat. These classes are not contradictory as their economic ownership, relations of production, and control of the labor power define them unambiguously.

Managers and supervisors, on the other hand, occupy contradictory positions between the proletariat and the bourgeoisie. Differently from the capitalists, they exert substantial but not complete control over the labor power and the means of production, while they do not own the means of production or do so to a minimal extent. They also differ from the proletariat, whose members do not own or control the means of production and exert no authority on others. As for the contradictory class locations between the bourgeoisie and the petty bourgeoisie, small employers are self-employed, own a limited amount of capital, and have only few employees. Wright thought along Marxist lines that white-collar employees have some autonomy in their immediate labor process. He concurred with Braverman's thesis (1974) that this class is undergoing a proletarization process. According to his empirical research, the proletariat in the United States is by far the largest social class (Wright, 1976, pp. 35–41, 1980, pp. 185–188).

Wright laid consistent emphasis in his class analysis on the Marxist notion of exploitation as distinct from the broader notion of domination. This notion "is a particularly important component of Marxian theory," as in keeping with it capitalism is based on its exploitation of the proletariat. It refers to "the social relations within which one person's activities are directed and controlled by another" (Wright, 2005a, p. 25), and which therefore "implies a set of opposing material interests" (Wright, 1985, pp. 56–57). Concerning exploitation specifically, in his early publication on class boundaries in advanced capitalist societies, Wright wrote: "The distinctive feature of capitalist production is the appropriation of surplus value through the exploitation of workers in the labor process" (1976, p. 35). Roughly 30 years later, he reiterated the same concept:

> The ingredient that most sharply distinguishes the Marxist conceptualization of class from other traditions is the concept of 'exploitation,' and second, that an exploitation-centered concept of class provides theoretically powerful tools for studying a range of problems in contemporary society. (2005a, p. 5)

Wright defined exploitation as a situation that satisfies the following criteria. First, capitalist and workers have different and antagonistic material interests as the members of the former class exploit the members of the latter; second, different access to particular productive resources from which others are excluded make exploitation possible; finally, the exploiters obtain material advantage from appropriating the labor effort of the exploited (1985, pp. 56–57, 2005a, pp. 23–24, 2005c, pp. 721–722). As he put it succinctly, "exploitation is thus a diagnosis of the process through which the inequalities in incomes are generated by inequalities in rights and powers over productive resources" (2005c, p. 721). Exploitation, thus defined, has three principal aspects or (in Wright's wording) dimensions, according to whether it is based on "control of capital, organization, and credential/skill-combined in various ways" (Wright, 1985, p. 148). Wright formulated different but consistent definitions on this concept.

These definitions emphasized, along with economic oppression, the transfer of labor power from the exploiter to the oppressed and the ensuing deprivation of the oppressed. For the labor effort of the oppressed and the surplus thus obtained, go to the oppressor who effectively claim them and need them for their own welfare. The exploiters and the exploited are mutually bound, since their social relations shape their ongoing interactions (Wright, 1985, pp. 37, 57–58, 63, 74–75, 81, 1997, pp. 10–12). The presence of exploitation in the class structure of countries that are advanced but otherwise quite different, such as Sweden and the United States, was an important result of a major comparative research Wright conducted with other sociologists in the 1980s (Wright, 1985, pp. 241–282, especially p. 278). Class analysis, as Wright conceived of it, revolves around the following set of definitional and theoretical statements:

(1) Class is defined by the objective location of people in income or wealth distribution; (2) Class is a source of subjective identity; (3) Class is a cause of unequal life chances; (4) Class is a source of antagonistic conflicts over unequal access to economic opportunities; (5) Class is a cause of historical variation in the social organization of inequalities; (6) Class is a source of social transformation to end capitalist economic oppression and exploitation; (7) Therefore, Marxist class analysis is both an explanatory concept and as an instrument of emancipation (2005b, pp. 180–191, 2015, pp. 121–122, 141–146). Wright argued accordingly that "class remains a significant and sometimes powerful determinant of many aspects of social life" (2015, p. 155). He referred in this connection to the persistence of several capitalist features such as class boundaries, economic inequality, extraction of labor efforts from the working class, and impact on individual subjectivity (2015, pp. 146–155).

Marxist class analysis – he argued – is superior to other theoretical traditions, for it is able to answer questions deemed to be of central relevance such as "[t]he nature of capitalism, its harms and contradictions, and the possibilities of its transformation" (2015, p. 3). Wright also called attention to important features of contemporary capitalism that to some extents have modified its nature. He pointed in this regard to the existence in today's capitalist countries of noncapitalist aspects that produce "hybrids of different kinds of economic relations" (2015, p. 245). These new attributes of capitalism include worker cooperatives, employee stock ownership plans, and financial participation in the firms by nonprofit organizations (2015, pp. 245–250). Such attributes make it possible to achieve a "positive class compromise" that preserves capitalism but uses private and public funds to finance social insurance and public goods (2015, p. 250). Wright's attention to processes of social mobility stemmed from his persuasion that "relative mobility patterns reflect general mechanisms associated with the advantages and disadvantages of class origins, barriers to entry to class destination, and cultural resources associated with the family of origin" (1997, p. 180).

His research on such processes has been premised on a class model that comprehends the classes of the bourgeoisie, the small employers, the petty bourgeoisie composed of self-employed people with no more than one employee, and the working class. This model is based on differences in the possession and the amount of such attributes as property, authority, and skill. Wright focused in his research on the comparison between some advanced capitalist countries with different degrees of state intervention in the economy. The United States and Sweden were most distinct in this regard the United States being capitalist with the least degree of state intervention. Property, rather than skill or authority, constitutes there the greatest obstacle to class mobility. More specifically, Wright inquired whether there are significant differences, for each of these countries, in the permeability of class boundaries for people that belong to distinct social classes. He found that the boundaries permeability was greatest for the authority boundary, while the property boundary was least permeable, and the skill boundary occupied an intermediate position in the permeability order (Wright, 1997; Western & Wright, 1994).

WRIGHT ON WEBER

Wright expressed a constant interest in Weber's class categories. They were sometimes jointly considered with Marxist class analysis. More frequently, however, they were distinguished from it and investigated for comparative purposes. Before focusing on an article by Wright that contains an in-depth analysis of Marx's and Weber's corresponding class theories (Wright, 2002), we shall mention other publications by this author that deal with this same subject. In *Classes*, Wright analyzed Weber's concept of class under the heading of "Alternative Class Theories" (1985, pp. 106–108). In this connection, he de-emphasized a frequent contraposition between Marx and Weber in terms of production relations for the former author and market and exchange relations for the latter, as both Marx and Weber in his view adopted a production-based definition of classes. Apparently in this sense, Wright wrote that "when Weber speaks of classes, he is speaking in a rather Marxian voice" (Wright, 1997, p. 29, note 22).

Subsequently and in a different context, Wright remarked that both Marx and Weber linked "status inequalities to attributes of birth" (Wright, 2010, p. 47, note 10). As he also stated, according to both these authors, though more emphasized by Weber, only in capitalism "economically based power plays the predominant role in determining the use of economic resources" (Wright, 2010, p. 121, note 9). Still, he pointed to what he considered as a real difference between these two authors; namely, that Weber viewed classes as determined by market exchanges in which labor power and skills are traded, whereas Marx viewed classes as generated by the exploitation of one class on the part of another. For Weber, then, "class is a central feature of social structure only in capitalism" (1985, p. 108), while for Marx, classes, thus defined, may be found not only in capitalism but also in other historically contingent social formations, for those formations were also based on the exploitation of the labor power of the dominated class. As Wright argued in *Class Counts* and elsewhere, Marxist and Weberian class traditions also differ in other respects (Wright, 1997, pp. 29–37; Wright & Cho, 1992, p. 86).

First, they use different analytical categories, namely, exploitation for Marxists and life chances for Weberians. While the former notion points to conflict within production, the latter refers to conflicts within the market. As Wright put it in a different context, the Weberian model of class analysis "only deals with the bargaining within exchange" (Wright, 2005a, p. 27). Weber therefore left out of consideration the study of classes in nonmarket societies and the link between production and exchange (Wright, 1997, p. 182). Second, while Weberian sociologists have devoted much less attention to the notion of class structure and exploitation in comparison to their Marxist counterparts, they have paid greater attention to the analysis of social mobility and life chances (Wright, 1997, pp. 31, 170–171). Wright's comparative article on Marx's and Weber's class theories (2002) referred to notions, such as class and exploitation, which had been presented and discussed in his previous publications.

In particular, Wright reiterated here what he considered "the central difference between Marx's and Weber's concept of class," namely, Weber's focus on market transactions and Marx's emphasis upon conflict over the performance and appropriation of labor effort that occurs after market exchanges are contracted (Wright, 2002, p. 846; see also 1985, p. 72). In this regard, Wright remarked that Weber's notions of status groups and corresponding lifestyles becloud the central importance of status groups as agents of exploitation processes (Wright, 2002, p. 847). Further, Wright stated that Weber's position toward the problem of work effort "is broadly in line with that of contemporary neoclassical micro-economics" (Wright, 2002, p. 849), notwithstanding Weber's awareness of the substantive irrationality inherent to the capitalist formally rational organization of the labor market.

WEBER ON EXPLOITATION

The thesis that Weber was aware of the substantive irrationality born into the capitalist labor market, but rather focused on its formal rationality, will be considered here in conjunction with Wright's other interpretive thesis, that Weber's notion of life chances exclusively refers to conflicts within the market rather than within production. The former thesis finds no textual support in Weber's *General Economic History*, which is a work Wright himself cited in his 2002 article. Toward the end of this work Weber stated that "the development of the concept of the calling quickly gave to the modern entrepreneur a fabulously clear conscience – and also industrious workers; he gave to his employees ... co-operation in his ruthless exploitation of them through capitalism" (Weber, 1927, p. 367, 1958, p. 313). In his use of the notion of exploitation, Weber referred here to the sphere of production, not to that of exchange.

The notion of exploitation (Weber used a variety of terms to designate it such as *Ausbeutung, Nutzung, Verwertung*), furthermore, occurs quite a few times in this work. Weber referred in this regard to the exploitation of peasants or craft workers in the Middle Ages on the part of the dominant powers (Weber, 1927, pp. 61, 72, 92, 94, 124–125, 1958, p. 68, 77, 93–94, 118) or to the exploitation of labor through the colonial trade rather than through market operation (Weber, 1927, p. 300, 1958, p. 258). In this discourse context, Weber made an appreciative citation of Marx (Weber, 1927, p. 71), thus pointing to his continuity with Marxist social theory. In *Economy and Society*, Weber mentioned "the exploitation of capitalist dependencies," apparently meaning the workers, on the part of corporate occupational organizations for their political purposes (Weber, 1971, pp. 325–326, 1978, p. 1397). In another passage of *Economy and Society*, Weber wrote that "for employers, there is always the possibility of transforming their exploitation of labor into a source of income" (Weber, 1978, p. 129).

Wright's Marxist argument that the dominant classes resorted to the exploitation of other classes to preserve or increase their power even before the onset of modern capitalism was in fact consonant with Weber's class analysis. This statement does not imply, however, that for Weber, classes are generated by the exploitation of one class at the hands of another, in keeping with Wright's thesis; neither does it imply, on the other hand, that Wright was mistaken in arguing that for Weber, classes are determined by the market. This argument, however, gives only a partial and incomplete account of how Weber referred to these sociological notions. While a detailed examination of Weber's class categories will not be conducted here (cf. Breen, 2005, pp. 32–34), some essential information should be provided on Weber's view of classes, life chances, and the market.

It should be underlined, first, that for Weber classes (*Klassen*) are, along with status groups (Stände) and political parties (*Parteien*), "phenomena of distribution of power within a community," power being defined as the chance for a person or plurality of persons of having their will prevail against the resistance of others who are also involved in this action. This statement implies that, in keeping with Weber, classes should not be considered separately from status groups and parties. Weber's classes are defined by having its members' life chances determined by their exchanges in the commodity or labor markets. Wright's interpretation is then to this extent correct. However, the two latter categories – status groups and parties – are not market-determined (Weber, 1972, p. 531, 1978, p. 927; cf. also Giddens, 1973, pp. 163–165). Wright's interpretation is therefore in this regard partial and incomplete. It is so in other regards as well. Reference should be made in this connection to Wright's omission to come seriously to grips in his class analysis with the Weberian notions of social class and social mobility.

This omission is surprising, as Wright wrote that the problem of common life chances of people involved in market exchanges "naturally leads to a concern with the intergenerational transmission of life chances" (Wright, 1997, p. 170). Intergenerational mobility is a subject with which Wright concerned himself extensively. Yet, he referred in this regard to Marxist and Bourdieu's social theories rather than to Weber and Weberian sociology (cf. especially Wright, 1997, pp. 171–173, who cited Bourdieu, 1984, 1985, 1987). According to Weber, a social class (*Soziale Klasse*) is defined by the easy and typical mobility between given sets of class situations, the presence of mobility boundaries outside of these sets (Weber, 1972, p. 177, 1978, p. 302), and is accordingly distinguished from market-determined classes. Weber did not investigate why there are in capitalist societies four social classes, and not a greater or smaller number of them (Mackenzie, 1982, pp. 65–67). Rather, he preferred to leave to empirical research the answer to this question.

Paying greater attention to this Weberian notion of social class might have enabled Wright not only to achieve a better understanding of Weber's analysis of the capitalist forms of inequality. It might have also led him to redefine his concept of exploitation in broader terms as the consequence of social boundaries that de facto prevent comparatively disadvantaged people to have their offspring provided with better life chances. Exploitation would then not just result from the appropriation of surplus labor; it would rather result from the social closure of mobility opportunities, which people that belong to relatively privileged sets of economic classes enact – deliberately or not – towards others who have lesser life chances. In keeping with Weber, exploitation then means that some collectivities have better life chances to the detriment of others, and that this social condition ensues from the intra and intergenerational transmission of inequality.

WEBER AND WRIGHT ON ORGANIZATIONS, "MIDDLE CLASSES," STATUS GROUPS, AND DEMOCRACY

We shall now present and compare Weber and Wright's writings on classes and status groups. Wright's interpretation and assessment of Weber's contribution to this field of studies is still going to be relevant, as shown at the end of this section. The formation and very existence of social classes, defined in terms of similar mobility opportunities for the members of any given social class, is closely related to the presence of status groups (Weber, 1972, p. 180, 1978, pp. 306–307). Status groups constitute the core of social classes. As Weber put it, "the status group (*Stand*) comes close to the social class (*Soziale Klasse*) and is most unlike the commercial class (*Erwerbsklasse*)" (Weber, 1972, p. 180, 1978, pp. 306–307). While commercial classes and in-general classes as defined by market-determined life chances arise out of common economic interests, status groups arise out of conventions that regulate the lifestyle of their members (Weber, 1972, p. 180, 1978, pp. 306–307). Their definitions are therefore mutually exclusive (Bendix, 1989, p. 150). Status groups and social classes are then sources of exploitation, as defined in terms of structured inequality stemming from the distinct life chances that pertain to each social class.

Thus defined, exploitation is neither a distinctive feature of capitalism nor is therefore a state of affairs that a socialist order, or mode of production, could do away with. This definition of exploitation shares with Wright's the exclusion and (to some extent) the appropriation principles. As Wright himself observed, "The rights and powers of people over productive assets" is instrumental in creating or upholding the position of the propertied bourgeoisie as the most privileged social class according to both Marx and Weber (Wright, 2005a, p. 23). Differently from Wright, however, Weber did not mention in this regard the appropriation of labor efforts as a source of privilege. The relative privilege of each of Weber's social classes presupposes that all the other social classes have their own particular life chances, market-determined privileges, and material and cultural interests. A given social class's possession of all these attributes prevents all other social classes from partaking of them, in keeping with a broader version of Wright's exclusion principle.

Weber's notion of exploitation differs from Wright's also in some other important respects. For Weber did not argue that actors (whether they be individuals, social classes, or status groups) necessarily have counterposed interests, as Wright's inverse interdependent welfare principle holds. Nor did Weber argue, as Wright did, that the privileged social classes draw their privilege from the material deprivation of others (Wright, 2005a, pp. 23–24). Thus, Weber's stance on capitalism and inequality departed substantially from Wright's. This conclusion holds notwithstanding Weber's concern with interests' conflicts and with their representation in capitalist societies. Interest groups such as those representing the business circles or the working class may find political representation by means of political parties rather than business associations; for only in Parliamentary democracies conflicts – whether social or otherwise – are overt and amenable to institutionalization (Weber, 1971, pp. 257–258, 275–276).

As stated, the appropriation of labor effort connotes Wright's conception of exploitation and therefore his view of inequality in capitalism; as capitalism has raised "exploitation based on property relations in means of production ... to an unprecedented level" (Wright, 1985, p. 82). Inequality has for Wright the broad sense of differential opportunity of possessing any "morally irrelevant attribute which interferes with a person's access to the necessary material and social means to live a flourishing life" (Wright, 2010, pp. 15–16). Capitalism, Wright maintains, "is fundamentally incompatible with the strong notion of equality of opportunity" (Wright, 2010, p. 52). By contrast, Weber's conception of structured inequality in opportunities and life chances revolves around the unequal distribution of power in different status groups and consequently in different social classes. The "bureaucratization of capitalism" supported the claims on the part of the diploma holders to obtain exclusive control of the privileged social and economic positions (Weber, 1972, p. 577, 1978, p. 1000).

In conjunction with a status order based on educational diplomas, bureaucratic organizations therefore promote processes of exploitation, in keeping with Weber's definition of this term. For Weber, then, exploitation so defined and social status are interlinked. Wright, it may be recalled, objected to Weber – among other strictures – that Weber had failed to discuss how status groups concur to capitalist exploitation. However, this objection was based on a Marxist, rather than a Weberian, definition of exploitation. Particular attention should be paid to Wright's organization and to credential or skill as dimensions of exploitation in addition to control of capital (Wright, 1985, pp. 283–284), for these are instances of exploitation as defined by both Weber and Wright. It is worthwhile to present and compare here the respective statements concerning the meaning which the two authors conferred to the notion of organization.

According to Weber, an organization (*Verband*) are social relationships to which outsiders have no or limited access and in which only specific individuals enforce its regulations (Weber, 1972, p. 26, 1978, p. 48). According to Wright, who focused on organization assets rather than on organizations per se, "organization assets consist in the effective control over the coordination and integration of the division of labor" (Wright, 1985, p. 151). Albeit mutually compatible, these conceptions of organization are distinct. Weber laid stress on its social closure while Wright considered organizations as an instrument of power over subordinates. Each of these conceptions, moreover, conforms to their different views of exploitation, for Weber emphasized lesser access to a privileged status position on the part of those lacking formal qualification requirements, whereas Wright pointed to various benefits that accrue to those able to appropriate others' labor efforts by means of organizations. Weber and Wright, furthermore, formulated partially different views on the defining features of the so-called middle classes.

On the one hand, they concurred with the assertion that the possession of marketable skills and credentials-based assets and expertise are sources of privilege connoting a stratum they called *Mittelklassen* (Weber) or "middle classes" (Wright). On the other hand, however, they pointed by this designation to partially distinct social categories. Namely, as for Weber, the middle classes comprehend such people as self-employed farmers, craftsmen, and frequently, public and private officials and the members of the free professions (Weber, 1972, pp. 178–179, 1978, p. 304); as for Wright, middle-class locations characterize managers as well as supervisors and experts. Middle-class locations are, in Wright's words, "contradictory locations and privileged appropriations locations among employees" (Wright, 1997, p. 24). The privilege of middle-class locations obtains because these class locations "designate an asset embodied in the labor power of people which enhances their power in labor markets and labor processes" (Wright, 1997, p. 23).

Briefly stated, for Weber, the middle classes constitute a unitary social class that comprehends a plural number of people and of market-determined classes. Their members share similar mobility opportunities, as is the case of the members of any other social class thus defined. For Wright, middle-classes members are connoted by their contradictory class location, namely, for their being at the same time exploiters and exploited, if exploitation is defined by the appropriation of others' labor efforts. Their respective conceptions of this social category are not incompatible but point to their distinct fundamental concerns. On Weber's part, there was a scholarly concern with the degree of social fluidity or closure in capitalist societies. With regard to Wright, there was, more importantly than a scholarly interest, a commitment to socialism, which he viewed as an alternative social order and which he defined as "democratic power over the allocation and use of productive resources". Alternatively but in an equivalent sense, socialism means for Wright "meaningful democratic control over both State and economy" (Wright, 2010, p. 39).

Socialism would transcend capitalism in such a way that "robustly expands the possibilities for realizing radical democratic egalitarian conceptions of social and political justice requires social empowerment over the economy" (Wright, 2010, p. 367). In socialism thus defined, exploitation as Wright conceived it would be contained or curbed altogether. The road to socialism could be paved by particular activities, which are conducted within the capitalist social and economic order, which Wright calls interstitial, and which introduce into this order elements of a social economy while abstaining from "the political struggle for radical social transformation" (Wright, 2010, p. 326). Instances are – among others – producers' and consumers' cooperatives, workers' factory councils, and equal-exchange organizations (Wright, 2010, Chapter 10).

Symbolic transformation differs from the interstitial one in that it refers to the workers' increasing power as a way to undermine through class struggle "the capacity of capitalists to unilaterally make decisions and control resources of various sorts" (Wright, 2010, p. 345). Wright views symbolic transformation as instrumental to achieve advances "in bottom up social empowerment within a capitalist society" (Wright, 2010, p. 337). By social empowerment, Wright means "direct social participation" by "ordinary people" in the state and in civil society (Wright, 2010, pp. 143, 161). It is considered an "emancipatory project" which instances of social capitalism giving labor some power in the firm management would approximate (Wright, 2010, pp. 213, 229). Positive class compromise between the capitalist and working classes, which would obtain in the course and by means of symbolic transformation, while not detrimental to the interests of the dominant classes, would open the way for a democratic, egalitarian, and socialist society (Wright, 2010, p. 361).

WEBER AND WRIGHT ON EMANCIPATION

As will be here maintained, such differences between these two authors originated from their distinct interpretation of the ultimate value of human emancipation, a value which they shared. Weber and Wright apparently concurred with Kant on the notion and the ideal of human emancipation. As Kant stated at the inception of his celebrated essay on *What Is Enlightenment?* Enlightenment is man's emergence from his self-imposed tutelage. Tutelage is for Kant the inability to use one's own understanding without another's guidance. Weber did not believe that the Enlightenment would still exert influence on people's minds and conducts. As he wrote toward the end of his essay on the *Protestant Ethic and the Spirit of Capitalism* (Weber, 2002), "Even the rosy temperament of asceticism's joyful heir, the Enlightenment, appears finally to be fading" (Weber, 2002, p. 124, 2012, p. 181). Weber was accordingly of the view that "the claims of the Enlightenment for science and human reason were over-pitched" (Whimster & Lash, 1987, p. 10). Nonetheless, Weber showed concern for the jeopardy of the human condition if capitalist and bureaucratic domination prevailed unchecked. The concern accorded with his persuasion that the emancipation from self-imposed tutelage should come from the citizens themselves by the agency of representative political institutions.

He expressed this concern especially in his political writings. As he wrote there, democracy and freedom, which these political institutions are meant to safeguard, "are in fact only possible if they are supported by the permanent, determined will of a nation not to be governed like a flock of sheep" (Weber, 1971, p. 64, 1994, p. 69). Democratic political institutions are based on universal suffrage, for ballots are "the most important although not the only feature of the modern Parliament" (Weber, 1971, p. 264, 1994, p. 101). Universal suffrage gives political representation to the neediest part of the population, namely, to those who require "bread, house and clothing" (Weber, 1971, p. 268) but who cannot afford them. By setting limits to universal suffrage and to democratic parliamentary representation, other forms of political representation would not promote the interests of the most disadvantaged. They would rather be subservient to the interests of a capitalist plutocracy along with those of a bureaucratic authoritarian State; for this, State would fall under the control of the authoritarian officialdom in league with heavy industry (Weber, 1971, p. 349, 1994, p. 1415).

Accordingly, emancipation meant for Weber deliverance from the sources of social oppression that may obtain in a capitalist society. They were, he argued, represented by the upper ranks of the public administration in conjunction with the reactionary interests that prevailed in German capitalism. Weber therefore advocated a political reform that would follow the model of British Parliamentary democracy; as was the case of Britain, but in his judgment not of Germany, a strong Parliament had the legitimacy that was provided by "the proud traditions of peoples which are politically mature and free from cowardice" (Weber, 1971, p. 405, 1994, p. 1461). Domination of powerful social classes and organizations could not be done away with entirely but kept under control by means of effective parliamentary institutions. The capitalist order would not be called into question but brought into agreement with representative democracy, as had been the case in Britain.

Socialism would be no solution, Weber maintained, to the problem of curtailed freedom in modern societies. Socialism "would, in fact, require a still higher degree of bureaucratic organization than capitalism" (Weber, 1971, pp. 322–323, 1978, pp. 1394–1395, see also 1971, p. 517; Gerth & Wright, 2007, pp. 87–88). It would accordingly preserve or even strengthen its authoritarian tendencies. In a speech delivered in 1907 at a meeting of the Verein für Sozialpolitik, Weber pointed to the bureaucratization of the Marxist German Social Democratic Party, which he called "a gigantic bureaucratic machine." He also pointed to the contrast between its radical ideology and its petty bourgeois leadership. Some years later, in *Parliament and Government in a Reconstructed Germany* (1918), Weber contrasted the workers' "unpolitical ethos of proletarian brotherhood and syndicalism" to the Social Democratic Party leaders' willingness to assume government responsibilities (Weber, 1978, pp. 1428–1429).

Accepting these responsibilities would put them in a predicament, for both the trade unions and the Social Democratic Party which would be asked to cooperate with public institutions (Weber, 1971, pp. 390–391). Weber viewed with favor the participation of the representatives of socialist parties or unions in administrative functions. In fact, in 1918, he declared himself very close to the "economically educated" members of the Social Democratic Party (Weber, 1971, p. 484). Still, he objected to its ideological and political seclusion and welcomed its participation in public and civic affairs. With reference to the experience of the socialist administration in the Sicilian city of Catania but also to similar cases in Germany, he maintained that these administrations might differ in their goals; however, the quality of the services which they provide to their constituencies does not vary in accordance with their value orientations (Weber, 1924, pp. 407–412). In other words, bureaucratic organizations are in his view inherently authoritarian irrespective of their ideologies and the social actors enacting roles in them, but the effectiveness of their performances is not thereby affected.

For Weber, as well as for Wright (Wright, 2010, pp. 81–85), bureaucratic organizations are inherently authoritarian and therefore set constrains on democracy. This agreement between the two authors has distinct origins, however. Weber's critical assessment of a capitalist society stemmed from his liberal values rather than from reservations on its viability. Wright concurred with Weber that socialism would involve bureaucratic domination so long, however, as reference is made to a version of socialism he called "statism." He meant thereby the authoritarian state domination when it is exerted over civil society (Wright, 2010, pp. 131–134). Wright emphasized, we recall, the importance of deep-rooted democratic practices – such as trade unions and civil associations – in civil society; for they preserve and consolidate democracy itself. "A deep democracy," he wrote, "is one in which the State is both controlled by the people and serve their interests" (Wright, 2010, p. 180).

This emphasis on deep democracy is consonant with Weber's vision and ideal of democracy and in particular with his aspiration to a civil and political society such as the British, since Britain provided his model of a well-functioning parliamentary democracy. In such a society, citizens – far from resembling a flock of sheep – would be active participants in associations such as unions, and in political life at the local and central level. Social empowerment was a value which both Weber and Wright cherished and shared. They also concurred in rejecting both "ruptural transformation" (Wright) and "revolution" (Weber). For ruptural transformation would be for Wright "more likely to involve some form of authoritarian statism" than a "radical democratic form of social empowerment" (Wright, 2010, p. 318); while a revolution would be for Weber "a serious misfortune" (*ein schweres* Unglück) since it would deliver Germany to foreign economic and military domination (Weber, 1971, pp. 484–485).

Accordingly, their aversion to social commotions stemmed from different reasons. Weber was concerned lest social and political freedoms would be thereby curtailed; whereas Wright foreshadowed its authoritarian and anti-democratic consequences that would hinder capitalist transformation into socialism. The two authors' different stance originated – it is here maintained – from their distinct interpretations of the Kantian value of emancipation from tutelage; as emancipation meant for Weber freedom from social and political oppression in general, while for Wright, it meant in a more specific sense freedom from capitalist oppression. Their divergent interpretations of this common value were in line with their, respectively, liberal and socialist persuasions. The following section will expand on this point.

WRIGHT'S SELECTIVE INTERPRETATION OF WEBER: A REASSESSMENT

By way of recapitulation, Wright concurred with Weber on the following items: (a) production-based definition of classes and (b) The social and economic relevance of ascribed status inequalities. However, he argued that the theoretical position on classes of Marxism in general, and his own in particular, differed from Weber's in these respects: (a) For Marx, classes are found in more than one historically contingent social formations; for Weber – according to Wright's interpretation – there are classes only in capitalism; (b) Weber neglected to consider the role of status groups in the exploitation process; (c) Weber analyzed the labor market from a neoclassical economic viewpoint and emphasized its formal rationality, rather than paying attention to its substantive irrationality; (d) Weber neglected to consider classes in nonmarket societies and did not investigate the relation between production and exchange; (e) Weber's focus on market transactions made him disregard the exploitation of labor in the production process.

With reference to these critical remarks, it has been here argued as follows: (a) Weber took repeated notice in his work *General Economic History* of the exploitation of labor in the production process; (b) For Weber, status groups and political parties are not determined by market exchanges; (c) Weber, like Wright, made frequent use of the notion of exploitation. However, differently than Wright, for Weber, this notion referred to the social closure of mobility opportunities rather than to the appropriation of surplus labor; (d) for Weber, therefore, exploitation is present in capitalism but is not its distinctive trait. As regards Wright's theses on Weber's neglect to pay sufficient consideration to exploitation in his class analysis, these three points would challenge all of them. At this juncture, one may wonder what textual basis Wright possessed in making his critical assessments on Weber's class analysis, and in particular in claiming that the theme of exploitation made there but a shadowy presence.

To the extent that Wright indicated the sources of his Weberian references in discussing the notion of exploitation, for he did not always do so (Wright, 1985, pp. 106–108, 300), Wright referred chiefly to Weber's essay on the *Protestant Ethic and the Spirit of Capitalism*, and to *Economy and Society* (Wright, 2002). He did quote Weber's *General Economic History*, referring to the coercion which workers, and all those without substantial property, must experience on the part of their employers under conditions of a market economy because they need a wage to cover their basic needs (Weber, 1958, p. 241). However, Wright neglected to consider a few other passages of Weber's *General Economic History* that had been previously quoted in this chapter. These passages might have prompted him a different interpretation of Weber's writings insofar as the subject of the exploitation of labor in the production process is concerned. One may wonder why Wright made such uneven references.

There can be no certainty in this regard, to be sure. Wright's selective interpretation of Weber could hardly be the consequence of any ideological or theoretical biases on his part that would make studying exploitation outside of the production process irrelevant. For Wright investigated how symbolic transformation, and therefore a lesser amount of exploitation, could be achieved in all "the arenas of power in society – the state, the economy, civil society" (Wright, 2010, p. 370). However, an indication that would account for his highly selective use of the Weberian textual sources may come from these two authors' different understanding of emancipation, a value both held and cherished. Emancipation, we recall, meant for Wright deliverance from capitalist oppression as epitomized by the exploitation of labor, so that people would cover their needs and thus be able to enjoy a flourishing life in a socialist society. It meant for Weber, in a more general sense, freedom from all social and political oppression so that all citizens would be enabled to actively participate in their political institutions.

Wright's selective interpretation of Weber flowed from their distinct interpretations of this common value. Exploitation is for Weber not just the appropriation of surplus labor, but it rather means in a broader sense any benefit, whether pursued or not, that accrues from the closure of mobility opportunities. Wright's radical proposal to do away finally with exploitation pursued the transformation of the capitalist mode of production into a socialist one. Weber's proposal, which was entirely consonant with his liberalism, did not aim at eliminating exploitation altogether, for he deemed this an impossibility. Rather, it aimed at containing and curtailing it by means of political reforms pursuant to the British model of parliamentary democracy. These reforms, he hoped, would be conducive to a greater access to higher positions in political and civil society on the part of the less privileged citizens.

SUMMARY AND CONCLUSION

This chapter has compared Erik Olin Wright's and Max Weber's notions of exploitation. To this end, it has: (1) briefly dwelt on the usage of this term on the part of some prominent contemporary sociologists, (2) reconstructed Wright's and Weber's class theories, (3) lingered on Wright's reception of Weber, and finally, (4) considered their respective notions of exploitation. This concept was denoted distinctively to the effect that Wright laid stress on the exploitation of the labor force and defined it in Marxist terms. For Weber, by contrast, exploitation meant obtaining benefits from a privileged position in a hierarchy of social classes as Weber conceived them in terms of common mobility opportunities on the part of his members. These different definitions stemmed, it has been argued, from Wright's and Weber's distinct understanding of emancipation as, respectively, deliverance from either class or social and political oppression. Wright's reading of Weber, insofar as exploitation is concerned, leaves out of consideration those passages of Weber's works in which this term is used, albeit in his own peculiar and broader sense. This chapter has underlined the importance of Wright's and Weber's value orientations, respectively socialist and liberal, for their formulation of this notion and for the object of their interest. There was no shadow of exploitation in Weber's class analysis; rather, he understood and used this term in a broader sense than Wright.

REFERENCES

Bendix, R. (1989). *Embattled reason. Essays on social knowledge* (Vol. 2). Transaction Publishers.
Bourdieu, P. (1984). *Distinction*. Routledge and Kegan Paul.
Bourdieu, P. (1985). The social space and the genesis of groups. *Theory and Society, 14*, 723–744.

Bourdieu, P. (1987). What makes a social class? On the theoretical and practical existence of groups. *Berkeley Journal of Sociology, 32,* 1–17.
Braverman, H. (1974). *Labor and monopoly capital.* Monthly Review Press.
Breen, R. (2005)Foundations of a neo-Weberian class analysis. In E. O. Wright (Ed.), *Approaches to class analysis* (pp. 31–50). Cambridge University Press.
Gerth, H., & Wright, M. C. (Eds.). (2007). *From Max Weber.* Routledge.
Giddens, A. (1971). *Capitalism and modern social theory.* Cambridge University Press.
Giddens, A. (1973). *The class structure of the advanced societies.* Harper & Row.
Kant, I. (1992). *An answer to the question: What is enlightenment?* Hackett Publishing Company. Originally published in 1784.
Mackenzie, G. (1982). Class boundaries and the labour process. In G. Anthony & G. Mackenzie (Eds.), *Social class and the division of labour* (pp. 63–86). Cambridge University Press.
Murphy, R. (1988). *Social closure. The theory of monopolization and exclusion.* Clarendon Press.
Ossowski, S. (1963). *Class structure in the social consciousness.* The Free Press of Glencoe.
Parkin, F. (1979). *Marxism and class theory. A Bourgeois critique.* Columbia University Press.
Poulantzas, N. (1975). *Political power and social classes.* New Left Review.
Weber, M. (1924). *Gesammelte Aufsätze zur Soziologie und Sozialpolitik.* Mohr.
Weber, M. (1927). *General economic history.* Greenberg.
Weber, M. (1958). *Wirtschaftsgeschichte.* Duncker & Humblot.
Weber, M. (1971). *Gesammelte Politische Schriften.* Mohr.
Weber, M. (1972). *Wirtschaft und Gesellschaft.* Mohr.
Weber, M. (1978). *Economy and society.* University of California Press.
Weber, M. (1994). *Political writings.* Cambridge University Press.
Weber, M. (2002). *The protestant ethic and the spirit of capitalism.* Roxbury.
Weber, M. (2012). *Religion und Gesellschaft. Gesammelte Aufsätze zur Religionssoziologie.* Wissenschaftliche Buchgesellschaft.
Western, M., & Wright, E. O. (1994). The permeability of class boundaries to intergenerational mobility among men in the United States, Canada, Norway and Sweden. *American Sociological Review, 59*(4), 606–629.
Whimster, S., & Lash, S. (Eds.). (1987). *Max Weber, Rationality and modernity.* Routledge.
Wright, E. O. (1976). Class boundaries in advanced capitalist societies. *New Left Review, 98,* 1–41.
Wright, E. O. (1980). Class and occupation. *Theory and Society, 9*(1), 177–214.
Wright, E. O. (1985). *Classes.* Verso.
Wright, E. O. (1997). *Class counts. Comparative studies in class analysis.* Cambridge University Press.
Wright, E. O. (2002). The shadow of exploitation in Weber's class analysis. *American Sociological Review, 67,* 832–853.
Wright, E. O. (2005a). Foundations of Neo-marxist class analysis. In W. E. Olin (Ed.), *Approaches to class analysis* (pp. 4–30). Cambridge University Press.
Wright, E. O. (2005b). Conclusion. If class is the answer, what is the question?. In E. O. Wright (Ed.), *Approaches to class analysis* (pp. 180–192). Cambridge University Press.
Wright, E. O. (2005c). Social class. In G. Ritzer (Ed.), *Encyclopedia of social theory* (pp. 717–723). Sage.
Wright, E. O. (2010). *Envisioning real utopias.* Verso.
Wright, E. O. (2015). *Understanding class.* Verso.
Wright, E. O., & Cho, D. (1992). The relative permeability of class boundaries to cross-class friendships: A comparative study of the United States, Canada, Sweden, and Norway. *American Sociological Review, 57*(1), 85–102.

A LOST HORIZON: REVISITING "THE SOCIETAL RATIONALIZATION OF THE ECONOMY" (TRANSLATOR'S INTRODUCTION)

Anthony J. Knowles

University of Tennessee – Knoxville, USA

ABSTRACT

This short essay situates The Societal Rationalization of the Economy: Guaranteed Minimum Income as a Constitutional Right *by Harry F. Dahms, published in 1992 (and included in this volume), in its historical context in Germany shortly after the unification of the Federal Republic of Germany (West Germany) and the German Democratic Republic (East Germany). The challenge of implementing a guaranteed minimum income served as an anchor for discussing a unique opportunity to create greater consonance between the quality and effectiveness of social policies and claims about how the latter were supposed to support democratic citizenship and equality. The essay provides a brief summary of Dahms' chapter, his take on the idea of a guaranteed minimum income, and the concept of the societal rationalization of the economy between socialism and neoliberalism.*

Keywords: Social policy; Germany; neoliberalism; G. W. F. Hegel; Eduard Heimann; Ralf Dahrendorf; Claus Offe; Jürgen Habermas

Appearing a few months after the fall of the Soviet Union, with Germany in the process of social, political, cultural, and especially economic reunification, "The Societal Rationalization of the Economy" by Harry F. Dahms attempted to deliver a crucial message amid a clear turning point not just for Germany but for all modern capitalist societies. On the one hand, what would be retroactively understood as the neoliberal turn – first started by the Reagan administration and Thatcher's premiership of the 1980s – had already shifted economic policy and popular ideology in the United States and Great Britain, generating ripple effects across the industrialized world. On the other hand, the collapse of the Soviet Union and its satellites meant that the longtime geopolitical and ideological rival of the capitalist West appeared to be vanquished once and for all. While proclamations of the "end of history" in the early 1990s (Fukuyama, 1992) may have made it seem as if discussions of capitalism and its possible alternatives had ended, at least for the foreseeable future, in reality, there was much discussion still to be had regarding the direction "triumphant" capitalism should take at a time when market capitalism prevailed in most of the world (e.g., Albert, 1993). Despite the de facto consensus that neoliberalism is still largely the dominant ideological and political paradigm today, we should not make this historical development retrospectively understood as a foregone conclusion. Indeed, "The Societal Rationalization of the Economy" and the – primarily German – literature it interfaced demonstrate that discussions over potential new directions and alternatives to "actually existing" capitalism were alive and well. Instead of the "end of history," Dahms and his contemporaries saw emergent possibilities to ameliorate poverty and push western industrialized societies in a more egalitarian direction, even if the tumult of the reunification process generated uncertainty for many Germans. Dahms contributed to this discussion through his analysis of the concept of the *guaranteed minimum income* – more commonly known as universal basic income (UBI) today – particularly in terms of justifying its constitutional and socio-legal viability. The article first appeared as the lead article of an issue of the German journal, *Soziale Welt*, in 1992, during the time when Ulrich Beck was editor.

To start, Dahms draws upon little known passages of pre-eminent continental philosopher G. W. F. Hegel's *Philosophy of Right* (1821/1958) to uncover insights regarding Hegel's understanding of poverty, social inequality, and property, as well as his justification of what would come to be known as the "welfare state." Dahms describes how Hegel wrestles with the problem of poverty in *bürgerliche Gesellschaft*, the hybrid of civil as well as bourgeois society, and how the responsibility of the modern state ought to go beyond reliance on individual charity or exhortations of personal responsibility. These intriguing propositions remain incomplete, however, leaving later scholars and theorists to pick up these lost threads. The failure to appreciate Hegel's insights here might be due to his work being commonly understood as philosophy rather than – or simultaneously – as social theory or sociology. Although Hegel's work heavily inspired the canon of one of the most important social theorists, Karl Marx, the critic of *bourgeois* society who was less concerned with its *civil* dimension (i.e., emphasizing capital, production, and economic classes over law, rights, and citizenship), mainstream considerations of Hegel, to the extent he is considered at all, typically treat him implicitly as pre-sociological. Nevertheless, Dahms takes Hegel's insights as a serious contribution that grapples with the problems of poverty, inequality, and the "welfare state" in modern society.

Dahms next identifies Eduard Heimann (1889–1967) as the theorist who appears to best continue Hegel's thought as formulated in his "theory of social policy" (1929/1980). Here, Heimann – a German Jewish economist who emigrated to the United States in 1933 and counted among the "reform economists" of the New School for Social Research – envisages the implementation of a robust program of social policy via "radical reforms" that provides strong social protections from the vicissitudes of economic change without endangering the dynamics and productive powers of modern industrial economies, ultimately resulting in a "social order of freedom" (Heimann, 1929/1980, p. 158ff). Heimann is less well known in the Anglosphere than similar German Jewish emigrés such as Theodor W. Adorno, Max Horkheimer, and Herbert Marcuse of Frankfurt School fame, but his core message of how carefully crafted social policy with an eye toward enhancing social freedom could powerfully shape the direction of capitalism was certainly pertinent after the fall of the socialist alternative and remains so today.

Following the discussion of Heimann, Dahms describes the patterns of economic inequality emerging toward the end of the 1980s – that would only continue to grow well into the present (see Piketty, 2014). From this background, discussions surrounding the guaranteed minimum income – primarily involving major German social theorists such as Ralf Dahrendorf, Claus Offe, and Jürgen Habermas – are raised to make the case for guaranteed minimum income as a crucial component of a comprehensive social policy program that can best be understood as a *constitutional entitlement* or, in a phrase more palatable in the American context, a *constitutional right*.[1] Ralf Dahrendorf, who had a storied career as a sociologist, politician, and university administrator, was Dahms' mentor when he was a student at the University of Konstanz. Claus Offe is a German sociologist and founding member of the Basic Income Earth Network who, in agreement with Dahrendorf, frames the guaranteed minimum income as a policy capable of ameliorating the legitimacy problems, or problems of the social contract, that emerge when social inequalities continuously expand, as they from the 1980s up through the present. During one of his regular stays as a visiting professor at the New School for Social Research in New York, Claus Offe was one of Dahms' professors, where the latter pursued his dissertation on Schumpeter's theory of entrepreneurship and wrote the first draft of this article for a seminar Offe taught at the time. Relatedly, Jürgen Habermas' theory of communicative action, spelled out by the leading Critical Theorist of the "second generation" of the Frankfurt School, is presented as a sophisticated theoretical framework in whose context the implications of the effects of a guaranteed minimum income for the relationship between the state, economy, and society can be understood, although Habermas would not refer to it explicitly until a few years later. Though Dahms does not reference this aspect of Habermas' theory explicitly in his article, the notion that a guaranteed minimum income would be a policy innovation intended to *counteract* the colonization of the lifeworld by the system is both implied and entirely consonant with Dahms' argument and analysis, as radical reforms directed at *decolonization*.[2] Finally, Dahms concludes by explaining how the implementation of a guaranteed minimum income can be framed as a step in the "societal rationalization of the economy." In other words, "the shift from 'capitalist' to 'post-capitalist' society" (p. 177) is contingent on "theoretically and practically ... [reassessing] *the status of the capitalist economic system within a society whose political and social legitimacy is based primarily on the objective of actualizing a genuine democracy that warrants the designation at the societal level"* (pp. 176–177 below; emphasis in original).

As this outline should make clear, "The Societal Rationalization of the Economy: Guaranteed Minimum Income as a Constitutional Right," primarily a contribution to social theory, is not first and foremost *about* the guaranteed minimum income. Rather, it is about whether and how the guaranteed minimum income would be compatible with a comprehensive social-policy regime aimed toward the progressive societal rationalization of the economy. This message was delivered at a critical moment when possibilities for *radical reforms* appeared to exist (e.g., how to reunify Germany successfully, or what direction the capitalist West should go in now that the Cold War purportedly had ended). Yet, such a theoretical framework is perhaps more important now, even and especially after decades of neoliberal hegemony. Indeed, perhaps Dahms' concept of the *societal rationalization of the economy* should be paired and analyzed in tandem with its "mirror darkly," an *economic rationalization of society* that appears to have occurred over the last half century. Evidence of an "economic rationalization of society" abounds and has been treated thoroughly elsewhere, typically under the heading of neoliberalism (e.g., Blyth, 2015; Brown, 2015, 2019; Crouch, 2011; Harvey, 2005). Though neoliberalism certainly fits the criterion of a manifestation of the "economic rationalization of society," both concepts have purchase at a higher level of theoretical abstraction, describing how social systems, institutions, and individuals come to orient themselves toward "social" or "economic" ends. Perhaps the twin concepts of societal rationalization of the economy and economic rationalization of society would prove to be a useful theoretical framework for diagnosing and analyzing society as well as orienting efforts for social change. Indeed, Dahms would further address these topics and their relation to basic income in his later work (see, Dahms, 1995, 1998, 2005, 2006, 2015). Throughout, Dahms makes the case that these concepts contribute theoretical and analytical value both within and beyond the debate and advocacy for a guaranteed minimum income.

This article is of interest to advocates and scholars of Universal Basic Income (UBI) particularly in the way it traces the intellectual foundations and debates for UBI within the German context. Anglo-American writers tracing the intellectual history of UBI frequently cite historical figures and programs such as Thomas Paine, the Speenhamland policy in Britain, Milton Friedman's negative income tax (Friedman, 2002/2002), or the failed attempt to pass a UBI under the Nixon Administration (Bregman, 2017; Livingston, 2016). "The Societal Rationalization of the Economy," meanwhile, though not merely or primarily an intellectual history, nevertheless details a distinctly German tradition of thought on UBI, that runs through Hegel, Heimann, Dahrendorf, Offe, and up to Habermas and contemporary critical theorists. The commonality among this group, however, is not different permutations of UBI as a policy, but the framework of social policy and the common understanding of the responsibility that modern civil society has to its members. It is only within this broader context, these

German scholars implicitly claim, that UBI can succeed. This characteristically German way of conceptualizing the relationship between social policy, social responsibility, and social theory could be a useful contribution to the discussion surrounding social policy and UBI in the English-speaking world. In this way, "The Societal Rationalization of the Economy" is valuable as an intellectual history, a framework that offers sophisticated theoretical concepts, and as an argument that captures the spirit of a major turning point in history. It also serves as an example of the kind of mindset necessary to constructively think through the social, economic, and political problems of the present.[3]

NOTES

1. Although the concept of government entitlements has become toxic in American discourse thanks to decades of neoliberal "personal responsibility" ideology (see, Brown, 2015), the concept of entitlements still largely holds legitimacy in the German context. In this translation, the term *rights* and *entitlements* are used interchangeably to best grasp how the guaranteed minimum income is being conceptualized in this debate, with the concept of rights having a comparatively amenable acceptance in American political discourse.

2. "Everyday consciousness sees itself thrown back on traditions whose claims to validity have already been suspended; where it does escape the spell of traditionalism, it is hopelessly splintered. In place of 'false consciousness' we today have a 'fragmented consciousness' that blocks enlightenment by the mechanism of reification. It is only with this that the conditions for a *colonization of the lifeworld* are met. When stripped of their ideological veils, the imperatives of autonomous subsystems make their way into the lifeworld from the outside – like colonial masters coming into a tribal society – and force a process of assimilation upon it. The diffused perspectives of their local culture cannot be sufficiently coordinated to permit the play of the metropolis and the world market to be grasped from the periphery" (Habermas, 1981/1987, p. 355).

3. I am indebted to Harry F. Dahms for the opportunity to translate his manuscript as well as the many suggestions, clarifications, and corrections he made to the final product. I would also like to thank Adrian Del Caro for his crucial support in fostering my translation skills and his many helpful comments.

REFERENCES

Albert, M. (1993). *Capitalism against capitalism*. Whurr Publishers.
Blyth, M. (2015). *Austerity: The history of a dangerous idea*. Oxford University Press.
Bregman, R. (2017). *Utopia for realists*. Back Bay Books.
Brown, W. (2015). *Undoing the demos: Neoliberalism's stealth revolution*. Zone Books.
Brown, W. (2019). *In the Ruins of Neoliberalism: The rise of antidemocratic politics in the west*. Columbia University Press.
Crouch, C. (2011). *The strange non-death of neoliberalism*. Polity Press.
Dahms, H. F. (1995). From creative action to the social rationalization of the economy: Joseph A. Schumpeter's social theory. *Sociological Theory*, *13*, 1–13.
Dahms, H. F. (1998). Beyond the carousel of reification: Critical social theory after Lukács, Adorno and Habermas. *Current Perspectives in Social Theory*, *18*, 3–62.
Dahms, H. F. (2005). Globalization or hyper-alienation? Critiques of traditional marxism as arguments for basic income. *Current Perspectives in Social Theory*, *23*, 205–276.
Dahms, H. F. (2006). Capitalism unbound? Peril and promise of basic income. *Basic Income Studies*, *1*, 1–7.
Dahms, H. F. (2015). Which capital, which Marx? Basic income between mainstream economics, critical theory, and the logic of capital. *Basic Income Studies*, *10*(1), 115–140.

Friedman, M. (2002). *Capitalism and freedom*. University of Chicago Press. (Original work published 1962).
Fukuyama, F. (1992). *The end of history and the last man*. Free Press.
Harvey, D. (2005). *A brief history of neoliberalism*. Oxford University Press.
Hegel, G. W. F. (1958). *Hegel's philosophy of right* (T. M. Knox, Trans.). Clarendon Press. (Original work published 1821).
Heimann, E. (1980). *Soziale Theorie des Kapitalismus*. Suhrkamp. (Original work published 1929).
Livingston, J. (2016). *No more work: Why full employment is a bad idea*. University of North Carolina Press.
Piketty, T. (2014). *Capital in the twenty-first century*. Harvard University Press.

THE SOCIETAL RATIONALIZATION OF THE ECONOMY: GUARANTEED MINIMUM INCOME AS A CONSTITUTIONAL RIGHT

Harry F. Dahms

University of Tennessee – Knoxville, USA

Translated by Anthony J. Knowles

ABSTRACT

The guaranteed minimum income is an idea that is consonant with a social-theoretical tradition which can be traced from G. W. F. Hegel via Eduard Heimann to contemporary social thinkers like Jürgen Habermas and beyond. It is the cornerstone of an expansive theory of social policy expressive of the changes in the relationship between economy and society over the long-term, which I am referring to here as the societal rationalization of the economy. By starting with Hegel's remarks on poverty in The Philosophy of Right (1821/1958), *the stage is set to examine the guaranteed minimum income as a policy project with strong constitutional implications. Like Hegel, Eduard Heimann did not address the idea of the guaranteed minimum income directly; yet, his arguably most important work,* Social Theory of Capitalism: Theory of Social Policy *(1929/1980), provides an excellent frame of reference for appreciating how the guaranteed minimum income exemplifies a radically reformist project of social policy that is pointing beyond inherently regressive social structures. In the writings of Ralf Dahrendorf and Claus Offe, a theory of social policy that treats the guaranteed minimum income as a constitutional right takes shape. This chapter concludes with an attempt at delineating how a guaranteed minimum income should aspire to be one important step toward the societal rationalization of the economy.*

Keywords: Universal basic income; G. W. F. Hegel; Eduard Heimann; Ralf Dahrendorf; Claus Offe; Jürgen Habermas

INTRODUCTION TO THE TRANSLATION (2024)

In its original form, this chapter was published in German (as the lead article in an issue of the journal, *Soziale Welt*; Dahms, 1992a). I have updated slightly the present version to emphasize the continuing relevance of social-theoretical insights put forth by purportedly abstract thinkers like G. W. F. Hegel and Jürgen Habermas, and more policy-oriented theorists like Eduard Heimann, Ralf Dahrendorf, and Claus Offe.[1] Their contributions have a lasting bearing on how the idea of a guaranteed minimum income (or in current terminology, universal basic income) exemplifies and illustrates a type of policy strategy intended to ground social and welfare policies in a manner that points beyond the status quo and transcends it in practice. Theoretically informed and oriented perspectives on practical policies are especially notable when the latter are designed to enable modern societies to tackle persistent problems and proliferating predicaments via socially rational approaches, to enhance their capacity to reinforce the framework of democratic institutions and processes, their legitimacy, and public support. To be sure, nothing is simple and straightforward in social, political, cultural, and economic affairs. The consequences resulting from the establishment of an ambitious guaranteed minimum income predictably would create a force field of intended and unintended consequences whose medium and long-term implications will be unpredictable, with unintended consequences likely outweighing intended effects, at least initially. In fact, once in existence, studying the effects of an ambitious guaranteed minimum income will reveal how much more research will be required to devise successful policies in terms of stated goals whose attainment is not merely momentary but characterized by staying power – even if citizens and politicians would want it to succeed, which often is not the case. For the time being, the existing public policy apparatus in modern societies is much more likely to work from implicit, more or less outdated assumptions, and with objectives in mind that are likely to perpetuate and replicate existing social, political, and economic structures, rather than critically reflecting on and transforming them. The increasingly effective populist practice of fostering, promoting, and relying on the more regressive instincts and inclinations among both humans and within institutions and organizations are prone to amplifying such implicit assumptions – and consistent with objectives that are inversely related to transcending a status quo whose problematic character is much more obvious today than it was three decades ago. Populist approaches to policy typically subvert and thwart rational and progressive consonance between stated goals and attained outcomes that go beyond the interests and privileges of specific segments of a given population. The evidence would suggest that the decline of this type of consonance is one of the defining features of politics and policy in the 21st century to date, with the gulf between stated goals and realized outcomes widening precipitously. Rising inequality, proliferating precariousness, intensifying climate change, and burgeoning willingness to rely on military conflicts to pacify or manage domestic populations and problems are just a few of the many examples that demonstrate the socially, politically, and economically constructed – and increasingly engineered – public policy failures.

In many ways, this journal article anticipated many of the challenges we are facing today, in terms of public policies in general, of social policies, and a kind of politics whose inability to tackle proliferating problems is undeniable (e.g., Chamayou, 2018/2021; Harvey, 2007). Most importantly, though, when this paper was completed, the horizon of the future appeared to be open, with the *societal rationalization of the economy*, as delineated below, representing a spectrum of opportunities to increase the convergence between the actuality of modern societies and their pronounced and regularly reiterated self-descriptions – how their members ought to perceive them. Yet, at the time, the foundations already had been well-established for a strengthening countermovement: the *economic rationalization of society*. In many regards and for decades, what social scientists have been observing, and countless humans have been experiencing, are consistent and determined efforts to subvert and hollow out "society," both as *modern* societies and as *democratic* societies. From this angle, this chapter might serve as a foil for remembering what "social policy" could have come to mean, with what kinds of consequences, for discerning the normalization of efforts to erode democracy, and for imagining what could and should have been, and where we might be today as a result.

INTRODUCTION (1992)

In light of the present economic, political, and social situation in the eastern part of Germany and its consequences for the "capitalist"western part, the future of social policy programs and projects in this country once again has become uncertain.[2] In the "recent pasts" of the two parts of Germany, problems of poverty and social inequality had lost some of their importance. Predictably, the consequences resulting from reunification will effect citizens of the former German Democratic Republic (GDR) – and to a lesser extent those of the Federal Republic of Germany (FRG) also – in different ways, and put these problems in modified form back on the political agenda (see Plum, 1990). Furthermore, the main consequence of the accelerating disintegration of communist social systems in Eastern Europe means that the foil for addressing poverty and social inequality, at least in practical regards, in categories of class antagonism, no longer exists: the horizon of the future opens and calls for new answers to social problems for which we have not yet found a satisfactory solution.

In this context, the purpose of this chapter is to discuss a topic that has met increasing interest in recent years, not only in the Federal Republic but also in other industrially developed Western societies: the *guaranteed minimum income*. However, the goal here is not to view the introduction of a guaranteed minimum income, no matter how high it may be set, as a definitive and reliable solution to the most fundamental social problems. After all, because of the economic consequences resulting from such an innovation in the present situation, it is difficult to estimate the reach of such a measure, and because a corresponding social contract consonant with and in support of such an innovation for now only exists in broad outline. A clear step in this direction potentially might have been successful under conditions of the more stable old Federal Republic that ended in 1990. After the incorporation of the five East German states, however, maintaining *business as usual* has become doubtful in many respects. If, furthermore, the imminent influx of people in the coming years from Eastern European countries and the republics of the former Soviet Union – as recently dramatically reported in *Der Spiegel* – is taken into account, then it would appear that the sociopolitically stable situation that experiments like the introduction of a guaranteed minimum income require may be irretrievably lost.[3] Therefore, the alternative attempt to draw conclusions for the further programmatic development of the guaranteed minimum income from the events of the past 2 years would currently make little sense. Instead, I will address this program, with a view beyond the current situation both into the past as well as into the perhaps not so distant future, because it promises to provide an answer to the question of the further development of the social welfare state and, accompanying with it, capitalism. My attempt at such an interpretation will draw on the sociopolitical implications that derive from the program of the guaranteed minimum income and point toward a newly developing relationship between economy, state, and society. In proceeding accordingly, I will be concerned with the constitutional and socio-legal aspect of this program, without the following being able or meant to aspire to legal standards.

The first section of this chapter draws attention to a widely neglected aspect of Hegel's *Philosophy of Right* that involves a surprising theoretical contribution, with implications for the justification of a guaranteed minimum income. The next section focuses on Eduard Heimann's attempt in the late 1920s to formulate a "theory of social policy," which may constitute the only effort at solving the strained relationship between equality and freedom in a manner that is inspired by Hegel's approach to the problem of poverty and social inequality. Skipping to the present, the third section provides a sketch of changes in poverty and the question of inequality in the most developed societies toward the end of the 1980s. The fourth section compares two attempts at constitutionally grounding a guaranteed minimum income in ways that neither Hegel nor Heimann were in the position to anticipate and approach conceptually. The concluding section endeavors to forge a theoretical link from Hegel and Heimann, via the present, into the future, along the lines of the "societal rationalization of the economy."

POVERTY IN CIVIL SOCIETY, OR: ON THE RELEVANCE OF A NEGLECTED ASPECT OF HEGEL'S *PHILOSOPHY OF RIGHT*

In his *Philosophy of Right*, Hegel (1821/1958) commented on a subject whose treatment subsequently almost entirely became the domain of his successor Karl Marx and the analytical and theoretical tradition he inaugurated, in terms of the antagonism of economic classes. In the section about property, in the appendix to § 49, Hegel commented on the problem of *social* inequality and the possibility of its abolition as follows:

> The equality which might be set up, e.g. in connexion with the distribution of goods, would all the same soon be destroyed again, because wealth depends on diligence. But if a project cannot be executed, it ought not to be executed. Of course men [*Menschen*, i.e., "humans"] are equal, but only *qua* persons, that is, with respect only to the source from which possession springs; *the inference from this is that everyone must have property. Hence, if you wish to talk of equality, it is this equality which you must have in view.* But this equality is something apart from the *fixing of particular amounts, from the question of how much I own. From this point of view it is false to maintain that justice requires everyone's property to be equal, since it requires only that everyone shall own property.* The truth is that particularity is just the sphere where there is room for inequality and where equality would be wrong. True enough, men often lust after the goods of others, but that is just doing wrong, since right is that which remains indifferent to particularity.[4]

The distinction between "humans" and "persons" therefore is significant because "humans" denotes individual subjects in the complexity of their identity as well as their relationship to the environment, the synthesis of generality and particularity in the freedom of particularity, while "persons" only characterizes the general aspect in the subject, i.e., the human being as *legal, social,* or *political* person. In the *Philosophy of Right*, Hegel apprehends the problem of social inequality within this coordinate system, with "human" and "person" as axes. While social equality could be enforced by political means, this would turn into injustice – not only because the equality attained cannot be maintained in the long run, but above all because the corresponding treatment would transform subjects into *objects*. At least partially, social inequality is a *function of individual distinctness*; it also constitutes the precondition for both individuality and subjectivity, while material equality created by force would degrade individuals into objects of state regulation, thus depriving them of their subjectivity in one fundamental regard. Humans would become "persons" and the potential multiplicity of their "essence" the item (*Gegenstand*) of external objectification. The formal equality which is the precondition for the membership of persons in a political community (*Gemeinwesen*) would, if applied to the economic realm, be driven so far that their existence as "person," which is an existence as "second nature," would become their "first" nature.

To be sure, for Hegel, this does not result in a short circuit: rather than allowing social inequality as the product of historical development to persist, it must be tackled *on a different* level. *It is not equal property that matters, but rather the presence of property*: "the inference from this is that everyone must have property.... [J]ustice ... requires only that everyone shall own property" (Hegel, 1821/1958, p. 237). All persons are equal insofar as they have the "right" to own property, but this *formal* equality as the right to concrete property does not require the *substantive* equality of the *extent of property*. However, these categories – formal and substantive – attain validity as soon as we apply them to law itself. It is not enough to guarantee all citizens a formal right to property, but rather what is necessary is a *substantive* right to property. Property thus does not only appear merely as a possibility in principle but as a category characterized by a substance, a *minimum level* of property. Only someone who in fact is able to dispose over a certain minimum amount of property can be a full member of civil society.

In the section "Police", Hegel (1821/1958, p. 146) expands further on this idea and its social implications. For Hegel, the meaning of "police" goes far beyond today's common usage. It is not only incumbent upon the police and its responsibility to maintain public safety and to enforce law and order in instances of breaches of the law in general, but also as far as *social* breaches of the law are concerned, i.e., when society commits offenses against the material security of single or several of its members. In fact, "police" denotes the entire anonymous apparatus of the state's administrative and executive system. What is today often pejoratively is denounced as "welfare state" therefore belongs to the area of responsibility of the "police," an area which, however, is not unambiguously delineated: "These details are determined by custom, the spirit of the rest of the constitution, contemporary conditions, the crisis of the hour, and so forth" (§ 234, p. 146). The responsibility of the "police" as guardian and protector of social order consequently cannot be determined once and for all: the concrete content of what is understood today as social policy is determined in every era from the specific social, political, and economic situation.[5]

In Hegel's *Philosophy of Right*, the dialectical relationship of the particular and the general and of rights and duties – both of the community toward the individual and of the individual toward the community – manifests as follows: civil society has to ensure the "subsistence" of its members, but it also can urge them to provide subsistence for themselves as far as they are able to do so (addition to § 240, p. 277). However: "It is not simply starvation which is at issue; the further end in view is to prevent the formation of a pauperized rabble" (p. 277). In civil society, "public authority" takes over the place that the family formerly had held (§ 241). While the state cannot entirely satisfy subjectively necessary aid, the latter also requires "regard for the special circumstances as those of disposition and love" (§ 242, p. 149), i.e., the support of the sphere of *morality* or, as one would say today, of philanthropy, foundations, or other nonstate organizations. Yet,

> Subjective aid, however, both in itself and in its operation, is dependent on contingency and consequently society struggles to make it less necessary…
>
> …There is still quite enough left over and above these things for charity to do on its own account. A false view is implied both when charity insists on having this poor relief reserved solely to private sympathy and the accidental occurrence of knowledge and a charitable disposition, and also when it feels injured or mortified by universal regulations and ordinances which are *obligatory*. Public social conditions are on the contrary to be regarded as all the more perfect the less (in comparison to what is arranged publicly) is left for an individual to do by himself as his private inclination directs. (p. 149)

Evidently, more than 180 years ago, Hegel already considered the "welfare state" a necessary complement to bourgeois society; the less that remains left to the responsibility of philanthropists, foundations, and other nonstate organizations, the better. After all, the amassing of riches has the downside of "…subdivision and restriction of particular jobs. This results in the dependence and distress of the class tied to work of that sort," which are the negative products of an economically successful civil society, "and these again entail inability to feel and enjoy the broader freedoms and especially the intellectual benefits of civil society" (§ 243, p. 150). And in the following paragraph, Hegel continues:

> When the standard of living of a large mass of people falls below a certain subsistence level [which regulates itself] as the one necessary for a member of the society – and when there is a consequent loss of the sense of [the right, the legality, and the honor that correlates with maintaining oneself through one's activity and labor] – the result is the creation of a *rabble of paupers*, which at the same time [and on the other hand is accompanied by greater ease to concentrate] disproportional [riches] in a few hands. (p. 150; the passages in brackets are my translation, as Knox's translation of this paragraph is oddly erroneous)

However, Hegel does not see a *satisfactory answer* to "[t]he important question of how poverty is to be abolished" which is "one of the most disturbing problems which agitate modern society" (addition to § 244, p. 278). Neither providing the needy with the means required to maintain a decent living standard outside of the system of wage labor that characterizes civil society, nor the direct mediation of provisions through job opportunities can solve the problem of poverty. Even the wealth that civil society already in Hegel's time was able to dispose over was not enough, in his estimation, to manage the excessive size of the rabble of paupers and of poverty (§ 245). Hegel did anticipate such a development that...

> ...[t]his inner dialectic of civil society thus drives it – or at any rate drives a specific civil society – to push beyond its own limits and seek markets, and so its necessary means of subsistence, in other lands which are either deficient in the goods it has over-produced or else generally backward in industry.... (§ 246, p. 151)

But the imperialist expansion of "*colonization*" (p. 392) leads neither to the elimination of poverty nor constitutive change in the logic of social development in civil society or even its social structure. Shlomo Avineri has impressively summarized this dilemma: "the only problem which remains open and unresolved according to Hegel's own admission is the problem of poverty."[6]

Since Hegel, has there been any progress in dealing with this problem that can be understood as a continuation of his thought? To answer this question, the following section first takes a brief look at the sociopolitical aspects of the work of Karl Marx that contributed to how Hegel's approach to the problem of poverty has been forgotten, to then turn to Heimann's *Social Theory of Capitalism* (1929/1980), which took the treatment of this problem to the next level.

ECONOMIC PROCESS AND SOCIAL INEQUALITY IN MARX AND IN THE WEIMAR REPUBLIC: HEIMANN'S SOCIAL THEORY OF CAPITALISM

Toward the end of the 19th century in the most progressive circles of modern societies, theoretical debates about social inequality were shaped largely by the opposition between capital and labor. The most serious consequence of this stance was, above all, the widespread impossibility of breaking out of the straitjacket of class theory. Either, positively, a progressive, i.e., socialist-Marxist perspective was adopted and social inequality seen as the inevitable and sole result of the domination of one class over another. Concordantly, the assumption was that it was only possible to solve the problem of social inequality within the coordinate system of class antagonism via its abolition in a classless society. Or negatively, a liberal, conservative, or even reactionary position was taken whose common denominator was to view capitalism affirmatively as a further expression of the eternal return of inequality among people, with the label "naturalness" being bestowed on inequality (Dahrendorf, 1961/1967). Almost without exception, inequality was being treated in absolute terms, and a "soft" solution to the problem was not being taken into consideration, for ideological reasons, either from a progressive or a conservative standpoint. In contrast, only theorists who sympathized with *both* a liberal and a social-democratic worldview in principle were in a position to avoid falling prey to either extreme.

Although Marx's "Critique of Hegel's Philosophy of Right" (Marx, 1843) was directly concerned with Hegel's *Philosophy of Right*, he did not deal with the paragraphs (Hegel, 1821/1958, §§ 230–249) discussed above. While the paragraphs Marx discussed (Hegel, 1821/1958, §§ 261–313) also are in the work's third part (*Ethical Life*, Hegel, 1821/1958, pp. 105–223), like those at stake here, the latter belong to the Section *Civil Society* (Hegel, 1821/1958, pp. 122–155), and those that Marx criticized to *The State* (Hegel, 1821/1958, pp. 155–223). Yet, Marx's criticism of Hegel's discussion of the role of private property, which was oriented in terms of the theory of state already adhered – as Avineri (1968, p. 13) put it – to the patterns characteristic of Marx's later thought. Hegel's remarks on the responsibility of civil society in the face of poverty in any case did not go hand-in-hand with Marx's critique, which primarily was oriented toward Hegel's political philosophy, nor did they offer a suitable target for his method. In contrast to many other passages in the *Philosophy of Right*, Hegel after all was successful here in offering not only a socio-theoretical expression and sociopolitical manifestation of his time but also in being far ahead of the latter. However, his remarks no longer fit into the project, already emerging at that time, of the far more radical critique of political economy to whose formulation Marx dedicated the rest of his life.[7]

Subsequent to Marx, Eduard Heimann's *Social Theory of Capitalism* (1929/1980) constitutes a singular high point as a sociopolitically oriented theoretical attempt to break out of the schema of the critique of political economy. Heimann assumes that social and political progress must take place simultaneously with the increasing revolutionization of the economic structure, without jeopardizing economic productivity. His "theory of social policy" – thus the book's subtitle – indeed can be interpreted as an attempt to give Marx's negative critique of capitalism a positively and practically oriented twist. As Bernard Badura wrote in an essay in the book's 1980 republication: Heimann's treatise constitutes, "for the time being, the last convincing attempt, to [embed] the analysis of social policy measures and programs in a comprehensive interpretation of modern capitalism, its origins, and possibilities for development" (Badura, 1980, p. V).

Heimann's theory belongs to debates within a theoretical "tradition" in the broader sense, which has its beginnings in social democracy and the theory of democratic socialism toward the end of the 19th century. Key proponents of this this tradition were economists, social theorists, and practitioners, such as Hugo Sinzheimer, Hugo Preuß, Ernst Fraenkel, Otto Kirchheimer, Rudolf Hilferding, Franz Neumann, Emil Lederer, and Adolf Löwe. The "spirit" of this tradition found clear expression in some articles of the constitution of the Weimar Republic, Germany's first "experiment" with democracy.[8] However, as it became apparent in the early years of the Weimar Republic, the effectiveness of this spirit was mainly limited to the formulation of these articles and did not extend to their implementation (cf. Articles 153, 156, 163, 165). Although Marx greatly inspired this theoretical school of thought, it cannot be seamlessly included with the tradition the latter monopolized in terms of class theory. Here, I will limit myself to Heimann's *Social Theory of Capitalism* as a kind of culmination point in this theoretical development by merging the "Marxian" and the "Un-Marxian" in a unique manner, while also bringing the Hegelian spirit of social policy up to date with contemporary developments, even though Heimann does not directly deal with the problem of social inequality.[9]

What, then, are the main features of Heimann's theory? He shared the *theoretically* fundamental view with Marxism that "capitalism is based on the mutilation ... of workers and that the liberation of the working class must be the work of the working class itself, because only it is 'interested' in continuous change" (Heimann, 1929/1980, p. 150). For Heimann, however, the aspect of *praxis* opens up in a different way: "[ev]idently one must believe in the compatibility of the socio-political achievements of capitalism with the future victory over capitalism, if one is pursuing social policy and at the same time wants socialism; one expects a series of partial victories instead of a decisive blow or with a decisive blow as the conclusion" (p. 315).

For Heimann, social policy in its "revolutionary-conservative double-sidedness" (p. 190) is the key to solving the social question – a question that cannot be solved once and for all. Heimann identified three historically consecutive stages of social policy: (1) the introduction of occupational health and safety measures (pp. 190–195), (2) the implementation of wage increases and unemployment benefits (pp. 196–204), and (3) the modification of the capitalist economy through social policy (pp. 204–215). At every stage, it is imperative that as much is demanded and enforced as is bearable for the economy without structural damage. A prerequisite for solving the social question is an economic structure that has already reached a certain level of productivity (even though it is not possible to predetermine this level with theoretical means). The sociopolitical "overcoming" of capitalism does not simply combat capitalism but instead presupposes it positively: "Relinquishing goods to the benefit of society is only possible within a certain scale of supplies [*Spielraum der Versorgung*], and social policy owes this to the unique productive powers of capitalism" (p. 210). This limitation has to start with the "social movement" itself, i.e.:

Whoever, like the social movement, laments the domination of things over people and wants to free people from the undignified position of being mere means to produce goods can and must be willing to sacrifice things when people are at stake. Humans do not live on bread alone, and to whatever small extent one may disregard the issue of supplies with regard to a well-fed citizen or a starved idealist, *the adjustment of thought is evidenced and proves itself only where the commitment to humans if need be is willing to make a sacrifice as far as the economy is concerned. Only here does the idea of the social triumph as directed at humans as living unities and not just at the consumer in them.* It is not necessary to certify an extra-economic and super-economic achievement of social policy, an increase in freedom, responsibility, and creative possibilities, in terms of favorable economic effects. (p. 208f; my emphasis)

Up to this point, the Hegelian and Marxian roots are basic to Heimann's thought. He draws the other half of the revolutionary-conservative double-sidedness from liberalism whose economic and social doctrines he regarded as a link in the "chain of the great acts of liberation" on which the modern world is built and "in which a new and overflowing feeling of life and vigor creates space for the realization of one's being" (p. 15). This liberal side of modernity, which Heimann refuses to abandon, constitutes the formal foundation of the liberation of workers: the *law* (*Recht*).[10]

According to Heimann, in a democratically constituted polity [*Gemeinwesen*] with a liberal parliamentary system, workers as citizens have a *right to freedom.* If the power structure of the economic system stands in the way of this freedom, it is the task of social policy to point toward a transition from material self-preservation as a necessity to liberal human dignity. The granting of equal opportunities for all must be presupposed because only through this granting can individual achievement become the measure of individual success (p. 28). This is the starting point of liberalism, a demand which cannot merely be paid lip service to. Heimann, like the young Marx, accepts the humanistic objectives of political liberalism and demands that they be compared to actual developments – their de facto political validity. If social reality lags behind the theoretically conceptualized or ideological program, the deployment of critique is a requirement. Heimann holds on to liberalism's strong attachment to freedom and at the same time points out that liberal economic theory is also a theory of society. Furthermore, liberal economic harmony must "comprise complete social freedom" (p. 29). The later Marx contributed to underestimating this aspect of liberalism. He recognized that only liberalism elevated "the worker to the legal person in its full meaning," but he regarded the corollary release of workers from their means of production as the basis of economic exploitation and social bondage in the midst of the purported order of freedom. In contrast, Heimann proposes conceiving "liberal liberation as an act of social policy also in the modern, concise sense of this word." There is no doubt that the workers themselves gained more than they had lost through the exploitation diagnosed by Marx. Like Hegel, Heimann also emphasizes that there can be no economic freedom without property: "in order to be able to live freely, one must have at one's disposal the resources necessary for one's keep" (p. 30).

How is it possible to achieve this economic freedom via property? At least in part as an expression of his time, Heimann's demand fits with the *large enterprise* as the frame of reference. In late 20th-century society, it is not only possible to speak of large enterprises with greater plausibility than in Heimann's time, even though approximately half of the gross national product is still provided by small businesses. In addition, the modern economic order (e.g., in the Federal Republic or in the United States; as in the case of franchises that are tied to large corporations) now has reached a level of societal organization that no longer allows a sharp separation of small and large businesses with regard to the political treatment of the problem of social inequality. If therefore we replace "large enterprise" with the term "economic system," in the sense in which the latter term was introduced into sociological terminology by Talcott Parsons and developed further by Niklas Luhmann, and also integrated into Jürgen Habermas's version of the critical theory of society, then the gap from Heimann's time to the present can be bridged seamlessly.[11]

> It is necessary to expand the organizational-techn[olog]ical creations of capitalism and to incorporate them into a social order of freedom. Into a social order of freedom because the individual freedom of small enterprise is antiquated; because disciplined collaboration in the large enterprise must be combined with the right to freedom; finally, because individual freedom within the large enterprise would either destroy large enterprises themselves, if individual freedom were generalized; or because it would – as individual freedom in large enterprises – once again destroy the freedom of others. The freedom of one must guarantee the freedom of the other. (pp. 158ff)

Finally, Heimann formulates the programmatic nature of social policy – its true potential – as follows:

> Income can be allocated; freedom, however, desires to be gained through vigorous use of energy and be applied every day. That is why genuine social policy must constantly cultivate working people's active will and develop their strength to be free. Domineering socialization from above cannot facilitate social freedom because it summons the strength of the worker only for a singular revolutionary overthrow, instead of unfolding it into achievement in freedom. ... However, when social policy is narrowed to a mere question of wages and the mental resilience of working people is forgone for the sake of how to attain wage increases, then here, too, welfare emerges instead of a liberal arrangement of working life.[12]

For Marx as well as for Heimann, the treatment of the social question involved the transformation of society for the purposes of liberating the real potential of human beings, albeit in different ways. What mattered to Marx was the radical reorganization of a society that exhibits both the working day and the exploitation of workers as its predominant structural characteristics. Heimann's idea of change in society was less radical: social policy as the reformist medium of transformation should not only cover up or conceal the grossest social blemishes but eliminate their causes. In the words of Claus-Dieter Krohn, in *Social Theory of Capitalism*, Heimann was:

> ... the first to develop a consistent theory of social policy that was no longer based, as in the past, on the idea of protecting the socially weak and insuring their welfare in complete isolation from the economic system but instead saw this protection as a powerful [dynamic] vehicle for transforming society. (Krohn, 1987/1993, p. 54)

Thus, the question presents itself of whether, at the end of the 20th century, the most developed Western European industrial societies in any way will draw upon the constitutional amendment unsuccessfully envisaged by Hegel or the radical-reformist social policy postulated by Heimann.[13] Yet, should the possibility exist of a program that integrates both a constitutional amendment and social policy reform? What would be the implications of such a constitutionally oriented social reform for the legal system and the self-legitimation of *democratic* societies which, in crucial regards, seem to be so closely related to the society described by Hegel and Heimann that they still, although by no means pre-eminently, deserve to be called "bourgeois" societies (see Dahms, 2006)? Furthermore, is it possible to extrapolate from the character of such an amendment, for theoretical purposes, an impetus that is symptomatic of the shift currently being observed in the coordinate system of the spheres of material and cultural production and reproduction?

HOW POVERTY AND SOCIAL INEQUALITY RE-EMERGE IN THE CONTEXT OF INSTITUTIONALIZED DEMOCRACY IN POSTANTAGONISTIC TWO-THIRDS SOCIETIES

While attempts to solve the problem of poverty and social inequality around the end of the 19th century and in most industrialized societies well into the 20th century were decisive aspects of social change, they appeared to lose in relevance during the 1970s. Class antagonism (especially as described by Marx in terms of "capitalists vs workers" or "bourgeoisie vs proletariat") for the most part ceased to be a determining factor in the direction of social development, even though its empirical basis remains. In addition, during late 1970s and early 1980s, the problem of social inequality itself largely disappeared from the political agenda or was low on the ranking list of social concerns and trigger points (Plum, 1990), i.e., during the years when neoliberal public policies began to gain momentum. Not surprisingly, attempts to eradicate social inequality completely were not particularly appealing to the citizens of modern western industrial societies at the time, given the general standard of living reached, and at least partially accounted for widespread acceptance of existing social structures. Already by the 1960s and even more so by the 1970s, a decisive segment of the population in the most developed countries no longer considered the communist-socialist alternative to the capitalist mode of production – and the social order that was supposed to be flourishing on top of it – a viable alternative in the foreseeable future.

Furthermore, supported by an economic climate presented as precarious, political and economic elites succeeded in scaling back the demands of labor unions to make their earlier achievements part of the status quo. Habermas has pointed out that the potential for conflict, which was concentrated on class conflict during the "development phase" of capitalist societies, shifted to a new potential for protest, which is "not being ignited because of problems of distribution, but by questions having to do with the grammar of forms of life" (1981/ 1987, p. 392).[14] Ulrich Beck explained this situation as follows:

> On the one hand, the relations of social inequality have remained largely *constant* during the post-war development of the Federal Republic. On the other hand, the living conditions of the population have radically changed. The peculiarity of the socio-structural development in the Federal Republic is the *'elevator effect'*: the 'class society' as a whole is being moved to a higher floor. Despite all the inequalities that are balancing out in new ways or persisting, a *collective increase* in income, education, mobility, law, science, and mass consumption is happening. As a consequence, subcultural class identities and ties are being thinned out or dissolved. At the same time, a process of *individualization* and *diversification* of life situations and lifestyles is unleashed that undermines the hierarchical model of social classes and strata and questions its reality.[15] (Beck, 1986, p. 122)

With the temporary disappearance of the problem of poverty and inequality from the political agenda in the late 1970s and early 1980s, even before the collapse of "actually existing socialism," the – perhaps only temporary – opportunity emerged to deal with the problem theoretically in a less rigid way than the coordinate system of class antagonism allowed. It is therefore not surprising that the discussion about the guaranteed minimum income developed during this time period (Gerhardt & Weber, 1984; Gorz & Sonenscher, 1980). Although poverty has threatened to become again a scourge of western societies since the mid-1980s (which it had not been for a few decades), and as "new poverty" appeared on the political agenda, it forms only one side of the problem (see Kopnarski, 1990). Another phenomenon that has gained increasing importance in these societies, especially in Western Europe, was and still is *unemployment*, sometimes also called "new unemployment," due to structural differences when compared to earlier forms of unemployment. New unemployment is symptomatic of a society in which the relationship between labor demand and supply tends to diverge: in the economically furthest developed societies the need for work decreases, since especially industry, but the economy in general also could fulfill its function just as well with fewer workers, and could perhaps even fulfill it better. Accordingly, Ralf Dahrendorf describes the situation toward the end of the 20th century in terms of a figure of thought from Hannah Arendt who had already assumed that labor society would run out of work, in her book, *The Human Condition* (Arendt, 1958/1998):

> Fewer people carry the yoke of the remaining paid employment more lightly...more people have incomparably more opportunities to engage in free activity... For centuries, work, including paid employment, was the scaffolding around which people have built their lives. Work has (among other things) determined the schedule of the day, the week, the year, and of life, including even the time that is not spent in the workplace as well...
>
> ...[P]aid labor, which used to be available in abundance, has turned into a scarce commodity. ... As it tends to go with scarce commodities, some have them in abundance, while others end up utterly empty handed. It remains a problem of distribution.... (Dahrendorf, 1987, p. 167; my translation)

The end of "work society" (Offe, 1984, especially pp. 13ff) announces itself where, despite a high level of social prosperity, a new group of marginalized (poor, homeless, unemployed, etc.) is forming, for whom the social, political, economic, and health-related certainties of the majority of the population no longer apply. These marginalized people have dropped out of the "two-thirds society" or "majority class," and poverty is re-establishing itself, albeit at a relatively higher level. Jürgen Habermas diagnosed this situation as follows:

> The utopian idea of a laboring society of independent producers has lost its persuasive power-and not only because the forces of production have lost their innocence or because the abolition of private ownership of the means of production has clearly not in and of itself resulted in the management of workers by themselves. Above all it is because that utopian idea has lost its point of reference in reality: the power of abstract labor to give structure and form to a society. (Habermas & Jacobs, 1985/1986, p. 4)

The discussion of a guaranteed minimum income uncoupled from work that began in the late 1970s can be understood in the most economically and industrially developed European societies as an expression of a situation in which technical, technological, and organization "know-how" in industry, and the service sector has reached a high level of both differentiation and perfection. This level has become so high that it is not enough to deflect the practical possibility of materially providing for all citizens with reference to the purportedly counterproductive consequences of any attempt to redistribute wealth.[16] The pioneers of this "movement," which certainly still is at a great distance from being recognized as "social" in Heimann's sense, for now are primarily intellectuals and academics. To advocates of a guaranteed minimum income among intellectuals and academics, the ideological walls between the dominant economic and political interest blocks are too rigid, with the concept of a guaranteed minimum income constituting an opportunity to break out of the hardened categories of "left" and "right" (Dahrendorf, 1987, p. 148). In this regard, the idea of a guaranteed minimum income certainly is reminiscent of Heimann's vision of a radical social reform. At the same time, the idea as such is not entirely new. Particularly the thesis that in societies whose production machine no longer requires full employment in order to function effectively, a reduction in the number of workers even could lead to productivity increases and cost savings, has a market-oriented tradition primarily in terms of a "negative income tax" (see Frey, 1983, p. 157ff; Jordan, 1986, p. 291; van Parijs, 1990). This leads to the question of the relationship between work and income; according to the concept of the guaranteed minimum income, work and income must be *uncoupled* as soon as a society is no longer able – or no longer needs – to provide work for everyone.

The discussion about the guaranteed minimum income belongs to "welfare state" discourse. Only in countries where the welfare state has been established far enough to warrant the designation, this debate has started to intensify, albeit still tentatively. This is the case primarily in some parts of Western Europe, and less so in the United States, despite astonishing efforts during the administration of Lyndon Johnson and the Great Society programs and the War on Poverty legislation, which were carried further to some extent during the Nixon administration.[17] There are two related reasons for differences between Western Europe and the United States: particularly on the European continent, a broad social consensus continues to prevail about a functioning welfare state being the safest guarantee for avoiding class conflicts (see Fach, 1990). On the other hand, criticisms of the welfare state since the mid-1970s tellingly seem to rest on an equally broad consensus: the size of the welfare state is excessive, it is too bureaucratic and inefficient, and it extends too far into the lives of individuals. The concept of a guaranteed minimum income offers an alternative here that could reveal a way out.

Without addressing the concrete details of implementation and the many facets and possibilities considered in the relevant literature (Büchele & Wohlgenannt, 1985; Dahrendorf, 1983; Jordan, 1986; Opielka & Vobruba, 1984; Schmid, 1986), suffice it to say that the program of a guaranteed minimum income is singular in that one far-reaching legislative act potentially could solve several troublesome structural problems. To list a few of the frequently mentioned and hoped for social consequences in the related literature:

- the problem of social marginalization could be put aside because stigmatized poverty and unemployment would disappear;
- the disciplinary character of the labor market would be suspended or curbed, depending on the size of the provision;
- it would allow a free play of forces in the labor market;
- it would provide the economy, at least at the level of large industry, with the possibility of radical rationalization, in several regards;
- the productivity of labor could increase due a higher level of voluntary choice and a lower level of coercion overall;
- it would give individuals the opportunity to engage with more activities outside of work;
- it would curtail the need for bureaucracy to intervene in all areas of life.

In short, it is possible that, to use the distinction introduced by Habermas, society would become *more relaxed* both at the level of the lifeworld as well as of the system. Thus, half a century after Heimann's *Social Theory of Capitalism*, the problem of social inequality again became the subject of creative thinking about the relationship of freedom and equality, social policy, and *social* rights. Below, we will encounter two endeavors to present the guaranteed minimum income as a constitutional step to solve the problems of poverty and unemployment.

THE SOCIAL QUESTION AS LEGAL QUESTION, OR: HOW CAN THE INTRODUCTION OF A GUARANTEED MINIMUM INCOME BE JUSTIFIED IN CONCERT WITH PREVAILING DEMOCRATIC NORMS AND VALUES?

Both Ralf Dahrendorf and Claus Offe have presented a social justice rationale for the minimum income with regard to the *legitimacy of social order in a democratic society*. What is this connection?

The Guaranteed Minimum Income as a Constitutional Right

At the end of the 1950s, Dahrendorf (1959/1968) critically engaged with Heimann's book, *Reason and Faith in Modern Society: Liberalism, Marxism, and Democracy*

(1955/1961).[18] In the essay, Dahrendorf reiterates Heimann's claim that "both varieties of 'social rationalism' – namely, liberalism or individualism, and Marxism or Communism – [have] failed" (Dahrendorf, 1959/1968, p. 179). He accepts Heimann's observation that "[l]iberty and equality are the two halves of democracy," and that "equal freedom is required for democracy" (Heimann, 1961/1955, p. 233). Ultimately, however, he gives this social-liberal argument a liberal twist: "the aims of social-liberal politics must above all be liberal, for equal liberty is above all liberty" (Dahrendorf, 1967/1959, p. 214).

More than 2 decades later, after "new poverty" emerged as a problem in the Federal Republic and other industrial societies, and after old and "new" unemployment had already become a politically accepted fact, Dahrendorf attempted another approach to the issue, viewing poverty and unemployment as problems that *democratically* constituted polities must actively grapple with. Social problems of this caliber cannot be reconciled with the legal and moral self-image of these polities:

> The new social question is no less than the question of the social contract, i.e. the basic agreement over the values and rules by which we want to live – an agreement that of course is implicit, at bottom just imagined, yet still alive in the institutions. This is the question of legitimacy. (Dahrendorf, 1987, p. 151)

In such a situation, in Dahrendorf's eyes, the solution cannot lie in a change in the economic system, but rather in the reconstitution of citizenship, i.e., in its adaptation to social developments that already have occurred. If the political participation rights of members of a democratically constituted polity are diminished by *structural* poverty or unemployment – i.e., if the latter are not attributable to individual responsibility – then the citizenship status of a considerable number of individual is endangered. In a democratic polity, such a condition immediately turns into a potential threat to the polity's legitimacy since not all members can see themselves as equal members of the polity. According to Dahrendorf, the guaranteed minimum income as a *constitutional right* of every citizen offers a possible way out from this dilemma (pp. 154ff), since the structurally marginalized can again become involved in the process of shaping the polity as equal citizens.

Furthermore, Dahrendorf brings into play a functional argument that is strongly reminiscent of Hegel: new poverty and new unemployment pose a threat that could endanger social cohesion. However, for Dahrendorf, this danger does not emanate from "feared revolts of the marginalized" (Schmid, 1986, p. 10) who do not represent a social class based on solidarity but rather form a kind of "Lumpenproletariat" in the Marxian sense – a social category, "which at most becomes the reserve army of occasional manifestations (revolts)" (p. 150). This does not mean minimizing the problem, quite the opposite – it is essential to prevent the "crumbling of the social contract":

> If material livelihood is not part of the basic rights of every citizen, then civil society will disintegrate. Put differently, decoupling income from work is indeed necessary to define the common floor on which everyone stands. Neither pure welfare nor reviving the saying that whoever does not work shall not eat is sufficient here. But this is no more than the necessary

condition to create a society that is worth living in. ... The guaranteed minimum income is as necessary as the other civil rights, i.e. equality before the law or universal suffrage. (p. 157)

Obviously, this line of argument not only goes with Heimann, it goes beyond him in terms of a sociopolitical clarity that is only attainable at the current level of productive forces and relations of production. While Heimann formulated the right to freedom and a decent life in general terms and assigned its implementation to social policy – however, without presenting practical suggestions, Dahrendorf now expressly makes the case for the constitutional realization of this freedom:

> A step is to be taken that, in its intention, is *irreversible*. Certainly, constitutions do not protect against tyrants, especially not against the media charisma of populist leaders. Yet, if constitutions are well-designed, they do embody the best achievements of a civilized society: that behind which no one does not want to fall. In the normal course of things, they tie the hands of political actors, and even in non-normal developments, they create an impediment to pernicious decisions. *In the broader sense, the minimum income also belongs into the constitution. It must be recognized as a basic element of citizenship rights because its rests in the determination of a starting position that no one is allowed to fall behind."* (p. 159; my emphasis)

What is at stake is not only that all members of a democratically constituted polity must be full citizens; it is also a crucial component of this citizenship that citizens can influence the shape of the democratically constituted polity themselves. The marginalized, poor, or unemployed members of society have lost the opportunity to participate in shaping the polity. Only the unconditional availability of the guaranteed minimum income appears to offer a solution for the reintegration of these members – which brings us back to Hegel: *everyone must have property*. Dahrendorf's proposal updates Hegel's findings for modern western industrial societies in the late 20th century: to ensure full membership in a democratically constituted polity, the guarantee of an economically secure existence independent of social and political circumstances, along with business cycles, in the form of a guaranteed income.

The Guaranteed Minimum Income and Protection Against the Socially Caused Vicissitudes of Life

In his essay *The Acceptance and Legitimacy of Strategic Options in Social Policy*, Offe (1990/1996) points out that during the 1980s, demands were being directed at providing those who are neglected by the market as well as the welfare state – the residual category of economic modernization – with social and economic security. These demands are an expression of a society in which the formation of free labor and capital markets exposes individuals to an array of typical risks:

> ...which extend to their material life chances and opportunities for societal participation. These risks consist in the fact that, because of physical disadvantage or weakness (such as old age, inappropriate qualifications, homelessness, the burden of family duties or conversely the absence of a familial support network, and lack of employment opportunities), individuals are unable to gain, maintain, or regain access to the predominant form of societal participation, earning an income through dependent wage labor. (Offe, 1990/1996, p. 184)

The causes of the emergence and prevalence of these structural life risks, which are typical for every capitalist industrial society, cannot be blamed on the wrongdoing of individuals. Therefore, those affected neither can be expected to master the consequences without further help, nor to simply accept this situation. This is because "these risks do not merely have objective social causes of risk, but harmful *collective consequences* as well" (Offe, 1990/1996, p. 184): the social and political order may be questioned in rebellious and revolutionary ways. Offe is referring here to the functional argument that we already encountered in Hegel and Dahrendorf: "the privatization of some of these risks is no longer tolerable, for functional as well as moral reasons" (Offe, 1990/1996, p. 184). The problem of these life risks in the form of impending poverty or unemployment is entering the realm of responsibility of central state power because it considerably exceeds the problem-solving capacity of the local services to the poor, cooperative aid funds, and non-state self-help (p. 185).

A "regime" of legally secured entitlements must therefore be established precisely where otherwise "assessment-dependent and individual case assistance had predominated hitherto" (p. 194). Moreover, these demands go hand in hand with the blossoming of self-help groups which, following the pattern of new social movements, demand an anti-paternalistic and nondiscriminatory "social policy from below." These demands aim to secure the granting of welfare (*Sozialhilfe*) – that entails a stigmatizing sacrificing of partly essential elements of the civil rights to freedom and privacy – by granting "a simple legal entitlement to services, transfer payments, and materially guaranteed autonomy of action" that "would independent of individual lifestyle, income-earning or and family histories, etc." (p. 195). Hence, the legal question emerges here too.

This legal aspect comes to bear even more explicitly in the justification of "trial arguments" which in Offe's view would have to be drawn upon for every "guaranteeist" solution (p. 196). These trial (or hypothetical) arguments are necessary because the decision for or against the introduction of a guaranteed minimum income constitutes just as radical a structural innovation as the granting of unconditional legal claims to materially assured autonomy of action, which solely are tied to citizenship status. In this case, "[t]he welfare state would extend to *all* citizens without distinction or condition the right to a material share, and thereby remove the means by which 'deserving' and 'normal' members of the community might be symbolically and materially distinguished from the less deserving and less normal" (Offe, 1990/1996, p. 196). Finally, Offe presents five trial arguments that are of critical importance for the justice discourse he outlined (pp. 197–199):

(1) "Special" and "normal" living conditions and behaviors could no longer be clearly distinguished; the discrimination of such lifestyles that do not conform to those commonly sanctioned as "normal" clearly would be subverted, if not prevented entirely.
(2) The granting of *legal* entitlements like the guaranteed minimum income often is judged as detrimental to the functioning of both the economy and the labor market. However, there are indications that this by no means necessarily would have to be the case.

(3) As soon as it is no longer possible to typify certain lifestyles, biographical patterns, the gendered division of labor, etc., in privileging or discriminatory fashion, social policy loses its conventional mandate to compel individuals, through positive or negative sanctions, to participate in the cultural anchoring of a hegemonic lifestyle.
(4) The introduction of "guaranteeist" forms of social policy should be "tolerable" if a society is so "rich" that it can afford such a "sacrifice." This argument, however, involves an ambivalent element: what happens if the level of wealth drops again, so that society can no longer afford a guaranteed minimum income? In this case, it would be possible to amend the argument in such a way that material guarantees constitute a quasi-punishment that society imposes on itself for blatant failings – and constitute an incentive dam against the extent of the punishment by means of suitable institutional innovations.
(5) Finally, it is necessary to consider that the omission of such a sociopolitical innovation could have worse consequences for the political culture and the general conditions of a society than its introduction.

In connection with the fourth argument, Offe points to its ambivalence due to implications as they are independent of business cycles: should the social level of prosperity fall back to an earlier level or remain at the same level after the introduction of this structural innovation, then attempts could be made to legitimate and execute the withdrawal of the innovation. Similar to Dahrendorf, Offe drives at the need to prevent such a retraction due to the business cycle and proposes to use *institutional deficiencies* as a criterion rather than material affluence: accordingly, the unconditional and constitutional granting of a guaranteed minimum income should function as a mechanism for negative sanctioning in the event of social failures.

To be sure, both aspects of the argument boil down to the same assumption that the introduction of a constitutionally guaranteed minimum must occur within the framework of a long-term, holistic *societal* policy. This societal policy must encompass the *safeguarding of the general level of prosperity* and the *stability of the economic process* and manifest as an integrated social and economic policy. Without such a long-term-oriented societal policy, the structural innovation proposed here lacks the "environment" it needs to survive and thrive. For this reason, it is important to embed the program of the guaranteed minimum income in the context of an expansive and long-term *theory of social policy*. This long-run perspective must be oriented toward the process of the *societal rationalization of the economy* that has accompanied the development of modern societies since the beginning of the Enlightenment, albeit in fractured and contradictory manner, to the point where its dynamic has been difficult to detect and discern. Subsequently, I will attempt to outline the main features of this process and its relevance for the program of the guaranteed minimum income.

THE GUARANTEED MINIMUM INCOME AS CONSTITUTIONAL RIGHT: A STEP IN THE SOCIETAL RATIONALIZATION OF THE ECONOMY

If one considers the multiplicity of possible implications and consequences of the introduction of a guaranteed minimum income, then this concept reveals itself as the cornerstone of a broad-based societal policy. In addition, the tradition that I attempted to delineate in the preceding sections suggests an outline for such a societal policy. While this tradition began in the early 19th century, its concrete form is seemingly becoming discernable only towards the end of the 20th century, following Marx's dictum that "mankind thus inevitably sets itself only such tasks as it is able to solve, since closer examination will always show that the problem itself arises only when the material conditions for its solution are already present or at least in the course of formation" (Marx, 1859/1977).

In terms of economic sociology, the process of modern societal development since the late 18th century resulted from tensions between the economy and society in which the state played the relatively subordinate role of mediator and of facilitator of growing prosperity. Accordingly, Adam Smith's *Wealth of Nations* (1776/2014) was a sort of socio-theoretical obituary of a world in which economy and society were still one: the sharp separation between economy, society, and the state was not only theoretically groundless; it arguably also was empirically and analytically not clearly identifiable. In *Economy and Society* (1922/2013), Max Weber described the Enlightenment as a process of differentiation and of the breaking apart of the political, economic, and social spheres. Following Smith, the endeavor to clarify the constellation of economy, society, and the state across time became a determining element in attempts to develop a general theory of society and has remained so to this day. Hegel's *Philosophy of Right* thus represents the attempt to reconcile the three spheres by means of philosophy. In Marx, the same attempt to too great an extent turned out in favor of society: according to his theory, the economy should merge into society and the state should similarly dissolve into it – hence the term "socialism." By contrast, in liberalism, it was assumed that the goal had to be the restoration of the relationship between state, economy, and society as it allegedly had been in the world of Adam Smith: as a unity of economy and society with a state reduced to a limited organization and coordination function. With Heimann's *Social Theory of Capitalism*, however, a clear shift in the conceptual relationship between economy, society, and the state is already emerging that is not least an expression of the more state-oriented German tradition.[19] For him, the social receives theoretical priority, although he does not neglect the economy: a modern, socially just and responsible society requires an efficient and strong economy. Without its continuously sustained productivity, it would not be possible to maintain and push further the level of prosperity that has brought about the achieved condition of social justice and responsibility. In this, the state plays the role of intermediary between the mutually supporting and complementary spheres of economy and society, as a promotor of an effective and successful economic process, and as guarantor of social rights and accomplishments.

In Jürgen Habermas's work, the relationship of economy, state, and society finally and arguably reaches a highly sophisticated socio-theoretical level. Since his first essay, his project has been preoccupied with the "dialectic of rationalization" (Habermas, 1954; cf. also Habermas, 1985b). In terms of his social theory, this dialectic unfolds as follows: with the increasing development and differentiation of modern Western societies comes a dual rationalization, which results, on the one hand, in the rationalization of the *lifeworld* and, on the other hand, in the rationalization of social subsystems – above all the state and the economy. In the lifeworld (which can be understood as a proxy for society in contrast to the economy and the state), a progressive transition from traditionally determined normatively regulated action to *communicative action* takes place. The latter is characterized by how participants in the lifeworld begin to act increasingly independently from established norms and values and instead determine for themselves which principles they are willing to live by. At the same time, a rationalization of the economy and state takes place in which the regulation of action does not manifest via traditional or communicative norms and values but via the steering media of money and power, which provide a much more effective and faster coordination mechanism. In both cases, we encounter two different types of societal rationalization in quality and direction. The communicative rationalization of the lifeworld has a predominantly defensive character: the issue is not about bringing the economy and state under the social and cultural imperative of the lifeworld but rather about protecting the lifeworld from the functional imperatives of the subsystems of economy and society (cf. Rödel, 1990, p. 158).[20]

Within this theoretical framework, in a 1985 essay, Habermas grappled with the possibility of utopia in the present and the understanding of social change resulting from this possibility. In the essay (based as it was on a lecture he gave to the Spanish parliament in 1984), he commented on the future of the social welfare state – and by implication social policy – as follows:

> The development of the social state has arrived at an impasse, and this has drained the energy from the utopian idea of a laboring society. The answers of the legitimists and the neo-conservatives reflect a *Zeitgeist* that is only defensive; they express a historical consciousness that has been robbed of its utopian dimension. Even the dissidents from "growth-society" remain on the defensive. Their answer could be turned to the offensive only *if the project of the social welfare state were not simply carried on or abandoned, but rather continued at a higher level of reflection.* (Habermas, 1985/1986, p. 14; second emphasis added)

The societal status of labor occupies a central position as a factor in this higher level of reflection. Hence, even for today's leading critical social theorist, the guaranteed minimum income comes into play:

> If the project of the social welfare state were to become reflexive and be directed not only to taming the capitalistic economy, but also to containing the state itself, it would obviously lose labor as its central point of reference. It would no longer be a question of circumscribing the full employment held up as a norm. Nor could such a project limit itself to introducing a guaranteed minimum income so as to break the spell that the labor market casts over the life histories of *all* working men and women-even over the growing and increasingly marginalized potential of those who only stand in reserve. (Habermas, 1985/1986, p. 14; second emphasis added)

According to Habermas, this step would indeed be revolutionary, but not revolutionary enough; not even, "if the lifeworld could be shielded not only against the employment system's inhuman imperatives, but also against the counterproductive side-effects of administratively providing for human life as a whole" (Habermas, 1985/1986, p. 14; second emphasis added). What matters for Habermas is the establishment of a new separation of powers between the state, economy, and the lifeworld (society). The role of *communication* is vital in the reformulation of this new separation of powers: "...what before was a presupposition or boundary condition for the utopian idea of a laboring society has today moved to the center of the discussion. And with this discussion theme, the utopian accents shift from the concept of labor to that of communication" (p. 16). Like Offe, Habermas regards the integrity and autonomy of lifestyles as the central goal of societal policy. Moreover, Habermas emphasizes the vitalization of the utopian impulse, because should the "utopian oases" dry up, then "a desert of banality and helplessness spreads" (p. 16). However, Habermas does not believe that "a differentiated economic system can be transformed from within in accordance with the simple recipes of workers' self-management," rather:

> The problem seems to be rather one of how capacities for self-organization can be sufficiently developed in autonomous public spheres for the goal-orientated processes of will-formation of a use-value orientated life-world to hold the systemic imperatives of economic system and state apparatus in check, and to bring *both* media-controlled subsystems into dependence on life-world imperatives. I cannot imagine that this would be possible without a gradual abolition of the capitalist labour market, and without a radical-democratic implantation of political parties in their public spheres.[21]

Subsequent to the collapse of "actually existing socialism" and its corollary attempts at total "societal" control over the organization and deployment of the means of production, Habermas asserts, there is hardly any doubt that the capitalist economic system that has prevailed in the most developed societies acts as the most optimal mechanism of material production and reproduction for the foreseeable future: "complex societies are unable to reproduce themselves if they do not leave the logic of an economy that regulates itself through the market intact" (Habermas, 1990, pp. 16–17). However, it cannot be assumed that *a single optimal model* of market economy can be implemented everywhere in the same way and with similar results. Instead, the free-market model leads to a spectrum of variants whose concrete formation depends on the particular social, cultural, and political context. For the purpose of illustration, this spectrum could be described conventionally as a continuum with the United States currently at one end and Sweden at the other. The United States would therefore be the most "capitalist" society, i.e., the modern society in which the imperatives of the economy exert the greatest influence over culture and politics, while Sweden would be the most "social," in which cultural values and political priorities limit the sphere of influence of the (still capitalistically organized) economy to a much larger extent. The Federal Republic model of the *social market economy* would accordingly occupy a point closer to the center of this continuum. Since the term "capitalism" in the sense of its conventional meaning could be applied to all societies on this continuum, the concept would have largely lost the analytically delimiting acuity that made it appear fruitful in social science discourse for so long – all the more so after the collapse of "actually existing socialism" in Europe. It is symptomatic that in *economic sociology* – since its resurgence during the mid-1980s, especially in the United States – the term "capitalism" increasingly is being replaced by concepts such as "political economy," "social economy," and "social market." This larger situation finally promises to provide a suitable framework for scrupulously investigating and describing the relationship between economy and society in the late 20th century, by means of sociological research directed at the economic system. The economy is, after all, the social subsystem whose true functioning for a long time and very successfully has been mystified and concealed by formalist theories in mainstream economics (see especially Bruyn, 1991; Etzioni, 1988; Fligstein, 1990; Granovetter, 2017; Swedberg, 1987, 1990; Zukin & DiMaggio, 1990).

Along these lines, it is both possible and necessary to interpret the evolving relationship between economy and society since the late 17th century as *societal rationalization of the economy*, on two separate levels: theoretically, as a movement from an economically shaped to a socially and culturally shaped societal form; and empirically, as a movement within specific societies with a *capitalist market economy* in which the interests associated with the "societal sphere" progressively have been gaining in importance. What is the character of this "societal sphere?" Is it more than a simple tautology? To answer these questions, it is useful to refer to two related debates that have been unfolding in recent years, especially within the theoretically oriented social sciences: the attempts to reformulate the concept of *civil society* (*bürgerliche Gesellschaft*) mostly, but not exclusively, in the English-speaking world, on the one hand, and the attempts to develop a concept of *self-reflexive modernity*, on the other.

The concept of civil society appears to have experienced intensifying interest in recent times because in the course of the 1970s and 1980s, social, cultural, and political phenomena have emerged that were not functions of material motives and interests alone, such as new social movements, citizens' initiatives, and self-help groups. For them, questions of social justice, social peace, the preservation of the natural environment, etc., are more important than personal, regional, national, or international advantages in an economic register (see Arato & Cohen, 1984; Cohen, 1982; Cohen & Arato, 1992; Keane, 1988; Rödel, 1990). These phenomena may serve as indicators of the increasing importance of social, cultural, and solidarity-oriented standards of value that imply a change in priorities from the individual level to the level of society as a whole. Amitai Etzioni summarized this change in terms of the "moral dimension" (Etzioni, 1988; see also Lowe, 1987). Ultimately, however, this development points to a reassessment of the role of the economy as a whole.

The attempts to formulate a concept of *self-reflexive modernity*, of *contemporary enlightenment*, are also symptomatic of this change (see especially Beck, 1986/1992; Beck, 1988; also Blumenberg, 1966-1976/1983; Gorz, 1989/2011; in a certain way also Habermas, 1981/1983 and 1981/1987). The history of the Industrial Revolution and of the economic development in capitalism was above all a history of the rationalization of the "economic problem," behind which the history of the democratic rationalization of political power was secondary.[22] Because economic rationalization, which has largely been confined to *technological* modernization, has thus far proceeded along a single track, what is necessary today is a more comprehensive rationalization of this rationalization itself. A societal rationalization that is oriented toward social accountability and personal responsibility provides the only means of preventing or reducing the further destruction of the natural environment. Insight into the destructive power of economic, cultural, and social modernization, in the form of both postmodern questioning of modern goals and standards and enlightened self-critique, leads to a heightened awareness of social priorities that are not reducible to economic and political power.

The societal rationalization of the economy can hence be understood as a *process of the progressive societal "overarching" of the capitalist economy*. How to characterize this overarching? Is there at present a structural principle that this societal rationalization would follow? In my view, there is currently only one "candidate": the debate over democracy, which has been reviving *in the West* for about half a decade (Cronin, 1989; Dahl, 1985, 1989; Gould, 1988; Lefort & Macey, 1988; Rödel et al., 1989; Wolin, 1989; Wolin, 1990). *Democracy* is the concept or "organizational principle" that is central to the self-understanding of modern societies. Paradoxically however, debates about democracy during the late 1980s largely remained unnoticed behind the clamor of postmodernism (Dahms, 1992b), which is all the more surprising as the only possible – or at least *desirable –* successor to "capitalist society" appears to be a truly "democratic society." If we consider this theoretical revival of the democracy-theoretical discussion as a symptom of a societal reorientation whose impact on practical politics has not yet taken shape, then the societal rationalization of the economy would be akin to *democratic* rationalization. Democracy would then be synonymous with the social values of freedom, equality, and solidarity. This democratic rationalization would not translate into upheaval of the economic system but in embedding the latter in a society whose normative and legitimizing identity is increasingly determined by its democratic character. Democracy as an organizational principle would therefore not be restricted to the domain of political rule but would be crucial for *modern society as a whole*. The two poles of modernity, capitalism and democracy, would thus once again offer starting points for quasi-utopian impulses, albeit neither in a revolutionary nor a subversive way. At the end of a century abundant in socially induced and mediated catastrophes, which brought about the construction of the widely visible memorials of anti-modern fascism and the "hypermodern" experiments of communism, we must bid farewell to the pathos of states of exception, however alluring or motivating they may be at the psycho-emotional level. It is thus fundamental to the concept of the societal rationalization of the economy that it must not center on the conversion of capitalist society into a socialist one. Instead, what is required, both theoretically and practically, is a *reassessment of the status of the capitalist economic system within a society whose political and social legitimacy is based primarily on the objective of actualizing a genuine democracy that warrants the designation at the societal level*. By contrast, what has taken hold is the reduction of the meaning of democracy to what Schumpeter (1942/2003) referred to as the "democratic method," in ways that are nationally specific, typically echoing bygone eras and circumstances. The implicit perpetuation of the "democratic method" as the only standard that matters amounts to nothing less than the *reification* of democratic governance and corollary mediations between citizens and the politicians who claim to represent them and to do their bidding (see Dahms, 1998). It is crucial for democracy's self-understanding that both the concept and especially the practice of democracy are open to further development and evolution.

This development model of capitalism and democracy amounts to a concept of capitalism that clearly contradicts its conventional version (e.g., Seldon, 1990). The character of the capitalist economic mode of production distinguished modern society from its predecessors since the end of the 18th century. However, what may succeed the established nexus between capitalist mode of production and democratic method will not necessarily – and probably not at all – be a radically different form of organization of the economic process (see, e.g., how Schumpeter, 1942/2003, approached and answered the question of whether "capitalism can survive"). If we understand the development of modern society in terms of the societal rationalization of the economy, then the shift from "capitalist" to "postcapitalist" society (cf. Dahrendorf, 1959) will not take place as a shift in the specific mode of production but as a change of the relative importance of the economy within society. Because "postcapitalist" society will continue to be based on the capitalistic organization of economic production – the realm of necessity is likely to remain a realm of capitalist necessity on which the realm of freedom has the potential of continuing to slowly expand (Marx, 1894/1968, p. 828). As Habermas puts:

> ... a secondary, although by no means *trivial* question then arises of how ... plan and market are coordinated with each other, how their relative weights in the interaction of state and economy can shift. This would be difficult for me to anticipate, even if I had a better knowledge of economics. For every intervention in complex social structures has such unforeseeable consequences that processes of reform can only be defended as scrupulous processes of trial and error, under the careful control of those who have to bear their consequences. (Habermas, 1985b, p. 255)

In the framework of the social rationalization of the economy, however, the question posed by Habermas about the new relationship between plan and market is not simply trivial but fraught with serious implications. "Better knowledge of economics" alone will be of little help when attempting to answer this question. After all, the project consists in assuming societal (a.k.a. democratic) "control" over the economy as "public control in a democratic society" (Lowe, 1987) or as "democratic economic policy" (Frey, 1983) – i.e., in the sense and for the purpose of a socially, culturally, and politically responsible orientation of economic decision-making. To name just one example: the decisions of large national and international economic corporations already often have consequences whose scope is able to compete with political decisions – which is why large businesses increasingly are approaching the challenges of democratic legitimation – although they currently operate largely without concrete control, in some countries more than in others. Concordantly, only a theory of social development based on a *complex* understanding of freedom on the one hand and of economic necessity and planning on the other will be in a position to take precautions against the potential for undesirable, destructive, as well as societally self-destructive consequences of large-scale economic decisions.

Thus, what is at stake is the treatment of a question and the theoretical development of a project for whose answer certain forces currently appear to be forming themselves anew: the current discussion of *civil society*, a revitalizing *democratic theory*, a renewal of *economic sociology*, and the development of a concept of *self-enlightening modernity*. The project of the societal rationalization of the economy can only succeed through the differentiated yet integrated analysis of the economic, social, and political conditions of a "social order of freedom" (Heimann, 1929/1980, pp. 158ff).

CONCLUSION

Despite the perspective delineated here, undoubtedly, one can find a multitude of arguments against the possibility of introducing a guaranteed minimum income. Above all, the future significance of the nation-state poses a question mark that obscures the view of the continuing development of Western societies. The introduction of a guaranteed minimum income in all likelihood is a step that initially would be confined to the national borders of an ethnically and culturally homogeneous state. Yet, this geographical and population-based unity of social and economic policy decisions is becoming increasingly problematic. Not only considering "the largest and longest wave of migration that the world has ever seen," which promises to be the most momentous for European nation-states; furthermore, national economies to an increasing degree are becoming dependent on developments in the international economy that are summarized in the term "globalization" (Gilpin, 1987; Kolko, 1988).[23] These developments make the possibility of a societal policy and concurrent social policies that are independent of specific internal environments (citizens vs legal immigrants, asylum seekers, and residents of other nations; economic situation; political climate) as well as external environments (neighboring countries, global economic climate, the influx of illegal immigrants) rather improbable. Then again, these "disruptive factors" could prove to be not all that significant; the rapid disintegration of national unity appears especially doubtful (see Richter, 1992). Even if they should turn out to be significant, they do not necessarily subvert the development of a theory of social policy that endeavors to bring about social, economic, and political reconciliation in modern societies; in fact, they make the determined pursuit of such a theory all the more important. Once states of emergency take hold and are being normalized, the leeway is lost to allow for reflection and experimentation in the direction of a socially, culturally, politically, and economically healthy and viable polity that functions in ways that are consistent with its citizens values and judgments.

Furthermore, the responsibility for slowing down the destruction of the global natural environment lies almost exclusively with the most developed Western societies, not because they would be "wiser" or "more reasonable" than others but because only they can *afford* the purported "luxury" of reconsidering not just their own future but also the future of planet Earth. Here, too, however, it may appear doubtful whether reconciliation of collective decision-making processes that are prone to perpetuating and aggravating further myriad conflicts is possible. *Undoubtedly*, in inherently fragile complex advanced societies, such efforts at reconciliation – internally and externally – will be necessary for survival and might facilitate "reasonable" approaches to tackling the most urgent problems pertaining to the long-term preservation of both life on the planet and democratically aligned modern civilization. In this context, the guaranteed minimum income may appear as a small and insignificant step toward solving problems of nearly "global" magnitude. Nevertheless, it must be assumed that *it offers the only currently visible program of a social "policy of détente" without which the necessary structural preconditions for a reasonable long-term solution to present and future problems is hardly imaginable.*

NOTES

1. I have refrained from adding many references that have become directly relevant to the central argument, aside from a small number where doing so enhances or illustrates a specific point, e.g., Chamayou (2018/2021), Dahms (1998), Dahms (2006), Granovetter (2017), Harvey (2007), Jouet (2017), Kaes et al. (1994), Koslowski (2000), Kruse (1994), Lipset (1996), and Meifort (2017).

2. "Capitalist society" is an increasingly inadequate concept that needs revision: the most and furthest developed societies of the West today call for more sophisticated and multidimensional descriptions and explanations. Therefore, this work partly should be understood as a contribution to efforts to reformulate "capitalism" as a concept.

3. "Anstrum der Armen," *Der Spiegel*, No. 37, September 9, 1991.

4. Hegel (1821/1958), p. 237 (emphasis mine). In the *Phenomenology of Spirit*, Hegel had written, "The universal being thus split up in to a mere multiplicity of individuals, this lifeless Spirit is an equality, in which all count the same, i.e. as persons," Hegel (1807/1977), section "Legal Status" in chapter "The *true* Spirit. The ethical order," p. 290. His explanation ends as follows: "The actuality of the self that did not exist in the ethical world has been won by its return into the '*person*'; what in the former was harmoniously one now emerges in a developed form, but as alienated from itself" (p. 294).

5. In the "addition" to § 234, Hegel signals caution: "Here nothing hard and fast can be laid down and no absolute lines can be drawn. Everything here is personal; subjective opinion enters in, and the spirit of the constitution and the crisis of the day have to provide precision of detail. In time of war, for instance, many a thing harmless at other times, has to be regarded as harmful. As a result of this presence of accident, of personal arbitrariness, the public authority acquires a measure of odium. When reflective thinking is very highly developed, the public authority may tend to draw into its orbit everything it possibly can, for in everything some factor may be found which might make it dangerous in one of its bearings. In such circumstances, the public authority may set to work very pedantically and embarrass the day-to-day life of people. But however great this annoyance, no objective line can be drawn here either" (p. 276).

6. "The extraordinary thing about Hegel's discussion of these social problems in the *Philosophy of Right* is that in an analysis which attempts to depict how modern society in its differentiated structure is able to overcome its problems through mediation, the only problem which remains open and unresolved according to Hegel's own admission is the

problem of poverty."Avineri (1972), p. 148, in the section, "Poverty and the limits of civil society," pp. 147–154.

7. Although Marx's comments on the "Debates on the Law on Thefts of Wood" (Marx, 1842) were written half a year earlier, the situation is so similar that a thorough discussion for the purpose of this work would not be fruitful.

8. For a recent related compilation of different kinds of pertinent and illustrating materials, see Kaes et al. (1994).

9. In Germany, this line of inquiry disappeared almost completely after 1933 and even after 1945 never really was able to gain a foothold as a theoretically informed and oriented tradition. Aside from a few exceptions (see below in this paper), the sociopolitical discussion of the post-war period up to the present has remained alarmingly nontheoretical. One of the reasons for this is due to the representatives of this school of thought being forced to emigrate to other countries subsequent to Hitler's rise to power, where they usually could continue their work – like Eduard Heimann and some of his colleagues at the New School for Social Research in New York. During the Weimar Republic, links were being been forged between social theory and sociopolitical practice that appeared promising, but due to the largely different sociopolitical and socioeconomic circumstances in which the proponents of this tradition found themselves during the years following 1933, this specific and necessary fertile ground no longer was available. See above all Krohn (1987/1993), especially the sections IV.3, VI, VIII, and Krohn (1988).

10. I should acknowledge the longstanding debate about how to translate the German "*Recht*" into English. Strictly speaking, "*Recht*" translates into "*right*," but "*Recht*" in German is more akin to "law" in English, with "*Recht*" inevitably being tied to and implying laws. "*Recht*" often is used as shorthand for the entire nexus involving rights, laws, and the legal system, including courts, law enforcement, constitutional law, and even education – as in Hegel's *Philosophy of Right* or in such works as Luhmann's *A Sociological Theory of Law* (1983/1985), which in German is titled *Rechtssoziologie* (1983), etc. "Right" in English typically is more specific, referring to rights, and while both inevitably imply the existence of a legal systems, laws, etc., they usually do not refer to the entire nexus. Meaning: what specifically is intended is more important than the particular terminology employed.

11. Parsons and Smelser (1956); Luhmann (1988); Habermas (1981/1983, 1981/1987). Despite the attention that Luhmann's version currently enjoys, Heimann's (1954; 1963) contributions to the systems analysis of modern society rarely are acknowledged. For a notable exception, Kruse (1994), esp. part III (pp. 68–99).

12. p. 319 – Since Heimann, little has happened theoretically with regard to issues of social rights in the German-speaking world, or modern societies generally, aside from debates about a guaranteed minimum income, universal basic income, or similar schemes. We should therefore mention the British sociologist T. H. Marshall (1950), who distinguished three types of rights the formation of which accompanied the process of historical developments in modern societies: *civil*, *political*, and *social* rights. By contrast, Dahrendorf argued that this development followed a different logic in Germany than in the United Kingdom. In Germany, civil and political citizenship rights were relatively underdeveloped and had receded behind the supremacy of the *rule of law*, which emphasized aspects and the interests of the state. At the same time, the consideration of "social" citizenship rights in Germany was ahead of most other European countries (Dahrendorf, 1965, p. 79 ff.).

13. The emphasis lies on Western European societies because in the United States, to harken back to Hegel's expression, "There is still quite enough left over and above these things for charity to do on its own account" (Hegel, 1821/1958, p. 149). This is manifested in the omnipresent role of foundations and donors for activities that do not seem to directly come about from capitalist economic interests, such as education and art.

14. Habermas illustrates the diversity of the possibilities for protest two pages later: the anti-nuclear and environmental movement, peace movement, citizens' initiative movement, alternative movement, minorities, the psychedelic scene with life aid groups and youth cults, religious fundamentalism, anti-tax protest movement, school protests of parent

associations, resistance to modernist reforms and the feminist movement. "Of international significance furthermore are the autonomy movements struggling for regional, linguistic, cultural, and also religious independence" (p. 393). As we have known since the conflicts in the former Yugoslavia and Soviet Union, ethnic and nationalist autonomy movements in the formerly socialist societies are coming more and more to the fore.

15. This is a new translation, for the present purpose, of the relevant passage in Beck's book. In 1992, an official "translation" of *Risk Society* appeared in English, but there are major discrepancies, especially as far as the structure, title, scope, and length of Chapter 3 are concerned ("Beyond Status and Class?" Beck, 1986/1992, pp. 91–102). Inexplicably, instead of including the translation of Chapter 3 in the original version ("Jenseits von Klasse und Schicht" – "Beyond Class and Strata," Beck, 1986, pp. 121–161), which includes the quoted passage, the third chapter in the English version is an entirely different text and does not include, for instance, an explicit reference to the intriguing image of the "elevator effect" – an expression that would be akin to "a rising tide lifts all boats" in English. To complicate matters further, there also is a chapter by Beck (1987; in a collection edited by Meja, Misgeld, and Stehr), entitled *Beyond Status and Class: Will There Be an Individualized Class Society?* – which is the translation of a combination of two different, previously published German articles written by Beck.

16. Internationally, the term "basic income guarantee" or "universal basic income" has gained currency; there is also a global umbrella organization for the promotion of the idea of a guaranteed minimum income, the "Basic Income Earth Network – B.I.E.N."

17. In the 1960s and early 1970s, the United States had the financial and political prerequisites to support large-scale practical research in this direction – see, for example, the experiments in connection with the New Jersey Income Maintenance Program: Kershaw and Fair (1976); Watts and Rees (1977a, 1997b); see also Skidmore (1977). That not only the money but also the ideologically necessary mindset is missing today is primarily due to the unwillingness of the American middle and upper classes to regard economic development and stability as a long-term and *socially* supportive project. See, e.g., Lipset (1996), esp. pp. 53–76, Gilens (1999), and Jouet (2017), esp. pp. 168–193.

18. This was 8 years before Dahrendorf joined the Free Democratic Party, entered politics, and became a prominent promoter of liberalism and one of the engineers of the "Social-liberal coalition" (between the Social Democratic Party of [West] Germany, SPD, and the Free Democratic Party, FDP) under Willy Brandt and Walter Scheel that came to power in 1969 (see Meifort, 2017, pp. 146–199).

19. See Part II of Koslowski (2000), pp. 93–271.

20. See Habermas (1981/1987), especially the "concluding reflections" following p. 301, where he also formulated a more complex version of Marshall's model of the development of rights (without explicitly referring to the latter); Habermas lists "four epochal juridification processes" (p. 357): bourgeois state – constitutional state – democratic constitutional state – social and democratic constitutional state (pp. 356–373). In the original, Habermas called them "global" rather than "epochal" processes.

21. Habermas (1985a, p. 103). While the motive to democratically subordinate the economy and state under the imperative of the lifeworld shines through here, Rödel, Frankenberg, and Dubiel (Rödel, 1990, pp. 155–165) have correctly pointed out that the idea of democracy hardly plays a role any longer in Habermas's *The Theory of Communicative Action* (1981/1983 and 1981/1987). Therefore, this last section will also be an attempt to explicate and extrapolate the implicit meaning that Habermas assigns to democracy, especially in the conflict between economy and society. (For Habermas's fully developed theory of deliberative democracy, which in German appeared in the same year as the original version of this article, see Habermas, 1992/1996.)

22. Keynes (1930/1963), p. 326: 1963, p. 326: "Assuming no important wars and no important increase in population, the economic problem may be solved, or be at least within sight of solution, within a 100 years. This means that the economic problem is not – if we look into the future – *the permanent problem of the human race.*" In this essay, Keynes analyzed the consequences of reducing daily working hours to "at most three hours," for

individuals and society, and thus, by implication, indirectly revealed the motivating criterion of his theoretical endeavors.

23. According to the Director General of the International Organization for Migration in Geneva, James Purcell, quoted in *Der Spiegel*, No. 37, September 9, 1991, p. 36.

REFERENCES

Arato, A., & Cohen, J. (1984). Social movements, civil society, and the problem of sovereignty. *Praxis International*, *3*, 266–283.
Arendt, H. (1958/1998). *The human condition*. University of Chicago Press.
Avineri, S. (1968). *The social and political thought of Karl Marx*. Cambridge University Press.
Avineri, S. (1972). *Hegel's theory of the modern state*. Cambridge University Press.
Badura, B. (1980). Heimanns demokratischer Sozialismus, eine Provokation moderner Sozialpolitik. In E. Heimann (Ed.), *Soziale Theorie des Kapitalismus: Theorie der Sozialpolitik* (pp. III–XXII). Suhrkamp.
Beck, U. (1986). *Risikogesellschaft. Auf dem Weg in eine andere Moderne*. Suhrkamp.
Beck, U. (1986/1992). *Risk Society: Toward a new modernity* (M. Ritter, Trans.). Sage.
Beck, U. (1987). Beyond status and class: Will there be an individualized class society? In V. Meja, D. Misgeld, & N. Stehr (Eds.), *Modern German sociology* (V. Meja & G. Schroeter, Trans., pp. 340–355). Columbia University Press.
Beck, U. (1988). *Gegengifte: Die organisierte Unverantwortlichkeit*. Suhrkamp.
Blumenberg, H. (1966-1976/1983). *The legitimacy of the modern age* (R. M. Wallace, Trans.). MIT Press.
Bruyn, S. T. (1991). *A future for the American economy: The social market*. Stanford University Press.
Büchele, H., & Wohlgenannt, L. (1985). *Grundeinkommen ohne Arbeit: Auf dem Weg zu einer kommunikativen Gesellschaft*. Europaverlag.
Chamayou, G. (2018/2021). *The ungovernable society: A genealogy of authoritarian liberalism* (A. Brown, Trans.). Polity.
Cohen, J. (1982). *Class and civil society: The limits of marxian critical theory*. University of Massachusetts Press.
Cohen, J., & Arato, A. (1992). *Civil society and political theory*. MIT Press.
Cronin, T. E. (1989). *Direct democracy: The politics of initiative, referendum, and recall*. Harvard University Press.
Dahl, R. A. (1985). *A preface to economic democracy*. University of California Press.
Dahl, R. A. (1989). *Democracy and its critics*. Yale University Press.
Dahms, H. F. (1992a). Die gesellschaftliche Rationalisierung der Ökonomie: Vom garantierten Mindesteinkommen als konstitutionellem Anrecht. *Soziale Welt*, *43*(2), 141–167.
Dahms, H. F. (1992b). Democracy and the post-enlightenment: Lyotard and Habermas. *International Journal of Politics, Culture, and Society*, *5*(3), 473–509.
Dahms, H. F. (1998). Beyond the carousel of reification: Critical social theory after Lukács, Adorno and Habermas. *Current Perspectives in Social Theory*, *18*, 3–62.
Dahms, H. F. (2006). Does alienation have a future? Recapturing the core of critical theory. In L. Langman & D. K. Fishman (Eds.), *The evolution of alienation: Trauma, promise, and the millennium* (pp. 23–46). Rowman and Littlefield.
Dahrendorf, R. (1959). *Class and class conflict in industrial society*. Stanford University Press.
Dahrendorf, R. (1959/1968). Liberty and equality: Reflections of a sociologist on a classical theme of politics. In *Essays in the theory of society* (pp. 179–214). Stanford University Press.
Dahrendorf, R. (1961/1967). On the origin of inequality among men. In *Essays in the theory of society* (pp. 151–178). Stanford University Press.
Dahrendorf, R. (1965/1957). *Society and democracy in Germany*. W. W. Norton.
Dahrendorf, R. (1983). *Die Chancen der Krise*. Deutsche Verlags-Anstalt.
Dahrendorf, R. (1987). *Fragmente eines neuen Liberalismus*. Deutsche Verlags-Anstalt.
Etzioni, A. (1988). *The moral dimension: Toward a new economics*. Free Press.
Fach, W. (1990). Wohlfahrt als Argument. Der Streit um den wirtschaftlichen Wert von Sozialpolitik. *Soziale Welt*, *41*(4), 441–453.
Fligstein, N. (1990). *The transformation of corporate control*. Harvard University Press.

Frey, B. S. (1983). *Democratic economic policy: A theoretical introduction*. Blackwell.
Gerhardt, K.-U., & Weber, A. (1984). Garantiertes Mindesteinkommen. Für einen libertären Umgang mit der Krise. In T. Schmid (Ed.), *Befreiung von falscher Arbeit. Thesen zum garantierten Mindesteinkommen* (2nd ed., pp. 18–70). Wagenbach.
Gilens, M. (1999). *Why Americans hate welfare: Race, media, and the politics of antipoverty policy*. University of Chicago Press.
Gilpin, R. (1987). *The political economy of international relations*. Princeton University Press.
Gorz, A. (1980/1982). *Farewell to the working class: An essay on post-industrial socialism* (M. Sonenscher, Trans.). Pluto Press.
Gorz, A. (1989/2011). *Critique of economic reason* (G. Handyside & C. Turner, Trans.). Verso.
Gould, C. (1988). *Rethinking democracy: Freedom and social cooperation in politics, economy, and society*. Cambridge University Press.
Granovetter, M. (2017). *Society and economy: Framework and principles*. Belknap Press: An Imprint of Harvard University Press.
Habermas, J. (1954). Die Dialektik der Rationalisierung. Vom Pauperismus in Produktion und Konsum. *Merkur, 8*(78), 701–724.
Habermas, J. (1981/1983). *The theory of communicative action. Vol. 1: Reason and the rationalization of society* (T. McCarthy, Trans.). Beacon Press.
Habermas, J. (1981/1987). *The theory of communicative action. Vol. 2: Lifeworld and system: A critique of functionalist reason* (T. McCarthy, Trans.). Beacon Press.
Habermas, J. (1985/1986). The new obscurity: The crisis of the welfare state and the exhaustion of utopian energies (P. Jacobs, Trans.). *Philosophy & Social Criticism, 11*(2), 1–18.
Habermas, J. (1985a). A philosophico-political profile. *New Left Review, I/151*, 75–105.
Habermas, J. (1985b). Dialektik der Rationalisierung. In J. Habermas (Ed.), *Die Neue Unübersichlichkeit* (pp. 167–212). Suhrkamp.
Habermas, J. (1990). What does socialism mean today? The rectifying revolution and the need for new thinking on the left. *New Left Review, I/183*, 3–22.
Habermas, J. (1992/1996). *Between facts and norms: Contributions to a discourse theory of law and democracy* (W. Rehg, Trans.). MIT Press.
Harvey, D. (2007). *A brief history of neoliberalism*. Oxford University Press.
Hegel, G. W. F. (1807/1977). *Phenomenology of spirit* (A. V. Miller, Trans.). Oxford University Press.
Hegel, G. W. F. (1821/1958). *Hegel's philosophy of right* (T. M. Knox, Trans.). Clarendon Press.
Heimann, E. (1929/1980). *Soziale Theorie des Kapitalismus*. Suhrkamp.
Heimann, E. (1954). *Wirtschaftssysteme und Gesellschaftssysteme*. JCB Mohr.
Heimann, E. (1955). *Vernunftglaube und Religion in der modernen Gesellschaft*. JCB Mohr.
Heimann, E. (1955/1961). *Reason and faith in modern society: Liberalism, Marxism, and democracy*. Wesleyan University Press.
Heimann, E. (1963). *Soziale Theorie der Wirtschaftssysteme*. JCB Mohr.
Jordan, B. (1986). *The state: Authority and autonomy*. Blackwell.
Jouet, M. (2017). *Exceptional America: What divides Americans from the world and from each other*. University of California Press.
Kaes, A., Jay, M., & Dimendberg, E. (Eds.). (1994). *The Weimar republic sourcebook*. University of California Press.
Keane, J. (Ed.). (1988). *Civil society and the state: New European perspectives*. Verso.
Kershaw, D., & Fair, J. (1976). *The New Jersey income-maintenance experiment, Vol. 1: Operations, surveys, and administration*. Institute for Research on Poverty Monograph Series. Academic Press.
Keynes, J. M. (1930/1963). Economic possibilities for our grandchildren. In J. M. Keynes (Ed.), *Essays in persuasion* (pp. 358–373). W. W. Norton & Co.
Kolko, J. (1988). *Restructuring the world economy*. Pantheon.
Kopnarski, A. (1990). *Gesichter der Armut. Armut im Wandel der Zeit—Ein Beitrag zur Ortsbestimmung der aktuellen Armut anhand der Ergebnisse einer empirischen Untersuchung in Konstanz*. Hartung-Gorre.
Koslowski, P. (Ed.) (2000). *The theory of capitalism in the German economic tradition: Historism, ordo-liberalism, critical theory, solidarism*. Springer.

Krohn, C.-D. (1987/1993). *Intellectuals in exile: Refugee scholars and the new school for social research* (R. Kimber & R. Kimber, Trans.). University of Massachusetts Press.
Krohn, C.-D. (1988). Deutsche Exil-Ökommen in den USA nach 1933. Das Beispiel der New School for Social Research. In I. Srubar (Ed.), *Exil, Wissenschaft, Identität: Die Emigration deutscher Sozialwissenschaftler 1933-1945* (pp. 142–163). Suhrkamp.
Kruse, V. (1994). *Historisch-soziologische Zeitdiagnosen in Westdeutschland nach 1945: Eduard Heimann, Alfred von Martin, Hans Freyer*. Suhrkamp.
Lefort, C. (1988). *Democracy and political theory* (D. Macey, Trans.). Wiley.
Lipset, S. M. (1996). *American exceptionalism: A double-edged sword*. W. W. Norton.
Lowe, A. (1987). In A. Oakley (Ed.), *Essays in political economics: Public control in a democratic society*. New York University Press.
Luhmann, N. (1983). *Rechtssoziologie*. Westdeutscher Verlag.
Luhmann, N. (1983/1985). *A sociological theory of law* (E. King & M. Albrow, Trans.). Routledge & Kegan Paul.
Luhmann, N. (1988). *Die Wirtschaft der Gesellschaft*. Suhrkamp.
Marshall, T. H. (1950). *Citizenship and social class*. Cambridge University Press.
Marx, K. (1842). *Debates on the law on thefts of wood* (C. Dutt, Trans.). Rheinische Zeitung. https://marxists.architexturez.net/archive/marx/works/1842/10/25.htm#n1
Marx, K. (1843/1970). *Critique of Hegel's philosophy of right* (A. Jolin & J. O'Malley, Trans.). Cambridge University Press. https://www.marxists.org/archive/marx/works/1843/critique-hpr/. Accessed on May 1, 2024.
Marx, K. (1859/1977). *A contribution to the critique of political economy*. Progress Publishers. https://www.marxists.org/archive/marx/works/1859/critique-pol-economy/preface.htm. Accessed on May 1, 2024.
Marx, K. (1894/1981). *Capital: A critique of political economy* (Vol. 3). Penguin Classics.
Meifort, F. (2017). *Ralf Dahrendorf: Eine Biographie*. C. H. Beck.
Offe, C. (1984). *"Arbeitsgesellschaft": Strukturprobleme und Zukunftsperspektiven*. Campus.
Offe, C. (1990/1996). The acceptance and legitimacy of strategic options in social policy. In C. Offe (Ed.), *Modernity and the state: East, west* (C. Turner, Trans., pp. 183–200). MIT Press.
Opielka, M., & Vobruba, G. (1984). *Das garantierte Mindesteinkommen*. Fischer.
Parsons, T., & Smelser, N. (1956). *Economy and society: A study in the integration of economic and social theory*. The Free Press.
Plum, W. (1990). Entstrukturierung und sozialpolitische Normalitätsfiktion. *Soziale Welt, 41*(4), 477–497.
Richter, E. (1992). *Der Zerfall der Welteinheit. Vernunft und Globalisierung in der Moderne*. Campus.
Rödel, U. (1990). *Autonome Gesellschaft und libertäre Demokratie*. Suhrkamp.
Rödel, U., Frankenberg, G., & Dubiel, H. (1989). *Die demokratische Frage*. Suhrkamp.
Schmid, T. (1986). *Befreiung von falscher Arbeit. Thesen zum garantierten Mindesteinkommen* (2nd ed.). Wagenbach.
Schumpeter, J. (1942/2003). *Capitalism, socialism, and democracy*. Routledge.
Seldon, A. (1990). *Capitalism*. Blackwell.
Skidmore, F. (1977). Publication of the New Jersey income experiment results. *Focus: Institute for Research on Poverty, 2*(1), 1–2. https://www.irp.wisc.edu/publications/focus/pdfs/foc21.pdf. Accessed on May 1, 2023.
Smith, A. (1776/2014). *The wealth of nations*. Shine Classics.
Swedberg, R. (1987). Economic sociology: Present and past. *Current Sociology, 35*(1), 1–144.
Swedberg, R. (1990). *Economics and sociology: Redefining their boundaries—Conversations with economists and sociologists*. Princeton University Press.
van Parijs, P. (1990). The second marriage of justice and efficiency. *Journal of Social Politics, 19*(1), 1–25.
Watts, H., & Rees, A. (Eds.) (1977a). *The New Jersey income-maintenance experiment, Vol. 2: Labor-supply responses*. Institute for Research on Poverty Monograph Series. Academic Press.
Watts, H., & Rees, A. (Eds.). (1977b). *The New Jersey Income-Maintenance Experiment, Vol. 3: Expenditures, health, and social behavior; and the quality of the evidence*. Institute for Research on Poverty Monograph Series. Academic Press.

Weber, M. (1922/2013). In G. Roth & C. Wittich (Eds.), *Economy and society: An outline of interpretive sociology*. University of California Press.
Wolin, S. S. (1989). *The presence of the past: Essays on the state and the constitution*. John Hopkins University Press.
Wolin, S. S. (1990). Democracy in the discourse of postmodernism. *Social Research*, *57*(1), 5–30.
Zukin, S. & DiMaggio, P. (Eds.) (1990). *Structures of capital: The social organization of the economy*. Cambridge University Press.

PART III

THE PROBLEM AND CHALLENGE OF HETERONOMY (APPLIED CRITICAL THEORY)

AUTHORITARIANISM FROM BELOW: WHY AND HOW DONALD TRUMP FOLLOWS HIS FOLLOWERS

David Norman Smith and Eric Allen Hanley

University of Kansas, USA

ABSTRACT

Controversy has long swirled over the claim that Donald Trump's base has deeply rooted authoritarian tendencies, but Trump himself seems to have few doubts. Asked whether his stated wish to be dictator "on day one" of second term in office would repel voters, Trump said "I think a lot of people like it." It is one of his invariable talking points that 74 million voters supported him in 2020, and he remains the unrivaled leader of the Republican Party, even as his rhetoric escalates to levels that cautious observers now routinely call fascistic.

Is Trump right that many people "like" his talk of dictatorship? If so, what does that mean empirically? Part of the answer to these questions was apparent early, in the results of the 2016 American National Election Study (ANES), which included survey questions that we had proposed which we drew from the aptly-named "Right-Wing Authoritarianism" scale. Posed to voters in 2012–2013 and again in 2016, those questions elicited striking responses.

In this chapter, we revisit those responses. We begin by exploring Trump's escalating anti-democratic rhetoric in the light of themes drawn from Max Weber and Theodor W. Adorno. We follow this with the text of the 2017 conference paper in which we first reported that 75% of Trump's voters supported him enthusiastically, mainly because they shared his prejudices, not because they were hurting economically. They hoped to "get rid" of troublemakers and "crush evil." That wish, as we show in our conclusion, remains central to Trump's appeal.

Keywords: Authoritarianism; prejudice; racial resentment; sexism; Theodor W. Adorno

SOLVING THE TRUMP PARADOX

Pundits, bemused by Donald Trump's apparent contradictions, have seldom been as insightful as Yascha Mounck and Daniel Ziblatt, who turned for insight to Max Weber early in Trump's 2016 campaign. The apparent paradox that perplexed so many, they wrote, is that Trump blended reactionary vitriol and violent pledges (e.g., "to kill the families of terrorists") with praise for Planned Parenthood and Canada's progressive state-run healthcare system.[1] The secret to this duality, they wrote, is Trump's status, not as a fascist in any ordinary sense, but as a demagogue, a role which Weber had anatomized with clinical accuracy in *Politik als Beruf*. Vanity, which tempts all politicians, is all the more tempting for the demagogue, who:

> ...is forced to count upon "effect." He is therefore constantly in danger of becoming an actor and taking lightly the responsibility for the outcome of his actions and of being concerned merely with the "impression" he makes....His irresponsibility... suggests that he enjoys power merely for power's sake without a substantive purpose. [And] because power is the unavoidable means, and striving for power is one of the driving forces of all politics, there is no more harmful distortion of political force than the parvenu-like braggart with power and vain self-reflection in the feeling of power...[2]

Mathew Yglesias, some months later, cited the same passage, but with the significant inclusion of the passage's closing phrase, rejecting "in general every worship of power *per se*."[3]

Another pundit, the veteran Republican political consultant Michael Maslansky, offered further insight in an article published in January 2016. Writing in *PR Daily*, Maslansky made clear that Trump is not the only Trumpian worshipper "of power *per se*": "He's made sexist comments, racist remarks... He has broken every rule [of political orthodoxy] and become stronger as a result." How? By emulating "the language of his audience." By finding "a simple, emotional way to put himself on the side of his audience members and leave them feeling like only he knows what they really want."[4]

From a marketing standpoint, the issue is how to zero in on the wishes of a target market. So what does Trump's audience, his target market, "really want"? In a second article, published the day before Mounck and Ziblatt published their article, Maslansky explained: "Our research is clear: the key to political persuasion, much like the key to selling, is to appeal to the audience's beliefs – not your own." Trump was successful because he knew what his market valued:

> [They] blame...political correctness run amok...They're conservative, but they don't identify as "conservative." That label isn't a core part of who they are. Above all, they long for a leader: someone strong and powerful, successful outside the Washington Beltway, and brave enough to say the things that (they think) need to be said.
>
> Through this lens, all the attacks on Trump backfire. Being called a bully is a compliment. Being called a false conservative is mere noise. Being attacked for outrageous comments is a sign he's doing something right![5]

Eight years later, as Trump's rhetoric grows ever more vengeful and totalitarian, his followers remain in lockstep with him. In March 2023, Trump vowed to be even harsher, more punitive: "In 2016, I declared, I am your voice. Today, I add: I am your warrior. I am your justice. And for those who have been wronged and betrayed, I am your retribution."[6] Among the betrayed, he now says, are the insurrectionary "J6 patriots," Biden's "hostages," whose pardons he promises.[7] Four months later, Trump's campaign circulated an email with a Nazi-like image of the Jewish financier George Soros, portrayed as Biden's globalist puppet master. A *New York Times* team found that Trump had sent his supporters "at least 790" emails in 2023 that depicted Soros or "globalists" more generally, as anti-MAGA conspirators – "a meteoric rise from prior years."[8]

By November 2023, former Republican stalwarts like Peter Wehner and Robert Kagan were sounding the alarm. Wehner, calling Trump's escalating rhetorical salvos "clearly fascistic," cited two now infamous speeches: "We pledge to you that we will root out the Communists, Marxists, fascists, and the radical-left thugs that live like vermin within the confines of our country." Immigrants, too, he had recently said, are "poisoning the blood of our country."[9] Kagan, one week later, published a widely noted article, "A Trump dictatorship is increasingly inevitable," citing the same speeches and arguing that liberals are deceiving themselves if they imagine that Trump's legal difficulties will hurt him politically. On the contrary, Kagan said:

> Trump will not be contained by the courts or the rule of law. On the contrary, he is going to use the trials to display his power. That's why he wants them televised. Trump's power comes from his following, not from the institutions of American government, and his devoted voters love him precisely because he crosses lines and ignores the old boundaries. They feel empowered by it, and that in turn empowers him.[10]

This was the context in which, a week later, Trump joined Sean Hannity for a Fox News town hall, where Hannity invited him to deny that he would be a dictator if he won a second term. Trump complied – "except or day one," he added. "I want to close the border, and I want to drill, drill, drill."[11]

Two weeks later, though he repeated his claim that immigrants are "destroying the blood of our country," Trump felt compelled to deny that he was channeling Hitler: "I never read *Mein Kampf*."[12] But unfazed by his critics – indeed, if Maslansky and Kagan are right, enjoying and profiting from their hostility – Trump persisted in protesting the unfairness of his treatment even when, on January 10, 2024, his attorney agreed in court that Trump's immunity was so absolute that he could not be prosecuted even if he ordered Seal Team 6 to assassinate a political rival.[13] His "Project 2025" allies in the Heritage Foundation, meanwhile, were now boasting about how radically they would deconstruct the administrative state in a second Trump presidency: "People will lose their jobs," in the tens or hundreds of thousands, when Trump eviscerates the civil service, the CEO of the foundation said. "Buildings will be shut down. Hopefully they can be repurposed for private industry."[14]

In March, Trump said that many undocumented workers who are accused of crimes are "not people."[15]

DICTATOR FOR A DAY

This din of claims and threats was in the air when reporter Eric Cortellessa interviewed Trump in April. Casually explaining his radical-right agenda for the moment when he achieved unfettered power – 11 million deportations, the deployment of the National Guard to suppress dissent, and more – Trump provoked Cortellessa to ask whether he feared repelling voters by saying, openly, that he would be a dictator "on day one."

> I ask him, Don't you see why many Americans see such talk of dictatorship as contrary to our most cherished principles? Trump says no. Quite the opposite, he insists. "I think a lot of people like it."

This, in a nutshell, is Donald Trump's theory of authoritarianism: "A lot of people like it."

The evidence supporting this contention is strong. Early evidence for Trump's ability to bottle the lightning of authoritarian wishes is provided below, in our report on voter attitudes in 2016. But recent evidence is available as well, in the form of a large, politically representative UMass/You Gov Poll: "Former President Donald Trump recently said that if elected, he would be a dictator only on the first day of his second term. Do you think that this is a good or bad idea for the country?" (UMass Amherst/UMass Poll, 2024). Asked that question, 76% of those who had voted for Trump in 2020 said yes. The same was true for 74% of Republicans and 71% of self-described conservatives – figures very close, as we will see below, to the percentages who described themselves as strong Trump supporters in the 2016 American National Election Study.

Further, more fine-grained analysis of the UMass data adds nuance to this picture. Contrary to popular expectations, poll respondents differed little by education level: Those whose education ended in high school were no more likely to regard a Trump dictatorship as "definitely good" than those with graduate school education (17% in both cases) and only fractionally more likely than those with "some college" (16%, vs. 13% for those with undergraduate degrees). Nearly as many less-educated respondents held negative views of a potential Trump dictatorship (57%) as did those with undergraduate degrees (63%). And, strikingly, differences in income levels proved to have no apparent significance whatever.[16]

What potentially undemocratic measures would Trump's supporters endorse? Here again, the UMass Poll is instructive. Two-thirds of all Republican respondents said they wanted to see the convicted January 6 rioters pardoned, while 76% said they would like to see President Biden impeached – and only 5% agreed that Trump is guilty of conspiring to overturn the 2020 election. Only 10% of Republicans agreed that a Trump dictatorship would be "definitely bad."[17]

These figures should give centrists who seek common ground with "moderate" Republicans pause. That, in fact, is precisely what Robert Kagan warned against in a second article on a potential Trump dictatorship, two days after Trump's interview with Sean Hannity. Trump in 2024, Kagan predicted, will portray himself as a "victim of persecution, [claiming] that Biden is a dictator...."

> By the time the trials get underway, that will be the standard Republican talking point. Today, it is just the most devoted Trumpers, but before long, we will see even respectable Republicans 'raising questions' about the prosecutions, to the point where the entire court proceeding will be delegitimized in the eyes of the ordinary Republican voter.
>
> What effect will that have on that small percentage of Trump supporters who now say they would drop their support if he were convicted? Those who cling to the hope that the trials will bring Trump down need to understand that the number of Republicans willing to abandon Trump because of a conviction, already small today, is going to be much smaller come spring. ...Republicans of all stripes [will] rally to the martyrdom of Trump.[18]

The accuracy of this prediction is no longer in doubt. Republicans, nearly across the board, accept the premise that Donald Trump is a martyr for their cause and, at the very least, are open to the idea of a Trump dictatorship.

Authoritarianism at the apex of the pyramid, in other words, seems to have a clear corollary at the base. This was the central finding of our 2017 paper, presented at the annual meeting of the American Sociological Association, which reported on the results of the Right-Wing Authoritarianism items that the American National Election Study (ANES) had included at our urging. That paper, "Voting for Trump," below, sheds light on Trump's appeal in ways that coincide with insights obtainable from a lecture in 1967 by Theodor W. Adorno – the principal author of *The Authoritarian Personality* (1950) – which appeared in print for the first time in 2019. We develop that point and further elaborate our account of Trump's demagogic appeal in our conclusion.

VOTING FOR TRUMP (2017)[19]

Since 1952, when the first ANES was conducted, the ANES has become the gold standard of randomized, nationally representative research into the attitudes of presidential and congressional voters. Surveys and interviews cover a wide and evolving range of subjects, investigating both attitudes and their demographic correlates (with respect, e.g., to income, employment status, marital status, and more). Many of the items that appear in these surveys and interviews are regularly deployed. But in each successive election year, there are generally new scales, as well.

In 2016, the ANES survey included two questions about attitudes toward leaders that we had proposed the year before. Those questions had proven to be powerfully predictive of attitudes toward ethnic and sexual minorities in 2012–2013, and in 2016, they proved to be no less powerful with respect to support for (and opposition to) Donald Trump. The aim of this presentation is to explain what we have learned as a result.

One overall result should be stressed at the outset – namely, that Donald Trump's support among white voters in the 2016 election can most immediately and meaningfully be explained as an expression of social and political attitudes, not, as many polls have suggested, as a consequence of education, income, age, gender, and marital status. It's true that his core constituency has a distinctive demographic profile. Trump's supporters, and especially his most enthusiastic supporters, are more likely than average to lack college degrees. They are also likelier than average to be older and male. But when we look simultaneously at voters' attitudes and demographic attributes, we find that attitudes matter most. Less educated white voters, like older voters and men, are only more likely to vote for Trump when they share his worldview.

We can say this with confidence thanks to a statistical procedure, well known to sociologists but not often discussed in public, called multiple logistic regression. The value of regression is that it allows us to look at many variables simultaneously, to see which ones have the most influence. Polls typically look at one issue at a time, which they report in percentages: Candidate X has risen 7% in the polls; support for policy Y is down by 12%. These are useful snapshots of trends over time, but they rarely give us enough data to fully understand any given trend or to allow us to grasp how one trend connects to another. Polls are great for day-to-day news reporting, but they leave many tiles out of the mosaic.

Multiple regression of the 2016 ANES election data enables us to take major strides toward completing the mosaic. We learn not only that attitudes mattered most for Trump voters but that specific attitudes toward minorities and women and leaders played especially significant roles in the election.

What We Examined

In order to cast a wide explanatory net, we explored the relative influence of 17 variables in all. Five of these are often-cited population variables – gender, marital status, age, education, and income – and a dozen are attitude variables.[20] Our intent in casting such a wide net was twofold: first, to identify the principal attributes that distinguish pro-Trump voters from non-Trump voters; and second, to learn what attributes distinguish enthusiastic Trump supporters from mild Trump voters.

To achieve this goal, we statistically tested the influence of our 17 variables on both outcomes (voting for Trump, and voting for Trump with enthusiasm) for all white voters in the ANES survey (1,883) for whom we have complete data. Of those voters, 51.99% (979) voted for Trump and 38.02% (716) voted for Trump with enthusiasm. When we look only at 979 white voters who voted for Trump, the latter number – 716 – translates into 73.14% of the 979 pro-Trump voters.[21]

In other words, over half of the white voters who were surveyed by the ANES voted for Donald Trump, and nearly three quarters of his vote came from enthusiastic supporters.[22]

Our main findings pivot around the attitudes that yielded these results. But we also have demographic facts to report, which we report below.

Was It the White Working Class?

The standard narrative about the election takes this form:

> Trump's core supporters are "white working class" voters without college degrees who have been left behind in a globalizing economy that places a higher priority on technology than on manual labor. These workers are likely to have lost their jobs, or to be vulnerable to competition from immigrants or workers abroad. Trump won their votes with a populist rhetoric that tapped into their personal financial woes and worries.[23]

This narrative does not withstand close scrutiny. A very large pre-election study showed that Trump's supporters were less likely to be jobless or employed part-time than other voters. This study also showed that, though somewhat more of Trump's supporters than other voters work in production (9.6%–8.2%), they tend to be skilled workers with above-average wages and below-average direct exposure to immigrant workers. Changes in employment growth from 2000 to 2015 at the level of the community had no impact on the vote – and, in fact, higher shares of employment in manufacturing for communities in 2000 predicted *less* support for Trump in 2016, not more.[24]

It is also worth noting that self-employment was associated with Trump support and that business ownership was modestly associated as well. The latter facts are relevant in several ways. The claim that the white working class formed the core of Trump's support is generally an inference from the fact that relatively few Trump voters have 4-year college degrees. But it's unwarranted to assume that noncollege voters are production workers. Currently, there are 18.5 million white production workers and roughly 14 million white service workers in the United States. But the grand total of white Americans without 4-year college degrees is much larger – 135 million. There are, in other words, over 100 million white Americans without bachelors' degrees who work neither in production nor in the service sector. Of that total, 17 million are small business owners, of whom the large majority are reliably Republican voters.[25]

It is also instructive to note that, in the primary elections, when Trump's support peaked at 30.39% among voters without high school diplomas, his voters averaged just 0.28 fewer years of education than other Republican voters and that they averaged 0.84 more years of school than their statewide peers.[26]

Nor is poverty a distinguishing feature of Trump supporters. In fact, Trump outpolled Clinton by a larger margin among voters with household incomes from $70,000 to $120,000 than among any other group.[27] The same pattern obtained during the primaries, when Trump won broad support across the board but, especially, among those with $50,000 to $110,000 in annual income.[28] Although, overall, Trump's primary voters had lower average incomes than other Republican voters ($81,570 vs $72,870), they were still significantly better off than the average US adult ($56,130) in 2016. In fact, the median income gap between Trump and other Republican primary voters ($8,700) was just 52% as great as the gap between Trump voters and average adults in their states ($16,740). In the primaries, Trump had more support at every level of education and income than any of his Republican rivals. In the general election, he showed less strength among the truly rich and the truly poor, who voted disproportionately for Hillary Clinton, but he held his own in the middle.

Divided by Worldviews

The findings above, which we derive from a variety of sources, take on a deeper meaning when we explore them in the light of what we learned from the 2016 ANES. Our statistical analysis shows that Trump voters were not only reasonably secure with respect to their finances, but, in addition, they *felt* reasonably secure. In 2016, *pocketbook worries did not distinguish Trump voters from others.*

Voters who felt financially insecure were just as likely to be Democrats as Republicans – a striking fact, since, in almost all other instances, attitudes differed across party lines. In general, attitudes overshadowed demographics. But attitudes toward personal finances were not among the dividing lines in the 2016 election.

Class, clearly, matters greatly. So does every other aspect of personal status and experience that influences voters' life chances. But contrary to the assumptions of many pundits and party strategists, whose devotion to the premise that economic self-interest is the central driver of politics bears a clear resemblance to vulgar Marxism, "kitchen table" issues have not proven decisive in this hour of culture war. What Trump's voting base wants, more than anything, is a domineering leader who will settle scores with their perceived enemies.

This, at least, is the conclusion that emerges from our analysis of the ANES data, which we reached by a series of steps. We began by setting aside attitude variables to look exclusively at the influence of demographics (age, education, etc.). We then examined the same demographics and a single attitude, to see what effect that might have. We then did the same thing with two attitudes, and we concluded our analysis by looking simultaneously at all of the five demographic variables and a dozen attitudes.

That exercise beamed a ray of life into pro-Trump voters. A parallel exercise, to differentiate strong from mild Trump supporters, proved equally enlightening. The tables below (1a–1d) show what we learned at each stage in this inquiry, showing raw percentages for each group of interest: strong Trump supporters, milder Trump voters, and voters who supported other candidates. Starting, in the opening tables, with demographics, we then move on to consider attitudes.

The demographic results are clearly complex. Numbers in **bold** text show the proximity between groups. These numbers show that Trump's partisans and his milder supporters resembled each other with respect to age, gender, and marital status while they differed in these respects from other voters. But differences between these two sectors of Trump's voting base nevertheless do appear, namely, with respect to education and income.

Table 1a. Differences Among White 2016 Voters *(Bivariate Distributions)*.

Voters	Strongly Pro-Trump	Mildly Pro-Trump	Not Pro-Trump
Male	**50.56**	**49.04**	43.69
Female	**49.44**	**50.95**	56.31
Married: No	**33.38**	**32.70**	37.28
Married: Yes	**66.62**	**67.30**	62.72
Age (in years)	**54.41**	**53.48**	50.31
College degree: No	33.66	48.67	**59.62**
Annual income	$79,000	**$98,100**	**$99,100**

Note: Mean values for Strong Trump Voters ($N = 716$), Mild Trump Voters ($N = 263$), and Other Voters ($N = 904$).

Table 1b. Prejudices Across the Spectrum of White 2016 Voters.

Attitudes Toward…	Strongly Pro-Trump	Mildly Pro-Trump	Not Pro-Trump
African Americans	7.60	6.57	3.83
Immigrants	6.74	5.53	3.57
Muslims	6.34	5.42	4.05
Reverse discrimination	4.92	4.16	2.50
Women	4.68	4.38	2.66

Note: Average scores per attitude, on 1–10 scales where 10 is the most negative attitude.

Table 1c. Authority-Relevant Attitudes on 1–10 Scales for White Voters in 2016.

Attitudes Towards…	Strongly Pro-Trump	Mildly Pro-Rump	Not Pro-Trump
Children	6.45	5.52	3.45
Domineering leaders	7.71	6.46	3.48

Note: Average scores per attitude indicate higher levels of support for authoritarian leadership.

Table 1d. Other Key Attitudes on 1–10 Scales Across the Spectrum of White 2016 Voters.

Attitudes Toward…	Strongly Pro-Trump	Mildly Pro-Trump	Not Pro-Trump
Health of the economy	6.54	5.48	3.66
Liberalism/conservatism	7.10	6.60	3.57
General religiosity	6.45	5.94	3.57
Fundamentalism	5.22	4.11	2.41

Note: Average scores per attitude, where 10 is the highest possible score.

We see that strong and mild Trump voters differ modestly in terms of gender, age, and marital status. Mild Trump voters are slightly younger and likelier to be married, and they are more likely to be women. But these differences are not great enough to put mild Trump voters in close proximity to non-Trump voters. The picture differs, however, with respect to education and income. Here, we see that mild Trump voters and non-Trump voters are both strikingly more affluent than strong Trump voters – and, in fact, mild Trump voters are just $1,000 less affluent in annual median income than non-Trump voters.

These contrasts disappear, however, when we turn to attitudes. Here, pro-Trump and non-Trump voters are divided by a chasm. We present the relevant data below in three small tables. We look first at measures tapping prejudices against four specific groups and then at an item alleging discrimination against whites. We then inspect a pair of measures which are often associated with authoritarianism, one of which is our own, and, finally, we examine a number of related attitudes.

In each of these instances, Trump voters and non-Trump voters are clearly divided with respect to prejudice.

Both of these measures, especially with respect to domineering leaders, markedly divide Trump from non-Trump voters.

Here too, in each of these four cases, Trump voters hold attitudes that significantly distinguish them from non-Trump voters.[29]

The impressive magnitude of the differences in Tables 1a–1d is shown by a separate calculation of the degree to which a 1-point increase in any of these attitudes, on a 10-point scale, would increase the chance of voting for Trump (See the Appendix Tables). We learn from that calculation that, for every one-point increase in support for domineering leadership, there is a 16.2% increase in the likelihood of voting for Trump. Similarly, an increase in prejudice toward women is associated with a 23.5% increase in pro-Trump voting while bias against immigrants yields an increase of 22% and bias against African Americans corresponds to a 19.4 increase. All these attitudes, and the others reported in the tables below, are powerfully predictive. As is readily apparent, even the largest contrast between strong and mild Trump supporters is smaller than any of the differences between Trump and non-Trump voters.[30]

Trump and non-Trump voters may not be wholly distinct in demographic terms, but they differ acutely in their opinions.

Attitudes Toward Children and Leaders

Our unique contribution to the 2016 ANES survey consists of a two-item Domineering Leader scale which we proposed to the ANES. We drew these two items from a well-known scale which has evolved steadily since Bob Altemeyer of the University of Manitoba first constructed it. Altemeyer introduced this scale in two books, in 1981 and 1988.[31] But by the 1990s, as he wryly noted, these books had unleashed a "flood" of only five publications by other authors.[32] That would soon change. But until 2012–2013, when a five-item version of Altemeyer's scale which we proposed was included in the ANES internet supplement to the 2012 survey, his items had been studied mainly in small samples of students, among others. The inclusion of the items we had proposed was thus a small breakthrough.

Below, we show the two items that we borrowed from Altemeyer which were included in the 2016 ANES survey. We call this the Domineering Leader scale:

Respondents are asked to agree or disagree, strongly or otherwise, with two statements:

(1) Our country will be great if we honor the ways of our forefathers, do what the authorities tell us to do, and get rid of the "rotten apples" who are ruining everything.
(2) What our country really needs is a strong, determined leader who will crush evil and take us back to our true path.

These items have been fixtures of Altemeyer's scales since he introduced them, respectively, in 1986 and 1994. They have proven their reliability and validity in an ever-widening circle of studies carried out by a growing number of scholars since RWA research began to take off in the 1990s. But until now, the degree to which this research has generalizable findings has been speculative, since nearly all the research has been conducted with convenience samples (primarily of students and, at times, their parents) rather than with nationally representative samples. When, in 1994, Altemeyer introduced our second item ("crush evil"), he surmised that, if the general public held views akin to those of his students, "tens of millions of North Americans" would favor giving domineering leaders, unburdened by democratic scruples, a free hand to crush their purported enemies.[33] We now know that he was prescient on this point. Donald Trump received nearly 63 million votes in 2016, and our data show that his supporters fervently agreed that "rotten apples" should be eliminated and "evil" crushed.

Why has it taken so long for Altemeyer's scale to enter the arena of representative national surveys? In part, because the ANES (and, to this day, the General Social Survey) long regarded a different scale as the default source of insight into the same mentality. In that research, respondents are asked to choose one trait from each of four pairs of childhood traits. We call this measure the Child Trait scale:

Please tell me which one you think is more important for a child to have:

(1) Independence or respect for elders?   (2) Curiosity or good manners?
(3) Obedience or self-reliance?   (4) Being considerate or well-behaved?

In 2016 as in previous election-year surveys, the ANES regards the underlined choices as the answers indicating a wish for domineering authority. But earlier this year, a political scientist reported that this scale was an ineffective predictor or support for Trump.[34] The implication, widely reported in the press, was that other attitudes mattered but that the wish for domineering authority did not.

We decided to see for ourselves. Our thesis was that the Domineering Leader scale would have greater explanatory power than the Child Trait scale. This hypothesis was inspired by our sense that support for domineering leaders who promise to "get rid" of troublemakers was likely to be more common and influential among right-wing voters than preferences for respectful, mannerly, and obedient children. We now know that, among white voters in the 2016 election, that thesis has been borne out.

The Child Trait scale has real strengths. We found in 2012 that respondents who prefer propriety to curiosity and consideration were modestly but significantly more likely than average to resent African Americans.[35] And at first glance, our data analysis, reported below, suggests that the Child Trait scale does in fact predict support for Trump. Tables 2a and 2b below display data on Trump voters in two columns, which we call Trials 1 and 2. In the first of these trials, we ignored attitudes and looked only at gender, income, marital status, age, and education. Our goal was to learn how these variables influenced pro-Trump voting.

Since higher numbers indicate stronger effects, we learn from Table 2a that education and marital status have sizable effects – and that age is also relevant.

Table 2a. Variables Relevant to Support for Trump Among White Voters, $N = 1{,}883$.

Voting for Trump	Trial 1	Trial 2
Population Variables		
Education (some college or less = 1)	0.834***	0.416**
Marital status (married = 1)	0.402**	0.404**
Age (years)	0.012***	0.007
Gender (male = 1)	0.097	0.019
Income (in tens of thousands USD$)	−0.013	0.000
Attitudes		
Children's traits		0.277***

Notes: In this simplified table and in the tables below, we omit standard errors, constants, and pseudo-r square figures.
Fuller data appear in the complete regression tables in the appendices.
*$p < 0.05$; **$p < 0.01$; ***$p < 0.001$.

(Since age is counted year after year, small numbers can have large cumulative effects, as they do in this case.)

To properly interpret Table 2a, we need to recall that asterisks, here and below, indicate *reliable* results. When numbers in these columns appear with asterisks beside them, they are likely to reflect statistically significant results. That is, we can rely on these results; we can have confidence that they are true. By that criterion, we see from Trial 1 that education and age have particularly significant effects as well as particularly strong effects. (The presence of three asterisks indicates that the probability of a misleading result is very low. Two asterisks also indicate a high probability of significance.) Hence, we can trust the finding that age and especially education are strongly associated with pro-Trump voting.[36]

This is how we know that voters without bachelors' degrees are disproportionately represented among Trump voters.[37] So, more modestly, are older voters and married voters.

In Table 2b, meanwhile, our aim is to distinguish strong from mild Trump voters by the same statistical method we used in Table 2a, and the result is similar.

We learn, from Trial 1 above, that education is powerfully predictive with respect to Trump voting, just as it had been for the decision to vote for Trump in the first place. And although the effects revealed in Table 2a were stronger, we learn from this trial that enthusiastic Trump voters were less affluent and less likely to have college degrees than their milder counterparts.

In short, these results reinforce what we had already deduced from the raw numbers – that, demographically, with respect to income and education, mild Trump voters more closely resemble non-Trump voters than they resemble strong Trump voters.

In the trials shown in Tables 2a and 2b, above, we report what we found with respect to the hypothesis that preferences for several childhood traits also have a

Table 2b. Variables Relevant to Strength of Support Among White Trump Voters, $N = 979$.

Voting Enthusiastically	Trial 1	Trial 2
Population Variables		
Education (some college or less = 1)	0.528**	0.430**
Marital status (married = 1)	0.354	0.378
Age (years)	0.002	0.002
Gender (male = 1)	0.208	0.183
Income (in tens of thousands USD$)	−0.036**	−0.034*
Attitudes		
Children's traits		0.097**

Note: $*p < 0.05$; $**p < 0.01$; $***p < 0.001$.

significant bearing on attitudes toward Trump. An initial inspection of the data lends this thesis some support. Factoring Child Trait responses into our analysis yields a strong and significant coefficient (0.277***) with a corresponding decrease (from 0.834*** to 0.416**) in the significance and strength of the variable "some college or less."[38] We found the same pattern, though to a lesser degree, with respect to the relative strength of pro-Trump enthusiasm among his supporters.

The implication here is that less educated voters are likelier than average to vote for Trump, and to vote for him enthusiastically, largely because they tend to prefer conventional, conforming children. It is true that once we have identified every less educated voter who prefers well-behaved, respectful children over creative, independent children, we have found a substantial percentage of pro-Trump voters. And if this were the end of the story, we might conclude that the Child Trait hypothesis had been proven correct, at least with respect to the 2016 election. But when we test that hypothesis by including a single additional measure – attitudes toward domineering leaders – a different story emerges. Demographics fade into the statistical background, and Child Trait preferences lose their predictive power (though they do remain statistically significant).[39]

Authoritarian Wishes and Domineering Leaders

We show that result in the tables below, where the Trial 3 column shows the effects of analyzing both Domineering Leader and Child Trait items. We do this first for Trump voting *per se* in Table 2c, and then again for strong versus mild Trump support in Table 2d.

The effects here are massive. The results for Trial 3 show that when we factor just these two attitude variables into the analysis, the only demographic variable that retains any strength is marital status, and even this has reduced reliability. Education, which had already declined sharply when only Child Trait items were taken into account, now falls to virtual inconsequence. Both attitudes, toward

Table 2c. Variables Relevant to Support for Trump Among White Voters, $N = 1883$.

Voting for Trump	Trial 1	Trial 2	Trial 3
Education (some college or less = 1)	0.834***	0.416**	−0.014
Marital status (married = 1)	0.402**	0.404**	0.369*
Age (years)	0.012***	0.007	0.007
Gender (male = 1)	0.097	0.019	0.115
Income (in tens of thousands USD$)	−0.013	0.000	0.015
Attitudes			
Children's traits		0.277***	0.121***
Domineering leaders			0.487***

Note: *$p < 0.05$; **$p < 0.01$; ***$p < 0.001$.

children and leaders, yield significant and reliable results, and the wish for domineering leaders, in particular, eclipses every other variable.

A parallel result emerges when, in Table 2d, we report the results of a fourth trial. Here, from the sample of 979 white voters who supported Trump in 2016, we see that the strength of support for Trump also varies significantly with attitudes toward children and, above all, domineering leaders.

These numbers tell a striking story. Once again, the wish for a domineering leader emerges, with undiminished statistical significance, as the main dividing line between strong and mild Trump voters; child trait preferences, meanwhile, fall by the wayside.[40]

This story becomes more nuanced, as we show below, when we take other variables into account. But the essential lessons of Table 2d retain their validity – namely, that strong Trump supporters are even more desirous of domineering leaders than mild Trump voters, though they are no likelier to prefer obedient children to self-determining children.

Of the results we have reported thus far, the one that most dramatically clashes with standard narratives is the relatively small role played by education, once we

Table 2d. Variables Relevant to Strength of Support Among White Trump Voters, $N = 979$.

Voting Enthusiastically	Trial 1	Trial 2	Trial 3	Trial 4
Education (some college or less = 1)	0.528**	0.430**	0.331	0.215
Marital status (married = 1)	0.354	0.378	0.371	0.399
Age (years)	0.002	0.002	0.002	−0.001
Gender (male = 1)	0.208	0.183	0.264	0.317
Income (in tens of thousands USD$)	−0.036**	−0.034*	−0.025*	−0.021
Children's traits		0.097**	0.048	−0.003
Domineering leaders			0.241***	0.150***

Note: *$p < 0.05$; **$p < 0.01$; ***$p < 0.001$.

explore attitudes as well. This is not to say that education is irrelevant – the disposition to vote for Trump is clearly most pronounced and widespread among voters without 4-year college degrees.

But what our results show is that the main reason these "less educated voters" are likelier than average to support Trump is that they are likelier than average to share his worldview.

By now, few observers would doubt that Donald Trump sees the presidency as an imperial office. What we learn from Table 3a, below, is that a great many of his partisans agree, and that support for a domineering president is, in general, far more widespread among less educated white voters than among college educated white voters.

What this shows is that, among white voters, education was strongly associated with the wish for a domineering leader. In the upper quartile of the distribution, less educated white voters expressed high enthusiasm for strong leaders who vow to silence troublemakers. A similar result is found, interestingly, in the upper quartile of college educated white voters as well, but to a lesser degree, since these high-scoring college educated voters were no more eager for domineering leadership than were noncollege voters in the middle of their distribution. And many voters with college degrees entirely disavow the wish for an imperial president. The median score for these voters (3.7) shows that they are likelier to oppose than support domineering leadership; the score at the 25th percentile reveals even stronger opposition.

It could easily seem that our scale items so powerfully predict support for Donald Trump because they so closely resemble his rhetoric. But these items were crafted decades before Trump entered politics, and they proved powerful in 2012, as they have innumerable times in smaller samples. The evidence suggests, rather, that Trump owes his success largely to the fact that he tailored his rhetoric to the wishes of his electorate.[41] When the Republican primary season began, there were 16 other candidates for the nomination – but none of them sounded like Donald J. Trump. None promised to stifle dissent or "get rid of" troublemakers with anything resembling his brash, brazen energy. Facing a choice between conventional Republicans and a fire-breathing bully, the primary voters chose the bully. The underlying wish that fueled this choice, our results show, was an outright preference for aggressive, punishing leadership, as shown by the responses to our Domineering Leader items.

Table 3a. Statistical Dispersion of Scores on a 1–10 Scale Measuring Attitudes Toward Leaders by Education, White Voters Only, $N = 1,883$.

	Some College or Less			Four-Year College Degree		
Percentiles	25th	50th	75th	25th	50th	75th
Domineering leader score (1 = low, 10 = high)	5.0	7.5	8.7	1.2	3.7	7.5
Number of cases		975			908	

Note: High scores indicate stronger support.

The strength of these items is not, strictly speaking, a surprise. Altemeyer and many others had used these items for decades before the ANES, at our urging, included them with three others from the RWA scale in the 2013 internet study that polled many of the same subjects who had been interviewed in the 2012 election survey.[42] We found, in our analysis of the combined 2012–2013 data, that over and above the effects of demographics and other attitudes the five items we had drawn from Altemeyer's full 20-item scale had large and significant effects on racial resentment and on negative attitudes toward African Americans.[43] We also found that for every one-point increase in scores on our scale, support for same-sex marriages and adoptions fell by 27.1% and 23.3%, respectively, and that support for civil unions fell by 20.0%.

One of the central takeaways from our research is in both 2012–2013 and 2016, attitudes proved stronger than demographics. That proved to be true in 2012–2013 with respect to prejudice, which we examined in the light of our five-item RWA scale, and it proved to be true again in 2016 with respect to presidential voting, which we assessed with the two RWA items that performed best in 2013.[44] Those two items, which accounted for 89% of the total variance in the 2013 results which we obtained with the five-item scale, also predicted anti-minority prejudice and homophobia with similar strength and significance.[45]

Crushing Evil and Eliminating Enemies

The Child Trait scale is generally regarded as a measure of submissiveness. The Domineering Leader scale, in contrast, measures the wish for a strong leader who will force *others* to submit. The premise is that evil is on the march and that minorities and liberals are winning the culture war. The government, which Trump voters believe should defend the old order, has become "politically correct," and even moral authority now appears to have been usurped by undeserving intruders. The wish for a domineering leader is the wish to see this evil crushed.

To what extent, then, do Trump supporters want to *submit* as well as dominate? Support for a bullying leader might appear to imply a wish to submit, but that support is not unconditional. Only leaders who fight usurpers are supported and only as long as they stay the course. Authorities who tolerate usurpers are regarded as usurpers themselves; the power they wield, so plainly nonauthoritarian, is denounced as false, fraudulent.

Ground-level insight into the mentality is available in Arlie Russell Hochschild's 2016 ethnography of Tea Party supporters in Louisiana. Interviews with 40 subjects enabled Hochschild to decode the structure of what she calls the "deep story" underlying the feelings her subjects were expressing. When she showed a précis of this deep story to those subjects, they generally said "Yes, that's it exactly"; "You read my mind."

This précis now takes the form of a vignette Hochschild calls "The Line-Cutters." Her subjects have the sense, she writes, that there are "people cutting in line" ahead of them. Many of these line-cutters are African American, beneficiaries of affirmative action. Others are women, immigrants, and refugees. And maddeningly, even as they cut in line, "You're asked to feel sorry for them." They "see President Barack Hussein Obama waving the line-cutters forward. He's on their side. In fact, isn't he a line-cutter too?...Obama is using the money in your pocket to help the line-cutters. He and his liberal backers have removed the shame from taking. The government has become an instrument for redistributing your money to the underserving. It's not your government anymore; it's theirs."[46]

This vignette matches the spirit of the survey questions that Tea Party supporters and right-wing Republicans have endorsed for years. In 2006, researchers found that a four-item RWA scale which includes our "rotten apples" item explained significant variance in support for Bush's invasion of Iraq.[47] Two recent studies via Amazon's Mechanical Turk found that short RWA scales strongly and significantly correlated with the intention to vote for Trump ($r = +0.46$ and $r = +0.47$, both $p < 0.001$).[48] One of those studies investigated RWA in relation to a nine-item Trump scale which included this strongly associated item: "It takes a macho guy like Trump, who doesn't let anyone push him around, to be President of the United States."[49]

A similar point emerged from a 2016 study which included this item: "Because things have gotten so far off track in this country, we need a leader who is willing to break some rules if that's what it takes to set things right."[50] Nearly three quarters of Trump supporters – 72% – agreed with this statement, far more than Republicans in general (57%), or voters who fear terror attacks (57%), or white voters with only some college (51%) or only a high school education (62%).[51]

Exit polls, similarly, show that pro-Trump voters wanted a president who will shake things up. Nearly two-fifths of the 24,558 subjects in the exit polls said that what they want most in a president is the ability to "bring change." This answer was given more often than the combined *total* of the next most frequent responses, experience (22%), and compassion (15%). In fact, so many Trump voters gave this answer – 85% – that they accounted for nearly 32% of the entire electorate.[52]

Barack Obama had promised change, too. But what he represented was not, in the aptly chosen words of Christopher Parker and Matt Barreto, the kind of change the Tea Party, or the MAGA crowd, could believe in.[53]

Preferences, Prejudices, and More

Aesop, long ago, set a precedent for today's right-wing morality tales when he contrasted ascetic, hard-working ants with indolent, free-loading grasshoppers. Today's right-wing moralists add a dimension to this story when they contrast tough, domineering leaders, who punish grasshoppers, with lax, enabling authorities who purportedly reward "takers" while punishing "makers." It seems, in short, that a preference for domineering leaders is often, at the same time a prejudice against *other* kinds of leaders. The wish to elevate a domineering leader, in other words, often coincides with a wish to punish *other*, liberal, democratic leaders. This kind of prejudice, this kind of wish, as we see from the 2016 Election Study, converges with several other familiar prejudices.

We learn, from the ANES data, that education is predictive with respect to hostility toward women and minorities, just as it is with respect to support for domineering leaders. This is clear from Tables 3b and 3c:

This shows that less educated voters express more across the board negativity, toward every group, at every percentile. This is also what we see in Table 3c with respect to domineering leaders and African Americans:

The parallels here are almost uncanny, especially for less educated voters, whose scores match exactly at the 25th and 75th percentiles. This is also roughly what we see, but with finer and more abundant detail, when we step back to examine the big picture that emerges when we statistically analyze all 17 of our variables at once.

The decisive influence exerted by attitudes could hardly be clearer. When all 12 attitude variables are taken into consideration, every single demographic variable fades into insignificance, with the modest exception of marital status. Child Trait attitudes lose their punch, and so do personal financial worries and non-fundamentalist religiosity.[54]

Of the remaining attitudes, eight remain robust predictors of pro-Trump support among white voters. These are: Conservative self-identification, support for domineering leaders, fundamentalist Christianity, and six kinds of negativity (toward African Americans, immigrants, Muslims, women, and the health of the economy). These attitudes were evoked by questions new and old.

Table 3b. Statistical Dispersion of Scores on Selected 1–10 Scales by Education, White Voters Only, $N = 1,883$.

	Some College or Less			Four-Year College Degree		
Percentiles	25th	50th	75th	25th	50th	75th
Attitudes Toward...						
African Americans	5.0	6.9	8.7	2.5	5.0	6.9
Immigrants	4.2	5.6	7.5	**2.7**	4.2	5.8
Muslims	3.9	5.2	7.2	**3.3**	4.6	5.8
Reverse discrimination	3.0	4.0	5.5	1.5	3.0	4.5
Women	3.1	4.3	5.4	1.7	3.2	4.4
Number of cases		975			908	

Note: Higher scores indicate more negative attitudes.

Table 3c. Statistical Dispersion by Education on 1–10 Scales White Voters Only, $N = 1,883$.

	Some College or Less			Four-Year College Degree		
Attitudes Toward...	25th	50th	75th	25th	50th	75th
Domineering leaders	5.0	7.5	8.7	1.2	3.7	7.5
African Americans	5.0	6.9	8.7	2.5	5.0	6.9

Table 4a. Trump Voting, White Voters Only, $N = 1,883$.

Voting for Trump	Trial 1	Trial 2	Trial 3	Trial 4
Education (some college or less = 1)	0.834***	0.416**	−0.014	−0.164
Marital status (married = 1)	0.402**	0.404**	0.369*	0.331
Age (years)	0.012***	0.007	0.007	0.001
Gender (male = 1)	0.097	0.019	0.115	−0.039
Income (in tens of thousands USD$)	−0.013	0.000	0.015	0.018
Attitudes Toward...				
Child traits		0.277***	0.121***	−0.042
Domineering leaders			0.487***	0.196***
African Americans				0.177***
Reverse discrimination				0.114
Immigrants				0.197***
Muslims				0.137*
Women				0.211**
Personal finances				0.002
Health of the economy				0.376***
Liberalism versus conservatism				0.486***
General religiosity				0.028
Fundamentalism				0.107*

Note: $*p < 0.05$; $**p < 0.01$; $***p < 0.001$.

Feelings about African Americans were elicited by means of the "racial resentment" scale, which has appeared in countless surveys, including many previous ANES surveys. Items of a similar nature were grouped into scales probing attitudes toward immigrants and Muslims. And since, for the first time, the ANES in 2016 included items tapping both "hostile" and "modern" sexism, we merged those scales and found, by factor analysis, that seven of those items work cohere. This enabled us to ascertain, as we show in Table 4a below, that expressions of gendered resentment also predict pro-Trump voting with strength and significance.[55]

On Balance

Overall, what the data we report in Table 4a reveal is that pro-Trump voting was driven by a wide spectrum of attitudes. Since these attitudes are most common among men and older, less educated voters, those groups loomed large in Trump's election. But our core finding about authoritarianism makes this finding *intelligible*. The reason Trump's base is disproportionately male, older, and less educated is that these groups are disproportionately eager to see domineering presidential action against line-cutters and rotten apples.

What, then, are we to make of the puzzling fact that, as we see in Table 4a, Trump voters are acutely pessimistic about the state of the economy and yet no more worried about their personal finances than other voters? The likely answer is that, as researchers have often shown, "sociotropic" attitudes toward the economy typically reflect partisan prejudices more than they do personal concerns. Voters who reject the incumbent president tend to judge the economy harshly – and that tendency is aggravated when the incumbent president is viewed harshly by voters whose racial resentfulness has been inflamed by what they see as political correctness. The latter finding has been reported by Michael Tesler, whose analysis of ANES data reveals that pessimism about unemployment was strongly and significantly associated with racial resentment in both 2012 (0.369***) and 2016 (0.416***). Republican partisanship and conservatism were also associated with economic pessimism, though to a lesser extent. And when party loyalties and political ideologies were held constant, racial resentment, by itself, accounted for nearly 40% of the abyss between the economic views of racial liberals and racial conservatives.[56]

Similar findings were reported by Jonathan Rothwell and Pablo Diego-Rosell, who found that macroeconomic attitudes are "endogenous to political preferences." They found, also, that economic pessimism is most common among older and lower income white voters, not because they are hurting more than others but as a function of their worldviews.[57]

Table 4b shows the results we obtain on this topic for Trump's strong partisans.

Table 4b. Variables Relevant to Strength of Support Among White Trump Voters, $N = 979$.

Voting Enthusiastically	Trial 1	Trial 2	Trial 3	Trial 4
Education (some college or less = 1)	0.528**	0.430**	0.331	0.215
Marital status (married = 1)	0.354	0.378	0.371	0.399
Age (years)	0.002	0.002	0.002	−0.001
Gender (male = 1)	0.208	0.183	0.264	0.317
Income (in tens of thousands USD$)	−0.036**	−0.034*	−0.025*	−0.021
Attitudes Toward...				
Child traits		0.097**	0.048	−0.003
Domineering leaders			0.241***	0.150***
African Americans				0.060
Reverse discrimination				0.195**
Immigrants				0.164**
Muslims				0.075
Women				−0.069
Personal finances				0.025
Health of the economy				0.177***
Liberalism versus conservatism				0.064
General religiosity				−0.060
Fundamentalism				0.156**

Note: $*p < 0.05$; $**p < 0.01$; $***p < 0.001$.

What we see here is that strong and mild Trump voters were divided from each other by four of the eight attitudes that also divided Trump's supporters from nonsupporters: anti-immigrant nativism, authoritarian support for domineering leaders, economic pessimism, and Christian fundamentalism. Trump partisans outscored his milder supporters on each of those scales, and that difference made a difference: The higher the score, the greater the chance of voting for Trump. (Interestingly, sexism and self-reported conservatism do *not* seem to have distinguished enthusiastic from mild Trump voters. In other words, these are attitudes they share.)

The role played by racial resentment in the Trump camp is complex. On the one hand, ordinary racial resentment is widespread among both strong and mild Trump voters, but at the same time, an anti-minority scale that we constructed from several items alleging discrimination against whites did clearly distinguish ardent from lukewarm Trump voters.[58] Ardent supporters were significantly likelier than other Trump voters to allege anti-white discrimination, in this way manifesting, it seems, a particularly acute sense of victimization by purported line-cutters.[59] The wish for a domineering leader, which is strongest among Trump enthusiasts, is also, it seems, the wish to overturn an inverted moral order.[60]

What Next?

Trump's presidency, chaotic from the start, has already sustained some bumps and bruises, and some of milder backers have begun to peel away. Polls show that independents and voters who switched from Obama to Trump are among those showing signs of incipient disaffection. But his already legendary base has remained largely unmoved by his travails, leading pundits to wonder, in alternating tones of doubt and hopefulness: What, if anything, could Trump do that would alienate his base?

Our findings suggest that, in fact, the only way Trump could disillusion his base would be to change his tune, to restrain or apologize for his hectic denunciations of liberals, immigrants, Muslims, and other culture-war enemies. As long as he continues to play the part of the domineering leader, thwarting line-cutters and punishing political correctness, he will retain their loyalty. And if, uncharacteristically, Trump did begin to show signs of faltering strength or resolve, that would disappoint his base but leave their appetite for domination undiminished. Trump could exit the scene, but the Trumpist wish to rid the world of evil would remain intact. Trumpism could survive, in other words, long after Trump left the stage.

In the meantime, as we have seen, more than a quarter of Trump voters were not among his enraptured supporters. A good percentage of the electorate is always gripped by some degree of ambivalence, and that makes voters' loyalties volatile – on both right and left. The next frontier is to better understand that challenging fact, so that we can better defend liberty and equality against their aroused, militant enemies.[61]

AFTERWORD: A STRIDENT MINORITY (2024)

Today, seven years after we first reported these findings, the faint note of hopefulness in the closing paragraph now seems dated. Ambivalence is still very real, and Trump's base, however strident, remains a minority. And yet. Year after year, month after month, we have seen Trump's grip on his base harden as his tone has grown unrelievedly grim. *New York Times* reporter Charles Homans reports anecdotally on the "stunning" shift in tone he has witnessed over the years, a shift that sociologist Bart Bonikowski confirms by advanced social-scientific methods.[62]

What explains this hardening tone and stiffening intransigence? One important clue, we think, lies in the power of what Bob Altemeyer memorably called "the other authoritarian personality."[63] Named "Social Dominance Orientation" by its discoverers, Felicia Pratto and Jim Sidanius, SDO was shown by Sam McFarland and Sherman Adelson to match RWA in its explanatory power vis-à-vis ethnocentrism.[64,65] And SDO and RWA differ significantly in characterological tenor.

Where high RWA scorers divide the world in moralistic, Manichaean fashion between good and evil, high SDO scorers divide humanity into winners and losers, calling themselves winners and, from the safety of anonymity, openly avowing the amorality of their narcissistic pursuit of self-interest. High SDO and RWA scorers are equally scornful of outsiders and the weak, and both are eager to see them trampled underfoot. But high SDO scorers are also scornful of high RWAs, whose moralism they see as weakness.[66] SDO narcissism is individual, while RWA narcissism orbits around group identities.

The wider significance of the SDO-RWA divide became apparent when panelists from the 2012 ANES internet sample were randomly reinterviewed in July 2013. Subjects in those interviews were asked to respond to four SDO items that we had also proposed to the ANES in 2011, alongside the five RWA items that the ANES also fielded in 2013. We soon learned that both scales were powerful, with robust, independent effects on bias, net of the effects of other variables. A 30-point RWA increase, for example, yielded a 7.98 increase in racial resentment, while a matching increase in SDO yielded a 6.81 point increase. And SDO proved stronger than RWA – or indeed, any of the other attitude variables or demographics – with respect to anti-Black affect and stereotypy. SDO was also the single strongest variable with respect to presidential vote choice. With all else held constant, the odds of voting for Romney instead of Obama rose 65% with a shift from the 25th to the 75th SDO percentile; for RWA, the same shift yielded a 54% increase in favor of Romney.[67, 68] SDO was also the variable most strongly associated with conservatism and anti-immigrant nativism.[69]

In 2016, when the ANES inexplicably omitted SDO items, other researchers found that SDO and RWA both played key roles in Trump voting.[70] Our strongest 2013 SDO item ("We should do what we can to equalize conditions for everyone") also proved effective in enhanced SDO scales pioneered by researchers including Jim Sidanius (SDO7) and Felicia Pratto (SSDO, with Sidanius).[71]

SDO's impact in 2016 was apparent in other surveys as well.[72] Factor analysis has shown that SDO subdivides into two factors. One of these, "Opposition to Equality," was found to predict Trump votes *per se*, while the other, "Group Dominance," predicted Trump support among white Republicans: "For each unit increase in group-based dominance, the odds of supporting Trump – rather than another Republican – increased by a factor of 1.34, holding all other variables constant."[73]

Surveys with large student samples also proved revealing.[74] In 2022, for example, SDO outperformed RWA with respect to racial resentment and anti-immigrant nativism in a survey of 504 sociology undergraduates and, in that same survey, was independently and strongly associated with sexism, both hostile and modern. RWA remained strong as well, especially vis-à-vis vote choice, where the probability of voting for Trump over Biden in 2024 rose 48% for every unit increase in RWA.[75]

RWA's strength was further shown when, in late 2019, the Monmouth University Polling Institute carried out a representative national test of Altemeyer's full 20-item RWA scale.[76] The results, he reports, were among the most significant ever recorded. Monmouth found that a five-item RWA scale which included our "crush evil" and "rotten apples" was very nearly as effective as the full 20-item scale.[77] In 2021, the same scales Monmouth had used were administered in the United States and seven other nations by Morning Consult, with similar albeit less dramatic results. Altemeyer, reviewing that survey, named "crush evil" and "rotten apples" as two of the three strongest items.[78] That survey also empirically established what many people have long intuited – that, currently, support for domineering leadership is significantly stronger in the United States than in most other major electoral democracies.

Even such influential exponents of the Child Trait scale as Stanley Feldman, Marc Hetherington, and Andrew Engelhardt now acknowledge RWA's relevance for inquiry into authoritarianism. In a 2023 paper, revisiting the 2016 ANES, they defend the suitability of the Child Trait scale for the study of authoritarianism by connecting it to our two key items. Without directly addressing our argument, above, they nevertheless report that, when they reviewed the Child Trait scale in conjunction with a scale anchored by our "rotten apples" and "crush evil" items, the two scales significantly covaried[79]:

> The tight fit between the childrearing battery and the two questions drawn directly from the RWA measure suggest that the childrearing and RWA approaches capture the same underlying concept. For the first item, "What the country really needs is a strong, determined leader who will crush evil and take us back to our true path," 17.5% of those scoring lowest (0) on the childrearing measure agree compared to 74.3% of those scoring high (4).

> On the second question, "Our country would be great if we honor the ways of our forefathers, do what the authorities tell us to do, and get rid of the 'rotten apples' who are ruining everything," agreement ranges from 23.3% to 78.3%.[80]

Engelhardt and his coauthors conclude, on this basis, that "Those high on the childrearing measure are expressing authoritarian, not socially conservative, beliefs." They thus construe covariance with our two principal RWA items as validation of the Child Trait scale: "If RWA taps authoritarianism," they write, "then the childrearing scale must, too."[81]

BEYOND THE NUMBERS

Given that Trump supporters average high scores on social dominance as well as on right-wing authoritarianism, what does that suggest about the dialectic between this particular domineering leader and his inveterate followers? Trump strikes most observers as supremely idiosyncratic – but if Theodor Adorno is right, he is, in fact, a classical modern demagogue, playing a traditional role and following a traditional script.

We saw earlier that, according to Max Weber, the more a demagogue is "compelled to count upon 'effect'," the greater is the danger that he will be reduced to a mere "actor," heedless of the consequences of his actions and "concerned merely with the 'impression' he makes." This, of course, sounds very much like a premonition of Donald Trump. But for Adorno, there is more to be said, namely, that what Weber called the ultimate "distortion of political force" – *the power-quest of* "the parvenu-like braggart with power" – is precisely the *role* the demagogue must play, in his hour on the stage, if he hopes to enjoy more than what Weber called the "glamorous semblance" of power.

For Adorno, as he first explained with respect to the radio preacher Martin Luther Thomas in 1943, the fascistic agitator must play the role of an iconoclastic outsider, boasting about his greatness and about the power of the movement he incarnates, and yet, at the same time, personifying every regular-guy failing.[82] He must be a towering figure yet "relatable."

The will and ability to personify those opposite traits, Adorno stresses, is rare yet essential for the upstart demagogue.[83]

In 2019, with Trump in office and incipient right-wing extremism on the rise in Germany and elsewhere, another, equally relevant Adorno text appeared in print. Originally a lecture, delivered by Adorno to the *Verbands Sozialistischer Studenten Österreich* on April 6, 1967, *Aspekte des neuen Rechtsradikalismus* warns about the dangers posed by forces like the nascent *Nationaldemokratische Partei Deutschlands*, which had just won eight seats in Hesse and 15 in Bavaria.[84]

Today, in yet another fraught moment, Adorno's characteristically acute analysis is timely yet again. His claim, in fact, is that modern demagogic success rests on principles which were as valid in 1967 as they had been in 1943 and, previously, in Hitler's Germany. Today, too, we can benefit from his insights into the personality type "which I referred to in *The Authoritarian Personality* as the 'manipulative type'." The defining character traits of the ideal-typical manipulator, as depicted by Adorno, closely resemble the traits associated by other, later researchers with "Machiavellians" (so-called by Richard Christie in the 1950s) and now, since the 1990s, with Social Dominators.[85] Manipulators seduce their followers by placing rational means in service to morally irrational ends, catalyzing repressed taboo-breaking wishes among the otherwise "authority-bound."

Manipulators, like SDOs, are not authoritarians in the traditional sense. Adorno identified manipulators as high scorers on the *F*-scale whose motives distinguished them from authoritarians *per se*. They, like conventionalists and conspiracists (Adorno's "cranks"), scored high on the precursor to the RWA scale without manifesting the telltale, twofold traits of the classical authoritarian, aggressiveness toward out-groups and submissiveness toward dominators.[86] Manipulators, who are "even more compulsive than the authoritarian," prey on those who wish for a dictator, achieving psychic balance, Adorno wrote in *The Authoritarian Personality*, by "narcissistic withdrawal into their inner selves, ...reducing outer reality to a mere object of action." Profoundly amoral, the manipulator treats others as means to ends, repressing "any urge to love" and revealing what Adorno's chief collaborator Else Frenkel-Brunswik called "an exploitive-manipulative type of power orientation" in interpersonal relationships, not least in "their relations to the opposite sex."[87]

Fortunately, true manipulators are rare: "In our sample, the conventional and the authoritarian types seem to be by far the most frequent."[88] But recently, the balance has begun to shift.[89] As the percentage of high RWA scorers dwindles, the percentage of high SDO scorers appears to be rising. That in itself is alarming, if Adorno was right that manipulators, unlike authoritarians, are susceptible to psychopathology and, in some cases, outright psychosis.[90] Altemeyer, meanwhile, has called attention to the rising number of "Double Highs," who score high on *both* RWA and SDO. Those Double Highs, he argues, are among the most dangerous of today's domineering leaders.[91] Capturing and manipulating repressed RWA energies, they have the potential to catalyze and lead mass right-wing movements.

SOCIAL DOMINATORS MARKET THEIR WARES IN THE AUTHORITARIAN MARKETPLACE

Manipulators, of course, cannot simply will such movements into existence. The objective conditions must permit the growth of a constituency *susceptible* to manipulation. Periodically, however, that prospect is realized, when "the potential offered by the objective conditions is seized and exploited" by an agitator capable of channeling and harnessing the wishes of an "authority-bound" base. About the indispensability of that base Adorno is very definite: "It is said again and again that these movements promise something to everyone."[92] Clearly, that claim contains an element of truth, given the vague generality of the agitator's typical promises.

> But it is [also] wrong in that there is a very specific and very pointed unity in this appeal to the authority-bound personality *[die autoritätsgebundene Persönlichkeit]*. You will never find a single statement that does not correspond to the pattern of the authority-bound personality. And when you expose the structure of this appeal to the authority-bound personality, it really makes the right-wing radicals white-hot, which I would say proves, at least, that you have struck a nerve in this structure.[93]

Manipulators – high SDOs, Machiavellians, Double Highs – need high RWAs as their base. They win that base by propaganda, which Adorno in 1967 called "the center" of radical-right agitation, "in a certain sense," he explained, its very substance. "This propaganda is less...the dissemination of an ideology [than] a technique of mass psychology. It is based on the model of the authority-bound personality, in the same way today as in the time of Hitler or in the movements of the 'lunatic fringe' in America or anywhere else."[94,95]

Adorno devoted much of *Aspekte* to the elaboration of a typology of the agitator's means of manipulation – the time-tested appeals that galvanize authority-bound listeners. This classificatory framing, which had been central to his earlier work on Martin Luther Thomas, Adorno regarded as a perennial challenge for democratic educators whose most vital need is to find a way to counter right-wing talking points by means of applied theory. In all, as Harry Dahms has shown, Adorno identified a dozen "nerve points" for resistance to right-wing manipulation.[96] Beyond the mere "bare-faced lie," these nerve points typically pivot around hostility toward those who are branded as enemies, usurpers, traitors – "system" politicians, who humbly confess the sins of the ethnocentric past and denigrate national symbols, sparking "fits of rage and acts of violence"; and opportunistic businessmen, who sell national assets to foreigners and encourage "foreign infiltration by guest workers." All these alleged misdeeds, Adorno concludes, activate *"der Komplex der* punitiveness," which, he says, is often infused with more than a hint of outright sadism.[97]

Adorno is well aware, as he repeatedly emphasizes, that the success of right-wing movements hinges on far more than propaganda and psychology alone. Many social and economic conditions must pre-exist, and converge, in ways that can be wholly fortuitous.[98] But the dialectic of call and response, manipulation and reception, is also essential. Oddly, many of Adorno's leading current expositors draw precisely the opposite conclusion, either (they think) from his own texts on authoritarianism or (they argue) in reaction to his errors.

Peter Gordon, who wrote the preface to Verso's new edition of *The Authoritarian Personality*, credited Adorno with a hermetically anti-psychological stance in an influential paper, first presented in April 2016, and since widely reprinted, on Adorno's significance for Trump and Trumpism: *"The Authoritarian Personality* Revisited: Reading Adorno in the Age of Trump." Gordon is categorical: "...what Adorno was identifying in fascism was not a structure of psychology or the political precipitate of a psychological disposition. Rather, it was a generalized feature of the social order itself....If Adorno was right...we might conclude as follows."

> Trumpism is not anchored in a specific species of personality that can be distinguished from other personalities and placed on a scale from which the critic with an ostensibly healthy psychology is somehow immune. Nor is it confined to the right-wing fringe of the Republican Party, so that those who self-identify with the left might congratulate themselves as not being responsible for its creation. Nor can it be explained as the Frankenstein's monster of a racism once deployed cynically as a dog whistle by both the Republican and Democratic Parties, and now expressed openly...[99]

Nearly every line that Adorno ever published about authoritarianism, demagogues, and character traits contradicts this conclusion.[100] In 1967, Adorno echoed long-held views when he said that, in psychoanalytic terms, he was convinced that, "of the forces mobilized here, the appeal to the unconscious desire for disaster, for catastrophe, is by no means the least significant."[101] What the demagogue offers, beneath the surface, is the promise of a *Götterdämmerung*. This attracts those among high scorers whose real-world challenges leave them destitute of hope: "I would add – and I am speaking especially to those of you who are rightly skeptical about any merely psychological interpretation of social and political phenomena – that this behavior is by no means purely psychologically motivated; it also has an objective basis."[102] Yet psychology matters, and greatly:

> All those who see nothing [to hope for] and do not want the social foundation to change have no alternative, really, but to say, like Richard Wagner's Wotan, "Do you know what Wotan wants? The End." Owing to his social situation, they want the demise, not of their own group, but if possible the destruction of the whole."[103]

Adorno was undoubtedly still enough of a Marxist to recall the triumphal final line of the *Internationale*: "We have been naught, we shall be all!"[104] His point here, in effect, is that authoritarians without hope – and he sees repressed despair as their truth – expect just the reverse. Framed as the other side of the coin of the original lyric, their ulterior fear, and conviction, is this: "We have been all, we shall be naught." Their nihilism, in short, is the wish to have their enemies join them in defeat.

Whatever we may now think of this inference, Adorno is unambiguous about the nihilism he detects just below the surface of right-wing supremacism. Reactionary prophets of crisis remind him, he says, "of the type of manipulated astrology one finds today, which I consider an extremely important and typical socio-psychological symptom, because, in a sense, they want the catastrophe, they feed off apocalyptic fantasies...."[105]

Aside from the unrepentant Gordon, who recently claimed that Trump's success in microtargeting heralds the hemorrhage of critique and the triumph of "epistemic passivity," few of Adorno's interpreters have been bold enough to claim *The Authoritarian Personality* as their charter for the disavowal of the self.[106] But that disavowal is common. Claudia Leeb, in *Contesting the Far-Right* (2024), puts Adorno's propaganda typology to excellent analytic use but faults him for giving too much weight to potential and actual autonomy: "...Adorno suggests that the mechanism that generates the libidinal bond between the demagogue and the followers is identification." Freud, however, has shown us "that introjection and not identification is what generates the libidinal bond between the leader and the followers."

> Fascist propaganda techniques make the followers "fall in love" with the fascist demagogue through a process whereby they incorporate the idealized leader into themselves, replacing their ego ideal with the internalized leader figure. ...[This] generates deindividualized subjects...who completely surrender themselves to the love object. Such subjects cease to be critical of anything the leader does and willingly carry out his commands.[107]

Graham Potts, writing in 2007 about Adorno and *The Apprentice*, takes a similar stance. "Adorno," Potts muses, "is of the opinion that the critical cognitive function that may reject this situation [of reification] has not been completely subsumed, and that individuals may resist this process 'within certain limits'...."[108] But Potts feels that *The Apprentice* has proven Adorno wrong. "What has happened since...Adorno wrote causes a considerable cloud of doubt to be cast upon this final, somewhat positive assertion":[109]

> What *The Apprentice* represents is the overcoming of the final obstacle to total unfreedom: the critical cognitive facilities of the individual.[110]

AUTONOMY REDEEMED

Clearly, Trump's act has proven impressive, not least to those in the hermeneutic circle around Adorno. The question this raises is familiar and perennial: To what extent has Trump changed hearts and minds, effecting, by what Freud regarded as hypnotic means, what Max Weber called *metanoia*?[111] Or has Trump succeeded to the extent that he has, conversely, by adapting to his audience? If the latter is true, then however much causal priority we may ascribe to Trump personally, the center of gravity in the relationship lies with the audience. He must tell them what they want to hear.

The latter, briefly, is Adorno's view.[112] In the 1946 essay in which he distilled his findings about Martin Luther Thomas into reflections on the larger significance of far-right propaganda, he compared the theatrics of the strutting, boasting demagogue to the "social phenomenon of the soap opera." The intent, in each case, is to put on a show, a captivating display of showmanship that gratifies the listener by its form as well as its content. "Show," he writes, "is indeed the right word."

> The achievement of the self-styled leader is a performance reminiscent of the theater, of sport.... They shout and cry, fight the Devil in pantomime, and take off their jackets when attacking 'those sinister powers.'[113]

However much the demagogue may resemble the audience – in the case of Double Highs, they would be likely to share RWA attitudes – they differ in at least one fundamental respect, namely, that demagogues "know no inhibitions in expressing themselves. They function vicariously for their inarticulate listeners by doing and saying what the latter would like to, but either cannot or dare not. They violate the taboos which middle-class society has put upon any expressive behavior on the part of the normal, matter-of-fact citizen."[114]

The transgressiveness of this performance is as much the point as anything the propagandist says overtly. The aim is to break the chains of convention, to desublimate repressed wishes. The rally itself, enjoyment of the performance and identification with the performer, is as much the object of the ritual as its official goal. Such rituals, of course, often have brutally real consequences, and demagogues often have real-world objectives in mind, beyond their own aggrandizement. But to succeed on either level, personally or socially, they must know how to perform, and here too, there are implicit rules.

Adorno stresses, for example, that effective agitators must resist the temptation to impress intellectuals. They must avoid "discursive logic" and fact-based argument, relying instead, "particularly in oratorical exhibitions, [on] what might be called an organized flight of ideas. The relation between premises and inferences is replaced by a linking-up of ideas resting on mere similarity, often through association by employing the same characteristic word in two propositions which are logically quite unrelated."

> This method not only evades the control mechanisms of rational examination, but also makes it psychologically easier for the listener to "follow." He has no exacting thinking to do, but can give himself up passively to a stream of words in which he swims.[115]

A second advantage of this untethered speech is that it can deceive intellectuals into seeing the demagogue's logical somersaults as evidence of mental deficiency. Intellectuals, in a way, are the demagogue's second target market; by flooding the air with spaghetti-like speech, demagogues win cheers from the like-minded and derision from their opponents; overestimation on the one hand and underestimation on the other. Both work to their advantage.

What demagogues need most, though, is support from the like-minded. They achieve this, Adorno says, by a hectic performance which is, above all, "a symbolic revelation of the identity [the performer] verbalizes, an identity the listeners feel and think, but cannot express.

This is what they actually want him to do, neither being convinced nor, essentially, being whipped into a frenzy, but *having their own minds expressed to them.*"[116]

Demagogues, in short, follow their followers. They prove that *they are the like-minded*, inflated replicas of their own listeners. This is the wisdom of the marketer, as we learned from Michael Maslansky. This is what Max Weber feared braggarts could achieve by their bragging. Often, they are high SDOs, posing as high RWAs – Machiavellians, in a sea of moralists.

THE DEMOCRATIC EDUCATOR MUST BE EDUCATED

Where does this leave us? Adrift, without a proven antidote for manipulation. But at least we have clues about the nature of that manipulation and some of its roots and branches. That in itself, Adorno says, is a step on the path to democratic insight. We know from hard experience "that these authority-bound characters are inaccessible, that they will not let anything get through to them."

> Nonetheless – and I must ask you to forgive me if I refer to *The Authoritarian Personality* once again – nonetheless it transpired that, simply by making a socio-psychological problem out of these personalities who behave in this way and not any other, by reflecting on them, and on the connections between their ideology and their psychological, their socio-psychological structures, by making this a problem, a certain naivety in the social climate has been eliminated....[117]

The very act of publishing *The Authoritarian Personality* brought the problem out of the shadows. The core premise of that book remains highly controversial, not least, Adorno says, because there is often stubborn resistance to the attempt to probe the depths of unconscious as well as conscious motivation: "if one brings these things up, people suddenly become very scientific; they explain that the [nature or even the reality] of the authority-bound personality, cannot be proved statistically with the necessary exactitude..."[118] Clearly, with representative national data now in hand, we have the means to better approximate that kind of exactitude, with respect not only to RWA and SDO but also, e.g., the inveterate sexism of the far right.[119]

We also now know that, while education is always relevant, its roles differ in different places. In the South and Midwest, Trump's high RWA appeal extended to all white voters, whether they were college educated or not. But in the Northeast, Trump was actually *less* popular with less educated white voters than Romney had been in 2012. And in the West, Trump was no more or less popular than Romney had been among white voters without college degrees. What mattered most, in each region, was prejudice and the wish for a domineering leader. That wish was unevenly distributed, both geographically and demographically, but wherever it was found, it drove support for Donald Trump.[120]

Findings like these, however statistically exact they may be, will always require interpretation, if we hope to achieve the kind of insight we need to arm us for the struggle against manipulation. On this subject, Adorno has yet another pertinent observation to offer: "Perhaps I can also remind you of one of the findings from our *Authoritarian Personality* research in America, which revealed that even prejudiced personalities, who were certainly authoritarian, repressive, politically and economically reactionary, when it came to their own transparent interests, transparent to themselves, reacted quite differently."

> So they were mortal enemies of the Roosevelt administration, for example, but with those institutions that were of direct benefit to them, such as tenant protection or cheaper medicines, that was where their anti-Rooseveltianism immediately stopped and they behaved relatively rationally. This split in people's consciousness strikes me as one of the most promising points of departure to counter the developments I have discussed.[121]

In this light, one of the features of Trumpism that anti-authoritarians have typically found most puzzling – the simultaneous rightism *and populism* displayed by many Trump voters – becomes more readily understood. Trump's less educated and less fortunate supporters have no objection to welfare programs which benefit *them*. What they object to is welfare for others, above all, as we know, minorities and immigrants.[122]

IN LIEU OF A CONCLUSION

We close now, as Adorno did, with a call to action. Returning to the premise that right-wing radicalism is not simply "a psychological and ideological problem but a very real and political one," Adorno insisted nonetheless, in 1967, that the demagogues' reliance on deception forces their opponents "to operate with ideological means," that is, by means of counter propaganda: "...that is why, alongside political struggle by purely political means, one must confront it on its own turf. But we must not fight lies with lies, [rather] we must counteract them with the full force of reason, with the genuinely unideological truth."[123]

> Perhaps some of you will ask me, or would like to ask me, what I think about the future of right-wing extremism. I think this is the wrong question, for it is much too contemplative.
>
> In this way of thinking, which views such things from the outset as natural disasters to be predicted, as if they were tornados or weather catastrophes, [we see] a form of resignation in which one effectively annuls oneself as a political subject, revealing a harmful, spectator-like relationship to reality.
>
> How these things will evolve, and the responsibility for how they will evolve – that ultimately lies in our hands.[124]

NOTES

1. Yascha Mounck and Daniel Ziblatt (2016).
2. Max Weber (1919, p. 51). The translation here is slightly different than the version of this passage cited by Mounck and Ziblatt, which is drawn from the standard English translation, in *From Max Weber* (1949, p. 116).
3. Matthew Yglesias (2016).
4. Michael Maslansky (2016a).
5. Michael Maslansky (2016b). A fuller account of Maslansky's research and the views he and other marketing professionals take with respect Trump's tireless salesmanship appears in David Norman Smith (2023).
6. Steve Bannon, in a recent *New York Times* interview, called this speech central to understanding Trump's current thinking and plans. See Charles Homans (2024).
7. Marianne LeVine et al. (2024).
8. Karen Yourish et al. (2024).
9. Peter Wehner (2023).
10. Robert Kagan (2023b).
11. Jill Colvin and Bill Barrow (2023).
12. Michael Gold (2023).
13. Amy Davidson Sorkin (2024). Trump's attorney had said that Trump could be prosecuted only if Congress impeached him for that assassination.
14. Lulu Garcia-Navarro (2024).
15. Marisa Iati (2024).
16. UMass Amherst/UMass Poll (February 7, 2024). Respondents with graduate education were outliers in this survey, since, while they included a typical number of those strongly in favor of a Trump dictatorship, a larger-than-average number (71%) were strongly opposed. https://www.umass.edu/news/article/plurality-americans-support-removing-trump-presidential-ballots-due-insurrection
17. UMass Amherst/UMass Poll (2024).
18. Robert Kagan (2023a).
19. An abbreviated version of this paper appeared in *Critical Sociology* under the title "The Anger Games," with most but not all of our statistical tables (Smith & Hanley, 2018). The present, unabbreviated paper provides the full text and all of our original tables. Some parts of the narrative have been lightly edited for stylistic reasons.
20. Several other attitudes we explored (e.g., toward small government and egalitarianism) had negligible effects.
21. These figures contrast slightly with the exit polls, but they tell essentially the same story.
22. We determined strength of support by means of the ANES item V162035 – POST: Preference strong for Pres cand for whom R voted.

23. See David Brooks (2016), who concluded, shortly after Trump clinched the nomination, that he had catalyzed a "coalition of the dispossessed" made up of workers who had "lost jobs, lost wages, lost dreams." See also the extended discussion of this theme by Joan C. Williams (2017).

24. Jonathan Rothwell and Pablo Diego-Rosell (2016, pp. 1, 14, 15, 18) and *passim*. Rothwell and Diego-Rosell show that, of the innumerable community- and zip code-level variables they probed in connection with voters' attitudes, employment was 70th on the list and holding a production job was just the 94th most significant. More important, they found, was that Trump voters tend to live in white enclaves with low population densities, high levels of reliance on social security income, high levels of disability and ill health (diabetes, but not obesity or drug-related deaths), higher mortality rates for middle-age whites and relatively low education levels.

25. See the census figures cited by Kim Moody (2017). It is also relevant that, as Jamelle Bouie notes (2016), the noncollege working class is now just 58% white, which is a historically low figure.

26. See Jeff Manza and Ned Crowley (2017, p. 14 and, pp. 23–24) (Tables A1 and A2).

27. Robert Griffin and Ruy Teixeira (2017) show that the second largest group of Trump voters had annual incomes ranging from $50,000 to $70,000.

28. See the analysis of pre-election voting by Manza and Crowley (2017, pp. 12–14 and 23–24).

29. Pocketbook worries slightly distinguished Trump from non-Trump voters but, statistically, insignificantly.

30. All the differences reported below are statistically significant, and most (including all of the Trump vs non-Trump differences) are significant at the highest level, $p < 0.01$.

31. Bob Altemeyer (1981, 1988).

32. See the full discussion of the RWA scale's history in Altemeyer (1996).

33. Altemeyer (1994, p. 134).

34. Thomas Wood (2017), reporting on the 2016 ANES data, found that Trump voters had slightly lower Child Trait scores than average Republican voters in recent elections, but that they scored high on racial resentment. While a shift from the 50th to the 75th percentile in the Child Trait scale corresponded to a 20% increase in racial resentment, the same shift corresponded to only a 3% shift in the likelihood of voting for Trump.

35. See Smith et al. (2015a).

36. By the same criteria, since zero asterisks suggest low reliability, we see in Trial 1 that gender and income have relatively low reliability as well as small effects.

37. On this point, the ANES results confirm one of the best-established results from the 2016 exit polls, namely, that less educated voters were disproportionately likely to vote for Trump. Our findings clarify those results by showing that less educated white voters were disproportionately likely to support Trump only because they tended to share his prejudices to an unusually high degree.

38. In counterpoint, we see that the relationship between Child Trait attitudes and marital status appears to be negligible.

39. Our data do not permit clear insight into rural voters, but we now have the *Survey of Rural America* (2017), which shows that rural support for Trump (54%) resembles the support he receives from white voters overall, and that his many of his rural backers appear to be mild supporters. When asked whether immigrants "strengthen" or "burden" the country, 48% replied "strengthen" and 42% said "burden." When asked whether the country is "losing out" due to racial discrimination, rural respondents divide evenly between those who say that discrimination against minorities is the main problem and those who allege discrimination against whites. Only 32%, however, say that needy people often fail to get government help, while twice as many (64%) say that government help often goes to those who are simply irresponsible.

40. Stanley Feldman, a key defender of the Child Trait scale and thesis that authoritarianism has submissiveness at it center, found (2017, forthcoming) that Trump's success in the 2016 primaries was positively associated with Child Trait scores but that a measure of intolerance and punitiveness had "a much larger marginal effect."

41. See now David Norman Smith (2023).

42. The 2012 study obtained a representative national sample by multistage area-probability sampling. Of that sample, a subset, recontacted via internet in 2013, was asked further questions, including five RWA items from Altemeyer's 20-item scale. These items included our Domineering Leader items. Since we explored these data with an interest in bias, we restricted our analysis to white respondents for whom we had nonmissing values or the core variables (N = 1,023) for the questions about African Americans. Similarly, for items concerning homophobia, we analyzed only those respondents who identified as heterosexual for whom we had nonmissing values for core variables (N = 1,378).

43. In 2012–2013, the ANES also included a four-item Social Dominance Orientation (SDO) scale that we had recommended that scale proved to be powerfully predictive of several forms of prejudice, especially overt racial stereotyping. Unfortunately, the 2016 ANES survey did not also include these SDO items.

44. See Smith et al. (2015b).

45. Thanks to Dr Brock Ternes for running these numbers for us.

46. Arlie Russell Hochschild (2016b): A longer version of this story appears in Hochschild (2016a, pp. 137–140). Here to the list of line-cutters she adds "overpaid public sector workers" and brown pelicans. And in light of the fact that, as we saw earlier, Trump voters have above average employment and income – and disability assistance – we can surmise that deprivation is in the eye of the beholder.

47. Linda Skitka et al. (2006, pp. 378–379). Besides the "rotten apples" item, Skitka's team used these three RWA items: "Our country desperately needs a mighty leader who will do what has to be done to destroy the radical new ways and sinfulness that are ruining us;" "Our country will be destroyed someday if we do not smash the perversions eating away at our moral fiber and traditional beliefs;" and "The way our country can get through future crises is to get back to our traditional values, put tough leaders in power, and silence troublemakers spreading bad ideas."

48. See Becky Choma and Yaniv Hanoch (2017), Jasper Van Assche and Thomas Pettigrew (2017), Thomas Pettigrew (2017).

49. Choma and Hanoch, "Cognitive Ability and Authoritarianism," 2017.

50. See the interesting discussion by Pavlos Vasilopoulos et al. (2015) of a similar item about the wish for a domineering leader in France in the aftermath of the terror attack on the satirical journal *Charlie Hebdo*.

51. Robert Jones et al. (2016, p. 23).

52. See the exit polls reported by CBS online.

53. Christopher Parker and Matt Barreto (2016).

54. Interestingly, as it happens, Rothwell and Diego-Rosell found that *irreligiosity* predicts anti-Trumpism.

55. Insight into sexism in the 2016 election came both before and after the election from Carly Wayne, Nicholas Valentino, and Marzia Oceno (2016, 2017). For analysis of the interaction of the main variables in gender bias, see Joseph Begany and Michael Milburn (2002).

56. Michael Tesler (2016, pp. 56–57).

57. Rothwell and Diego-Rosell (2016), *op. cit.*, p. 3. For further insight, they cite Carol Graham, whose most complete study on this topic (2017) appeared after they had reported their findings.

58. While the intensity of economic pessimism distinguishes strong from mild Trump supporters, this is true to a far lesser extent than it is in the contrast between pro- and non-Trump voting. Given Tesler's finding about the connection between economic pessimism and racial resentment, the smaller influence of pessimism might be linked to the smaller influence of racial resentment in the strong versus mild relationship.

59. It may be relevant that one of the anti-immigrant scale items strongly suggests line-cutting as well – namely, that immigrants "take jobs away from people already here."

60. Martin Gilens (1999), offers an exceptionally incisive account of this worldview.

61. The contrast between strong and mild Trump supporters could be studied in many ways. Emily Ekins (2017) conducted a latent class analysis, which groups survey respondents into trait-based clusters, using longitudinal data from a proprietary database. Ekins' analysis suggests that Trump voters subdivide into four large clusters and one small one – a finding that would be well worth pursuing further, along with other suggestive indicators such as, e.g., the fact that suburban voters fell midway between rural and urban voters in just about every key category examined in the *Survey of Rural America*.
62. Homans (2024), Bart Bonikowski, Yuchen Luo and Oscar Stuhler (2022).
63. Bob Altemeyer (1998).
64. Pratto et al. (1994).
65. Sam G. McFarland and Sherman Adelson (1996).
66. Altemeyer's original essay on these convergences and contrasts (1998, *op. cit.*) is still the single best overview. On Manichaean moralism in relation to authoritarianism, see David Norman Smith (2004).
67. The same shift yielded a 130.0% increase in the belief that Obama favored minorities over whites.
68. Christopher Altamura (2018).
69. We derived the five-item RWA scale from a proprietary survey conducted by Robert McWilliams in 2005 for the Libertarian Party, which granted us access to these data. On this research, see Smith et al. (2011).
70. Jake Womick, John Jost et al. (2019), Diana C. Mutz (2018).
71. See, e.g., Agnieszka Golec de Zavala et al. (2017), Danny Osborne et al. (2017), Felicia Pratto et al. (2013), Małgorzata Kossowska et al. (2011).
72. Jake Womick, John Jost et al. (2019), Philip Dunwoody and Sam G. McFarland (2018).
73. Jake Womick, John Jost et al. (2019), Diana C. Mutz (2018) also reports a NORC panel study which showed an increase in SDO from 2012 to 2016.
74. We thank Dr Lisa-Marie Wright for collaborating on this survey with us, and doctoral candidate Brenden Oliver for assisting with the data analysis. Full results will be published later in a multiply-authored paper.
75. David Norman Smith, Eric Hanley et al. (2023).
76. Monmouth also administered the full 16-item SDO scale, but since the results have not yet been analyzed, we're working on that now
77. Patrick Murray (2020).
78. A measure of moral traditionalism was what Bob Altemeyer in 2023 calls the third "heavy hitter" among the Morning Consult items.
79. Engelhardt, in 2019, cited "The Anger Games" (Smith & Hanley, 2018) as a representative example of the literature tracing the division between pro- and anti-Trump voters to polarization with respect to racial attitudes. See also Smith and Hanley (2017).
80. Engelhardt et al. (2023, p. 539). They also report factorial coherence, finding that the "RWA-style questions measure a single underlying factor: the first principal components eigenvalue is 2.69 and the second is 0.85. We estimated a simple two-factor latent variable model; one factor for the four childrearing items and a second for the six RWA-like items. The model is an excellent fit to these data, with an estimated correlation between the two factors of 0.77. The latent factor measured by the childrearing items is highly correlated with the RWA scale."
81. Engelhardt et al. remain critical of the RWA scale, alleging that our items are too similar to far-right rhetoric to count as predictors of support for rightist parties. But our scale was constructed not to explain radical-right resurgence, as they evidently think, but rather, as per Adorno, to explain "generalized prejudice" (sexism, racism, nativism, ethnocentrism, etc.) *indirectly*, construed as elements of an overall *syndrome* of attitudes and traits. And RWA has often been shown to bear on *ordinary* political choices, not simply on political extremism.
82. Theodor W. Adorno (2003 [1943]).

83. Among the few sustained attempts to apply these categories, as presented by Adorno (2000 [1943], 2003 [1943]), the recent dissertation by Pamela Jean Rooks (2022) stands out. This massive study of Martin Luther Thomas's contemporary Gerald Winrod – the "Jayhawk Nazi" – builds on analyses like Adorno's, while offering many complementary insights.

84. The details here are drawn from Harry F. Dahms (2020) and from Michael Schwarz's editorial notes to Theodor W. Adorno (2019).

85. Christie (1958) introduced this concept in an unpublished paper, *A Quantification of Machiavelli*, which he used as the basis for collaborative research on the "climate" of values among medical students; see Christie and Robert Merton (1958). He subsequently coedited an influential book on the subject (Christie & Florence Geis, 1970), and more recently since Delroy Paulhus and Kevin Williams (2002) introduced the notion of the "Dark Triad," Machiavellianism has often been linked to narcissism and psychopathy. Jim Sidanius has noted the potential intersection of Dark Triad traits and Social Dominance Orientation more than once (see, e.g., Sidanius et al., 2015).

86. On the full spectrum of psychological types and syndromes, see T. W. Adorno (1950). On the contrast between conventionalism and authoritarianism, see also David Norman Smith (2019, 2023).

87. T. W. Adorno (1950, p. 753), and, in Adorno et al. (1950), see Else Frenkel-Brunswik (1950, p. 400).

88. T. W. Adorno (1950, p. 753).

89. This shift is most evident in the results of surveys we have conducted since 1998 in a very large introductory sociology course. The details of that research will appear in future publications.

90. It is often said that authoritarianism is treated as a form of pathology in *The Authoritarian Personality*. But in fact, the authors stress that authoritarianism poses a society-wide danger precisely because it is *not* pathological – because it is entirely ordinary, diffused, to varying degrees, across every sector of society. When they tested this thesis with a small sample of subjects with clinically diagnosed pathologies, they found that these subjects were no more ethnocentric, e.g., than the general populace.

91. Altemeyer (2003, 2004), cf. John W. Dean (2006), Dean and Altemeyer (2021).

92. T. W. Adorno (2020 [1967], p. 30). In what follows, we will cite this English edition of Adorno's text in modified form, introducing subtleties of nuance from the German original (Adorno, 2019 [1967]). We will call the latter edition *Aspekte*; we will cite the English version as *Aspects*.

93. In conversation with students in December 1967, Adorno noted that his colleague, the critical sociologist Helge Pross, had been bitterly attacked by right-wing extremists for carrying out a survey. See Michael Schwarz, *op. cit.*, from Rolf Tiedemann, ed., (2000, p. 163).

94. *Aspekte*, p. 28.

95. Else Frenkel-Brunswik (1950, p. 400).

96. Dahms, "Adorno's Critique of the New Right-Wing Extremism: How (Not) to Face the Past, Present, and Future," pp. 149–150. Cf. the thesis by Perttu Ahoketo (2021), which discusses 11 instances of the far-right rhetorical tricks that Adorno identifies in *Aspekte*.

97. Theodor Adorno (2020 [1967], p. 28). In what follows, we will cite this English edition of Adorno's 1967 text in lightly modified form, introducing some subtleties of nuance from the German original (Adorno, 2019 [1967]), which we will call *Aspekte*. The English version will be called *Aspects*.

98. Adorno, who says this often in *Aspekte*, in *The Authoritarian Personality* and elsewhere, is echoed on this point in insightful papers by John Abromeit (2018) and Christian Fuchs (2017).

99. Gordon (2018, p. 68) makes the same point, with equally little evidence: "If Adorno was right, then Trumpism cannot be interpreted as an instance of a personality or a psychology, but must be recognized as the thoughtlessness of the entire culture. It is a thoughtlessness and a penchant for standardization that today marks not just Trump and his followers but nearly all forms of culture, and nearly all forms of discourse."

100. Gordon capitalizes on his role as editor of the Verso edition of *The Authoritarian Personality* (Adorno et al., 2019 [1950]) to preface the volume with a formerly unpublished text, drawn from the archives (Adorno, 2019 [1948]) which Gordon regards as evidence of Adorno's suppressed critique of the entire agenda of the volume, with "startling" implications that "threatened the basic premises of the *Authoritarian Personality* study as an exercise in political psychology..." (Gordon, 2019, p. xxxiv). In fact, Adorno's archives include many unpublished texts and research memoranda on authoritarian personality traits and political psychology from the 1940s, many of which explicitly endorse those very "basic premises." The same is true for many of Adorno's subsequently published texts, including those cited here. And when Adorno published a volume of his chapters from *The Authoritarian Personality* in German translation (Adorno, 1955), he incorporated just one hitherto unpublished text, his critique of the demagogue Martin Luther Thomas (Adorno, 1955 [1943]).
101. *Aspekte*, p. 10.
102. *Aspects*, p. 9.
103. *Aspects*, pp. 10–11.
104. This is the closing couplet of the first stanza.
105. *Aspects*, p. 10.
106. After stressing the influence of the "psychographic" consultancy Cambridge Analytica, which had promoted Trump in 2016, Gordon (2022) warned that the algorithmic "endgame in the colonization of the lifeworld" is approaching. "Human beings are increasingly prone to submit to the authority of the given and it is this epistemic passivity when confronted with social norms that explains our readiness to embrace political authoritarianism. This is what I meant when I said that *The Authoritarian Personality* can be read as a social epistemology – a study of the psychological disposition that inclines us all to accept social reality without criticism" (27). Cambridge Analytica's founder, as it happens, credited Trump's success not to microtargeting but to his demagogic skill, audacity, and indefatigability. For details, see David Norman Smith (2023).
107. Leeb (2024, p. 72) highlights the fatalism and defeatism inherent in this point: "This difference is critical to keep in mind," she writes, "as it shows us how Freud challenged any notion of a mass as composed of 'free individuals,' that is, as autonomous subjects who carry out their own wills."
108. Graham Potts (2007, p. 3).
109. Graham Potts (2007, p. 2).
110. Graham Potts (2007, p. 2).
111. Max Weber (1968, pp. 1111–1158).
112. See again David Norman Smith (2023) (*passim*).
113. Adorno (1946, p. 131).
114. Adorno (1946, p. 131).
115. Adorno (1946, pp. 129–130).
116. Adorno (1946, p. 132) (italics ours).
117. *Aspects*, p. 38.
118. *Aspects*, p. 29.
119. Eric Hanley (2021).
120. David Norman Smith and Eric Hanley (2020).
121. *Aspects*, p. 37.
122. See again David Norman Smith (2019).
123. *Aspekte*, pp. 39–40.
124. *Aspects*, p. 40.

REFERENCES

Abromeit, J. (2018). Frankfurt school critical theory and the persistence of authoritarian populism in the United States. In J. Morelock (Ed.), *Critical theory and authoritarian populism* (pp. 3–27). University of Westminster Press.

Adorno, T. W. (1946). Anti-semitism and fascist propaganda In E. Simmel (Ed.), *Anti-semitism: A social disease* (pp. 125–138). International Universities Press.

Adorno, T. W. (1955). *Studien zum autoritären Charakter*, translated by Milli Weinbrenner. Suhrkamp.

Adorno, T. W. (1955 [1943]). Die psychologische Technik in Martin Luther Thomas' Rundfunkreden. In T. W. Adorno (1955), *Studien zum autoritären Charakter* (pp. 360–483). Suhrkamp.

Adorno, T. W. (2000 [1943]). *The psychological technique of Martin Luther Thomas' radio addresses*. Stanford University Press.

Adorno, T. W. (2003 [1943]). The psychological technique of Martin Luther Thomas' radio addresses. In T. W. Adorno, *Gesammelte Schriften in 20 Bänden: Band 9: Soziologische Schriften II* (pp. 9–141). Suhrkamp.

Adorno, T. W. (2019 [1948]). Remarks on *The authoritarian personality*. In T. W. Adorno, E. Frenkel-Brunswik, D. J. Levinson, & R. N. Sanford (2019 [1950]), *The authoritarian personality* (P. E. Gordon (Ed.)) (pp. xli–lxv). Verso.

Adorno, T. W. (2019 [1967]). *Aspekte des neuen Rechtsradikalismus. Ein Vortrag, mit einem Nachwort von Volker Weiß*. Suhrkamp.

Adorno, T. W. (1950). Types and syndromes. In T. W. Adorno, E. Frenkel-Brunswik, D. Levinson, & R. N. Sanford (Eds.), *The authoritarian personality* (pp. 744–783). Harper & Bros.

Adorno, T. W. (2019). *Vorträge 1949-1968* (Michael Schwarz, (Ed.)). Suhrkamp.

Adorno, T. W. (2020 [1967]). *Aspects of the new right-wing extremism* (Wieland Hoban, Trans.). Polity Press.

Adorno, T. W., Frenkel-Brunswik, E., Levinson, D. J., & Sanford, R. N. (2019 [1950]). *The authoritarian personality* (P. E. Gordon (Ed.)). Verso.

Adorno, T. W., Frenkel-Brunswik, E., Levinson, D. J., & Sanford, R. N. (1950). *The authoritarian personality*. Harper & Brothers.

Ahoketo, P. (2021). *Kriittinen katsaus suomalaisiin QAnon-salaliittodiskursseihin*. Bachelor's thesis. Tampere University.

Altamura, C. (2018). *Dialectic of dominance: Authoritarianism(s) and the 2012 election*. Master's thesis. Department of Sociology, University of Kansas.

Altemeyer, R. (1981). *Right-wing authoritarianism*. University of Manitoba Press.

Altemeyer, B. (1988). *Enemies of freedom*. Jossey-Bass.

Altemeyer, B. (1994). Reducing prejudice in right-wing authoritarians. In M. P. Zanna & J. M. Olson (Eds.), *The psychology of prejudice*. Lawrence Erlbaum.

Altemeyer, B. (1996). *Authoritarian specter*. Harvard University Press.

Altemeyer, B. (1998). The other 'authoritarian personality'. *Advances in Experimental Social Psychology*, *30*, 47–92.

Altemeyer, B. (2003). What happens when authoritarians inherit the Earth? A simulation. *Analyses of Social Issues and Public Policy*, *3*(1), 161–169.

Altemeyer, B. (2004). Highly dominating, highly authoritarian personalities. *The Journal of Social Psychology*, *144*(4), 421–448.

Altemeyer, B. (2023, May 31). The April 2021 morning consult eight nation survey: Into the weeds, deeply. https://theauthoritarians.org/the-april-2021-morning-consult-eight-nation-survey/

Begany, J., & Milburn, M. (2002, July). Psychological predictors of sexual harassment. *Psychology of Men and Masculinity*, *3*(2), 119–126.

Bonikowski, B., Luo, Y., & Stuhler, O. (2022). Politics as usual? Measuring populism, nationalism, and authoritarianism in U.S. Presidential campaigns (1952–2020) with neural language models. *Sociological Methods & Research*, *51*(4), 1721–1787.

Bouie, J. (2016, May). What Pundits keep getting wrong about Donald Trump and the working class. *Slate*. https://slate.com/news-and-politics/2016/05/what-pundits-keep-getting-wrong-about-donald-trump-and-the-working-class.html

Brooks, D. (2016, March 18). No, not Trump, not ever. *New York Times*. https://www.nytimes.com/2016/03/18/opinion/no-not-trump-not-ever.html
Choma, B. L., & Hanoch, Y. (2017, February). Cognitive ability and authoritarianism. *Personality and Individual Differences, 106*, 287–291.
Christie, R. (1958). *A quantification of Machiavelli*. Unpublished.
Christie, R., & Geis, F. L. (1970). *Studies in Machiavellianism*. Academic Press.
Christie, R., & Merton, R. K. (1958). Procedures for the sociological study of the values climate of medical schools. *Academic Medicine, 33*(10), 125–153.
Colvin, J., & Barrow, B. (2023, December 7). *Trump's vow to only be a dictator on 'day one' follows growing worry over his authoritarian rhetoric*. Associated Press.
Dahms, H. F. (2020, July). Adorno's critique of the new right-wing extremism: How (not) to face the past, present, and future. *disClosure: A Journal of Social Theory, 29*, 129–179.
Dean, J. W. (2006). *Conservatives without conscience*. Penguin.
Dean, J. W., & Altemeyer, B. (2021). *Authoritarian nightmare: The ongoing threat of Trump's followers*. Melville House.
Dunwoody, P., & McFarland, S. G. (2018). Support for anti-muslim policies: The role of political traits and threat perception. *Political Psychology, 39*(1), 89–106.
Ekins, E. (2017, June). *The five types of Trump voters*. Democracy Fund Voter Study Group. https://www.voterstudygroup.org/reports/2016-elections/the-five-types-trump-voters
Engelhardt, A. M., Feldman, S., & Hetherington, M. J. (2023). Advancing the measurement of authoritarianism. *Political Behavior, 45*(2), 537–560.
Feldman, S. (2020). Authoritarianism, threat, and intolerance. In E. Borgida, C. Federico, & J. Miller (Eds.), *At the forefront of political psychology*. Routledge.
Frenkel-Brunswik, E. (1950). Sex, people, and self as seen through the interviews. In Adorno, T. W., Frenkel-Brunswik, E., Levinson, D. J., & Sanford, R. N. (2019). *The authoritarian personality*, with a preface by Peter Gordon. Verso.
Fuchs, C. (2017). Donald Trump - A critical theory-perspective on authoritarian capitalism. *tripleC, 15*(1), 1–72. http://www.triple-c. at CC-BY-NC-ND
Garcia-Navarro, L. (2024, January 21). Inside the heritage foundation's plans for 'Institutionalizing Trumpism'. *New York Times*. https://www.nytimes.com/2024/01/21/magazine/heritage-foundation-kevin-roberts.html
Gilens, M. (1999). *Why Americans hate welfare*. University of Chicago Press.
Gold, M. (2023, December 19). Trump, attacked for echoing Hitler, says he never read 'Mein Kampf'. *New York Times*. https://www.nytimes.com/2023/12/19/us/politics/trump-immigrants-hitler-mein-kampf.html
Golec de Zavala, A., Guerra, R., & Simão, C. (2017, November 27). The relationship between the Brexit vote and individual predictors of prejudice. *Frontiers in Psychology*. https://doi.org/10.3389/fpsyg.2017.02023
Gordon, P. E. (2018). *The Authoritarian Personality* revisited: Reading Adorno in the age of Trump. In W. Brown, P. E. Gordon, & M. Pensky (Eds.), *Authoritarianism: Three inquiries in critical theory* (pp. 45–84). University of Chicago Press.
Gordon, P. E. (2019). Introduction. In T. W. Adorno, E. Frenkel-Brunswik, D. J. Levinson, & R. N. Sanford (2019 [1950]), *The authoritarian personality* (P. E. Gordon (Ed.)). Verso.
Gordon, P. E. (2022). Realism and Utopia in The Authoritarian Personality. *Polity, 54*(1), 8–28.
Graham, C. (2017). *Happiness for all?* Princeton University Press.
Griffin, R., & Teixeira, R. (2017, June). *The story of Trump's appeal*. Democracy Fund Voter Study Group. https://www.voterstudygroup.org/reports/2016-elections/story-oftrumps-appeal
Hanley, E. A. (2021). Sexism as a political force: The impact of gender-based attitudes on the presidential elections of 2012 and 2016. *Social Science Quarterly, 102*(4), 1408–1427.
Hochschild, A. R. (2016a, September-October). I spent 5 years with some of Trump's biggest fans. Here's what they won't tell you. *Mother Jones*. https://www.motherjones.com/politics/2016/08/trump-white-blue-collar-supporters/
Hochschild, A. R. (2016b). *Strangers in their own land*. The New Press.

Homans, C. (2024, April 27). Donald Trump has never sounded like this. *New York Times.* https://www.nytimes.com/2024/04/27/magazine/trump-rallies-rhetoric.html

Iati, M. (2024, March 16). Trump says some undocumented immigrants are 'Not People'. *Washington Post.* https://www.washingtonpost.com/politics/2024/03/16/trump-immigrants-not-people/

Jones, R. P., Cox, D., Dionne, E. J., Galston, W. A., Cooper, B., & Lienesch, R. (2016, June 23). *How immigration and concerns about cultural changes are shaping the 2016 Election.* Public Religion Research Institute.

Kagan, R. (2023a, December 7). The Trump dictatorship: How to stop it. *Washington Post.* https://www.washingtonpost.com/opinions/2023/12/07/robert-kagan-trump-dictatorship-how-to-stop/

Kagan, R. (2023b, November 30). A Trump dictatorship is increasingly inevitable. *Washington Post.* https://www.washingtonpost.com/opinions/2023/11/30/trump-dictator-2024-election-robert-kagan/

Kossowska, M., Trejtowicz, M., de Lemus, S., Bukowski, M., Van Hiel, A., & Goodwin, R. (2011). Relationships between right-wing authoritarianism, terrorism threat, and attitudes towards restrictions of civil rights: A comparison among four European countries. *British Journal of Psychology, 102*(2), 245–259.

Leeb, C. (2024). *Contesting the far right: A psychoanalytic and feminist critical theory approach.* Columbia University Press.

LeVine, M., Arnsdorf, I., & Morse, C. E. (2024, March 23). Trump escalates solidarity with Jan. 6 rioters as his own trials close. *Washington Post.* https://www.washingtonpost.com/elections/2024/03/23/trump-jan-6-rioters-rhetoric-campaign/

Manza, J., & Crowley, N. (2017). Working class hero? Interrogating the social bases of the rise of Donald Trump. *The Forum, 15*(1), 3–28.

Maslansky, M. (2016a, January 28). Communication strategies from Donald Trump. *PR Daily.* http://www.prdaily.com/Main/Articles/Communication_strategies_from_Donald_Trump_20052.aspx

Maslansky, M. (2016b, February 29). Why attacks on Trump fail. *The Huffington Post.* https://www.huffpost.com/entry/why-attacks-on-trump-fail-what-to-do-about-it_b_9333090

McFarland, S. G., & Adelson, S. (1996). An omnibus study of individual differences and prejudice. In *Presented at the annual meeting of the International Society of Political Psychology*, Vancouver, Canada, July 3.

Moody, K. (2017, January 11). Who put Trump in the White House? *Jacobin.* https://jacobin.com/2017/01/trump-election-democrats-gop-clinton-whites-workers-rust-belt

Mounck, Y., & Ziblatt, D. (2016, March 1). Donald Trump isn't a fascist; He's a demagogue. *Vox.* https://www.vox.com/polyarchy/2016/3/1/11140876/trump-demagogue

Murray, P. (2020, August 25). Authoritarian tendencies in the American electorate (Part 1). https://www.monmouth.edu/polling-institute/2020/08/25/authoritarian-tendencies-in-the-american-electorate-part-1/

Mutz, D. C. (2018, March 26). Status threat, not economic hardship, explains the 2016 presidential vote. *Proceedings of the National Academy of Sciences.*

Osborne, D., Milojev, P., & Sibley, C. G. (2017). Authoritarianism and national identity: Examining the longitudinal effects of SDO and RWA on nationalism and patriotism. *Personality and Social Psychology Bulletin, 43*(8), 1086–1099.

Parker, C. S., & Barreto, M. A. (2014). *Change they can't believe in: The tea party and reactionary politics in America.* Princeton University Press.

Paulhus, D. L., & Williams, K. M. (2002, December). The dark triad of personality: Narcissism, Machiavellianism, and psychopathy. *Journal of Research in Personality, 36*(6), 556–563.

Pettigrew, T. F. (2017). Social psychological perspectives on Trump supporters. *Journal of Social and Political Psychology, 5*(1), 107–116.

Potts, G. (2007, Spring). Adorno on 'The Donald': Reality television as culture industry. *Problèmatique, 11*(1), 1–10.

Pratto, F., Çidam, A., Stewart, A. L., Zeineddine, F. B., Aranda, M., Aiello, A., Chryssochoou, X., Cichocka, A., Cohrs, J. C., Durrheim, K., Eicher, V., Foels, R., Górska, P., Lee, I-C., Licata, L., Liu, J. H., Li, L., Meyer, I., Morselli, D., ... & Henkel, K. E. (2013). Social dominance in context and in individuals: Contextual moderation of robust effects of social dominance

orientation in 15 languages and 20 countries. *Social Psychological and Personality Science, 4*(5), 585–597.
Pratto, F., Sidanius, J., Stallworth, L. M., & Malle, B. F. (1994). Social dominance orientation: A personality variable predicting social and political attitudes. *Journal of Personality and Social Psychology, 67*(4), 741.
Rooks, P. J. (2022). *The 'Jayhawk Nazi' of Kansas: Gerald Winrod, antisemitism, and the evangelical far right 1925-1944.* PhD, Department of Sociology. University of Kansas.
Rothwell, J., & Diego-Rosell, P. (2016, November 2). Explaining nationalist political views: The case of Donald Trump. *Gallup Working Paper.* https://papers.ssrn.com/sol3/papers.cfm?abstract_id=2822059
Sidanius, J., Pratto, F., Ho, A. K., Kteily, N., Sheehy-Skeffington, J., Henkel, K. E., Foels, R., & Stewart, A. (2015, October). The nature of social dominance orientation. *Journal of Personality and Social Psychology, 109*(6), 1003.
Skitka, L. J., Bauman, C. W., Aramovich, N. P., & Scott Morgan, G. (2006). Confrontational and preventative policy responses to terrorism. *Basic and Applied Social Psychology, 28*(4), 375–384.
Smith, D. N. (2004). Authority fetishism and the manichæan vision. In L. Langman & D. K. Fishman (Eds.), *The evolution of alienation* (pp. 91–114). Rowman & Littlefield.
Smith, D. N. (2019, May). Authoritarianism reimagined: The riddle of Trump's base. *The Sociological Quarterly, 60*(2), 210–223.
Smith, D. N. (2023, November 29). The agitator supplies what the base demands: Trumpism before and after Donald Trump. *Critical Sociology.* [Online First]. https://doi.org/10.1177/08969205231 2089
Smith, D. N., & Hanley, E. (2017, September 28). *The anger games* [online overview]. Association for Critical Sociology website. http://criticalsociology.org/the-anger-games-who-voted-for-donald-trump-in-the-2016-election-and-why/
Smith, D. N., & Hanley, E. (2018, March). The anger games: Who voted for Donald Trump in the 2016 election, and why? *Critical Sociology, 44*(2), 195–212.
Smith, D. N., & Hanley, E. (2020). The heart of whiteness: Patterns of race, class, and prejudice in the divided midwest. In B. Warf (Ed.), *Political landscapes of Donald Trump* (pp. 111–128). Routledge.
Smith, D. N., Hanley, E., & McWilliams, R. (2011). RWA, SDO, and Voter choice: Short reliable scales. A Proposal to the American National Election Study for the 2012 Times Series Study.
Smith, D. N., Hanley, E., Willson, S., & Alvord, D. R. (2015a). Authoritarianism, social dominance, and homophobia. *Presented to the meeting of the International Society for Political Psychology,* San Diego, July 6.
Smith, D. N., Hanley, E. A., Willson, S., & Alvord, D. (2015b). Authoritarianism, social dominance, and generalized prejudice. *American National Election Study proposal.* http://www.electionstudies.org/onlinecommons/2016TimeSeries/Authoritarianism.pdf 2015
Smith, D. N., Hanley, E., Altamura, C., & Oliver, B. (2023). Support for dominating leaders: Items for the 2024 ANES pilot study. Proposed to the American National Election Study.
Sorkin, A. D. (2024, January 10). Trump's bizarre immunity claims should serve as a warning. *The New Yorker.* hhttps://www.newyorker.com/news/daily-comment/trumps-bizarre-immunity-claims-should-serve-as-a-warning
Tesler, M. (2016). *Post-racial or most racial? Race and politics in the Obama era.* The University of Chicago Press.
Survey of Rural America. (2017, June). The Washington Post/Kaiser Family Foundation.
Tiedemann, R. (Ed.) (2000). *Frankfurter Adorno Blätter VI.* edition t+k.
UMass Amherst/UMass Poll. (2024, February 7). Plurality of Americans support removing Trump from presidential ballots due to insurrection clause, according to new national UMass Amherst Poll. https://polsci.umass.edu/trump-and-gop-toplines-crosstabs-feb-7-2024
Valentino, N., Wayne, C., & Oceno, M. (2017). Mobilizing sexism: The interaction of emotion and gender attitudes in the 2016 presidential election. *Presented at the 2017 American Political Science Association meeting.*

Van Assche, J., & Pettigrew, T. F. (2016). *Comparative American and European far-right voters*. Unpublished paper, Department of Development, Personality and Social Psychology. Ghent University.
Vasilopoulos, P., Marcus, G. E., & Foucault, M. (2015, November 21). Emotional responses to the Charlie Hebdo attacks. https://ssrn.com/abstract=2693952
Wayne, C., Valentino, N., & Oceno, M. (2016, October 23). How sexism drives support for Donald Trump. *Washington Post*. https://www.washingtonpost.com/news/monkey-cage/wp/2016/10/23/how-sexism-drives-support-for-donald-trump/
Weber, M. (1919). *Politik als Beruf*. Duncker & Humblot.
Weber, M. (1949 [1919]). Politics as a vocation. In M. Weber, H. H. Gerth, & C. Wright Mills (Eds.), *From Max Weber* (pp. 77–128). Oxford University Press.
Weber, M. (1968). Charisma and its transformation. In M. Weber (Ed.), *Economy and society: An outline of interpretive sociology* (Vol. 2, pp. 1111–1157). Bedminster.
Wehner, P. (2023, November 22). Have you listened lately to what trump is saying? *The Atlantic*. https://www.theatlantic.com/ideas/archive/2023/11/trump-becoming-frighteningly-clear-about-what-he-wants/676086/
Williams, J. C. (2017). *White working class*. Harvard Business Review Press.
Womick, J., Rothmund, T., Azevedo, F., King, L. A., & Jost, J. T. (2019). Group-based dominance and authoritarian aggression predict support for Donald Trump in the 2016 U.S. presidential election. *Social Psychological and Personality Science*, *10*(5), 643–652.
Wood, T. (2017, April 17). Racism motivated Trump voters more than authoritarianism. *Washington Post*. https://www.washingtonpost.com/news/monkey-cage/wp/2017/04/17/racism-motivated-trump-voters-more-than-authoritarianism-or-income-inequality/
Yglesias, M. (2016, July 11). How Max Weber explains the 2016 election. *Vox*. https://www.vox.com/2016/7/11/12053146/max-weber-hillary-clinton
Yourish, K., Ivory, D., Valentino-DeVries, J., & Lemonides, A. (2024, May 9). How republicans echo antisemitic tropes despite declaring support for Israel. *New York Times*. https://www.nytimes.com/2024/05/09/us/antisemitism-republicans-trump.html

APPENDIX: STATISTICAL TABLES

Many of the statistical tables in the main text, above, appear in abbreviated form. In this appendix, Tables 5, 6, 7, 7a, 8, 9, 9a. Te present the full, unabbreviated versions of these tables, plus a table of odds ratios. Readers who also wish to see the full attitude scales can request them from David Smith, emerald@ku.edu.

Table 5. Sample Means and Standard Deviations of Variables Included in Our Analyses of Presidential Choice and Strength of Support for Trump in 2016.

	White Voters in 2016		White Trump Voters in 2016	
	Mean	SD	Mean	SD
Outcomes				
% Who voted for Trump	0.520	0.500		
% Who voted for Trump enthusiastically			0.731	0.443
Demographic Variables				
% Male	0.470	0.499	0.502	0.500
Average age	52.3	17.2	54.2	17.0
Education (some college or less)	0.518	0.500	0.623	0.485

(Continued)

Table 5. *(Continued)*

	White Voters in 2016		White Trump Voters in 2016	
	Mean	SD	Mean	SD
Income (tens of thousands USD)	**9.13**	7.38	**8.41**	6.83
Marital status (married = 1)	**0.648**	0.478	**0.668**	0.471
Attitudes Toward...				
Child traits	**4.88**	3.25	**6.20**	2.24
Domineering leaders	**5.50**	3.20	**7.37**	2.24
African Americans	**5.65**	2.92	**7.32**	2.01
Reverse discrimination	**3.65**	2.01	**4.71**	1.60
Immigrants	**5.05**	2.39	**6.41**	1.88
Muslims	**5.11**	2.16	**6.09**	2.07
Women	**3.67**	1.87	**4.60**	1.55
Personal financial concerns	**5.01**	2.35	**5.61**	2.25
The health of the economy	**5.01**	2.31	**6.25**	2.04
Liberalism versus conservatism	**5.34**	2.61	**6.97**	1.86
General religiosity	**5.00**	3.94	**6.32**	3.57
Fundamentalism	**4.79**	2.84	**6.15**	2.38
Number of Cases		1,883		979

Note: For simplicity, we have substituted the term "outcomes" here for "dependent variables" and the term "causal factors" for "independent variables."

Table 6. Mean Values of Independent Variables Included in Analysis by Presidential Vote Choice in 2016, White Voters Only, $N = 1,883$.

Voted For...	Trump	Another Candidate	Difference
Demographic Variables			
Gender: Male	50.15	43.69	6.46
Gender: Female	49.85	56.31	−6.46**
Education: Some college or less	62.31	40.38	21.93***
Education: BA or higher	37.69	59.62	−21.93***
Marital status: Not married	33.20	37.28	−4.08
Marital status: Married	66.80	62.72	4.08
Age (years)	54.17	50.31	3.86***
Household income ($10,000 USD)	8.41	9.91	−1.50***
Attitudes Toward...			
Child traits	6.20	3.45	2.75***
Domineering leaders	7.37	3.48	3.89***
African Americans	7.32	3.83	3.49***
Reverse discrimination	4.72	2.50	2.22***
Immigrants	6.41	3.57	2.84***
Muslims	6.10	4.05	2.05***
Women	4.60	2.66	1.94***

Table 6. (*Continued*)

Voted For…	Trump	Another Candidate	Difference
Personal financial concerns	5.61	4.36	1.25***
The health of the economy	6.26	3.66	2.60***
Liberalism versus conservatism	6.97	3.57	3.40***
General religiosity	6.32	3.57	2.75***
Fundamentalism	4.92	2.41	2.51***

Notes: *$p < 0.05$; **$p < 0.01$; ***$p < 0.001$.

Table 7. Logistic Regression Coefficients From Four Models (Called "Trials" in the Main Text) Predicting Pro-Trump Voter Choice in 2016, White Voters Only.

	Model 1	Model 2	Model 3	Model 4
Demographic Variables				
Education (some college or less = 1)	**0.834****	**0.416****	−0.014	−0.164
	(0.116)	(0.125)	(0.150)	(0.206)
Marital status (married = 1)	**0.402****	**0.404****	**0.369***	0.331
	(0.128)	(0.137)	(0.154)	(0.213)
Age (years)	**0.012****	0.007	0.007	0.001
	(0.003)	(0.004)	(0.004)	(0.005)
Gender (male = 1)	0.097	0.019	0.115	−0.039
	(0.114)	(0.122)	(0.142)	(0.192)
Income (in tens of thousands USD$)	−0.013	0.000	0.015	0.018
	(0.008)	(0.009)	(0.011)	(0.015)
Attitudes Toward…				
Child traits		**0.277****	**0.121****	−0.042
		(0.021)	(0.021)	(0.035)
Domineering leaders			**0.487****	**0.196****
			(0.030)	(0.040)
African Americans				**0.177****
				(0.052)
Reverse discrimination				**0.114**
				(0.072)
Immigrants				**0.197****
				(0.060)
Muslims				**0.137***
				(0.047)
Women				**0.211****
				(0.068)
Personal financial concerns				**0.002**
				(0.045)
The health of the economy				**0.376****
				(0.055)
Liberalism versus conservatism				**0.486****
				(0.054)

(*Continued*)

Table 7. *(Continued)*

	Model 1	Model 2	Model 3	Model 4
General religiosity				0.028
				(0.032)
Fundamentalism				0.107*
				(0.049)
Constant	−1.175	−2.141***	−4.011***	−10.212***
	(0.231)	(0.261)	(0.322)	(0.701)
Pseudo *R*-squared	0.049	0.149	0.328	0.588
Number of cases	1,883	1,883	1,883	1,883

Notes: *$p < 0.05$; **$p < 0.01$; ***$p < 0.00$.
Model 1 = Demographics.
Model 2 = Demographics + Child Trait attitudes.
Model 3 = Demographics + Attitudes toward child traits + Domineering leaders.
Model 4 = Demographics + All attitudes.
Standard Errors in Parentheses.

Table 7a. Odds Ratios From Models Predicting Presidential Vote Choice in 2016, White Voters Only.

	Model 1	Model 2	Model 3	Model 4
Demographics				
Education (some college or less = 1)	2.304	1.516	0.986	0.849
Marital status (married = 1)	1.495	1.498	1.447	1.393
Age (years)	1.012	1.007	1.007	1.001
Gender (male = 1)	1.102	1.012	1.122	0.961
Income (tens of thousands USD)	0.987	1.000	1.016	1.018
Attitudes Towards...				
Child traits		1.320	1.128	0.959
Domineering leaders			1.628	1.216
African Americans				1.194
Reverse discrimination				1.121
Immigrants				1.217
Muslims				1.147
Women				1.235
Personal financial concerns				1.002
The health of the economy				1.457
Liberalism versus conservatism				1.626
General religiosity				1.029
Fundamentalism				1.113
Number of cases	1,883	1,883	1,883	1,883

Note: Odds ratios corresponding to coefficients significant at the 0.05 level in italics.

Table 8. Mean Values of Independent Variables Included in Analysis by Strength of Support for Trump in 2016, White Trump Voters Only.

Level of Support for Trump	Strong	Mild	Difference (Strong vs. Mild)
Demographics			
Gender: Male	50.56	49.01	1.51
Gender: Female	49.44	50.95	−1.51
Education: Some college or less	66.34	51.33	15.01***
Education: BA or higher	33.66	48.67	−15.01***
Marital status: Not married	33.38	32.70	0.68
Marital status: Married	66.62	67.30	−0.68
Age (years)	54.41	53.48	0.94
Household income ($10,000 USD)	7.90	9.81	−1.91***
Attitudes Toward...			
Child traits	6.45	5.52	0.93***
Domineering leaders	7.71	6.46	1.24***
African Americans	7.60	6.57	1.03***
Reverse discrimination	4.92	4.16	0.75***
Immigrants	6.74	5.53	1.21***
Muslims	6.34	5.42	0.93***
Women	4.68	4.38	0.30**
Personal financial concerns	5.74	5.27	0.47**
The health of the economy	6.54	5.48	1.05***
Liberalism versus conservatism	7.10	6.60	0.50***
General religiosity	6.45	5.94	0.51*
Fundamentalism	5.22	4.11	1.11***

Notes: *$p < 0.05$; **$p < 0.01$; ***$p < 0.001$.

Table 9. Logistic Regression Coefficients From Four Models (Called "Trials" in the Text) Predicting Strength of Support for Trump in 2016, White Trump Voters Only.

Causal Factors	Model 1	Model 2	Model 3	Model 4
Demographics				
Gender (male = 1)	**0.208**	**0.183**	**0.264**	**0.317**
	(0.173)	(0.174)	(0.178)	(0.193)
Age (years)	**0.002**	**0.002**	**0.002**	**−0.001**
	(0.005)	(0.005)	(0.005)	(0.006)
Education (some college or less = 1)	**0.528****	**0.430****	**0.331**	**0.215**
	(0.181)	(0.181)	(0.184)	(0.197)
Income (tens of thousands USD$)	**−0.036****	**−0.034***	**−0.025***	**−0.021**
	(0.014)	(0.014)	(0.012)	(0.013)
Marital status (married = 1)	**0.354**	**0.378**	**0.371**	**0.399**
	(0.198)	(0.201)	(0.201)	(0.216)

(Continued)

Table 9. *(Continued)*

Causal Factors	Model 1	Model 2	Model 3	Model 4
Attitudes Toward...				
Child traits		0.097**	0.048	−0.003
		(0.031)	(0.032)	(0.035)
Domineering leaders			0.241***	0.150***
			(0.039)	(0.043)
African Americans				0.060
				(0.051)
Reverse discrimination				0.195**
				(0.068)
Immigrants				0.164**
				(0.057)
Muslims				0.075
				(0.047)
Women				−0.069
				(0.065)
Personal financial concerns				0.025
				(0.042)
The health of the economy				0.177***
				(0.051)
Liberalism versus conservatism				0.064
				(0.056)
General religiosity				−0.060
				(0.031)
Fundamentalism				0.156**
				(0.053)
Constant	0.559	0.029	−1.470**	−4.825***
	(0.349)	(0.396)	(0.481)	(0.752)
Pseudo *R*-squared	0.029	0.040	0.082	0.173
Number of cases	979	979	979	979

Notes: $*p < 0.05$; $**p < 0.01$; $***p < 0.001$.
Model 1 = Demographics.
Model 2 = Demographics + Child Trait attitudes.
Model 3 = Demographics + Attitudes towards child traits + Domineering leaders.
Model 4 = Demographics + All attitudes.
Standard Errors in Parentheses.

Table 9a. Odds Ratios From Models Predicting Strength of Support for Trump in 2016, White Trump Voters Only.

	Model 1	Model 2	Model 3	Model 4
Demographics				
Age (years)	1.002	1.002	1.002	0.999
Gender (male = 1)	1.232	1.202	1.303	1.374
Education (some college or less = 1)	1.696	1.536	1.392	1.240
Income (tens of thousands USD)	0.964	0.967	0.975	0.979
Marital status (married = 1)	1.425	1.460	1.449	1.490
Attitudes Toward...				
Child traits		1.102	1.049	0.997
Domineering leaders			1.179	1.162
African Americans				0.979
Reverse discrimination				1.215
Immigrants				1.178
Muslims				1.078
Women				0.934
Personal financial concerns				1.025
The health of the economy				1.193
Liberalism versus conservatism				1.066
General religiosity				0.942
Fundamentalism				1.169
Number of cases	979	979	979	979

Note: Odds ratios corresponding to coefficients significant at the 0.05 level in italics.

PROJECT 2025 ENVIRONMENTAL POLICY: POSTFACTUAL ECOCATASTROPHE

Robert J. Antonio

University of Kansas, USA

> There is no future in which climate change will not impinge on all political questions. Climate is reshaping the terrain on which we will be fighting for years to come, and we only have begun to consider what this will mean.
>
> (Battistoni & Mann, 2023, p. 77)

ABSTRACT

This chapter focuses on the conservative Heritage Foundation's "Project 2025" and especially its comprehensive **Mandate for Leadership**, *which provides a detailed plan for fundamental policy and administrative changes to be instituted in a Trump second term. It advocates an unparalleled concentration of executive power, elimination of the independence of the civil service and Department of Justice from the office of the president, and institution of permanent dominance of Trumpian conservatism. The specific focus is on the* Mandate's *proposed antienvironmental policies, which are weaved throughout the document and are designed to roll back sweepingly previous climate-change and environmental protection policies. Stressing maximal usage, production, and export of fossil fuel, the Trumpian "energy dominance agenda" is in polar contradiction to climate science policy aimed at decarbonizing the economy and society and averting catastrophic climate change and a "Hothouse Earth." The* Mandate's *postfactual discourse combined with its advocacy of an all-powerful president and conspiratorial vision of the "woke" left as public enemy has definite protofascist overtones.*

Keywords: Climate change; environmental policy; energy dominance; fascism; Trump

Climate change policy has been a widely discussed facet of "Bidenomics." The Biden Administration's 2022 Inflation Reduction Act (IRA) provided at least $370 billion to subsidize development of environmental technologies intended to cut greenhouse gas (GHG) emissions.[1] They also passed substantial regulatory legislation to do the same. New oil and gas drilling must be averted to meet the 2015 Paris Agreement's target of limiting global temperature rise to 2° Celsius (C) (3.6° Fahrenheit) above preindustrial levels and hopefully to 1.5°C (2.7°F) to protect low-lying coastal regions and small island nations (Abnett, 2021).[2] The 2023 United Nations (UN) Emissions Gap Report said we are on track to rise 3.0°C this century, which would insure ecological catastrophe (Dickie, 2023). In 2024, researchers reported that the global economy is already "committed" to a 19% reduction in the next 26 years regardless of "future emission choices" and that "damages already outweigh the mitigation costs required to limit global warming to 2°C by sixfold over this near-term time frame..." (Katz et al., 2024, pp. 551, 556). The European Court of Human Rights ruled that states are required to protect their citizens from climate change damage; they must employ regulations and other measures to adapt to and mitigate global warming and set targets and timetables to reduce GHG, achieve carbon neutrality, and limit irreversible damages (Blattner, 2024). Awareness has grown that we are approaching a climate emergency that requires major collective action to ensure nation-state and transnational regulation aimed to avert ecocatastrophe (Poushter et al., 2022).

The keystone legislation of the Biden Administration "Green New Deal," the IRA was designed to mitigate climate change, reduce other global environmental problems, accelerate economic growth via reindustrialization, and replace fossil fuel energy with renewable, sustainable, nonpolluting alternatives. The Biden Administration has instituted other substantial environmental regulations.[3] However, it also permitted new oil leases and spurred increased crude oil production aimed to reduce domestic gasoline prices, weaken the power of the Organization of Oil Producing Countries (OPEC), and blunt Republican critiques of Democratic energy policy. By the third year of the Biden presidency, the United States (US) produced more oil in a year than any country ever, exceeding top producers Russia and Saudi Arabia, and peak US production under President Trump.[4] The United States also has been the top liquefied natural gas exporter under Biden (Halper & Olorrunipa, 2023; Tankersley & Friedman, 2023).

Although the IRA is landmark US climate legislation, it is by no means sufficient to cope effectively with the climate crisis and other global environmental problems (Battistoni & Mann, 2023, pp. 56–58). Moreover, the IRA included major concessions to the fossil fuel industry.[5] For example, it provided, "incentives in green tech, with no direct mechanisms to reduce fossil fuel use" and stipulated that leases of federal land for renewable energy projects must offer land for oil and gas development (Battistoni & Mann, 2023, p. 68). By creating green tax credits, moreover, Biden Administration environmental policy has been highly profitable for Wall Street as well as for green energy industries (Tankersley & Friedman, 2023). Dylan Riley and Robert Brenner (2022) argue that the IRA manifests a fundamental transformation in the US social structure of accumulation – a shift to "political capitalism" designed to redistribute income and wealth upward and boost rates of return by means of concentrated political power rather than through productive investment. Riley and Brenner (2022, p. 6) point to major tax cuts, privatized public assets, quantitative easing, sharply reduced interest rates, and much increased state spending aimed to benefit capital with modest trickledown to the general public (e.g., "Trump's CARES Act, Biden's American Rescue Plan, the Infrastructure and CHIPS Act, and the Inflation Reduction Act"). Even if the shift falls short of the regime change theorized by Riley and Brenner, the recent trend toward huge state investments and subsidies has accelerated growth, profit margins, and stock-market values.[6]

Authoritarian, right-wing, populist strongmen, and ethnoracial nationalists have surged globally for more than a decade. Their parties often have denied anthropogenic climate change or have been skeptical about the severity of the process and veracity of climate science. They usually have opposed regulation aimed to curb GHG emissions and decarbonize the fossil fuel regime.[7] Holding that climate agendas fashioned by liberal democratic polities impose burdensome costs on nonelite citizens, populists promise to protect ordinary people and vanquish predatory elites that enhance their power and wealth by restricting consumer choice and political freedom. They hold that liberal elites stir "climate hysteria" to legitimize their top-down policy regimes and charge that the UN Intergovernmental Panel on Climate Change (IPCC) and other organizations, scientists, activists, and politicians, who support transnational cooperation, regulation, and governance of climate change and other global environmental problems, sacrifice national sovereignty to globalist elites (Serhan, 2021). Trumpism is the leading US political manifestation of this hard-right drift.[8]

This chapter focuses on the conservative Heritage Foundation's "Project 2025" and especially its comprehensive (circa 900 page) *Mandate for Leadership*, which maps radical political policy and administrative changes to be instituted immediately after a Trump re-election. It advocates concentrating unparalleled executive power, politicizing the civil service, and instituting permanent hard-right political dominance and cultural hegemony in the United States.[9] Although explaining the overall thrust and aims of Project 2025, the paper focuses specifically on its antienvironmental politics. Rollback of Biden Administration and previous climate-change and environmental protection policies is a central theme weaved throughout the overall plan.

A MORE ILLIBERAL TRUMP SECOND TERM ON THE RISE?

Heritage framed similar policy statements for Republican administrations since the Reagan presidency, and they contend that President Trump largely embraced their first-term proposals. Headed by former Trump Administration officials, the expressed aim in the new *Mandate* is to rein in the liberal "administrative state" or "deep state" by concentrating political power more than ever before in the office of President and insuring lasting dominance by a right-wing populist regime. Heritage President, Kevin D. Rodgers, describes the mission of his organization and Project 2025 to be "institutionalizing Trumpism" (Garcia-Navarro, 2024). Director of Project 2025, Paul Dans (2023, p. xiv), holds that its ultimate aim is to reverse the "long march of cultural Marxism through our institutions..." He implies the liberal leaning left embedded in the "deep state" have cultural Marxist roots deeply resistant to change.

Heritage intends to eliminate the institutional guardrails that blocked realization of Trump's first-term agenda and avert challenges to his policy initiatives, outright refusals to obey, and insults, which the former president faced from key appointees in his first term.[10] The *Mandate* would provide re-elected Trump or another new Republican president with a concrete plan to be completed in the first 180 days of the new administration and a systematically vetted list of potential loyalist appointees (Edsall, 2024). Reversal of the Biden climate-change and environmental agenda is a centerpiece of this document, which calls for scuttling the "Green New Deal" as mandated by the IRA and deployed in various executive orders and legislation. The *Mandate* advocates eliminating subsidies for clean energy, electronic vehicles, and other green technologies and ending regulatory blocks to fossil fuel extraction, refinement, usage, and export. It argues that ending subsidies for green energy and lifting restrictions on fossil fuel would accelerate US economic growth and political–economic dominance by maximizing energy availability and reducing domestic prices for its most "reliable," "abundant" forms.

The *Mandate* asserts that for decades, progressives have sapped executive power by delegating it to the deep state bureaucracy, and that liberal-leaning civil servants and their agencies have been increasingly "weaponized against the public and the president." It contends that Trump or another new conservative president would have an "existential need for aggressive use of the vast powers of the executive branch" to strengthen the weakened presidency, set fundamentally new policy directions, and dismantle the deep state. The *Mandate* holds that an "unaccountable bureaucratic managerial class and radical left ideologies" have captured the Department of Justice (DOJ) and see activities unaligned with liberal beliefs as possible violations of federal law (Hamilton, 2023, pp. 545–546). It claims that the Biden Administration DOJ's "radical liberal agenda," stressing diversity, equality, and inclusion (DEI) drives "affirmative discrimination" and sidetracks DOJ from executing its core constitutional duties to protect public safety and insure rule of law. The *Mandate* contends that Biden Administration "weaponization" of DOJ has been buoyed by a politicized Federal Bureau of Investigation (FBI), which has helped propagate Democratic Party lies about Trump's supposed collusion with Russia, undercut Republican charges about Hunter Biden's laptop, and diminished free speech in the social media by monitoring alleged "misinformation" and "disinformation" and warning about "foreign influences" (Hamilton, 2023, pp. 545–546). Advocating "top-to-bottom" change, the *Mandate* holds that the DOJ should be under the president's "direct supervision and control" to ensure that it executes his or her political agenda (Hamilton, 2023. pp. 547, 557–559).

The *Mandate* contends that the next Republican president must fundamentally reorganize and shift the foci of the DOJ Civil Rights Division – i.e., redirect its energies to lawful matters from its Biden era obsession with enforcement of discriminatory DEI laws and practices. For example, the *Mandate* argues that DOJ should redirect its efforts to upholding laws that protect first amendment rights, criminalize providers and distributors of abortion pills by mail, protect against voter fraud, and restrict illegal immigration (Hamilton, 2023, pp. 560–567). The *Mandate* also charges that the Green New Deal undercuts the rule of law and empowers the deep state. Trump claims to be the "voice of the people" – the only one capable of ensuring retribution against their elitist leftist oppressors and transforming the top-down bureaucracy to serve the people's needs. Designed to facilitate a Trump second term, the *Mandate* claims that concentrating executive power in the president's hands would return power to the American people (Vought, 2023, pp. 43–44). This equation is reminiscent of fascist ideology, which contended that strongman political actions and decisions ultimately manifest the tacit affirmation or collective will of a solidary politicized citizenry and thereby is democratic (Reiff, 2022; Schmitt, 1996 [1932]).

Numerous Trump critics have analyzed his many, authoritarian moves during his 2016 presidential campaign and presidency, culminating in the January 6th debacle and overall failed self-coup (Antonio, 2022). His critics have warned that his winning a second term would unleash even more radical antidemocratic moves (Savage, Swan, & Haberman, 2023). Jonathon Swan (2022a, 2022b) illuminated the shift at Heritage from Bush conservatism to "New Right" ideas and organizations, which aligned with Trump's populist "America First" agenda and led to Project 2025. Swan stressed a nascent plan to dismantle the administrative state, based on the "Schedule F" executive order, which Trump made less than a month before the 2020 presidential election, and Biden later rescinded. If Trump was reelected, this executive order would have allowed him to reassign up to an estimated 50,000 civil servants, who could be construed to influence policy formation, as "Schedule F employees." In a second term, Trump would have stripped higher level nonpartisan civil servants of their strong employment protections and replaced them with political loyalists expected to execute his will obediently. Twentieth-century progressives, the *Mandate* claims, appointed civil servants that shared their liberal views and provided them with excessive employment protections and political authority, which insured reproduction of the liberal political culture that eventually hardened civil service bureaucracy into the deep state. As Swan expected, the *Mandate* contends that the only way to end this "woke" domination of the liberal administrative state is to reinstate Schedule F as soon as the next Republican president's term in office begins (Devine et al., 2023, pp. 73, 80–81; Swan, 2022a). The Project 2025 Presidential Personnel Database vetted thousands of potential Schedule F employees prior to the 2024 election to ensure identification of Trump loyalists, who would be ready to be appointed shortly after the inauguration. White House staff would oversee these new political appointees to ensure they are complying with the presidential agenda (Swan, 2022b; Swan & Haberman, 2023).

Discussion of the *Mandate's* advocacy of concentrated executive power increased in summer 2023 as Trump became the leading 2024 Republican presidential candidate. Critics began to warn that he and his allies aimed to make him "dictator." Provocative statements by Trump inflamed the growing controversy over the *Mandate*. For example, he promised to invoke the Insurrection Act, which authorizes "limitless discretion" to the president to use the military against civilian authorities or to quell civil unrest (Nunn, 2023). He also asserted that he would use DOJ and the FBI against his political enemies, including his own former staff, officials, and lawyers, who did not serve him well or turned against him (Arnsdorf et al., 2023). Trump declared that he would conduct sweeping nationwide raids to apprehend undocumented immigrants, incarcerate them in huge camps, and then deport them *en masse* (Savage, Haberman, & Swan, 2023). Threatening to overthrow the international order, he asserted that he would "'encourage' Russia 'to do whatever the hell they want'" to European allies that do not pay enough to support their own defense and implied that he would not abide by the National Atlantic Treaty Organization (NATO) obligations of mutual defense (Baker, 2024). However, he threatened to use military force in Mexico against the drug cartels and in the United States against undocumented immigrants and in Democratic run cities to stem crime (Swan et al., 2023). Neoconservative pundit and Brookings Institute Senior Fellow Robert Kagan (2023a) composed a systematic argument, which was convincing to many readers, in a *Washington Post* op-ed about the inevitability of a Trump dictatorship, stirring affirmations and denials of his authoritarian aims.[11] Interviewing Trump on *Fox News*, Sean Hannity tried hard to motivate him to deny Kagan's accusations. Trump said he would be a dictator only on day one to shut down the border and allow drilling everywhere (Graham, 2023). In spring and summer 2024, The Democratic Party made Project 2025 a major campaign issue by contending it was a plan for Trumpian dictatorship. Trump then claimed that he knew nothing about it. *The Economist* (2023) asserted that Donald Trump "poses the biggest threat to the world in 2024," and Biden declared that a Trump second term would pose a grave threat to democracy (Viser, 2024).

REVERSING THE BIDEN GREEN NEW DEAL: TRUMP'S "ENERGY DOMINANCE" AGENDA

Although skeptical about climate change, the *Mandate* does not engage climate science or attempt rebuttal of its findings or IPCC summations of them. It simply declares policies aimed to mitigate climate change to be a left-wing, "woke" political agenda that manifests Biden Administration climate "fanaticism." It says the next Trumpian administration must conduct "a whole-of-government unwinding" or reversal that ends federal support for Biden climate policies and scrubs their profuse facets "from all policy manuals, guidance documents, and agendas..." (Vought, 2023, p. 61). The Heritage position presupposed by the *Mandate* is that climate change may be happening but has mild, manageable effects. Contradicting the vast majority of climate scientists and IPCC reports, Heritage analysts hold that total elimination of GHG would reduce global temperatures extraordinary little this century, while the economic costs of mitigation would inflict much greater damage than climate change itself. Heritage modeling found that eliminating all US carbon dioxide emissions would cut global temperature by only 0.2 degrees by 2100; if the 37 Organization for Economic Co-operation and Development (OECD) advanced capitalist nations did the same, it would result in a mere 0.5-degree reduction, which contradicts massively all IPCC projections (Dayaratina et al., 2022).

Heritage writers hold that rejoining the Paris Agreement and pursing its GHG targets would increase unemployment, cut manufacturing jobs, reduce family incomes, and raise household electricity costs steeply. In their view, the Biden climate agenda costs millions of jobs across diverse economic sectors (Dayaratina et al., 2022). The *Mandate* holds that environmental problems are best managed by free-market policies, which accelerate economic growth and scientific/technological progress. It calls for US withdrawal from the UN Framework Convention on Climate Change and Paris Agreement (Walton et al., 2023, p. 708).[12] It also rejects private sector programs, such as corporate social responsibility, common-good capitalism, socially responsible investment, and stakeholder theory for justifying diminished primacy of profit maximization for social ends, including climate change mitigation, environmental justice, and sustainable development (Burton & Bowes, 2023, p. 832).[13]

Environmental battles have long ensued over extensive federal lands in US western states. The federal government owns 80.1% of Nevada, 60.9% of Alaska, and 45.9% of 11 coterminous western states (Congressional Research Service, 2020). The *Mandate* asserts that the Department of Interior once managed these lands in a bipartisan fashion, consistent with statutory requirements for balanced usage permitting more extensive economic and recreational activities. Aiming to please supporters in the environmental movement, the *Mandate* contends, President Carter imposed more restrictive policies limiting these activities on federal land. Sympathetic to western state efforts to seek divestitures of federal lands and open them to a wider range of economic and recreational activities (late 1970s and early 1980s "Sagebrush Rebellion"), President Reagan reversed Carter policies in the region. The *Mandate* holds that Presidents Clinton and Obama restored and intensified the Carter *War on the West* by imposing even more restrictive environmental regulations that sharply limited economic and recreational uses. It argues that Biden's "radical climate agenda" made matters worse. Rescinding the Trump "Energy Dominance Agenda," Biden Interior Secretary Deb Haaland overhauled resource management to block fossil fuel production on federal lands and stress monumental increases in solar and wind energy. The climate science consensus holds that burning fossil fuels is the primary driver of dangerous climate change, and that consequent policy agendas must stress sharp reductions of their usage and decarbonization. By contrast, the *Mandate* calls for ending Biden's "war on fossil fuel" and reinstating the Trumpian Energy Dominance agenda, which stresses maximizing fossil fuel production and usage to ensure provision of cheap, abundant, reliable energy, increase US energy sector exports and profitability, accelerate overall economic growth, and foster US geopolitical dominance (Pendley, 2023, pp. 518–523; Trump, 2023).

The *Mandate* says that a Trumpian Department of Interior would remove restrictions on lease sales for onshore and offshore oil production, do the same for mining in coal producing states, rescind the Biden Administration's restrictive rules for Bureau of Land Management (BLM) waste management and critical habitat exclusions of the Endangered Species Act, and sharply increase oil and gas production on Alaska public lands (Pendley, 2023, pp 522–529). The *Mandate* holds that the next Republican administration must vacate Biden's 30 × 30 initiative, which plans to protect at least 30% of our lands and waters for conservation. The *Mandate* also contends that the next Republican administration should reinstate Trump's reviews facilitating efforts to downsize extensive protected areas of National Monuments and to repeal the Antiquities Act of 1906, which allows the president to take emergency actions to protect scenic rivers, wilderness, endangered species, and unique natural places. The *Mandate* calls for reform of the National Environmental Policy Act (NEPA) which requires federal agencies to assess environmental and social and economic impacts of projects on federal lands or publicly owned facilities before issuing permits. It also holds that the government should stop relying on species specialists, who are self-interested and have ideological bias favoring species they study and hope to preserve, in enforcing the Endangered Species Act (Pendley, 2023, pp. 532–534). For example, Pendley (2023, p. 533) asserts that "the work of the Fish and Wildlife Service is the product of 'species cartels' afflicted with groupthink, confirmation bias, and a common desire to preserve the prestige, power, and appropriations of the agency that pays and employs them."

Long dominated by left political ends, the *Mandate* argues, the Environmental Protection Agency (EPA) must cease being an "all-powerful energy and land use regulator," and become more responsive to state and local needs. It contends that the Biden EPA has operated in a "top-down, coercive" fashion, forging entirely out of reach standards to transition away from natural gas, oil, and coal to "unreliable renewables," and consequently driving "job-killing" regulatory legislation, depressing economic growth, and expanding bureaucracy. Dominating the EPA, the *Mandate* holds, "embedded" climate activists expand federal interference across the entire economy, without congressional support, and their exaggerated claims about climate change inflame public fears and justify "liberty-crushing" regulation, eroded property rights, and higher prices (Gunasekara, 2023, pp. 417–419). The *Mandate* advises eliminating the Office of Environmental Justice and External Civil Rights, Office of Enforcement and Compliance Assistance, and Office of Public Engagement and Environmental Education. It holds that the new regime ought to ensure advisory boards expand the "diversity of scientific opinions," and that, on day one, Trump should issue an executive order to assess, reorganize, and downsize the EPA. It holds that political appointees responsible to overhaul the EPA will be vetted, assembled, and prepared to act before the new president takes office (Gunasekara, 2023, pp. 421–423). The *Mandate* asserts that the politically biased *Global Change Research Act of 1990*, which requires research into climate change and its impacts, and reports to Congress every four years on these matters must be reformed or scuttled (Gunasekara, 2023, p. 439). The emphasis throughout the EPA chapter is that the rules for reportage and regulation of GHG and for other types of pollution are far too stringent and were motivated by left-wing political manipulation rather than by unbiased deliberation of "sound science." It stresses emphatically that the EPA should be radically reformed and overseen strictly by political appointees of the president.

Author of the EPA chapter, Mandy Gunasekara, was previously a senior advisor and Chief of Staff to Trump EPA heads. She also worked for anti-environmentalist Oklahoma Republican Senator Jim Inhofe and brought him a snowball that he famously displayed on the Senate floor as "evidence" that climate change is a hoax. She is married to an oil industry lobbyist and has long ranted against "woke" climate policies of the left. She helped convince Trump to withdraw from the Paris climate agreement and roll back environmental regulation. She was a founder of Satoshi Action Fund supporting Bitcoin mining, which demands an enormous amount of fossil fuel energy in its operations (Dance, 2023; Eilperin & Dennis, 2020). She was a founder and president of the Energy45 dark-money PAC, which promotes Trump energy policies and is part of a climate change denialist coalition, who claim that any possible impacts will be "mild and manageable," "global prosperity is actually driven by fossil fuels," "fossil fuel is 'cheap energy,'" and fossil fuel can solve the energy "needs of the world's poor…" (Oreskes, 2019).

The *Mandate* contends that a Trumpian Department of Energy (DOE) would reverse artificial energy scarcity driven by ideologically extreme green politics, which aim to end fossil fuel use and channel taxpayer money into "intermittent wind and solar development." It contends that a new Republican president should prioritize American "energy security" by maximizing access to "abundant, reliable, affordable energy" and employing all types of energy (including nuclear energy). However, the government should let the market work and not pick winners and losers by regulating and pouring federal money into favored green energy projects. The *Mandate* asserts that the Infrastructure Investment and Jobs Act (IUA) and IRA, which provide federal money for politicized investment in renewable energy, must be repealed. It holds that the DOE should reassert its "core mission" stressing pursuance of energy security and related national security matters, American energy interests in global markets, and employment of the best science to achieve these ends (McNamee, 2023, pp. 363–367). The *Mandate* advocates abandoning efforts to reduce GHG emissions in "fossil fuel extraction, transport, and combustion" and slashing federal support for carbon capture. It advises eliminating the Office of Fossil Fuel and Carbon Management and related applied energy programs, Office of Energy Efficiency, and Office of Clean Energy Demonstration, and Renewable Energy and most programs of the Grid Development Office, which stress shifting to renewables and reduced carbon generation (McNamee, 2023, pp. 376–381). The *Mandate* holds that efforts to achieve "net-zero" carbon emissions and a clean energy economy by 2050 are futile and destructive, and that offices, regulations, and subsidies serving these ends should be eliminated.

The *Mandate* contends that the Biden Administration Department of Agriculture (USDA) made "climate change, renewable energy and equity" its primary goals while it diminished the importance of "efficient production." It holds that the left derides the American agriculture and food system and does not respect farmers and others who contribute to the reliable, resilient US food supply chain.

Consequently, it argues that the USDA endorses too readily UN sustainable development policies and supports misguided programs to transition to "organic" and "climate-smart" production, which lose sight of the relationship between "efficiency and affordability." The *Mandate* asserts that the US food and agricultural system works effectively and should not be transformed or burdened with more regulatory legislation. In a second term, it holds that Trump must break with UN and other international programs for sustainable development (Bakst, 2023, pp. 292–293). It calls for narrowing USDA foci away from its current emphasis on climate and environment and stressing instead removing foreign trade restrictions on American agricultural goods, employing "sound science" to promote delivery of affordable, abundant food, staunchly opposing excessive government intervention, and defending proven agricultural practices, individual dietary choices, and property rights (Bakst, 2023, pp. 291–292).

The Biden Administration's "anti-fossil fuel climate agenda" raised fuel economy standards beyond levels that can possibly be met by traditional internal-combustion engine (ICE) vehicles the *Mandate* charges. Justified by the Clean Air Act, it argues, the EPA established overly strict fuel economy limits to reduce carbon dioxide emissions of new vehicles and compel American consumers to shift to electronic vehicles (EVs), even though they prefer ICE vehicles (Furchtgott-Roth, 2023, p. 627). The *Mandate* holds that the Biden Administration made the transition to EVs a primary goal of the Department of Transportation (DOT), which it supports with generous government subsidies. It claims that raising fuel economy standards increases auto prices and discourages consumers from buying newer, safer cars. The shift to EVs, Heritage argues, undercuts ICE auto production, which has been a pivotal foundation of the US industrial base, key driver of overall economic growth, and a provider of millions of jobs (Furchtgott-Roth, 2023, pp. 625–626). They contend that regulatory interventions restrict consumer choices, eliminate jobs, and motivate Americans to drive old unsafe, polluting vehicles. Additionally, the *Mandate* asserts that the shift to EVs would require extremely costly changes in the US power grid and damage national security by making the US dependent on China and other nations for rare earth minerals required for EV batteries. Additionally, the *Mandate* claims that stringent fuel economy limits and a transition to EVs would not reduce long-term global temperatures. It contends that a second Trump Administration would increase vehicle milage limits and eliminate political pressure and subsidies for a transition to EVs (Furchtgott-Roth, 2023, pp. 627–628).

The *Mandate* argues that the Department of Commerce (DOC) has been damaged by "regulatory capture" from the left, consequent "ideological drift," and loss of focus on its primary responsibility to foster economic growth and meet the needs of the business sector. It holds that the next Trump Administration must review DOC with a focus on "consolidation, elimination, and privatization" to reverse the Biden era "precipitous economic decline" and compete with China (Gilman, 2023, p. 663). The *Mandate* asserts that the National Oceanic and Atmospheric Administration (NOAA), which is the biggest DOC agency except for decennial censuses, normally accounts for more than half of the DOC budget and personnel. The *Mandate* charges that the "colossal operation" of NOAA's six main offices predict, manage, and ultimately plan "the unplannable" and drive "the climate change alarm industry."[14] It asserts that NOAA should be "broken up and downsized," and that its role as provider of environmental information, stewardship, scientific research could be done more effectively and objectively by commercial operations (e.g., AccuWeather). Offices providing applied science important for public safety and business, such as the National Hurricane Center and Environmental Satellite Service, would be preserved pending review and ensuring they do not take sides in the climate debate. However, the *Mandate* calls for cutting or eliminating environmentally protective facets of other NOAA offices The *Mandate* contends that the Office of Oceanic and Atmospheric Research (OAR) climate change research is a hotbed of "climate alarmism" and therefore must be shut down (Gilman, 2023, pp. 675–676). Consistent with Project 2025's overall goal of concentrating executive power, the *Mandate* holds that NOAA and other scientific agencies must be "wholly in sync with Administration policy" and overseen by political officials who have been screened to insure loyalty to the executive (Gilman, 2023, pp. 677–678). The energy dominance goal of a new Trumpian regime precludes climate science as we now know it.

The *Mandate* asserts that the Department of Treasury should stress free-market principles and low taxes, moving away from progressive taxation toward a flat tax, cutting corporate tax rates from 21% to 18%, slashing estate and gift taxes, reducing Internal Revenue Service personnel and audits, softening financial regulation, and other policies that benefit high income taxpayers. It suggests that congress should require a two-thirds majority to raise taxes and consequently make it difficult for the federal government to raise revenue for social and environmental ends (Walton et al., 2023, p. 698). The *Mandate* says that Treasury's recent emphases on "equity" and "climate change" must be eliminated. A Trumpian Treasury, it contends, would repeal tax increases for the Inflation Reduction Act and thereby undercut the Biden climate change agenda (Walton et al., 2023. p. 696). It also advocates shutting down the "Climate Hub Office," which is supposed to coordinate Treasury efforts "to inform, guide, incentivize, and mobilize financial flows for climate mitigation and adaptation," related projects with global and domestic partners, and efforts to achieve net-zero emissions by 2050. The *Mandate* also advises that a new Trumpian regime should withdraw from climate change agreements and rely on economic growth and market driven scientific and technological advances to cope with and advert "extreme weather events." A new Trump Administration would promote the fossil fuel industry, withdraw from the Paris Agreement and UN Framework on Climate Change, and terminate federal support for environmental, and social governance and private sector "responsible investment" (Walton et al., 2023, p. 709).

CONCLUSION: CLIMATE AND ENVIRONMENT: THE FRONTLINE IN PROTOFASCIST POSTFACTUAL POLITICS

When the Trump as dictator discourse heated up in fall 2023, his campaign distanced him from Project 2025 (LeVine et al., 2023). Trump asserted that he did not agree with all *Mandate* proposals and was not bound by them. However, given Heritage's strong support for him and his "lack of interest in detailed planning," the *Mandate* might well dictate policy if he wins again in 2024 (Edsall, 2024). His claim to total immunity from criminal prosecution (which has been given substantial support from the 2024 US Supreme Court "Immunity decision") transparently manifested his belief that the executive should have unchecked concentrated power (Savage, 2024). His comments to the press and campaign's formal policy plans articulated in "Agenda47"[15] upheld *Mandate* policies (Haberman et al., 2023).[16] In 2024, Trump hosted Hungary's hard-right, populist Prime Minister Viktor Orbán at Mar-a-Lago after he visited Heritage (he did not visit sitting President Biden). Orbán concentrated executive power and de-democratized Hungary. His vision of "illiberal democracy" was eagerly embraced by the Make America Great Again (MAGA) wing of the Republican Party and Trumpian base. Praising Orbán to the Mar-a-Lago crowd, Trump celebrated his governing style – "'This is the way it's going to be, and that's the end of it. Right?' Trump said, 'He's the boss'" (Riccardi & Spike, 2024; Weber, 2022). A *Time* interviewer asked the former president, "Don't you see why many Americans see such talk of dictatorship as contrary to our cherished principles?" On the contrary, Trump declared – "I think a lot of people like it" (Cortellessa, 2024).

Orbán has called EU climate change policies a "utopian fantasy" that drives up energy prices (Abnett & Strauss, 2021). Trump follows in the Hungarian leader's tracks. Trump repeated emphatically many times that "drill, baby, drill" and "energy dominance" will be among his top priorities of his next administration. Ranting about the evils offshore wind energy (e.g., "killing whales and driving marine mammals 'crazy'"), Trump told potential doner oil and gas industry executives, attending a Mar-a-Lago dinner, that he would treat them better than Biden has, and he would "do much of what they wanted starting 'on Day 1'" Trump asked the fossil fuel CEOs to donate a billion dollars to his campaign so that he could dismantle the Biden Administration environmental agenda and realize the kind of policies portrayed in the *Mandate* (Joselow & Dawsey, 2024a; 2024b). He outlined similar points emphatically in an Agenda47 video. Should Trump win a second term, he and his loyal appointees would attempt to enact by congressional actions (if his party wins congressional majorities) and by executive orders the antienvironmentalist policy regime articulated in detail in the *Mandate* and Project 2025.

The *Mandate* positions on climate change and environment manifest one side of a sharp political divide that has grown more extreme for more than a decade between those supporting or leaning toward the Republican and Democratic parties. Even "seeing" the local effects of climate change is related to party affiliation or lean. This political divide is moderated among younger voters. Seventy-eight percent of Democrats or leaners consider climate change as a major threat compared to twenty-three percent of Republicans and leaners (only thirteen percent consider it a top priority). However, more than two-thirds of Americans prioritize development of renewable energy sources and the effort to become carbon neutral by 2050 rather than expand fossil fuel production. And two-thirds of Americans hold that corporations and large businesses are not doing enough to reduce climate change, and 56% believe the federal government is not doing enough (Tyson et al., 2023). Despite the political polarization over policy, the Project 2025 environmental plan conflicts with majority American views of climate and environment and constitutes an extreme agenda. However, Heritage and MAGA Republicans advocate employing much more concentrated political power and much enhanced information control to institute and legitimate their agenda and suppress political backlash to it.

Professor of government and sociology at Harvard, Theda Skocpol, portrays Project 2025 and related plans for a second Trump presidency, "... detailed plans to take full control of various federal departments and agencies from the very start and to use every power available to implement radical ethnonationalist regulations and action plans." She says it is a "full prep for an authoritarian takeover, buttressed by the control Trump and Trumpins now have over the G.O.P. and its apparatuses." (quoted in Edsall, 2024). Trump's political speeches have become more apocalyptic emphasizing a nation in decay and on the verge of collapse from immigrants, urban criminals, globalists, and especially the Marxian left, empowered by Biden and other Democrats. Charles Homans (2024) contends that Trump's "us versus them" rhetoric has never been this extreme and that no American presidential candidate (even segregationist George Wallace) spoke like this at their rallies. For example, Trump promises the "great silent majority" of "forgotten" Americans to "root out the communists, Marxists and radical-left thugs that live like vermin within the confines of the country" (quoted in Homans, 2024).

Ethnonationalist and fascist "strongmen" have routinely vilified public enemies to justify their concentrating power and employing antidemocratic, coercive, and violent methods to "save the nation" or "real citizens." Nazi era political theorist Carl Schmitt (1996 [1932], pp. 27, 67) contended that such "friend–enemy" discourse can unify nations by accusing, demeaning, and isolating the "other" or "stranger," who is "existentially something different and alien." He identified "moments in which the enemy is, in concrete clarity, recognized as enemy" as the "high points of politics," which unify and "militarize" the formerly fragmented, possessive-individualist, deracinated, depoliticized masses of declining liberal democracies. Schmitt argued that sovereigns' right to declare a "state of exception" justifies their installing dictatorship, which often has expressed or tacit popular "acclimation" and therefore is "democratic" (Schmitt, 1988 [1926], pp. 16–17). Schmitt's friend–enemy politics has helped inspire and justify later forms of neofascism, including Trumpism and other types of hard-right populism (Antonio, 2000, 2019).

Climate change–driven heatwaves, fires, droughts, and floods in many parts of the globe marked 2023. Temperatures in Phoenix Arizona exceeded 110° Fahrenheit (F) for 31 straight days; coastal waters in the Florida Keys reached 100°F in July; Antarctic winter sea ice reached its historic low; intense fires ravaged Maui and Greece; and July was the hottest month in 120,000 years. UN Secretary-General António Guterres declared famously that the era of "global boiling" has arrived (Harlan, 2023). Scientists have been shocked by the extremity of the climatic anomalies and speed of the changes and disappointed by the absence of concerted political action to address the accelerating climate emergency. The 2023 UN Conference of the Parties (COP28) agreed to transition away from fossil fuels, but without a timetable or mandatory reduction targets (Watts, 2023). A study led by top climate scientist, James Hansen, held that climate change is likely to exceed 1.5° Celsius (C) above preindustrial temperatures this decade and 2.0°C before 2050 (Hansen et al., 2023). Other scientists held that exceeding the ~2°C threshold and possibly even ~1.5°C could surpass multiple tipping points in vital ecosystem processes, generate a cascade of feedback that generates a state change in the Earth System toward an irreversible "Hothouse Earth Pathway" or climate endgame for our species (Steffen et al., 2018, p. 3). Vastly, increased fossil fuel usage and climate change has been ultimately driven by extraordinary growth in the size and intensity of the global economy and population relative to the biosphere (Daly, 2018). Fundamental change has occurred during the post-1950 "Great Acceleration" of economic growth, worldwide expansion of capitalism, and enormous global population growth. Scientists tracking Earth System processes and approaching tipping points hold we already have exceeded planetary boundaries for six of nine major processes, are approaching limits of two others, and are now "well outside the safe-operating space" for our species and for many other living things.[17]

Trumpian plans to concentrate executive power and forge an energy dominance program, based on maximizing fossil fuel production and usage, would be a suicidal route to a Hothouse Earth. The sociocultural, political, ideological, and technological barriers blocking effective climate adaptation and mitigation domestically and internationally are enormous and have been described by many critics from diverse vantage points.[18] Scientific findings even more rigorous and effectively communicated cannot overcome by itself the political polarization over climate change and other global environmental problems, fossil fuel sector and overall corporate money, lobbying power, and propaganda, and continuous flow of grossly distorted information on internet and the social media. Trumpian environmental politics and energy dominance agenda has arisen in a "post-truth" political culture. Yale historian, Timothy Snyder (2021), argues:

> Post-truth is pre-fascism, and Trump has been our post-truth president. When we give up on truth, we concede power to those with the wealth and charisma to create spectacle in its place. Without agreement about some basic facts, citizens cannot form the civil society that would allow them to defend themselves.
>
> (Snyder, 2021, December 28)

Climate change and the environment are on the frontlines of the battle against post-truth political culture and for democracy against emergent fascism. In any of today's culture wars, can there be anything more at stake? The spread of youth-oriented global social movements pushing back against environmental degradation offer some political promise and hope for the future. Defending democracy, resisting neofascism, and averting a consequent descent into barbarism is necessary to sustain the planet, humanity and other life forms with whom we share the planet.

NOTES

1. The 2021 Infrastructure Investment and Jobs Act (IUA) also contained major environmental provisions (e.g., about clean water, electronic vehicle charging stations, climate

change adaptation, wildlife crossings and conservation, and power grid development) (Buttle, 2023).

2. Influenced by the El Niño weather pattern (which releases heat from seas) and other transitory factors in 2023, global temperatures exceeded the 1.5°C target for the year. It would take about a decade averaging at this level to determine if we have permanently exceeded this target. The Earth has warmed about 1.2°C–1.3°C averaged over several years (Zhong, 2024).

3. In April 2024, Biden set the first national drinking water standard to ban cancer causing PFAS pollution (EPA Press Office, 2024), limited oil and gas drilling in over 13 million acers of the National Petroleum Reserve in Alaska (Joselow, 2024), and instituted new power plant rules that will close almost all coal-fined power plants by 2040 (Davenport & Friedman, 2024).

4. Biden promised during his presidential campaign to forbid new oil and gas drilling on federal lands, but later permitted the ConocoPhillips Willow Project on the North Slope of Alaska. This development was bitterly opposed by environmental groups but had the support of unions and indigenous groups because of its potential to create jobs and revenue (McGrath, 2023).

5. Biden's much more expensive, comprehensive "Build Back Better Act," which combined climate change and redistributive social protection support, passed the then Democratic Party controlled House of Representatives but failed in the Senate, where Democrats then held a razor-thin majority. Fossil fuel industry advocate, Democratic Senator Joe Manchin (WV), refused to support the bill. His consequent negotiations with Senate Majority Leader Chuck Schumer (NY) compromised IRA climate policy (Cochrane & Friedman, 2023; Waldman, 2022).

6. See Barker (2023), for a critique of Riley and Brenner's argument about political capitalism.

7. A Pew Research Center survey reports European support for climate change is lower in right-wing populist parties (Poushter et al., 2022). Mapping European populist party views about climate change, Schaller and Carius (2019) hold that they usually argue that policies aiming to restrict fossil fuel usage are economically harmful, unfair to middling and low-income strata, and ineffective ecologically. They contend that such policies drive economic decline and erode national sovereignty and do not take account of scientific dissent about anthropocentric climate change. Also see Conversi (2024) on related material.

8. Trumpism has benefitted from the strong support of white Christian nationalists (Gorski & Perry, 2022; Kagan, 2024).

9. *The Mandate for Leadership* is one of "four pillars" of Project 2025. The other three include a personnel database of potential conservative political appointees (aimed to speed the appointment process and ensure loyalty to the president), Presidential Administration Academy (online "educational system" taught by people from the Trumpist conservative coalition), and Playbook forged by "agency teams" to draft immediate transition plans (Dans, 2023, p. xiv).

10. Trump's top advisors sometimes publicly mocked his views, behavior, or ability to grasp issues. For example, Defense Secretary, Jim Mattis, held that the president acted like a "fifth-or six-grader"; Secretary of State, Rex Tillerson said he was a "moron"; White House Chief of Staff, John Kelly and Treasury Secretary, Steven Mnuchin called him an "idiot," and National Security Advisor, H. R. McMaster, said he was a "dope" (Morin, 2018).

11. The first Kagen op-ed drew 19,000 comments and was widely discussed by many other political columnists. His "grim" picture inflamed fears so quickly and sharply that he wrote a second op-ed a week later addressing ways the dictatorship could be stopped (Kagan, 2023b). However, this did not allay fears or halt discussion of a possible Trump dictatorship.

12. Trump quit the Paris Agreement, and President Biden rejoined it in day one of his administration (Blinken, 2021).

13. I list Burton and Bowes (2023) in the text and references as coauthors for simplicity's sake even though their names do not appear together under the *Mandate* chapter title (Financial Regulatory Agencies). They are listed separately within the chapter ahead of the separate sections they composed.

14. NOAA's main offices are – The National Weather Service, National Ocean Service, Oceanic and Atmospheric Research, National Environmental Satellite, Data, and Information Service, National Marine Fisheries Service, and Office of Marine and Aviation Operations and NOAA Corps (Gilman, 2023, p. 675).

15. See links to Agenda47 Trump videos on various facets of his presidential policy agenda at Agenda47 | Donald J. Trump (donaldjtrump.com).

16. Trump's *Time* interview about his governance style in a possible second term also converges with core themes of Project 2025 (Cortellessa, 2024).

17. The processes are climate change, biosphere integrity (biodiversity), stratospheric ozone depletion, ocean acidification, biogeochemical flows; land system change, freshwater change, atmospheric aerosol loading, and novel entities (synthetic chemical released into the environment, which have not been safety tested) (Richardson et al., 2023). For related studies see, e.g., Kemp et al. (2022), and Willcock et al. (2023).

18. For example, see Brulle (2000), Hansen (2009), Hulme (2009), Klein (2014), and Mann (2021).

REFERENCES

Abnett, K. (2021, November 9). Explainer: what's the difference between 1.5°C and 2°C of global warming. *Reuters.* https://www.reuters.com/business/cop-whats-the-difference-between–15c-2c-global-warming-2021-11-07

Abnett, K., & Strauss, M. (2021, October 21). 'Utopian fantasy': Hungary's Orban dismisses EU climate policy plans. *Reuters.* https://www.reuters.com/world/europe/utopian-fantasy-hungarys-orban-dismisses-eu-climate-policy-plans-2021-10-21/

Antonio, R. J. (2000). After postmodernism: Reactionary tribalism. *American Journal of Sociology*, *106*, 40–87.

Antonio, R. J. (2019). Reactionary tribalism redux: Rightwing populism and ge-democratization. *Sociological Quarterly*, *60*, 201–209.

Antonio, R. J. (2022). Democracy and capitalism in the interregnum: Trump's failed self-coup and after. *Critical Sociology*, *48*, 937–965. https://doi.org/10.1177/08969205211049499

Arnsdorf, I., Dawsey, J., & Barrett, D. (2023, November 6). Trump and allies plot revenge, Justice department control in a second term. *Washington Post.* https://www.washingtonpost.com/politics/2023/11/05/trump-revenge-second-term/

Baker, P. (2024, February 11). Favoring foes over friends, Trump threatens to upend the international order. *New York Times.* https://www.nytimes.com/2024/02/11/us/politics/trump-nato.html

Bakst, D. (2023). Department of agriculture. In P. Dans & S. Groves (Eds.), *Mandate for leadership* (pp. 289–318). Heritage Foundation.

Barker, T. (2023). Some questions about political capitalism. *New Left Review*, *140/141*, 35–51.

Battistoni, A., & Mann, G. (2023). Climate Bidenomics. *New Left Review*, *143*, 55–77.

Blattner, C. E. (2024). European ruling linking climate change to human rights could be a game changer-here's how. *Nature*, *628*, 691. https://www.nature.com/articles/d41586-024-01177-3

Blinken, A. J. (2021, February 19). The United States officially rejoins the Paris agreement. *U.S. Department of State.* https://www.state.gov/the-united-states-officially-rejoins-the-paris-agreement

Brulle, R. J. (2000). *Agency, democracy, and nature.* MIT Press.

Burton, D. R., & Bowes, R. (2023). Financial regulatory agencies. In P. Dans & S. Groves (Eds.), *Mandate for leadership* (pp. 829–844). Heritage Foundation.

Buttle, R. (2023, October 27), Green energy in the bipartisan infrastructure law: Opportunities for small businesses. *Forbes.* https://www.forbes.com/sites/rhettbuttle/2023/10/27/green-energy-in-the-bipartisan-infrastructure-law-opportunities-for-small-businesses/?sh=648bd6e829157sh=648?

Cochrane, E., & Friedman, L. (2023, September 21). Manchin's gas pipeline deal irks both parties, snarling spending bill. *New York Times*. https://www.nytimes.com/202209/2022us/politics/Manchin-pipeline-spending-bill-html

Congressional Research Service. (2020). Federal landownership: Overview and data. https://crsreports.congress.govR42346

Conversi, D. (2024, April 9). Eco-fascism: An oxymoron? Far-right nationalism, history, and the climate emergency. *Frontiers in Human Dynamics*, 6. https://doi.org/10.3389/fhumd.2024.1373872

Cortellessa, E. (2024). How far Trump would go. *Time*. https://time.com/6972021/donald-trump-2024-election-interview/

Daly, H. (2018). Ecologies of scale. *New Left Review* (Interview by B. Kunkel), 109, 81–104.

Dance, G. J. X. (2023, February 3). Anxiety, mood swings, and sleepless nights: Life near a bitcoin mine. *New York Times*. https://www.nytimes.com/2024/02/03/us/bitcoin-arkansas-noise-pollution.html

Dans, P. (2023). The 2025 presidential transition project. In P. Dans & S. Groves (Eds.), *Mandate for leadership* (pp. xiii–xiv). Heritage Foundation.

Davenport, C., & Friedman, L. (2024, April 25). Five things to know about Biden's new power plant rules. *New York Times*. https://www.nytimes.com/2024/04/25/climate/joe-biden-climate-global-warming.html

Dayaratina, K., Tubb, K., & Kreutzer, D. (2022, June 16). The unsustainable costs of President Biden's climate agenda. *The Heritage Foundation*. https://www.heritage.org/energy-economics/report/the-unsustainable-costs-president-bidens-climate-agenda

Devine, D., Kirk, D. D., & Dans, P. (2023). Central personnel agencies: Managing the bureaucracy. In P. Dans & S. Groves (Eds.), *Mandate for leadership* (pp. 69–85). Heritage Foundation.

Dickie, C. (2023, November 20). Climate on track to warm by nearly 3C without aggressive actions, UN finds. *Reuters*. https://www.reuters.com/sustainability/climate-energy/climate-track-warm-by-nearly-3c-without-greater-ambition-un-report-2023-11-20/

Economist. (2023, November 17). Donald Trump poses the biggest danger to the world in 2024. *Economist*. https://www.economist.com/leaders/2023/11/16/donald-trump-poses-the-biggest-danger-to-the-world-in-2024

Edsall, T. B. (2024, April 3). Trump backers are determined not to blow it this time around. *New York Times*. https://www.nytimes.com/2024/04/03/opinion/leonard-leo-heritage-trump-2025.html

Eilperin, J., & Dennis, B. (2020, February 14). She pushed Trump to exit the Paris climate agreement and roll back environmental rules. And she's returning to EPA as chief of Staff. *Washington Post*. https://washingtonpost.com/climate-environment/2020/02/14/she-pushed-trump-exit-paris-climate-agreement-rollback-environment-rules-shes-returtning-epa-chief-staff/

EPA Press Office. (2024, April 10). *Biden-Harris administration finalizes first-ever national drinking water standard to protect 100 m people from PFAS pollution*. United States Environmental Protection Agency. https://www.epa.gov/newsreleases/biden-harris-administration-finalizes-first-ever-national-drinking-water-standard

Furchtgott-Roth, D. (2023). Department of transportation. In P. Dans & S. Groves (Eds.), *Mandate for leadership* (pp. 619–640). Heritage Foundation.

Garcia-Navarro, L. (2024, January 21). Foundation's plans for 'institutionalizing Trumpism'. *New York Times*. https://www.nytimes.com/2024/01/21/magazine/heritage-foundation-kevin-roberts-html

Gilman, T. F. (2023). Department of commerce. In P. Dans & S. Groves (Eds.), *Mandate for leadership* (pp. 663–689). Heritage Foundation.

Gorski, P. S., & Perry, S. L. (2022). *The flag and the cross*. Oxford University Press.

Graham, D. A. (2023, December 6). Trump says he'll be a dictator on 'Day One'. *Atlantic*. https://www.theatlantic.com/ideas/archive/2023/12/trump-says-hell-be-a-dictator-on-day-one/676247/

Gunasekara, M. M. (2023). Environmental protection agency. In P. Dans & S. Groves (Eds.), *Mandate for leadership* (pp. 417–448). Heritage Foundation.

Haberman, M., Swan, J., & Savage, C. (2023, November 13). Trump campaign officials try to play down contentious 2025 plans. *New York Times*. https://www.nytimes.com/2023/11/13/us/politics/trump-campaign-2025-statement-html

Halper, E., & Olorrunipa, T. (2023, December 31). U.S. oil production hit a record under Biden. He seldom mentions it. *Washington Post.* https://www.washingtonpost.com/politics/2023/12/31/us-oil-production-has-hit-record-under-biden-he-hardly-mentions-it/

Hamilton, G. (2023). Department of justice. In P. Dans & S. Groves (Eds.), *Mandate for leadership* (pp. 545–579). Heritage Foundation.

Hansen, J. (2009). *Storms of my grandchildren.* Bloomsbury.

Hansen, J. E., Sato, M., Simons, L., Nazarenko, L. S., Sangha, I., Kharecha, P., Zachos, J. C., von Schuckmann, K., Loeb, N. G., Osman, M. B., Jin, Q., Tselioudis, G., Jeong, E., Lacis, A., Ruedy, R., Russell, G., Cao, J., & Li, J. (2023). Global warming in the pipeline. *Oxford Open Climate Change, 3,* kgad008. https://doi.org/10.1093/oxfclm/kgad008

Harlan, C. (2023, December 31). The climate future arrived in 2023. It left scars across the planet. *Washington Post.* https://www.washingtonpost.com/climate-environment/2023/12/31/2023-record-heat-temperatures/

Homans, C. (2024, April 27). Donald Trump has never sounded like this. *New York Times.* https://www.nytimes.com/2024/04/27/magazine/trump-rallies-rhetoric.html

Hulme, M. (2009). *Why we disagree about climate change.* Cambridge University Press.

Joselow, M. (2024, April 19). Biden limits oil drilling across 13 million acres Alaskan Arctic. *Washington Post.* https://www.msn.com/en-us/money/markets/biden-limits-oil-drilling-across-13-million-acres-of-alaskan-arctic/ar-AA1nhZHg

Joselow, M., & Dawsey, J. (2024a, April 17). Trump rails against wind energy in fundraising pitch to oil executives. *Washington Post.* https://www.washingtonpost.com/climate-environment/2024/04/17/trump-wind-power-oil-executives/

Joselow, M., & Dawsey, J. (2024b, May 9). What Trump promised oil CEOs as he asked them to steer $100 billion to his campaign. *Washington Post.* https://www.washingtonpost.com/politics/2024/05/09/trump-oil-industry-campaign-money/

Kagan, R. (2023a, November 30). A Trump dictatorship is increasingly inevitable, we should stop pretending. *Washington Post.* https://www.washingtonpost.com/opinions/2023/11/30/trump-dictator-2024-election-robert-kagan/

Kagan, R. (2023b, December 7). The Trump dictatorship: How to stop it. *Washington Post.* https://www.washingtonpost.com/opinions/2023/12/07/robert-kagan-trump-dictatorship-how-to-stop/

Kagan, R. (2024, April 24). We have a radical democracy. Will Trump voters destroy it? *Washington Post.* https://www.washingtonpost.com/opinions/2024/04/24/trump-tyranny-christian-nationalist-democracy/

Katz, M., Levermann, A., & Wenz, L. (2024). The economic commitment to climate change. *Nature, 628,* 551–557. https://doi.org/10.1038/s41586-024-07219-0

Kemp, L., Xu, C., Depledge, J., & Lenton, T. M. (2022). Climate endgame: Exploring catastrophic climate change scenarios. *PNAS, 119*(34), e2108146119. https://doi.org/10.1073/pnas.2108146119

Klein, N. (2014). *This changes everything.* Simon & Schuster.

LeVine, M., Arnsdorf, I., & Dawsey, J. (2023, December 6). Trump 'dictator' comment reignites criticism his camp has tried to curb. *Washington Post.* https://www.washingtonpost.com/elections/2023/12/06/trump-comments-dictator-campaign-president-2024/

Mann, M. E. (2021). *The new climate war.* PublicAffairs.

McGrath, M. (2023, March 13). Willow project: Biden walks political tightrope over Alaska oil project. *BBC.* https://www.bbc.com/news/world-us-canada-64944535

McNamee, B. L. (2023). Department of energy and related commissions. In P. Dans & S. Groves (Eds.), *Mandate for leadership* (pp. 363–416). Heritage Foundation.

Morin, R. (2018, September 4). 'Idiot,' 'dope,' 'moron': How Trump's aids insulted the boss. *Politico.* https://www.politico.com/story/2018/09/04/trumps-insults-idiot-woodward-806455#:~:text=The%20comments%20came%20after%20Tillerson,security%20team%20and%20Cabinet%20officials&text=At%20a%20dinner%20in%20July,idiot%2C%E2%80%9D%20BuzzFeed%20News%20reported

Nunn, J. (2023, November 17). Trump wants to use the military against his domestic enemies. Congress must act. *Brennan Center.* https://www.brennancenter.org/our-work/analysis-opinion/trump-wants-use-military-against-his-domestic-enemies-congress-must-act

Oreskes, N. (2019, November 11). The greatest scam in history: How energy companies took us all. *Common Dreams.* https://www.commondreams.org/views/2019/11/11/greatest-scam-history-how-energy-companies-took-us-all

Pendlay, W. P. (2023). Department of interior. In P. Dans & S. Groves (Eds.), *Mandate for leadership* (pp. 517–544). Heritage Foundation.

Poushter, J., Fagan, M., & Gubbala, S. (2022). Climate change remains top global threat across 19-county survey. *Pew Research Center.* https://www.pewresearch.org/global/2022/08/31/climate-change-remains-top-global-threat-across-19-country-survey/

Reiff, M. R. (2022, November 8). The conversation: Why do some people think fascism is the greatest expression of democracy? *UC Davis.* https://www.ucdavis.edu/blog/curiosity/conversation-why-do-some-people-think-fascism-greatest-expression-democracy

Riccardi, N., & Spike, J. (2024, March 8). Trump meets with Hungary's leader, Viktor Orbán, continuing his embrace of autocrats. *AP.* https://apnews.com/article/trump-orban-hungary-conservatives-autocrats-biden-97d6998f747d3543f2f1df069b0f9165

Richardson, K., Steffen, W., Lucht, W., Bendtsen, J., Cornell, S. E., Donges, J. F., Drüke, M., Fetzer, I., Bala, G., von Bloh, W., Feulner, G., Fiedler, S., Gerten, D., Gleeson, T., Hofmann, M., Huiskamp, W., Kummu, M., Mohan, C., Nogués-Bravo, D., . . . & Rockström, J. (2023). Earth beyond six of nine planetary boundaries. *Science Advances, 9,* eadh2458. https://www.science.org/doi/pdf/10.1126/sciadv.adh2458?trk=public_post_comment-text

Riley, D., & Brenner, R. (2022). Seven theses on American politics. *New Left Review, 138,* 5–27.

Savage, C. (2024, April 24). Trump's immunity claim joins his plans to increase executive power. *New York Times.* https://www.nytimes.com/2024/04/24/us/trump-immunity-president-supreme-court.html

Savage, C., Haberman, M., & Swan, J. (2023, November 11). Sweeping raids, giant camps, and mass deportations: Inside Trump's 2025 Immigration plans. *New York Times.* https://www.nytimes.com/2023/11/11/us/politics/trump-2025-immigration-agenda.html#:~:text=Former%20President%20Donald%20J.,they%20wait%20to%20be%20expelled

Savage, C., Swan, J., & Haberman, M. (2023, December 4). Why a second Trump presidency may be more radical than his first. *New York Times.* https://www.nytimes.com/2023/12/04/us/politics/trump-2025-overview.html

Schaller, S., & Carius, A. (2019). *Convenient truths: Mapping climate agendas of right-wing populist parties in Europe.* Adelphi. https://adelphi.de/en/publications/convenient-truths

Schmitt, C. (1988 [1926]). *The crisis of parliamentary democracy.* MIT Press.

Schmitt, C. (1996 [1932]). *The concept of the political.* University of Chicago Press.

Serhan, Y. (2021, August 10). The far-right view of climate politics. *Atlantic.* https://www.theatlantic.com/international/archive/2021/08/far-right-view-climate-ipcc/619709/

Snyder, T. (2021, December 28). The American abyss. *New York Times.* https://www.nytimes.com/2021/01/09/magazine/tump-coup-html

Steffen, W., Rockström, J., Richardson, K., Lenton, T. M., Folke, C., Liverman, D., Summerhayes, C. P., Barnosky, A. D., Cornell, S. E., Crucifix, M., Donges, J. F., Fetzer, I., Lade, S. J., Scheffer, M., Winkelmann, R., & Schellnhuber, H. J. (2018). Trajectories of the Earth system in the anthropocene. *PNAS, 115,* 8252–8259. https://doi.org/10.1073/pnas.1810141115

Swan, J. (2022a, July 22). A radical plan for Trump's second term. *Axios.* https://www.axios.com/2022/07/22/trump-2025-radical-plan-second-termz

Swan, J. (2022b, July 23). Trump's revenge. *Axios.* https://www.axios.com/2022/07/23/donald-trump-news-schedule-f-executive-order

Swan, J., & Haberman, M. (2023, April 20). Heritage foundation makes plans to staff next G.O.P. administration. *New York Times.* https://www.nytimes.com/2023/04/20/us/politics/republican-president-2024-heritage-foundation.html

Swan, J., Haberman, M., & Savage, C. (2023, December 26). How trump and his allies plan to wield power in 2025. *New York Times.* https://www.nytimes.com/article/trump-2025-second-term.html#:~:text=Trump%20is%20planning%20to%20revive,even%20decades%20after%20settling%20here

Tankersley, J., & Friedman, L. (2023, November 27). Biden's absence at climate summit highlights his fossil fuel conundrum. *New York Times.* https://www.nytimes.com/2023/11/27/climate/biden-cop28-climate-dubai.html

Trump, D. J. (2023, September 3). Agenda47: America must have the #1 lowest cost energy and electricity on Earth. https://www.donaldjtrump.com/agenda47/agenda47-america-must-have-the-1-lowest-cost-energy-and-electricity-on-earth

Tyson, A., Funk, C., & Kennedy, B. (2023, August 9). What the data says about Americans' views of climate change. *Pew Research Center.* https://www.pewresearch.org/short-reads/2023/08/09/what-the-data-says-about-americans-views-of-climate-change/#:~:text=Overall%2C%2037%25%20of%20Americans%20say,a%20Center%20survey%20from%20January

Viser, M. (2024, January 6). Biden, in Valley Forge speech, hits Trump hard as threat to democracy. *Washington Post.* https://www.washingtonpost.com/politics/2024/01/05/biden-trump-threat-to-democracy/

Vought, R. (2023). Executive office of the President of the United States. In P. Dans & S. Groves (Eds.), *Mandate for leadership* (pp. 43–67). Heritage Foundation.

Waldman, S. (2022, February 8). How Manchin used politics to protect his family coal company. *Politico.* https://www.politico.com/news/2022/02/08/manchin-family-coal-company-00003218

Walton, W. L., Moore, S., & Burton, D. R. (2023). Department of the treasury. In P. Dans & S. Groves (Eds.), *Mandate for leadership* (pp. 691–716). Heritage Foundation.

Watts, J. (2023, December 29). World will look back at 2023 as year humanity exposed its inability to tackle climate crisis, scientists say. *Guardian.* https://www.theguardian.com/environment/2023/dec/29/world-will-look-back-at-2023-as-year-humanity-exposed-its-inability-to-tackle-climate-crisis?share=linkedin

Weber, P. J. (2022, August 4). Autocratic Hungarian leader Orban hailed by US conservatives. *AP.* https://apnews.com/article/2022-midterm-elections-donald-trump-dallas-marjorie-taylor-greene-3c5a43ea6cd3a3472a05f48d3b527a76

Willcock, S., Cooper, G. S., Addy, J., & Dearing, J. A. (2023). Earlier collapse of Anthropocene ecosystems driven by multiple faster and noisier drivers. *Nature Sustainability*, 1333–1342. https://doi.org/10.1038/s41893-023-01157-x

Zhong, R. (2024, February 8). Have we crossed a dangerous warming threshold? What to know. *New York Times.* https://www.nytimes.com/2024/02/08/climate/global-warming-dangerous-threshold.html

FILMMAKING AS PEDAGOGY AND PRAXIS: AN INTERVIEW WITH GARRY POTTER[1]

Daniel M. Harrison

Lander University, USA

ABSTRACT

The author conducted this interview about film, pedagogy, and praxis with filmmaker and sociologist Dr Garry Potter in May 2023. Potter is the author of Dystopia: What Is to Be Done? *(2010, New Revolution Press),* The Philosophy of Social Science: New Perspectives *(2017, Routledge), and* The Bet: Truth in Science, Literature, and Everyday Knowledges *(2020, Routledge). He is also the writer, producer, and director of more than 20 films, including:* Luxury Eco-Communism *(2020),* Sociology at the End of the World *(2018),* Contract Faculty: Injustice in the University *(2016),* Ideology: Marx, Althusser, Gramsci *(2015),* Marx's Theory of Alienation and Species Being *(2013), and* Whispers of Revolution *(2012). This interview covers, inter alia, Potter's background and intellectual biography, his training as a theorist and filmmaker, and his reflections on film both as educational tool and vehicle for social change.*

Keywords: Filmmaking; praxis; education; social change; radical cinema

Daniel Harrison (DH): You came of age in Canada in the 1970s. How did growing up in this time and place impact you?

Garry Potter (GP): I actually went to high school in the States and stayed in Seattle for a while after that. In the early 1970s I visited Victoria, BC, and thought I'd stepped into a time warp. Some place the end of the 1960s in 1969 with Altamont, which may be correct; anyway, they were well gone by 1972.

However, the 1960s hippy era was alive and well in Victoria. The thing is I really liked the 1960s era and thus decided to live in Victoria and also attend university there. I stayed for a decade, where I thought the 1960s were still continuing all that time and that Victoria was a very special place, which I still believe.

DH: Why did you decide to go to graduate school at the University of Essex?

GP: It was a two-part process. First, I met a woman doing graduate research at UVic and then followed her back to Wivenhoe in Essex. Wivenhoe was I believe another very special place. Many graduates of Essex University never left the area. Wivenhoe was also the home of an eclectic bunch of artists. So, university lecturers, students, former students, and artists formed the dominant culture of this small village. The social rules of the rest of the UK were turned upside down. There were some very rich businesspeople in the village, but they were only allowed to drink with us under two conditions: first, they had to pay for the drinks; and secondly, they had to defer to our leftie politics. I stayed in Wivenhoe for 18 years, the place gradually undergoing a process of what I called "normalization" and some others spoke of as "Stepfordization".

DH: What was your experience at Essex? How was the sociology department at that time?

GP: I got to know many professors at Essex long before I began my PhD there. Academia and the intellectual world has its fashions and at the time Althusser was *the Man*. People across many disciplines, both grad students and professors all felt that "they had to come to grips with Althusser." A reading group was set up. It turned out I was the only one who had much knowledge of Marx. These people all needed to read some *Capital* before they could approach *Reading Capital*. Anyway, being formally the least educated in the group, this experience made me think I should do a PhD So I did. After completion of it, I of course, wished to be a professor at Essex and for the next 8 years or so, I sort of was. Actually what I was, was what came to be known as an adjunct professor or a sessional (in the US and Canada respectively). It was referred to as "part-time lecturer" in the UK, a label which really annoyed me, as I sometimes carried the heaviest teaching load in the department. I was desperately seeking and failing to find a full-time position and thus during most of my time post PhD at Essex I was a very bitter man. It was only some years later that I came to realize that the Essex sociology department was actually pretty wonderful. It received the highest research rating in the country and overall there was an extraordinarily lively intellectual scene there. We also received the highest teaching rating possible, which along with the research rating had considerable irony, as we all disapproved of the rating system. We had a department party to celebrate our teaching rating and one of the professors remarked: *"Well, if they want shit, we've shown them we can shovel it in bucketfuls!"* the thing is, this was never said publicly and should have been.

DH: Your films advocate a sort of socialist or leftist praxis. In contemporary politics, much of the action today comes from the political right. What has changed?

GP: I am a committed Marxist and have been since my early 20s when I first read Marx. Lenin and Trotsky and Althusser came later. Most of the world has been changing and not in a good way. This is particularly true of the US and UK. For me, the saddest aspect of that occurred in the UK. The election of Reagan and Thatcher marked the beginning of Neo-liberalism as policy. However, unlike the US the UK had a strong labor movement and a working-class political party. When I first moved there, I was amazed that people like Tony Benn were allowed on television. However, the Labour Party had been on a rightward trajectory for decades prior and culminated in Tony Blair taking control of the party leadership. I left the LP; however, many good people stayed and simply endured the Blair years. Many came back with the advent of the accident that brought Jeremy Corbyn to power. I was back in Canada by this time and watched with sadness and anger, as he was poisonously attacked by the media and betrayed by his own party. Today we have Tony Blair Mark II in the form of Keir Starmer. It is very sad. US politics is dominated by the absence of any real left and tens of millions of fascist leaning lunatics on the one hand, and a mainstream media and an intentionally liberal wishy washy (except for war mongering) democratic party on the other. There is a serious confusion in the US; all sides see liberals as being left. They are not. Fascism looms!

DH: How did you become interested in filmmaking? What sort of training have you had in film production?

GP: I have no formal training in film production. Essentially it was advances in film editing technology that brought me to filmmaking. I taught myself Final Cut Pro. It is utilized by many Hollywood editors. Ergo, I became able, with respect to some things at least, to use some of the same quality level of equipment as the top of the profession and match them in production values. With some exceptions, my films are mainly made through editing a collage of downloaded clips.

DH: What has been your experience shooting original documentary footage?

GP: Well actually I have very little experience doing so. In the film you mentioned, *Contract Faculty*, I had a partner – Stephen Svenson – who carried most of the load as far as camera work. My strengths have always been script wring and editing.

DH: In many of your films, you rely on the "fair use" of images and sounds. How are these found and determined?

GP: This is quite a tricky topic. The blurb I put at the end of all my films concerning "educational fair use" is for a potential defense against accusations of copyright. So far, I've never had to use it. When you upload a film to YouTube, they have a program to search for potential illegal use of downloaded images and video clips. I kind of use them as my test case. This program has often flagged up clips in my films; however that does not necessarily result in a problem. Once YouTube has identified a possible issue, they contact the copyright holder giving them three choices. First, they could make a demand that the clip be removed. This has never happened to me. Secondly, they can monetize it, giving them a cut or maybe even the whole amount of any money the film makes. This has only happened to me once. Early on in my filmmaking career I was advised to stay away from Disney material as they are very litigious. I was also advised not to use any music clips, even very short ones. And I do so very rarely; most of the music I use is composed by my wife. The one time the music clip was monetized was when I used about a minute of Rage Against the Machine's version of "Street Fighting Man."

DH: How did you get involved with Insight Media?

GP: I'm no longer involved with Insight. A woman named Elana Joffe, at that time head of video acquisitions, started me with Insight. However, she moved over to Films Media Group (now owned by Infobase) and I followed her there. At FMG I received a co-production contract. Meaning that whatever films I signed over would not be wholly exclusive in terms of sales and distribution but split, whereby I could distribute them through my own company, Social Theory Films.

DH: How long have you been working with Liza Nicklin?

GP: Liza Nicklin is actually my wife. I had a professional Hollywood narrator (Phoebe Craddock) for my first six or seven films. Liza was developing her electronic music composition skills at this time and while she thought Phoebe's voice was good, she believed the sound engineering to be kind of shabby. She also reminded me that she had gone to acting school and thought she could do a good job with the narration. So, we gave it a go and she has done all the narration and sound engineering subsequently, as well as composing most of the music. Twenty-four films is the present total.

DH: What do you hope to accomplish with your films?

GP: Ah, grand hopes and dreams and a sad reality. I wish to educate and inform, which I have done to a small extent. But I'm always hoping for a much, much bigger audience than I actually get. I lack the means, i.e. the money, to do much in the way of advertising. Thus, a small distribution, very disappointing when you want to change the world.

DH: Approximately how long does it take you to make one (e.g. half an hour) film, including the planning, the writing of narrative, editing, post-production, etc.?

GP: It takes me about 5–6 months.

DH: Other than Marx, what are some important theoretical foundations of your approach to sociology, filmmaking, and politics?

GP: Lenin and Trotsky and Gramsci. Outside of the Marxist milieu, I would add Bourdieu and Merleau-Ponty

DH: What films, books, and other resources might you recommend for viewers/readers to learn more about contemporary class struggle?

GP: I initially got the question wrong and started a list of great political films and books of the past: *The Killing Floor* (1984, directed by Bill Duke); *Matewan* (1987, directed by John Sayles), *The Battle of Algiers* (1966, directed by Gillo Pontecorvo), *Z* (1969, Costa-Gavras), *Missing* (1982, Costa-Gavras) and *The Grapes of Wrath*, the novel (1939, written by John Steinbeck) NOT the film (1940, directed by John Ford). The film is a good example of how Hollywood twists powerful revolutionary messages. All Americans should read *A People's History of the United States* by Howard Zinn. Of course, there is also a lot of good contemporary stuff. For example, David McNally and John Clark have recently come out with new books. Following Richard Wolff's twitter feed would also be a good idea.

DH: Have you made any films about gender inequality or feminism, or about the sociology of race/ethnicity? If not, are you planning on doing so?

GP: The short answer is no and no. And the short answer as to why not is that I'm not really qualified, in terms of possessing the requisite knowledge, to do so. However, I have another project, which is still in the thinking it through stage, of an analysis of ways I believe the contemporary left has gone wrong. This will include a critique of intersectionality without much of a class dimension, mixed with a "political correctness" praxis based upon liberalism.

DH: In order to make their points, your films attempt to appeal to the viewing audience's intellect and also their emotions. How do you balance these approaches?

GP: Well, first of all most of my films present an analysis, and in the more political ones a prescription, with an argument supporting that prescription of what needs to be done. I feel I need to give some elements of hope and in that the emotive fuses with the prescriptive. I also consciously search for clips containing humour.

DH: At times, it seems that your work advocates a kind of righteous indignation against the status quo. Do you worry that the messages in your film might be co-opted by the political right and that they may be seen as encouraging political conflict and/or violence? Why/why not?

GP: There are strong elements of legitimate grievance within the far right; they just mistake who are their real enemies. As my films concentrate upon making that very thing clear – in my last one, I actually name names – I'm not very worried about being coopted by the right. "[P]olitical conflict and/or violence"? I do encourage these things. Fight the fascists? Yes! Fight the power? Yes! "No War but the Class War!" is a slogan I quite literally endorse.

DH: Your filmic style might be critiqued for being too modernist/realist/representational, in that many of your techniques seem to mirror cultural forms in the "bourgeois" film industry – e.g. 'Voice of God' narration; spectacular images; quick jump cuts; heart-pumping music tracks, etc., which can potentially reify the very social structures which need to be transformed. To what extent do you think that, in order to be successful at 'changing minds' the visual and sound elements of cinema also need to be broken down and recreated? I am thinking here of the filmic equivalent to Hegel's "severe style," Brecht's *Verfremdungseffekt*, and Godard's attempts at radical cinema, etc.

GP: I understand your point here and I reject the argument. I don't believe that "spectacular images" or "heart pumping music tracks" reify the social structures that need to be transformed. I think that many of the attempts at disrupting the form of cinema have been failures except in the eyes of pseudo-radical bourgeois film critics. As to learning about how the power structures of the world work, people come out of such films going "Huh?" or "What?" People lie saying the disruption of form was really interesting, when they were actually thinking it was really boring.

DH: Can you speak about the intended and unintended impact of your film-work? Have you accomplished what you set out to do when you started making films?

GP: As stated earlier, my films are, broadly speaking, of two sorts. First, there are what I call educational films. These synopsize and explain the ideas of many of the world's greatest thinkers and social theorists. They are, as it were, designed for the classroom. As such, I would say they were quite successful. I have had a great deal of praise for them from both students and teachers.

Sadly, with respect to what I consider to be my political films *Luxury Eco-Communism* (2020), *Whispers of Revolution* (2012), etc. – it is a different story. I had hoped to really make an impact upon the world with them. Yet only a relatively small number of people have seen them. Filmmaking, like book writing, requires, it seems, promotion well beyond self-promotion, if one is going to affect anything. I wished, of course, to contribute to changing the world.

DH: What are your thoughts about agency, action, and/or activism in contemporary societies and filmmaking as a kind of praxis?

GP: Agency is, of course, necessary for directed social change to occur. And in that sense my films are, of course, a form of praxis. But the relationship between structure and agency is different depending upon one's place in a hierarchical structure.

Let me use climate change as an example. The almost universal conceptual utilization of one's "carbon footprint" shows the lack of possibility for effective individual agency by ordinary people. It has been a powerful ideological trope for a misdirection of responsibility. Most people would be surprised to know that the concept was developed as a part of an advertising campaign put forward by Big Oil. A relatively small number of people – 2,000, maybe 3,000 people – have enormous personal agency with respect to climate change. They make the decisions, which the rest of us experience as structural realities.

Let me return to my filmmaking with regard to this. My praxis (though I still think it worth doing) is largely ineffectual whereas Hollywood and Madison Avenue are extremely powerful. However, both for myself and people in general, however weak and ineffectual are our attempts at social change, we have no choice but to try. And collective action is, of course, preferable to merely individual efforts.

NOTE

1. This interview was conducted over Zoom and email and has been edited for brevity and clarity.

INDEX

Action theory, 109–110, 131, 170, 213
   definition, 97–99
   future open possibilities, 99–100
   studies, 97–99
Adorno, Theodor W., 148–149
Agency
   accountability, 29–31
   applied critical theory, 8–12
   blaming, 104–105
   change structures, capacity to, 24–29
   as concept, 4–7
   deliberation, 19–24
   dignity, 29–31
   intention, 19–24
   inverting reasons and causes, 110–115
   meaning, 19–24
   problems, 108–110
   radically expanded, 107–108
   social science publications with, 44
   social theory, 8–12
   sociological theory, 8–12
   sociology. *See* Sociology
   21st Century, 6–7
   structure, definition, 105–106
   theoretical sociology, 8–12
   What Do We Need, 118–119
   What Do We Use, 119
Agency-like-beliefs, 123
Agentic dimension, 18
Agenticness, 22, 24
Agent-structure problem, 45
Alexander, J. C., 17, 81, 85
Amasyali and van den Berg (A&vdB), 77–79, 81–84, 91–95, 97, 100, 107
Animism, 108
Anti-establishment romanticism, 44–45

Anxiety epidemics, 7
Applied critical theory, 8–12
Archer, Margaret, 22–23, 110–111
Asymmetric life chances, 130
Attributions of agency, 95–96
Authoritarianism
   autonomy redeemed, 216–217
   on balance, 207–209
   children and leaders, attitudes toward, 198–201
   crushing evil and eliminating enemies, 204–205
   democratic educator, 217–218
   dictator, 192–193
   preferences, 205–207
   prejudices, 205–207
   social dominators market, 213–216
   strident minority, 210–212
   Trump, Donald, 190–191
   voting, 193–209
   wishes and domineering leaders, 201–204
Author-meets-critics, 11
Autonomy redeemed, 216–217

Barnes, B., 78, 123
Becker, Gary, 109
Beliefs, 81, 112
Biden administration, 238–242, 247
Bidenomics, 238
Bittner, Rudiger, 109
Blaming, 104–105
Bounded agency, 82
Bureau of Land Management (BLM), 243–244

Causality, 118
Causes, inverting, 110–115

Children and leaders, attitudes toward, 198–201
Choices, 47, 49, 81, 123
Civil society, 156–159
Cold War, 150
Colonization, 159
Constitutional entitlement, 149–150
Constitutional rights, 149–150, 167, 169
Constitutive elements, 18
Creativity, 81
Critical theory, 8–9, 12
Crushing evil and eliminating enemies, 204–205
Cultural dope, 16
Curiously abstract, 78–79

Dahms, Harry F., 147–148
Dahrendorf, Ralf, 149–150
Decolonization, 149–150
Deliberation, 19–24
Democracy, 137–140
Democratic educator, 217–218
Dennett, Daniel, 108–109
Desires, 112
Determinism, 16–17, 24, 26, 92, 95
 empirical turn, 93–94
 paradoxes of, 93–94
Dictator, 192–193
Dignity, 29–31
Diversity, 121–122
Dodds, E. R., 107–108
Domineering leaders, 201–204
Durkheim, E., 10, 99

Economic rationalization of society, 154
Economic system, 162–163
Economy, societal rationalization of, 172–178
Elder, G. H., 123
Emancipation, 140–142
Emirbayer, M., 98, 121
Empathy, 114
Empirical turn, 92–93

attributions of agency, 95–96
People Like Us (PLUs), 95–96
structure gets a pass, 96–97
Energy dominance, 242–247
Environmental Protection Agency (EPA), 244–245
Epistemological certainty, 84–85
Epistemological solutions, 92–93
Erich Fromm's Sane Society, 108
Exclusion, 130
Exploitation, 135–137
 asymmetric life chances, 130
 exclusion, 130
 monopolization, 130

False consciousness, 120
Federal Republic (FRG), 155
Filmmaking, 257–263
Footnoted conceptualizations
 epistemological certainty, 84–85
 probabilistic science, 79–80
 probabilistic thinking, 84–85
 profitably engage with, 82–84
 sociological social psychology, 80–82
Footnotes, 82–84
Frankfurt School psychoanalytic sociology, 108
Freedom, 92, 95, 123
 empirical turn, 92–93
 ontological and epistemological solutions, 92–93
Free will, 83–84, 119
Friedman, Milton, 150–151

German Democratic Republic (GDR), 155
Giddens, Anthony, 16–17, 44, 81
Gleeson, S., 48–49
The Greeks and the Irrational, 107–108
Guaranteed minimum income
 as constitutional right, 167, 169, 172, 178

Index 267

socially caused vicissitudes of life, protection against, 169–171

Hanley, Eric Allen, 11–12
Hegel, G. W. F., 10, 156, 159
Heimann, Eduard, 148–149
Heimann's social theory of capitalism, 159–164
Heimann's theory, 161–163
Heritage Foundation's Project 2025, 238–239, 242, 247, 250
Hirvonen, H., 48
Hitlin, S., 123–124
Hood, K. E., 82
Horkheimer, Max, 148–149
Human dignity, 29, 31, 120
Husso, M., 48

Illiberal democracy, 247–248
Inferences, 111–112
Inflation Reduction Act (IRA), 238
Inner agent, 106–107
Institutionalized democracy in postantagonistic two-thirds societies, 164–167
Intentional stance, 108–109
Intentions, 19, 24, 81
Interaction, 46
Internal-combustion engine (ICE), 246
Inverting reasons and causes, 110–115

Jacobides, M. G., 54

Lewin, Kurt, 80–81
Loyal, S., 78

Madama, I., 54
Martin, J. L., 78, 80
Marx, Karl, 10, 159
Middle classes, 137–140
Mische, A., 98, 121
Monios, J., 54
Monopolization, 130
Mouzelis, N. P., 25, 27

Naturalness, 159–160
Neoinstitutionalist literature, 54
Neoliberalism, 150
Normative approval, 47–63

Observation, 111–112
Offe, Claus, 149–150
Ontological solutions, 92–93
Organization for Economic Co-operation and Development (OECD), 242–243
Organizations, 137–140

Paret, M., 48–49
Paris Agreement, 243
People Like Us (PLUs), 95–96
Phenomenological experience of freedom, 123
Philosophy of Right, 156–159
Policy entrepreneurs, 54
Political agency, 48–49
Post-capitalist society, 149–150
Postfactual ecocatastrophe, 238–239, 242, 247, 250
Potter, Garry, 257–263
Poverty, 156, 159, 164, 167
Prejudices, 205–207
Probabilistic science, 79–80
Probabilistic thinking, 84–85
Protofascist postfactual politics, 247–250
Psychological predispositions, 83
Public authority, 158

Radically expanded agency, 107–108
Radical reforms, 148–150
Ranganathan, M., 48–49
Reasons, inverting, 110–115
Reassessment, 142–144
Redundant description, 47–63
Revolutionary-conservative double-sidedness, 161–162
Right to freedom, 162

Sampling, 46
Seiffge-Krenke, I., 48
Selective interpretation, 142–144
Self-contradictorily, 119
Self-efficacy, 123
Sense of agency, 123
Shanahan, M. J., 82
Simmel, G., 94–95
Simmel, Georg, 10
Smith, David, 11–12
Snyder, Timothy, 250
Social accountability, 29–31
Social dominators market, 213–216
Social inequality, 164–167
Social policy, 148–151, 154
Social science, 120
Social theorists, 8
Social theory, 8–12
Social Theory of Capitalism, 160–161
Societal rationalization of the economy, 147–151, 154
Sociological literature
 agency for all, 58–63
 choice within structural limits, 53–58
 making a difference, 49–53
 making choices as agency, 47–49
 methods, 45–46
 normative approval and back again, 47–63
 redundant description, 47–63
Sociological social psychology
 environments, 80–82
 psychological predispositions, 80–82
Sociological theory, 8, 12, 98–99
Sociology, 84, 118–119, 123
 accountability, 29–31
 change structures, capacity to, 24–29
 deliberation, 19–24
 dignity, 29–31
 intention, 19–24
 meaning, 19–24
Status groups, 137–140
Strawson, P., 107

Strident minority, 210–212
Structural limits, 53–58
Structural psychological dispositions, 83
Structure, definition, 105–106

Theoretical sociology, 8–12
Theory of social policy, 160
Thunberg, Greta, 121
Trump, Donald, 11–12, 190–191, 193–195, 198, 201, 204–205, 209–210, 212–213, 216–218, 239, 242, 247, 250
Turner, S. P., 79

UN Intergovernmental Panel on Climate Change (IPCC), 239
United States Sentencing Commission, 49

Variation, 121–122
Voluntarism, 16–17, 23, 29–30, 119
Voluntaristic theory of social action, 16
Voodoo narrative, 109
Voting, 193–209

Ward, Lester F., 10
Watson, G., 107
Weber, Max, 10–11, 19–20, 80, 134–135
 democracy, 137–140
 emancipation, 140–142
 exploitation, 135–137
 middle classes, 137–140
 organizations, 137–140
 reassessment, 142–144
 status groups, 137–140
Web of Science's Core Collection, 45
Welfare state, 148, 166–167
Wilhelm, Georg, 10
Wilmsmeier, G., 54
Winter, S. G., 54
Wishes/domineering leaders, 201–204

Work society, 165–166
Wright, Erik Olin, 134–135
   democracy, 137–140
   emancipation, 140–142
   middle classes, 137–140
   organizations, 137–140
   reassessment, 142–144
   status groups, 137–140
Wright's class theory, 130–134